Immigration Detention, Risk and Human Rights

Maria João Guia • Robert Koulish •
Valsamis Mitsilegas
Editors

Immigration Detention, Risk and Human Rights

Studies on Immigration and Crime

Springer

Editors
Maria João Guia
Coimbra, Portugal

Robert Koulish
College Park, Maryland
USA

Valsamis Mitsilegas
Department of Law
Queen Mary University of London
London, United Kingdom

ISBN 978-3-319-24688-8 ISBN 978-3-319-24690-1 (eBook)
DOI 10.1007/978-3-319-24690-1

Library of Congress Control Number: 2016931369

Springer Cham Heidelberg New York Dordrecht London

Printed on acid-free paper

Springer International Publishing AG Switzerland is part of Springer Science+Business Media (www.springer.com)

Preface

In recent years, with the European Union, the Schengen space and the space of Security, Freedom and Justice in force, European law converged to measures aiming to fight irregular immigration, rising in Europe. Some of the measures taken included the criminalisation of entering illegally in a certain member state or remaining illegally there after a legal entrance. Most of the European member states have this measures installed, except Portugal, Spain and Malta (which do not criminalise the illegal entrance and permanence of migrants, neither with a fine nor with an imprisonment—even though Spain does criminalise illegal permanence) and France, which does not criminalise illegal permanence but only entrance (FRA, 2014: 4–5). In fact, the Returns Directive (2008/115/EC) states in its article 15 that third-country migrants may be held in detention up to 6 months, a period that may extend to a maximum of 18 months. This procedure must follow a set of legal procedures, but it is always a moment of privation of individual freedom, which carries on over the migrant's shoulders the weight of their choice to look up for a better life, endeavouring a lot of dangers, vulnerabilities and social and personal difficulties.

We are very happy to present you this book, which was only possible with the effort, dedication and reflection of all authors who have worked hard with us. We have tried to provide you with a set of different reflections of the topic of detention of immigrants and that has been working as an offence to human rights. The way in which migrants became a risk to European space has been a great challenge to policies around irregularity. We can never, anyway, forget that migrants are human beings, deserved of respect and a respectful treatment.

This book is thus a compilation of the reflections of 18 authors who have discussed their thoughts with us during international conferences and workshops, mainly during the I CINETS conference held in Coimbra, Portugal, on the 11th and 12th of October 2012.

CINETS (Crimmigration Control International Net of Studies—www.crimmigrationcontrol.com) is an international non-profit group that got together their effort to enlarge knowledge around crimmigration control over migrants in different approaches. This is the third CINETS book published in English, and many others will be organised in the next years.

We will now provide a brief summary of the chapters in this book, and we thank authors once again for all the energy they have put into their papers to make this book possible.

Robert Koulish starts this book with an article introducing the topic. His analysis focuses on sovereignty connected with crimmigration control and the exceptionalism that helps shape the criminalisation of non-citizens. It examines how sovereign bias is revealed through unaccountable and disproportionate enforcement and detention policies and practices, even with state of the art risk technologies.

Michael Flynn examines discrepancies in the "liberal epoch" that includes a vast closeted immigration detention system that conceals information that the public has a right to know. Flynn also focuses on the "face-off between sovereign rights and human rights".

Valsamis Mitsilegas offers a more complicated relationship, where the *Returns Directive* may place limits on the enforcement authority of member states, but member states offer a flanking manoeuvre to "counter the loss of state control over movement" (Mitsilegas 2005). In the chapter "Immigration Detention, Risk and Human Rights in the Law of the European Union. Lessons from the Returns Directive", V. Mitsilegas delves deeper into the relationship to demonstrate that the criminalising intent of the Returns Directive can indeed be tempered by appeals to European law. In the chapter "Immigration Detention and Non-removability Before the European Court of Human Rights", Marloes A. Vrolijk examines whether repeated detention of irregular migrants is a violation of human rights. The chapter hones in on the tension between sovereign bias and the human rights of migrants.

Galina Cornelisse suggests that even with international law constraints on state sovereignty for immigration purposes, E.U. member states continue to treat undocumented migrants as a threat to sovereignty and respond accordingly to this perceived threat. Cornelisse examines the tension between sovereignty, the European Court of Human Rights (ECtHR) and the Court of Justice (CJEU). She compares the two courts in terms of their susceptibility to the logic of sovereignty. Of the two courts, she observes the CJEU is the one less susceptible to sovereign bias.

In the chapter "Trapped Between Administrative Detention, Imprisonment, and Freedom-in-Limbo", Charles Gosme critically examines the Court of Justice of the European Union to delve into one category of irregular migrants that has fallen through the cracks of CJEU rulings. He similarly finds weaknesses in the international courts' constraints. He examines the "residual category of irregular migrants", which consists of persons who have fallen through the cracks when the CJEU singled out non-citizens who would be permissible targets for imprisonment.

Larissa Leite, in the chapter "Immunity from Criminal Prosecution and Consular Assistance to the Foreign Detainee According the International Human Rights Law", examines the bias of Brazil's sovereign immunity. Leite addresses a separate question of immunity from prosecution and consular assistance granted to detainees. Leite argues that foreign nationals who receive the benefit of consular assistance are subjected to better treatment than citizens for the same criminal act.

In the chapter "Understanding Immigration Detention in the UK and Europe", Elspeth Guild examines the contested terrain between European court decisions and immigration detention in the U.K. She documents the UK's reliance on administrative detention in the face of the recent international law framework.

In the chapter "Women's Immigration Detention in Greece: Gender, Control, and Capacity", Mary Bosworth, Andriani Fili and Sharon Pickering incorporate feminist theory to critically analyse immigration detention in Athens, Greece. Bosworth argues that "detention (is)... a lightning rod for public opinion, deployed as a cynical political tool to demonstrate the government's determination to salvage Greek national pride". Bosworth substantiates the argument with results from an ethnography that highlights egregious conditions of immigrant detention for women in Greece.

In the chapter "Changing Practices Regarding the Implementation of Entry Bans in Belgian Migration Policy Since 1980", S. De Ridder and M. van der Woude examine crimmigration of irregular migration in the Belgium Migration Act. Specifically, they focus on how the *Returns Directive* provides opportunity for the member state to enhance the crimmigration in the detention context.

In the chapter "Crimmigration Policies and the *Great Recession*: Analysis of the Spanish Case", José Ángel Brandariz García examines crimmigration in Spain during the "Great Recession" of 2008–2009. Brandariz Garcia tackles the conflict between sovereignty and neoliberalism to reveal neoconservative politics embedded within the sovereign bias. This is followed by Katia Cardoso, chapter "'Immigrants as Detainees': Some Reflections Based on Abyssal Thinking and Other Critical Approaches", which critically examines immigration detention as political spaces particularly prone to abuse.

Next, in the chapter "Mandatory Immigration Detention for U.S. Crimes: The Noncitizen Presumption of Dangerousness", Mark Noferi critically examines the sovereign bias in mandatory detention statutes, along with the cultural presumption of dangerousness that informs such legislation in the first place along with over-enforcement by immigration authorities. Noferi highlights presumed dangerousness in the context of mandatory detention. As Noferi demonstrates, as a result of the 1996 immigration law (IIRIRA), while a single minor mistake of judgment can land immigrants in mandatory detention and removal proceedings, citizens have much less to lose for committing an analogous offence in the criminal process.

Christina Fialho argues for opening immigration detention to the light of day, particularly for purposes of visitation. Daylight is perhaps the most effective palliative to the abuses resulting from sovereign bias. Gabriel Teixeira examines irregular migration in the context of Arizona's SB 1070, ruled mostly unconstitutional by the Supreme Court. Teixeira addresses questions of dual sovereignty, federalism and constitutional constraints on Arizona's draconian immigration law.

We have aimed with this book to provide you with more information and reflections over risk and detention of migrants, under a human rights approach.

We intend with this information to provide tools for those who have means to take decisions on this field to reflect upon measures that have been taken, and also to raise public awareness on what has been happening in law and in action to migrants who cross borders irregularly.

A last word of gratitude to all authors and those who have been helping us to make this book a tool to raise awareness.

Acknowledgements

Maria João Guia would like to express her gratitude to João Pedroso, António Casimiro Ferreira and Alexandra Aragão for all the suggestions and comments on her projects and to Tokyo Foundation, where she feels very honoured to be a SYLFF Fellow.

Coimbra, Portugal — Maria João Guia
College Park, MD, USA — Robert Koulish
London, UK — Valsamis Mitsilegas
2015

Abbreviations

A/RES	Assembly Resolution
ACLU	American Civil Liberties Union
AEDPA	Anti Terrorism and Effective Death Penalty Act
AVID	Association of Visitors to Immigrant Detainees
BEDEX	Brigade for Expulsion of Foreign Criminals
CCA	Corrections Corporation of America
CIMT	Crime involving moral turpitude
CITs	Centros de Instalação Temporária (Temporary Installation Centres)
CIVIC	Community Initiatives for Visiting Immigrants in Confinement
CJEU	Court of Justice European Union
CPT	Committee for the Prevention of Torture
CVP	Community Visitation Program
DEVAS	Project on the Detention of Vulnerable Asylum-Seekers in the European Union
DHS	Department of Homeland Security
DOJ	Department of Justice
DOS	Department of State
ECHR	European Convention of Human Rights
ECJ	European Court of Justice
ECtHR	European Court of Human Rights
EID	Enforcement Integrated Database
EOIR	Executive Office of Immigration Review
ERO	Enforcement and Removal Operations
EU	European Union
FAO	Food and Agriculture Organization of the United Nations
FOIA	Freedom of Information Act
FRONTEX	European Union Agency
GMR	Global Migration Group
HB	House Bill
HRC	The Human Rights Committee

HRF	Human Rights Foundation
IACtHR	Inter-American Court of Human Rights
ICCPR	International Covenant on Civil and Political Rights
ICE	Immigration and Customs Enforcement
ICE-PBDS	Performance-Based National Detention Standards
ICIRR	Illinois Coalition for Immigrant and Refugee Rights
ICJ	International Court of Justice
IDC	International Detention Coalition
IIRIRA	Illegal Immigration Reform and Immigrant Responsibility Act
ILC	International Law Commission
ILO	International Labour Organization
INA	Nationality Act
INE	Spanish National Statistics Institute
INS	Immigration and Naturalization Service
IOM	International Organization for Migration
IRCA	Immigration Reform and Control Act
JRS	Jesuit Refugee Service
KYR	Know Your Rights
MCACC	Middlesex County Adult Correction Centre
NGO	Non Governmental Organization
NIF	National Immigration Forum
NPM	New public management
ONHCR	United Nations Office of the High Commissioner for Human Rights
PBNDS	Performance-Based National Detention Standards
RCA	Risk Classification Assessment
RHC	Recurso em *Habeas Corpus*
SB	Senate Bill
SCOTUS	Supreme Court of the United States of America
SEF	Serviço de Estrangeiros e Fronteiras (Immigration and Borders Service)
SIS	Schengen Information System
TCNs	Third country nationals
TPI	Tribunal Penal International
UHSA	Unidade Habitacional de Santo António
UNESCO	United Nations Educational, Scientific and Cultural Organization
UNHCR	United Nations High Commissioner for Refugees
USC	United States Code
VCCR	Vienna Convention on Consular Relations
VCDR	Vienna Convention on Diplomatic Relations
WCDF	West County Detention Facility

Contents

Contributors

Mary Bosworth is Professor of Criminology and Fellow of St Cross College at the University of Oxford and, concurrently, Professor of Criminology at Monash University, Australia. She has published widely on immigration detention and imprisonment, including, most recently, *Inside Immigration Detention* (OUP, 2014). Mary is currently heading a 5-year project on "Subjectivity, Identity and Penal Power: Incarceration in a Global Age" funded by a Starter Grant from the European Research Council and a 3-year International Leverhulme Network on External Border Control funded by the Leverhulme Trust. She is the Director of Border Criminologies (http://bordercriminologies.law.ox.ac.uk), the UK Editor-in-Chief of *Theoretical Criminology*, a co-editor of *Routledge Studies in Criminal Justice, Borders and Citizenship* and a member of the editorial board of the Clarendon Studies in Criminology.

José A. Brandariz-García earned a Ph.D. in Criminal Law (1999, University of A Coruña, Spain), and he is currently Professor of Criminal Law at the University of A Coruña, Spain. He has authored and edited more than 15 books and dozens of journal articles and book chapters on penalty issues, and he has lectured on these topics in universities of some 15 European and American countries. He has extensively analysed crimmigration policies and devices, particularly in relation to the Spanish context. His main publications in this field are the books *Criminalización racista de los migrantes en Europa* (co-edited with Salvatore Palidda; Comares, 2010), *Sistema penal y control de los migrantes* (Comares, 2011) and *Políticas y prácticas de control migratorio* (co-authored with Marta Monclús-Masó; Didot, 2015).

Katia Cardoso is a researcher at the Centre for Social Studies and member of the Humanities, Migrations and Peace Studies Group. She is a Ph.D. student in the Doctorate Programme "Post-colonialisms and Global Citizenship" at the University of Coimbra. Katia obtained her master's degree in African Studies by ISCTE and has a B.Sc. in International Relations by the School of Economics of the University of Coimbra. Her current research interests include youth violence, youth in Africa, post-colonialisms, deportation and Cape Verdean diaspora.

Galina Cornelisse L.L.M (Leiden University), Ph.D. 2007 (European University Institute), is a lecturer in European and International Law at the Vrije Universiteit Amsterdam. Previously, she taught Constitutional Law at Utrecht University. She has published widely on European and international immigration laws, with a specific focus on detention, including a monograph titled *Immigration Detention and Human Rights: Rethinking Territorial Sovereignty* (Martinus Nijhoff, 2010). Her most recent publications include "State Borders, Human Mobility and Social Equality: from Blueprints to Pathways", in: Weber, L. (ed) *Rethinking Border Control for a Globalising World.* Routledge (2015), and "What's wrong with Schengen: Border disputes and the Nature of integration in the Area without internal Borders" Common Market Law Review 51: 741–770 (2014).

Steven De Ridder is a teaching assistant at the Criminology Department of the Vrije Universiteit Brussels, Belgium, and a doctoral researcher with the research group Crime and Society (CRiS—research line of Penalty and Society). In July 2009, he graduated as Master in Criminology with a master's thesis entitled 'Right on the Run? The Reception of Unaccompanied Minors in Belgium'. Since October 2009, his research activities have related to the presence of irregular migrants in Belgian prisons. More particularly, the decision-making processes regarding release from prison and expulsion are the central focus of his research. His research activities are under supervision of Professor Dr Kristel Beyens and Professor Dr Sonja Snacken.

Christina M. Fialho is an attorney and the co-founder/executive director of Community Initiatives for Visiting Immigrants in Confinement (CIVIC), a non-profit working to end the isolation and abuse of people in U.S. immigration detention. Previously, she researched and wrote for the Global Detention Project, co-founded the first detention visitation program in California and assisted in defending immigrants before U.S. Immigration Courts and the Court of Appeals for the Ninth Circuit. She is a 2012 Echoing Green Fellow, Board Member of the ACLU of Southern California and Steering Committee Member of Detention Watch Network. Her work has been published by *Refugee Survey Quarterly*, *Forced Migration Review*, the *Huffington Post* and the *Washington Times*, among others.

Andriani Fili is the Leverhulme International Network Facilitator at the Centre for Criminology, University of Oxford. With master's degrees in Criminology and Criminal Justice (University of Oxford) and Gender and Social Policy (LSE), she has a range of experience working in the non-profit sector mainly in Greece with migrants and refugees. As a researcher she has been involved in a variety of projects concerning border policing, gender and immigration detention. Her future interests include exploring the Greek-Turkish border reception facilities and also expand the research on immigration detention in Greece.

Michael Flynn is the Executive Director of the Global Detention Project (www.globaldetentionproject.org/) in Geneva, Switzerland. He holds a B.A. in Philosophy from DePaul University and an M.A. and Ph.D. in International Studies from the

Graduate Institute of International and Development Studies. Flynn previously worked as a project director at the Institute for Policy Studies in Washington, D.C.; as a project coordinator at the Graduate Institute's Programme for the Study of Global Migration; and as an associate editor of the Bulletin of the Atomic Scientists. His work has been supported by the Geneva International Academic Network, the Swiss Network for International Studies, the Pew International Journalism Program and the Fund for Investigative Journalism.

Charles Gosme recently obtained a Ph.D. in Public Law at the Sciences Po Doctoral School, following the defence of his thesis entitled "Limbo spaces between illegal and legal stay: resulting from EU management of non-removable third country nationals". He teaches two courses entitled "European Law on Foreigners" and "European Law on Asylum Seekers and Irregular Migrants" to undergraduate students at Sciences Po. He is also the leader of an Immigration & Asylum project, in partnership with Paris-based NGOs, under the framework of the Sciences Po Law School Clinic. This project involves the provision of legal aid to irregular migrants and asylum seekers, as well as empirical research on targeted groups of migrants. He has acquired some expertise in his field of study through the provision of legal aid to imprisoned and non-imprisoned third-country nationals, as well as through the writing of numerous works relating to immigration and asylum law, most notably of an empirical study on the deterrent effect of administrative detention on irregular migrants in France.

Maria João Guia is a Ph.D. (summa cum laude) in Law, Justice and Citizenship at the twenty-first century at the University of Coimbra, Portugal, and the author of the thesis "Immigration, 'Crimmigration' and violent crime. The convicted inmates and the representations of Immigration and Crime". She is Associate Researcher at the Centre of Human Rights, at the Faculty of Law, University of Coimbra. Her most recent edited book is 'The Illegal Business of Human Trafficking' (Springer, 2015). Maria was appointed in 2012 as a SYLFF Fellow for her leadership and organisational skills and was (until December 2015) an independent external expert of the European Commission on the area of Security, Freedom and Justice and currently the Director of CINETS (www.crimmigrationcontrol.com).

Elspeth Guild is Jean Monnet Professor and personal at Queen Mary University or London and Radboud University, Nijmegen. She is also a partner at the London law firm Kingsley Napley and an Associate Senior Research Fellow at the Brussels-based think tank, the Centre for European Policy Studies. She has specialised in immigration and asylum law for more than 10 years and is the author of numerous books on the subject. She advises both European Union institutions and the Council of Europe on issues around free movement of persons, immigration and asylum.

Robert Koulish, Ph.D., is Director of MLAW Programs, undergraduate law programming at the University of Maryland in the College of Behavioural and Social Sciences, Joel J. Feller Research Professor of Government and Politics, at the University of Maryland, College Park, MD 20742. He is Lecturer at Law at UMD Carey School of Law. He is the author of *Immigration and American Democracy:*

Subverting the Rule of Law (2010) and academic and law review articles, book chapters and op/ed columns about crimmigration, detention, immigration privatisation and risk. Website: http://mlaw.umd.edu

Larissa Leite is the coordinator of the Protection Area of the Reference Centre for Refugees, which is a project of Caritas Arquidiocesana de São Paulo with the UNHCR. With master's degree in Economic and Environmental Law, she is also doctor in Human Rights by University de São Paulo (Brazil). Author of articles and book, she focuses in Criminal Law, Criminal Procedure, Refugee Law and Immigration Law. Her most recent research has been on Refugee Law and Due Process. As a professor, she has taught in Brazilian Colleges, besides coordinating the implementation of the Master Department in the Catholic University of Mozambique.

Valsamis Mitsilegas is Professor of European Criminal Law, Director of the Criminal Justice Centre and Head of the Department of Law at Queen Mary University of London. He is Co-coordinator of the European Criminal Law Academic Network (ECLAN) and a member of the Commission's Expert Group on European Criminal Policy. From 2001 to 2005, he served as legal adviser to the House of Lords European Union Committee. He is the author of 4 monographs and over 80 articles in the fields of European, economic and transnational criminal law; immigration and asylum law; and the relationship between security and human rights, in particular the right to privacy. His latest book is 'The Criminalisation of Migration in Europe' (Springer, 2015).

Mark Noferi is Enforcement Fellow at the American Immigration Council, a non-partisan research organisation in Washington, D.C. His research focuses on criminal immigration connections and immigration enforcement, detention and due process. Mr. Noferi has published in the Journal of Civil Rights & Economic Development, Michigan Journal of Race & Law and American Journal of Criminal Law; advised an economic cost-benefit study of a national immigration appointed counsel system; and spoken frequently at conferences and presented testimony. Mark earned his J.D. from Stanford Law School and B.A. from Boston College and clerked for the Hon. Harold Baer, Jr., in the Southern District of New York.

Sharon Pickering is an Australian Research Council Professorial Future Fellow and Professor of Criminology. She is currently Head of School, Social Sciences at Monash University and Director of The Border Crossing Observatory, an international research centre hosting a network of scholars researching borders, security, crime and justice www.borderobservatory.org. Professor Pickering researches irregular border crossing and has written in the areas of refugees and trafficking with a focus on gender and human rights. She leads a series of Australian Research Council projects focusing on the intersections of security and migration, deportation, and police and community responses to Prejudice Motivated Crimes. She has worked extensively with government agencies and law enforcement and with local and international NGOs. She has previously worked in Northern Ireland, on counter-terrorism policing, and human rights and women in South East Asia.

Gabriel Haddad Teixeira is a professor of Criminal Law and International Rights at Centro Universitário de Brasília (UniCEUB), with a master's degree in "Law of International Relations", line of research "International Protection of the Human Person". Also, he is a Criminal Lawyer.

Maartje van der Woude L.L.M., M.Sc., is Associate Professor of Criminal Law and Criminal Procedure at the Institute for Criminal Law & Criminology at Leiden Law School, the Netherlands. In her research, Van der Woude is interested in the interplay between political decision-making, decision-making by more street-level criminal justice actors and the boundaries set by the rule of law and international human rights. Within this broad spectrum, she tends to focus on uncovering and understanding rationales behind decision-making processes, as well as on the (un) intended effects of decision-making. She seeks these effects on a more theoretical and normative level by questioning the impact of decision-making on procedural justice, systemic inequality and the fundamental principles underlying criminal law and criminal justice. Her current research aims at a deeper understanding of the process of crimmigration, the growing merger of crime control and immigration control. Over the past couple of years, this has resulted in a growing body of empirical and more theoretical (inter)national publications focusing on unravelling crimmigration in the Netherlands and the EU. In her current research project, *Crimmigration and Multi-level Discretionary Decision-making in EU Borderlands*, she seeks to uncover the politics of internal border control in the EU through the spectrum of crimmigration.

Marloes Vrolijk is currently working as a legal employee for the Dutch Refugee Council and teaching social science at a bilingual high school in the Netherlands. Her paper is a shortened version of her master thesis, which was written for the completion of a Master of Laws (*cum laude*) in Public International Law at Utrecht University, the Netherlands (2011–2012). She also completed a Master of Arts (*cum laude*) in the Sociology of Law at the International Institute for the Sociology of Law in Oñati, Spain (2012–2013). There she focused upon socio-legal theory and legal limbo situations of *non-removable* irregular immigrants. Her (research) interests in immigration, immigration detention and legal limbo situations result from her internship at Amnesty International on the topic of immigration detention in the Netherlands (2010–2011).

Sovereign Bias, Crimmigration, and Risk

Robert Koulish

Abstract This chapter is part of a larger research project. It examines the proenforcement tilt of crimmigration with reference to sovereign bias. Sovereign bias alludes to how the nation-state wields extraordinary power over noncitizens at territorial borders and within boundaries. It favors politics over law, and the state over immigrants. It occurs where political actors have final say over legal matters, and governmental authority is nearly unconstrained by constitutional norms. As much as plenary powers have tempered in recent years, sovereign bias continues to drive an exceptional path for immigration at the intersection of law and crime. Following a brief examination of crimmigration enforcement and detention, the chapter documents sovereign bias in ICE's risk classification assessment for detention, where secret computer algorithms are responsible for recommending the mass detention of hundreds of thousands of noncitizens without due process.

1 Sovereign Bias

The pro-state anti-immigrant tilt in immigration law originates in the Court's early examinations of federal immigration policy. The Court could have and in my opinion should have found a basis for regulating immigration in the Constitution but instead linked immigration to the ambiguous international law concept sovereignty, which provides very few limits on state power.

> To preserve its independence, and give security against foreign aggression and encroachment, it is the highest duty of every nation, and to attain these ends nearly all other considerations are to be subordinated... (*Chae Chan Ping* 1889, 623).

As the Courts constructed federal powers over immigration that derived from sovereignty, they decided on plenary powers, which means congress would have unlimited power over immigration (Legomsky 1984). In Wong Wing v. U.S. (1896), the Court reaffirmed plenary powers over government decisions to detain. The Court in the 21st century continues to defer to the plenary powers that derive

R. Koulish
MLAW Programs and the Department of Government and Politics, University of Maryland, College Park, MD, USA
e-mail: rkoulish@umd.edu

M.J. Guia et al. (eds.), *Immigration Detention, Risk and Human Rights*,
DOI 10.1007/978-3-319-24690-1_1

from sovereignty particularly when it comes to immigration detention and removal. Whether it's the Court minority in Zadvydas v Davis (2001) or the Court majority in Demore v Kim (2003), pro-state anti immigrant arguments continue to refer to these early cases that recognize congress' nearly unrestrained power to regulate the admission of migrants into the USA (Benson 1997). Hence congress can still discriminate against noncitizen in the immigration context on the basis of race from Chae Chan Ping, gender from Fiallo v. Bell, and political opinion from Kleindienst v Mandel. Presumably, congress retains the power to exclude on the basis of religious affiliation as well. As discussed in this chapter, sovereign bias also informs immigration detention practices.

Justice Brandeis' dissent in the non-immigration case *Olmstead v United States* warns of the consequences of such unchecked government power. "If the Government becomes lawbreaker," he said, "it breeds contempt for the law; it invites every man to become a law unto himself; it invites anarchy." Brandeis' warning clearly applies to the immigration apparatus that oppresses immigrants almost per whim, due to the sovereign bias that washed over the Court more than a century ago.

In terms of immigration law it is the government—not the immigrant—that has subverted the rule of law. The rule of law would have required procedural safeguards for immigrants subject to crime control measures and perhaps would ensure the decriminalization of what are ostensibly civil offenses. At the intersection of crime and immigration, crimmigration law ensures neither.

2 Crimmigration

Crimmigration is a term of art coined by Juliet Stumpf in 2006. It applies to the intersection of immigration law and criminal law and embeds criminal enforcement authority within a civil regulatory regime (Legomsky 2007). Stephen Legomsky recognized the politicalization of immigration law when he observed, "Those features of the criminal justice model that can roughly be classified as enforcement have indeed been imported. Those that relate to adjudication—in particular, the bundle of procedural rights recognized in criminal cases—have been consciously rejected" (Legomsky 2007, p. 472).

Mitsilegas (2015) understands it in Europe as "the threefold process whereby migration management takes place via the adoption of substantive criminal law, via recourse to traditional criminal law enforcement mechanisms including surveillance and detention, as well as via the development of mechanisms of prevention and preemption." Cesar Cuauhtemoc Garcia Hernandez observes that crimmigration law reimagines people as deviants and security risks in the absence of an existential threat. "They are people to be feared, their risk assessed, and the threat they pose managed" (2014, p. 1457). The term crimmigration also serves as an organizing tool for critical immigration scholarship about immigration structures, processes, interactions, and norms giving rise to the criminalization of immigrants and immigration.

In the first volume of this series, Stumpf summarized "two horns" of crimmigration, which subverts rule of law principles (2013). The first horn extends the net of removable offenses for noncitizens, it justifies rounding up, mandatorily detaining, and then removing noncitizens as criminal aliens and aggravated felons even with nonviolent offenses committed long ago, including minor drug or comparative offenses for which they have already paid their criminal debt. The second horn criminalizes civil offenses, jailing people, for example, for "improper entry by an alien" offenses that are no more serious than a misdemeanor for underage tobacco chewing (8 U.S.C. 1325; Lydgate 2010). Similarly under the *Secure Communities* initiative and its successor *Priority Enforcement Program (PEP)* (Morton 2014), noncitizens can be detained almost any time law enforcement stops their car and runs a search.

Their vulnerability as foreigners and racial and ethnic minorities is exacerbated by exaggerated state powers and a paucity of rights at the intersection of crime and immigration.

3 Securitization Frame

Securitization introduces a useful frame for exploring sovereign bias. (Welch 2007). It suggests that within this enforcement machinery *naming* the threat to public safety rather than the threat itself can trigger the deployment of immigration enforcement machinery (Simon 2007).

As Ole Waever observes,

> What then is security? With the help of language theory, we can regard "security" as a speech act. In this usage, security is not of interest as a sign that refers to something more real; the utterance itself is the act. By saying it, something is done (as in betting, giving a promise, naming a ship). By uttering "security" a state representative moves a particular development into a specific area, and thereby claims a special right to use whatever means are necessary to block it" (1995, p. 55).

Securitization puts a postmodern spin on immigrant dangerousness and immigration crises. It does not refer to something necessarily real. Rather, as Ulrich Beck suggests, it is not about actual sources of danger but the perceptions of it. "Is it not spies, communists, Jews, Turks, or asylum seekers from the Third World who are ultimately behind it?" (1992, p. 75). Following Beck's idea, the concept sovereign bias is about: 1) naming the crisis; 2) blaming immigrants as (dangerous) perpetrators; 3) complaining about ineffective government controls; 4) deploying additional enforcement and control measures; and 5) disempowering immigrants. Sovereign bias has as much to do with a politics and culture of exclusion as with law.:

Consider the following examples of naming, blaming and complaining in recent news headlines.

In summer 2014, when I first heard about a crisis at the US–Mexico border, caused by thousands of Central American minors and mothers arriving at the border to escape organized violence in northern triangle countries, I thought the Administration was naming a crisis caused by violence in Central America. It wasn't until I read several news articles that it became clear that the crisis was the arrival of the refugees themselves, who, rather than fleeing violence, were being perceived as threatening pubic safety in the USA. Feeling both cynically amused and horrified at my country's lack of empathy and its trigger happy responses to human rights tragedies, the administration expedited the children's and their mothers' return to the violence in Central America, where many people subsequently died at the hands of gang violence.

It was mind boggling to see a humanitarian tragedy morph into a failure to adequately enforce laws and the border, victims were misidentified as criminal aliens, gang members, and rapists, with no empirical evidence to support these the rationale for these mass removals.

In July 2015, Karen Steinle was shot and killed in San Francisco. Her death triggered a political campaign against 'sanctuary cities,' a pejorative term constructed by anti-immigrant activists. Within 3 weeks of Karen Steinle's unfortunate death, the House of Representatives introduced and passed H.R. 3009, referred to as Enforce the Law Against Sanctuary Cities Act, sponsored by Duncan Hunter (R-Ca).

The legislation would freeze federal allocations to a state or local government with a law or procedure that undermines provisions of the Immigration Reform and Immigration Responsibility Act (IIRIRA) of 1996. The House passed the bill, which at the time of writing, is in the Senate. At about the same time Donald Trump's presidential campaign gained steam as the candidate fueled anti-immigrant panic by referring to Mexicans as "rapists," and calling for removal of 11 million undocumented immigrants from the USA—within 18 months.

Both H.R. 3009 and Trump's calls for draconian immigration restrictions, which as of fall 2015 are driving the GOP presidential race, rest upon misleading claims tying undocumented immigrants to criminality.

4 Immigration Detention Case-Study

Evidence of sovereign bias in mass immigration detention exists in the fact immigration detentions top the list of federal imprisonment generally. Naming, blaming and complaining about the dangerousness of immigrants helps rationalize mass detention. Expedited removal procedures assure the daily detention of thousands of immigrants, along with bed quotas that assure detention of tens of thousands daily, and other mandatory detention policies that assure the detention of thousands more for prior crimes regardless of when the crimes were committed or whether they connote dangerousness. Those mandatorily detained have no right to a bond hearing even though many are not risky. In many ways, as discussed in this section, mandatory detention is triggered by little more than sovereign bias. The following brief case study which is part of a larger research project examines sovereign bias in ostensibly risk based detention determinations that contribute to athis well documented crisis in mass detention.

In FY 2012, DHS detained a record 477,523 adult noncitizens, an over fivefold increase since the enactment of IIRIRA (Department of Homeland Security (DHS)

2012; Meissner et al. 2013). The annual number has increased by nearly 25 % since the Obama Administration began in 2009 (Meissner et al. 2013).

In fiscal year (FY) 2014, ICE spent nearly $2 billion on detention in approximately 250 detention facilities across the country, including county jails, privately run contract facilities, and federal facilities (Department of Homeland Security 2014, p. 39). ICE has estimated the average cost of detaining an immigrant, not accounting for personnel and operational expenses, to be $119 per day (or over $43,000/year). The allocation for immigration enforcement is greater than allocations for all other federal criminal enforcement combined; large numbers of immigrants rounded up in the process are actually long-term residents, many of them with families and jobs and who pose no risk to public safety. Contracts with Corrections Corporation of America (CCA) and GEO Group, the two largest private immigration detention corporations, enhance financial incentives to grow immigration detention.

ICE detention priorities converge with securitizing rationales to detain "violent criminals, felons, and repeat offenders as ICE's highest immigration enforcement priority" (Morton 2011, pp. 1–2). In November 2014, DHS Secretary Johnson clarified ICE detention priorities further. Today, Priority One includes those convicted of "aggravated felonies" or a state felony (other than an offense containing immigration status as an element); Priority Two includes those convicted of three misdemeanors arising out of separate incidents or a "significant misdemeanor," generally including convictions for over 90 days, or certain domestic violence, DUI, burglary, firearms, sexual abuse, and drug crimes. Priority Three includes those with recent removal orders issued after January 1, 2014 (2014 Johnson Priorities Memo at 3–4). Such priorities are similar to those the Court referred to in *Demore v Kim* (2003) invoking the shadow of plenary powers in deciding for mandatory detention without a bond hearing. While circuit courts in *Demore* (2003) determined it was unconstitutional to detain without a bond hearing, the Supreme Court reinforced—post 9/11—sovereign bias as it supported mandatory detention that for pretrial immigrants would be unacceptable if applied to citizens.

5 Mandatory Detention

In 1996, Congress mandated in the Illegal Immigration Reform and Immigrant Responsibility Act (IIRIRA) that ICE "shall take into custody" pending removal individuals who have committed a broad category of crimes, "when the alien is released" from criminal custody (INA § 236(c); 8 U.S.C. § 1226(c); see 8 C.F.R. § 236.1(d)(3)). Based on the mandatory detention provisions in Section 1226(c) in Title 8 of the United States Code, certain noncitizens who are deportable or inadmissible to certain crimes are mandatorily detained pending proceedings to remove them from the USA. These crimes include "aggravated felonies" and "crimes involving moral turpitude" under immigration law (8 U.S.C. §

1226(c))—some of which can be quite minor[1]—as well as controlled substance offenses. This mandatory detention provision potentially applies to any noncitizen, including lawful permanent residents (8 U.S.C. § 1226(a), (c)).

Once detained, certain noncitizens may ask an immigration judge to reconsider the applicability of the mandatory detention statutes (see 8 C.F.R. 1003.19(h)(2)(ii)), but such review, called a Joseph Hearing, is limited in scope and addresses only whether the individual's criminal history fits within the scope of the mandatory detention statute. It is widely contended that prolonged detention under mandatory detention without the possibility for review of the government's justification of the detention by a neutral magistrate reinforces plenary powers and raises important constitutional concerns.

As *Demore* (2003) demonstrated, mandatory detention policies detain without bond those who have a right to be in the country—legal permanent residents—and are still fighting their case. Many of these individuals have stable families, jobs, and strong community ties, which suggest they are neither a flight nor a public safety risk (Koulish and Noferi 2015). The circuit courts in *Demore* (2003) applied rule of law norms to assess the request for bond hearing. A recent study on immigration risk assessment demonstrates that a bond hearing for those mandatorily detained could likely result in widespread release for low-risk immigrants currently in bricks and mortar detention (Koulish and Noferi 2015).

6 Bed Quota

Sovereign bias exists in the immigrant detention bed quota where political actors have the final say over how many immigrants get detained. Each year, Congress appropriates moneys for ICE's detention budget (H.R. 5855, Rep. No. 112–492, 112th Cong., 2d Sess. 81 (2012)). In 2007, Congress created language in the Senate Appropriations Bill introducing the bed mandate for immigration detention. Originally, the bed mandate was for about 27,000 beds. Since FY 2012, Congress has mandated detention of 34,000 noncitizens on any one day (Department of Homeland Security (DHS) 2014), a fivefold increase in detention since FY 1995 (then 7475 on average).

When considering how the plenary power doctrine may inform the bed quota, consider the following quote from an editorial posted by Bloomberg, which suggests that the bed quota policy for immigrants would not be acceptable if applied to citizens:

> Imagine if Congress mandated that an arbitrary number of jail cells be filled with prisoners-regardless of the crime rate. Authorities would be required to incarcerate people, no matter the circumstances or the affront to human rights. That's basically the state of immigration detention in the United States (The Editors of Bloomberg View, September 26, 2013).

[1] An "aggravated felony" could encompass marijuana possession, a bar fight, or shoplifting, while a "crime involving moral turpitude" could encompass subway turnstile jumping or a disorderly persons offense. 8 U.S.C. §§ 1226(a), (c).

The sovereign attribute of applying laws to immigrants that could not be applied to citizens is in full display as members of congress toy with bed quotas as if immigrants were little more than the "alien horde" the Court named in 1889.

7 Expedited Removal

Sovereign bias is also present in expedited removal proceedings as the government hastily removes immigrants, without providing access to an immigration judge or counsel. Expedited removals constituted 44 % of all removals from the USA in FY 2013 (193,032 individuals) (Department of Homeland Security (DHS) 2013). Statutes mandate detention of those subjected to expedited removal until they are actually removed (8 U.S.C. § 1225(b)(1)(B)(iii)(IV)).

Expedited removal is perhaps the most direct way in which ICE mandatorily detains and removes nonviolent offenders, almost per whim. Expedited removal applies to "arriving aliens" DHS encounters at or within 100 miles of a border with insufficient or improper documents (8 U.S.C. §§ 1225(b)(1) (A)(i), 1182(a)(6)(C), (7)(A)(i)(I)). It defines "arriving aliens" as those "who have not been admitted or paroled into the United States, and who are unable to prove continuous physical presence in the United States for the 2-year period immediately prior to the date of the determination of inadmissibility." Expedited removal gives immigration authorities discretion to remove certain "arriving aliens" "without further hearing or review." The decision whether to apply expedited removal is in the sole and unreviewable discretion of the Attorney General, referring back to *U.S. ex rel Knauff v Shaughnessy's* statement that it is "due process as far as an alien entry is concerned" (at 44, 1950).

8 The Immigration Risk Classification Assessment (RCA)

The Risk Classification Assessment (RCA) is a computerized tool, adapted from analogous criminal justice tools. It is designed to set priorities for and standardize ICE's use of detention. The risk tool assesses public safety and flight risk and recommends detention or release, the amount of bail (if any), and detention or supervision levels. It makes determinations in an ostensibly objective manner.

In October 2009, Dr. Dora Schriro issued a report recommending that ICE implement risk assessment, as part of a larger reform of the immigration detention system (Schriro 2010). Schriro envisioned that risk assessment would improve the uniformity of ICE detention. Then DHS Secretary Janet Napolitano adopted Schriro's recommendation. ICE implemented the risk assessment in several stages. It piloted the RCA in summer 2012 in Baltimore and Washington, D.C., and completed national deployment in January 2013. ICE subsequently made changes to the RCA process, scoring, and decision logic in August 2013 and January 2014.

Congressional members of both parties have stated support for DHS' introduction of risk assessment. Internal ICE objections to risk assessment have been muted. Immigrant and human rights advocates have largely supported risk assessment as well. Some NGOs, though, have raised concerns that the tool is overweighted towards detention. Others have expressed concern regarding asylum seekers subjected to expedited removal and recommended that ICE perform RCA again after an individual passes a credible fear interview and is transferred into a judicial removal proceeding. Recently, DHS' Inspector General called RCA "not effective in determining which aliens to release or under what conditions" and expressed concerns that ICE is not improving RCA's predictive capabilities, among others.

The risk tool operates a computerized risk-based recommendation whether to detain. There is no review of the risk determination before an immigration judge. The logic of risk suggests the risk tool surveys the population of immigrants and compares it against the norm, assesses those in custody through abstract data points, and then makes a recommendation that is binding on most immigrants. The purpose of the risk tool is to detain "outliers from the norm," to be removed from the country.

Risk recommendations are computed by an algorithm that is designed to track, flag, and analyze risk profiles (Noferi and Koulish 2014). The lack of transparency in the risk assessment increases the likelihood that risk profiles discriminate. On the basis of political whim, and securitized naming of existential dangerousness. The secret algorithm shares characteristics of sovereign bias as it tilts towards state power to undermine immigrant rights in a manner that lacks accountability, transparency and predictability (Noferi and Koulish 2014). Because of the secrecy of the algorithm, researchers can only speculate on the potential direction this new plenary power might take.

For example, recent research about the immigration risk tool reveals that it is responsible for ICE overdetaining immigrants. Every immigrant is categorized as a risk. The computer recommends the release of only 1 %. Only 2 % are categorized as a low risk, and 83 % of immigrants in custody are detained (Koulish and Noferi 2015).

Risk is computed in terms of both public safety and flight. Only 5 % are categorized as low flight risk, and 95 % are medium or high risk. In the public safety category, 38 % are low risk, 41 % are medium risk, and 58 % are high risk. There is little difference in risk factors between those detained and released (Koulish and Noferi 2015).

Of particular interest is how risk correlates to mandatory detention, ostensibly the category for the most dangerous immigrants. But no correlation exists between risk and mandatory detention. Those mandatorily detained have much lower flight risk and only a slightly higher public safety risk. For 60 % of those in mandatory detention, the criminal conviction responsible for mandatory detention is not the reason immigrants are in ICE custody, raising the question whether those mandatorily detained immigrants are indeed dangerous. Not only are those mandatorily detained not more dangerous than nonmandatorily detained immigrants, but also there are substantial mitigating factors that should be accounted for. Of all the categories of immigrants in ICE custody (mandatory detention, discretionary detention, and release), those mandatorily detained have the highest percentage of long-term residency, family in the USA, work authorizations, and property ownership (Koulish and Noferi 2015).

The findings suggest that risk is disaggregated from dangerousness. Worse, there is no way to ensure that the RCA's legal analysis is correct. Since the algorithm is secret, researchers cannot discern whether the RCA is correct in naming those mandatorily detainable.

The RCA must engage in complicated legal analysis. Consider that even a straightforward analysis of the violent offense of murder, rape, or sexual abuse of a minor under INA subsection 101(a)(43)(A), for example, would require distinguishing among at least 150 different ways of being subject to mandatory detention under this one subsection.[2] In the state of Maryland, for example, there are at least ten different ways to commit murder in the first degree. The complexity of analysis required is sure to test the algorithm's rigor.

Next, the algorithm must compare the state offense against federal law. A state offense amounts to a charged federal offense if it (1) is indivisible and a strict categorical match or (2) is divisible and is matched under a modified categorical approach (see Matter of Chairez-Castrejon 2014). In the Fourth Circuit, for example, for a state offense to be considered an aggravated felony, all elements of the state offense must be the same as or narrower than the elements of the generic federal offense (U.S. v Royal 2013).

A soon-to-be-published analysis of the mandatory detention cases by Koulish and Noferi suggests that the RCA questionably identifies state offenses as mandatorily detainable offenses under federal immigration law (on file with author).

In one case, a 22-year-old male from India was in custody in Baltimore, Maryland. He had been charged by a state court with robbery and received a 3-year sentence. Once in immigration custody, he was charged as mandatorily detainable for having committed an aggravated felony under INA 237(a)(2)(A)(ii), for the commission of a violent crime of violence under INA 101(a)(43)(F). Robbery in the state of Maryland retains its common law definition, crafted by the Supreme Court of Maryland. The Fourth Circuit never decided whether the Maryland Robbery offense amounts to a crime of violence for the purpose of the INA. The Maryland robbery definition would not always fall within the federal crime of violence definition. In this case, the Fourth Circuit infers only ambiguously that robbery is a crime of violence, and yet the RCA is programmed to provide a binary yes/no response as the basis for mandatory detention recommendation.

A second case involves a 22-year-old male from Paraguay who had been convicted of the crime of larceny, potentially a mandatorily detainable offense involving a crime involving moral turpitude. The RCA algorithm must determine

[2] Consider multiplying three parts to this offense by 50 state criminal codes.

whether a larceny conviction is a CIMT under 212(a)(2)(A)(i) (I).[3] Larceny is a common law term defined as fraudulent taking of another's property. The Fourth Circuit has ruled that a fraudulent taking is not included within the federal definition of theft, and therefore a categorical analysis would suggest it does not match the federal definition of theft and therefore does not amount to a CIMT under immigration law (Matter of Silvia-Trevino 2008; Omargharib v. Holder 2014). This immigrant should not have been mandatorily detained.

Clearly the risk tool has failed, in Dora Schriro's words, to better tailor ICE detention to individuals warranting it (2009). She had hoped the risk assessment would help reduce the severity of custody, given immigration detainee's "low propensity for violence" compared to criminal detainees.

The secretive and unaccountable workings of the RCA, along with its pro-enforcement bias, are indicative of sovereign bias. Although it may invite controversy to hold classic immigration cases responsible for bias in a twenty-first century risk tool I believe sovereign bias remains the source of much that seems intractably oppressive in crimmigration law. I refer to the chapters in this volume to help substantiate the role sovereign bias plays as the source of deep patterns of anti immigrant bias throughout the US and other immigration systems. As the chapters in the volume tell different stories, these different depictions of oppression find a shared source in sovereignty. Still, I can imagine more implausible reasons for systemic anti-immigrant bias in immigration law, than alluding to the ghosts of plenary powers and the sovereign bias that persists in reproducing instances of anti-immigrant oppression in one fact of crimmigration after another.

Further, I would argue that until immigration enforcement explicitly removes sovereign bias by directly reversing the doctrine of plenary powers and securing immigration law be judged within the rubric of constitutional norms, sovereign bias is likely to continue to inform risk and other reforms per political whim. Until immigration law is brought inside the juridical, immigration controls will continue to operate both within and outside the juridical.

9 Conclusion

In this chapter, I examined crimmigration through the lens of sovereign bias, defined as actions taken in the shadow of the plenary power doctrine. Immigration is one of the few policy issues and legal fields that share more characteristics from the logic of sovereignty than from the rule of law. This central feature, I believe, establishes a lens for interpreting the exceptional and seemingly aberrant features of

[3] Under INA 212(a)(2)(A)(i)(I), a noncitizen committed a crime involving moral turpitude if he is "convicted of, or [] admits having committed, or who admits committing acts which constitute the essential elements of ... a crime involving moral turpitude... or an attempt or conspiracy to commit such a crime."

immigration law enforcement and detention. Immigration law is highly unusual because of the state's unique relationship to noncitizens, how this relationship gets codified in law, and the culture that both results from and socially reproduces this peculiar imbalance of power.

More than a century ago, the courts interpreted immigration law through sovereignty, from which the plenary power doctrine would recognize inordinate powers in the political branches over the regulation of immigration. Similarly, immigration procedures in the immigration court system were subsequently designed with a prosecutorial bias against immigrants. State-of-the-art enforcement technologies breathe new life into this anachronistic doctrine of sovereign power.

The chapter has demonstrated sovereign bias in immigration detention, specifically in mandatory detention statutes, bed quota mandates, and risk classification assessments. While plenary powers linger in parts of the detention determination process, new technologies of power such as the risk classification assessment reintroduce a postmodern version of sovereign bias where plenary powers continue to hide out within a black box algorithm.

References

Beck U (1992) Risk society: towards a new modernity. Sage, Thousand Oaks

Benson L (1997) Back to the future: congress attacks the right to judicial review of immigration proceedings. Conn Law Rev 12(1411):1412

Department of Homeland Security (2012) Immigration enforcement actions. DHS, Washington, DC

Department of Homeland Security (2013) Immigration Enforcement Actions

Department of Homeland Security (2014) U.S. Immigration and Customs Enforcement Salaries and Expenses, FiscalYear 2015 Congressional Justification, 81

Hernández G, Cuauhtémoc C (2014) Immigration detention as punishment. UCLA Law Rev 61 (5):13–41

Koulish R, Noferi M (2015) Immigration detention in the risk classification assessment era. Migration Policy Institute, Washington, DC

Legomsky SH (2007) The new path of immigration law: asymmetric incorporation of criminal justice norms. Immigr Nationality Law Rev 28:679

Lydgate J (2010) Assembly-line justice: a review of operation streamline. Calif Law Policy Brief 481–544

Meissner D, Kerwin D, Muzaffar C, Bergeron C (2013) Immigration enforcement in the United States: the rise of a formidable machinery. Migration Policy Institute, Washington, DC

Mitsilegas V (2015) The criminalisation of migration in Europe: challenges for human rights and the rule of law. Springer, New York

Morton J (2011) Morton memo exercising prosecutorial discretion. http://www.ice.gov/doclib/secure-communities/pdf/prosecutorial-discretion-memo.pdf

Morton J (2014) Morton memo on secure communities. http://www.dhs.gov/sites/default/files/publications/14_1120_memo_secure_communities.pdf

Noferi M, Koulish R (2014) The immigrant detention risk assessment. Georgetown Immig Law J 29:45

Schriro D (2010) Improving conditions of confinement for criminal inmates and immigrant detainees. Am Crim Law Rev 47:1441

Simon J (2007) Governing through crime. Oxford University Press, Oxford
Stumpf J (2006) The crimmigration crisis: immigrants, crime, and sovereign power. Am Univ Law Rev 56:367
Waever O (1995) Securitization and desecuritization. In: Lipschutz R (ed) On security. Columbia University, New York, pp 46–86
Welch M (2007) Moral panic, denial and human rights: scanning the spectrum from overreaction to under-reaction. Crime, social control and human rights: from moral panics to states of denial: essays in honour of Stanley Cohen 92–104

Statutes

Antiterrorism and Effective Death Penalty Act (AEDPA). Pub. L. No. 104–132, 110 Stat. 1214
Illegal Immigration reform and Immigrant Responsibility Act (IIRIRA). Pub. L. No. 104–208; 110 Stat. 3009

U.S. Cases Cited

Chae Chan Ping, 130 U.S. 581 (1889)
Matter of Chairez-Castrejon, 26 I&N Dec. 349, 354 (BIA 2014)
Demore v. Kim, 538 U.S. 510 (2003)
Fiallo v Bell, 430 U.S. 787 (1977)
Fong Yue Ting v U.S., 149 U.S. 698 (1893)
Jean v Nelson, 472 U.S. 846 (1985)
Kleindienst v Mandel, 408 U.S. 753 (1972)
Knauff v Schaughnessy, 338 U.S. 537 (1950)
Matter of Silva-Trevino, 2008 BIA LEXIS 37, 2 (B.I.A. 2008)
Nishimura Ekiu v U.S., 42 U.S. 631 (1892)
Oceanic Steam Navigation Co. v Stranahan (214 U.S. 320 (1909)
Omargharib, 2014 U.S. App. LEXIS 24289 (4th Cir. Dec. 23, 2014)
Olmstead v United States, 277 U.S. 438, 485 (Brandeis, J., dissenting)
Orantes Hernandez v Thornburg, 919 F. 2d. 549 (1990)
Plyler v Doe, 457 U.S. 202 (1982)
United States v. Royal 731 F.3d 333, 342 (4th Cir. 2013)
Wong Wing v. United States, 163 U.S. 228 (1896)
Zadvydas v. United States, 533 U.S. 678 (2001)

Sovereign Discomfort: Can Liberal Norms Lead to Increasing Immigration Detention?

Michael Flynn

Abstract Many liberal democracies betray a noticeable discomfort when it comes to public scrutiny of immigration detention, neglecting to release comprehensive statistics about it, cloaking detention practices in misleading names and phrases, and carefully choosing which activities they define as deprivation of liberty. On the other hand, these same countries have labored to expand their detention activities and to encourage their neighbors to do the same. What explains this simultaneous reticence towards and embrace of immigration detention? This paper argues that a largely unrecognized variable influencing the evolution of immigration detention has been the promotion of some key human rights norms, which has helped spur states to adopt new institutions dedicated to this practice while at the same time prompting them to shift the burden of global migration to countries on the periphery of the international system.

1 Introduction

> A comfortable, smooth, reasonable, democratic unfreedom prevails in advanced industrial civilization (**Herbert Marcuse**, One-Dimensional Man)

The T. Don Hutto Residential Center is not a nursing home. Nor is it a shelter for runaway children or a halfway house for recovering addicts. It is a privately run for-profit immigration detention facility located near Austin, Texas, that confines undocumented female immigrants who are slated for deportation by the U.S. Department of Homeland Security's Immigration and Customs Enforcement (ICE). Why is a migrant detention center hidden behind a name? Answering this riddle can provide important clues about the forces shaping immigration detention policies today, particularly the role played by the promotion of human rights norms.

M. Flynn (✉)
Global Detention Project, Geneva, Switzerland
e-mail: michael.flynn@globaldetentionproject.org

M.J. Guia et al. (eds.), *Immigration Detention, Risk and Human Rights*,
DOI 10.1007/978-3-319-24690-1_2

2 Adapting to Human Rights

In October 2009, Manfred Nowak, then the UN Special Rapporteur on Torture, argued at a press conference that because states were failing in "their obligations to respect the basic dignity of human beings in detention," it was time to adopt a UN treaty on the rights of detainees (Nowak 2009). Among the vulnerable populations Nowak referred to were irregular migrants held in administrative detention, whose plight the UN High Commissioner for Human Rights Navi Pillay had claimed a month earlier—in September 2009—represented "one of today's most critical human rights challenges" (Pillay 2009).

These pronouncements by two high-profile human rights advocates operating at the international level about the rights of immigration detainees highlight the intensifying global attention this practice has received in recent years. They also reflect an important factor influencing the evolution of immigration detention—the diffusion (or spreading) of human rights norms relevant to the protection of noncitizens deprived of their liberty for reasons stemming from their immigration status. As states increasingly turn to detention to control their borders and immigrant populations, this practice is attracting the attention of an expanding number of rights advocates operating at the national, regional, and international levels.[1]

The diffusion of immigration-related human rights has been fostered by the emergence since World War II of what some scholars call the "liberal epoch," a period that has seen the adoption of numerous international treaties that provide specific protections for noncitizens, like the UN Refugee Convention. As Lahav (2003, p. 90) writes, "The 'liberal epoch' of human rights norms that facilitated humanitarian migration alongside labour recruitment . . . contrasts with the preceding period. One only needs to recall the expulsions of 400,000 Poles from Germany in 1885–1886, or the exclusion of Chinese immigrants before the turn of the century in the United States to realize the normative evolution that has taken place in the migration policy domain."

Sustaining the notion of a "liberal epoch" requires employing careful caveats that take into account the sometimes awful and inhuman conditions in which migrants can be detained across the globe, as well as the totalitarian conditions under which much of the globe lived during the purported formative years of this epoch. Nevertheless, Lahav points to an important aspect of contemporary international relations that needs to be considered when discussing the evolution of immigration detention regimes.

According to many scholars of globalization, sovereign states are gradually "losing control" over their discretion on how to treat foreign-born residents because

[1] Two of the more outstanding cases of increasing detention regimes are those of the United States and the United Kingdom. By 2009, the total U.S. immigration-related detention capacity was 33,400, up from 27,500 in 2006 and 6785 in 1994 (GDP 2009). In the United Kingdom, detention capacity increased from approximately 250 in 1993 (Bacon 2005) to nearly 3500 by 2011 (GDP 2011).

of the "emergence of an international human rights regime that prevents nation-states from deciding who can enter and leave their territory" (Guiraudon and Lahav 2000, p. 164). This paper aims to provide a subtler assessment of the impact of human rights norms. While it is indeed the case that certain norms—for example, the UN Refugee Convention's prohibition against *refoulement* of people who face persecution in their home countries—have the effect of constraining state freedom of action with respect to certain categories of foreigners, the human rights framework relevant to noncitizens includes a host of norms that provide specific protections to immigration detainees without calling into question the states' sovereign right to detain or expel them. Additionally, while the right to personal liberty is one of the most powerful norms in the international community, states have developed a number of techniques to avoid scrutiny of their adherence to this principle when it comes to the treatment of migrants.

This face-off between sovereign rights and human rights is resulting in a peculiar evolution of the detention phenomenon in which states employ adaptive mechanisms of adherence and avoidance. In other words, in their efforts to digest the bitter pill of human rights norms, states neither lose control nor gain more control. Rather, they adapt. It is this process of adaptation—or resilience—that this paper endeavors to explore.

3 Hutto

In April 2010, I visited Hutto at the invitation of U.S. Immigration and Customs Enforcement (ICE).[2] For several years preceding my visit, the facility—which previously had been called the Hutto Family Residential Facility—was notorious for being one of only two U.S. sites used to detain families in what critics described as punitive conditions. Named after one of the U.S. pioneers in prison privatization and cofounder of the company that today owns Hutto (the Corrections Corporation of America),[3] Hutto is located in a former prison that was converted to a family detention center in 2006 at the behest of Congress.

[2] The author, in his capacity as lead researcher of the Global Detention Project, visited the T. Don Hutto Residential Center on 19 April 2010 at the invitation of the head of the Juvenile and Family Residential Management Unit of ICE's Detention and Removal Office (Dougherty and Lorenzen-Strait 2010).

[3] T. Don Hutto cofounded with Tom Beasley and Robert Crants the Corrections Corporation of America (CCA) in 1983. In 1984, CCA opened the country's first privately run detention center using a former hotel called the Olympic Motel. This temporary facility, which according to CCA was opened at the behest of INS, was replaced soon thereafter by the Houston Processing Center, "CCA's first design, build and manage contract from the U.S. Department of Justice for the Bureau of Immigration and Customs Enforcement (formerly the Immigration and Naturalization Service) in Texas" (CCA website, "A Quarter Century of Service to America").

Before Hutto opened, either detained families in the U.S. tended to be released from custody to await the termination of their immigration cases, or family members were placed in separate facilities: children were placed in the custody of the Office of Refugee Resettlement; parents were confined in detention centers. According to one account, when "Congress discovered this, it took immediate action to rectify the situation to ensure that ICE's practices were in keeping with America's tradition of promoting family values" (Women's Commission for Refugee Women and Children and Lutheran Immigration and Refugee Service 2007, pp. 1–2). In short, detaining families at Hutto was apparently meant to protect an important human right—the right to family life.

Almost overnight Hutto sparked heated debate in the United States about the treatment of undocumented immigrant children and families.[4] In 2007, the American Civil Liberties Union (ACLU) successfully settled a lawsuit it had brought against ICE, which contended that conditions inside the detention center violated standards for the treatment of minors in federal immigration custody. Two years later, in 2009, the Obama administration announced that it was officially ending the detention of children and families at Hutto and converted the center into an adult female-only detention facility.

By the time I arrived at Hutto in April 2010, the facility had undergone an intense makeover, becoming a centerpiece in the Obama administration's efforts to put a kinder, gentler face on detention (thus my invitation to visit it). Such was its apparent transformation from derided jailer of children to friendly lock up of immigrant women that one detainee I spoke with—a woman from Honduras who had previously been detained at other Texas detention centers—asked if I knew of any way to ensure that she would be detained again at Hutto in the event that she was apprehended during her next attempt to come to the United States (where her U.S.-born children lived).[5]

To reach Hutto, you have to drive through a low-income neighborhood located on the outskirts of the small town of Taylor, Texas. After passing several blocks of run-down homes and abandoned barns, you come upon a large open field, at the end of which is a set of buildings surrounded by fences and barbed wire. Inside, the

[4] Helping spearhead local opposition to Hutto was an Austin, Texas-based group called Grassroots Leadership, http://www.grassrootsleadership.org/.

[5] It is important to note that while Hutto undertook a number of important reforms, the facility has continued to be plagued by scandals related to the treatment of detainees. In August 2010, for example, the ACLU launched an investigation into the alleged sexual abuse of detainees by CCA employees. In an August 2010 press release, the ACLU stated: "The sexual abuse of numerous immigration detainees at Hutto underscores the systemic failures that continue to plague our nation's broken immigration detention system. The irony is that ICE touts Hutto as a flagship facility, emblematic of its commitment to reform. Clearly, that commitment is shallow. ICE has ignored repeated calls for increased and independent oversight and accountability of its immigration detention facilities and the private contractors like CCA who run them, and tragedies like this are the unfortunate result. It is time for ICE officials to live up to their promise of creating a 'truly civil' immigration detention system that does not tolerate the abuse and degradation of its detainees."

detention center is comprised of several pods—or living areas—each with two levels of individual cells and an open area in the center. There are also a central cafeteria, a large gym, a library, a computer room, medical facilities, and outdoor recreation areas. Through the wide and high-ceilinged hallways, one can observe inmates walking about freely from one section of the facility to the next, which they are allowed to do from early morning to early evening, when they must return to their cells.

During my visit, I was introduced to numerous staff representing both the Corrections Corporation of America and ICE and given a personalized tour by the facility warden and a representative of ICE based at the facility.[6] The tour included a visit to one of the pods. When we entered the pod, all the female detainees—apparently on cue and under orders—stood and began to clap, bringing a beaming smile to the face of the male warden.

After the tour, I sat with numerous facility staff, including several on-site medical personnel, to discuss my impressions. I acknowledged that Hutto appeared to be a well-ordered and humanely operated incarceration facility and pointed out that surely the inmates at Hutto received better medical care than the people living in the surrounding community. One staff member commented that the working environment at Hutto was extremely warm and positive and that this attitude had a positive impact on the demeanor of the detainees. I commented that while all the staff I had encountered indeed seemed quite cheerful, this fact struck me as disconcerting given the nature of their jobs. The warden then explained that the facility was able to have such an open and relaxed security environment because the women detained there were handpicked based on their nonthreatening profiles and track records. I asked why, if the women were not a threat, they were detained at such high costs in the first place, to which one of the staff responded—not without reason—that that was a question for the policy makers.

4 Sovereign Discomfort

The peculiarities of Hutto are not unique to that facility. In fact, across the globe today one can find immigration detention centers hiding (and disclosing) their identities, operating under the management of a diverse array of state and nonstate actors, and performing the apparent dual functions of assuaging public concern about immigration while signaling to would-be irregular migrants and asylum seekers that they are not welcome.

As with Hutto, the names of many of these facilities reveal contradictory official attitudes: Turkey previously called its migrant detention centers "guesthouses"; Mexico uses "migratory stations" (*estaciones migratorias*) for the "temporary

[6] The author's visit to Hutto was overseen by ICE Supervisory Detention and Deportation Officer George Robertson.

housing" (*alojamiento temporal*) of migrants; Hungary has "guarded shelters," Italy has "welcome centers" (*centri di accoglienza*), and France has "centers of administrative retention" (*centres de rétention administrative*).

Of course, not all countries use such creative terminology to describe their detention operations, but most states appear to view the penal nature of immigration detention as a source of embarrassment, a phenomenon I term *sovereign discomfort*.

This unease manifests itself in numerous ways and has long been at the heart of immigration detention regimes. For instance, what explains the paltry amount of statistical details regarding detention regimes? "A first difficulty that one encounters when attempting to present an overview of the use of immigration detention by [EU] Member States is to obtain reliable figures," writes Cornelisse. "If states do keep statistics, they are often rather reticent to make them available to the public" (Cornelisse 2010, p. 7).

States commonly seek to delink detention from incarceration, despite the obvious affiliation between the two. A somewhat surprising example of this is provided by the Bahamian Department of Immigration on its website "Apprehension, Detention, and Deportation,"[7] which states: "While there may be widespread debate on the whole concept of detention, through its Detention Centre, the Department of Immigration maintains its stance that its centre is not a prison, but fundamentally acts as a holding facility for individuals who are found in contravention of the Immigration Rules and Regulations."

Bahamian legal traditions and detention policies have been shaped by two of the more important detaining countries in the world, the United Kingdom and the United States. And both of these countries—as well as other common law countries like Australia—have struggled to find legal justifications for this practice, in part because of what Wilsher terms the "uncomfortable recognition of the dissonance between immigration detention and liberal legal orthodoxy" (Wilsher 2011, p. 56).

Thus, while detention centers have clear symbolic and political roles, states have endeavored—sometimes with the backing of rights actors—to soften the sharp edges of this practice, including by framing detention efforts with what Herbert Marcuse might characterize as a smile, *à la* Hutto.

This leads to a central question: can the promotion of liberal norms have an unintended deleterious impact on how states confront the challenges of irregular immigration?

5 Institutionalization and Diffusion

Two outstanding characteristics of contemporary immigration detention are the gradual institutional entrenchment (or *deepening*) of detention regimes in the nation-state—as observed, for example, in the shift from criminal prisons to

[7] http://www.bahamas.gov.bs, in the Department of Immigration section.

dedicated immigration facilities—and the spreading (or *widening*) of this practice across the globe.[8] These developments appear to be driven by two processes: (1) the diffusion of normative regimes aimed at protecting non-nationals (2) and the externalization of interdiction practices from core states of the international system to the periphery. As a result, we are witnessing the emergence of dedicated immigration detention regimes even in countries where there is little evidence of systematic efforts to detain as recently as 10 years ago.

Several recent cases help illustrate this argument. In early 2011, an official with the UN High Commissioner for Refugees described the Berks County Family Shelter in Leesport, Pennsylvania—the similarly misleadingly named sister facility to Hutto which for many years was the only site in the United States that detained families—as the embodiment "of the best practices for a truly civil immigration detention model." The official explained that "UNHCR believes strongly that the vast majority of asylum seekers should not be detained," but in the event that asylum seekers are detained, Berks was the model to follow (UN High Commissioner for Refugees 2011).

By all accounts, Berks operates in a humane and "nonpenal" manner, especially when compared to former operations at Hutto. However, while it is clearly important to applaud improvements in the treatment of detainees, is it a good idea for the international community's premier agency protecting asylum seekers to provide its imprimatur to efforts—even limited ones—to detain them, including children? UNHCR, as a political *and* humanitarian entity, by necessity must at times walk a thin line between its treaty-based mandate and the desires of its state partners. But this thesis argues that this sort of encouragement from a leading humanitarian agency provides "normative cover" for detention practices, shielding the state from uncomfortable questions regarding the right to liberty and helping entrench immigration detention into the institutional framework of the nation-state.

Similarly, rights actors frequently focus their detention-related advocacy on promoting the proper treatment of detainees and applauding efforts by states to differentiate between criminal incarceration and the administrative detention of irregular migrants and asylum seekers. However, there is cause for concern that the emergence of specialized detention regimes can lead to increased use of detention in the face of growing international migration.

In contrast to the United States, most European countries ceased some time ago to use criminal facilities for the purposes of immigration detention, and the recent EU Returns Directive provides that member states must use specially planned facilities for confining people as they await deportation. But the process of shifting

---

[8] The terms "deepening" and "widening" are frequently used in the context of the European Union to describe, respectively, the increasing levels of integration of its member states and its growing number of members. This paper adopts the terms to signify phenomenon with respect to immigration detention—the integration (or institutionalization) of detention practices in the nation-state and the expanding number of states as well as nonstate actors involved in this technology of immigration control—though not restricted to the European Union.

from informal to formal detention regimes, which has occurred over the last two decades, has paralleled the growth in immigration detention in this region.

Is there a connection between these two developments? The case of Ireland is illustrative. Ireland's immigration detention estate has been notable for two main reasons—its exceedingly small number of detainees each year (numbering in the low hundreds) and the fact that it has no official facility to confine migrants. However, in 2006, after an official visit to the country, the Council of Europe's Committee for the Prevention of Torture admonished Ireland for detaining failed asylum seekers slated for deportation in prisons. The CPT pointed out that this treatment violated norms established in the European Convention on Human Rights. The CPT then recommended that Ireland build a facility that would be dedicated to this purpose. In its response, the government of Ireland promised to do just that, stating that it was in "ongoing discussions with the Irish Prison Service . . . with the aim of providing a separate purpose built facility for immigration offenders at the new complex that conforms to best international standards."

As journalist Fernandes (2007, p. 199) once wrote regarding the U.S. "immigration-industrial complex": "With the increase in prison beds to house immigrants comes the pressure to fill them." Ireland thus represents an important test case for the future: when the country shifts to specialized facilities, will there be an uptick in the numbers of people detained?

At the same time that detention operations are becoming increasingly specialized in destination countries, these states are endeavoring to export interdiction efforts to other countries, raising questions about the evasion of their normative responsibilities. A case in point is the West African nation of Mauritania, which in 2006 opened its first dedicated detention center for irregular migrants in the port city of Nouadhibou with assistance provided by the Spanish Agency for International Development Cooperation. The center, which assisted Mauritania's efforts to crack down on migrants using the country en route to the Canary Islands, was set up in a former school restored by Spanish authorities. Before 2006, in the rare instances that migrants were arrested by the police, they were typically held at police stations (Amnesty International 2008).

Spain's involvement in establishing the detention center led to questions over who controled the facility and guaranteed the rights of the detainees.[9] While the center was officially managed by the Mauritanian National Security Service, Mauritanian officials "clearly and emphatically" stated to a Spanish human rights organization in October 2008 that Mauritanian authorities performed their jobs at the express request of the Spanish government (European Social Watch 2009).

The Mauritania case reflects a broader trend of core countries attempting to deflect migratory pressures by externalizing immigration controls to states that are not considered main destinations of migrants and where the rule of law is often

[9] This type of hybrid detention management situation raises a number of important questions about the evolving nature of sovereignty vis-à-vis contemporary immigration control and management. For a discussion of this, see Adler-Nissen and Gammeltoft-Hansen (2008).

weak. This raises questions about the culpability of liberal democracies in the abuses detainees suffer when they are interdicted before reaching their destinations. Observers have expressed similar concerns with respect to the numerous efforts to thwart the arrival of asylum seekers, such as EU discussions on extraterritorial processing centers, Australia's "Pacific Solution," and U.S. Caribbean interdiction policies.

6 Unintended Consequences

Ultimately, this paper argues that states' responses to liberal norms—as these are embodied in relevant international treaties like the UN Refugee Convention and the UN Covenant on Civil and Political Rights—are helping accelerate the institutionalization of detention in core destination countries and leading to the externalization of detention pressures and practices from the core to the periphery. On the one hand, norms regarding the proper treatment of detainees (those related to security of person) appear to be driving many destination countries to create specialized institutions that receive the blessing of rights watchdogs. At the same time, however, states increasingly seek to externalize interdiction efforts so as to circumvent pressure stemming from norms that call into question the state's right to detain and deport, such as the right to liberty and prohibition of *refoulement* (for a fuller treatment of this argument, see Guiraudon and Lahav 2000).

What is at stake here is our understanding of the role human rights promotion plays in shaping state efforts to detain and deport undocumented migrants. Some scholars have argued that the practice of immigration detention is generating a normative discourse about the rights of noncitizens that has the potential to undermine the territorial basis of sovereignty and thereby "transform the international and domestic legal order into one that is more true to some of its underlying universalistic ideals" (Cornelisse 2010, p. 29).

The indications discussed here seem to point to a different conclusion: that the promotion of the rights of migrant detainees reaffirms the territorial sovereignty of the nation-state in such a way as to ensure the increasing institutionalization and propagation of immigration-related detention into the foreseeable future.

The right to personal liberty is one of the most powerful norms in the international community. As such, liberal states often betray a distinct discomfort when locking people up outside criminal processes. This sovereign discomfort takes on a number of peculiarities vis-à-vis the administrative detention of noncitizens for immigration-related reasons. States disguise the practice by using misleading terminology. They frequently limit access to detainees and fail to make available detailed statistics about detention. They selectively apply human rights norms that do not call into question the sovereign's right to detain and deport. They export detention pressures to the exterior so as to avoid norm-based responsibilities, like admitting asylum seekers. They endeavor to characterize many of the people subject to this form of detention in such a way as to spur public fears, and thereby justify locking migrants up. And, finally, they increasingly create legal institutions that criminalize irregular migration, thereby shifting this form of detention from an administrative to a criminal law framework.

For rights actors concerned about the growth of immigration detention, there may be an important lesson to be learned from this assessment. There appears to be a problematic aspect to the narrow promotion of the rights of migrant detainees. As such, migrant rights advocates arguably should consider deemphasizing discourses that focus only on improving the situation of noncitizens in state custody and reemphasizing the taboo against depriving anyone of his or her liberty without charge. Instead of spurring states to create special institutions—or standard operating procedures—for keeping migrants in their custody, advocates should work to ensure that any limitation on freedom remains the exception to the rule.

References

Adler-Nissen R, Gammeltoft-Hansen T (eds) (2008) Sovereignty games: instrumentalizing state sovereignty in Europe and beyond. Palgrave, New York

Amnesty International (2008) Mauritania: nobody wants to have anything to do with us. Amnesty International, 1 July 2008

Bacon C (2005) The evolution of immigration detention in the UK: the involvement of private prison companies. RSC Working Paper No. 27. Refugee Studies Centre, Department of International Development, Queen Elizabeth House, University of Oxford

Cornelisse G (2010) Immigration detention and human rights: rethinking territorial sovereignty. Martinus Nijhoff, Leiden

Corrections Corporation of America (nd) A quarter century of service to America http://cca.com/our-history. Accessed 26 Aug 2014

Dougherty D, Lorenzen-Strait A (2010) Interview with Michael Flynn in Washington, D.C. on 16 Apr 2010. Global Detention Project, Geneva

European Social Watch (2009) Spain: the externalisation of migration and asylum policies: the Nouadhibou Detention Center. European Social Watch

Fernandes D (2007) Targeted: homeland security and the business of immigration. Seven Stories Press, New York

Global Detention Project (2009) United States detention profile. Global Detention Project, Geneva www.globaldetentionproject.org/fileadmin/docs/United_States_Detention_Profile_2009.pdf. Accessed 26 Aug 2014

Global Detention Project (2011) United Kingdom detention profile. Global Detention Project, Geneva. www.globaldetentionproject.org/fileadmin/docs/UK_Detention_Profile_2011.pdf. Accessed 26 Aug 2014

Guiraudon V, Lahav G (2000) A reappraisal of the state sovereignty debate: the case of migration control. Comp Polit Stud 33(2):163–195

Lahav G (2003) Migration and security: the role of non-state actors and civil liberties. United Nations Population Division, New York: UN/POP/MIG/2003

Nowak M (2009) Press conference by United Nations Special Rapporteur on Torture on 20 October 2009. UN Department of Public Information, New York

Pillay N (2009) Opening remarks at the panel discussion on human rights of migrants in detention centers at the UN Human Rights Council. Geneva, 17 September 2009

UN High Commissioner for Refugees (2011) In rural Pennsylvania, a model of civil immigration detention. UNHCR, 6 January 2011

Wilsher D (2011) Immigration detention: law, history, politics. Cambridge University Press, Cambridge

Women's Commission for Refugee Women and Children and Lutheran Immigration and Refugee Service (2007) Locking up family values: the detention of immigrant families

Immigration Detention, Risk and Human Rights in the Law of the European Union. Lessons from the Returns Directive

Valsamis Mitsilegas

Abstract By focusing on the provisions of the Returns Directive and the case law of the Court of Justice in the field, this chapter will analyse the legal framework of immigration detention under the Returns Directive and flag up in particular measures and practices targeting migrants as high-risk individuals under EU law. The chapter will be based on a twofold categorisation of the relationship between immigration detention, the Returns Directive and EU law: firstly, the chapter will focus on the limits that the Returns Directive as such poses on the criminalisation of migration at national level; secondly, the chapter will address the limits placed by EU law on Member State enforcement action when implementing the Returns Directive. It will be demonstrated that the criminalisation focus of the Directive can be tempered when the latter is placed within the broader context of the general principles of European Union law.

1 Introduction

The adoption of the EU Returns Directive has triggered a political and legal debate on the regulation and consequences of the detention of migrants in Europe. At both the legislative and the judicial levels, EU institutions have had to grapple with a number of questions related to the need to ascertain the key objectives of legislation on return and the related issues of the conditions and limits of detention of migrants and the relationship between immigration detention and fundamental rights. These issues have arisen in particular in the context of the implementation of the Returns Directive by Member States, with the Court of Justice already having been the recipient of a number of preliminary references by national courts concerning the applicability, limits and scope of the Returns Directive. These references have arisen in particular in cases involving the detention of third-country nationals who were deemed by national authorities to be high-risk individuals. Legal issues related to the relationship between immigrant detention and return have moreover transcended the stage of the implementation of the Returns Directive *per se* and

V. Mitsilegas (✉)
Department of Law, Queen Mary University of London, London, UK
e-mail: v.mitsilegas@qmul.ac.uk

M.J. Guia et al. (eds.), *Immigration Detention, Risk and Human Rights*,
DOI 10.1007/978-3-319-24690-1_3

now extend to instances where EU Member States have chosen to criminalise migration in their domestic law in addition to, and independently from, any EU law measures in the field.

National initiatives to criminalise migration have led to a series of preliminary references by national courts to the Court of Justice of the European Union, which was confronted in a series of cases with questions regarding the compatibility of domestic criminal law provisions with the Returns Directive. By focusing on the provisions of the Directive and the case law of the Court of Justice in the field, this chapter will analyse the legal framework of immigration detention under the Returns Directive and flag up in particular measures and practices targeting migrants as high-risk individuals under EU law. It will be demonstrated that the criminalisation focus of the Directive can be tempered when the latter is placed within the broader context of the general principles of European Union law. The analysis in this chapter will be based on a twofold categorisation of the relationship between immigration detention, the Returns Directive and EU law: firstly, the chapter will focus on the limits that the Returns Directive as such poses on the criminalisation of migration at national level; secondly, the chapter will address the limits placed by EU law on Member State enforcement action when implementing the Returns Directive. A contextual analysis of the Returns Directive and the legal framework established by it on immigration detention is essential, prior to analysing the way in which immigration detention, risk and human rights issues have been tackled by the Court of Justice.

2 The Returns Directive in Context

The Returns Directive constitutes a major development of the European Union *acquis* in relation to immigration enforcement. Two features of the Directive are key in contextualising and analysing its impact on immigration detention in EU law: the first feature is the achievement by the Directive of a high level of harmonisation of aspects of immigration enforcement at EU level, and the second feature is that the Directive contributes to the criminalisation of migration at EU level, in particular by including specific legal provisions on immigration detention. The high level of harmonisation is evidenced by the very title of the measure in question, a Directive 'on common standards and procedures in Member States for returning illegally staying third-country nationals'[1] and is confirmed by the opening Article of the Directive according to which it sets out common standards and procedures to be applied in Member States for returning illegally staying third-country nationals, in accordance with fundamental rights as general principles of

[1] DIRECTIVE 2008/115/EC OF THE EUROPEAN PARLIAMENT AND OF THE COUNCIL of 16 December 2008 on common standards and procedures in Member States for returning illegally staying third-country nationals, OJ L348/98, 24.12.2008.

Community law as well as international law, including refugee protection and human rights obligations.[2] Unlike EU measures in the field of granting rights to migrants and in particular asylum seekers, where EU action has taken initially the form of minimum standards, the Returns Directive thus reflects a consensus by EU institutions on the need to adopt common rules on immigration enforcement. This consensus is the outcome of different priorities by the different EU institutions involved in the legislative process leading to the adoption of the Returns Directive. Member States have been traditionally keen to adopt at EU level strong standards on immigration enforcement. In the heavily securitised Hague Programme of 2004, the European Council 'called for the establishment of an effective removal and repatriation policy based on common standards for persons to be returned in a humane manner and with full respect for their human rights and dignity' and for the start of Council discussions on minimum standards for return procedures, including minimum standards to support effective national removal efforts, taking into account special concerns with regard to safeguarding public order and security.[3]

The securitised approach on returns by Member States is here evident, and it is noteworthy that the EU legislative outcome has surpassed the initial Council ambition for the adoption of mere minimum standards in the field. The achievement of a high level of harmonisation has been facilitated by the integrationist ambitions of the European Commission and the European Parliament, which acted as a co-legislator in the adoption of the Returns Directive (Acosta 2009, pp. 19–39). The Commission in its proposal for the Returns Directive justified the adoption of common standards by arguing that co-operation among Member States is likely to be successful if it is based on a common understanding on key issues and that common standards should be set in order to facilitate the work of the authorities involved and to allow enhanced co-operation among Member States. According to the Commission, in the long term such standards will provide the ground for adequate and similar treatment of illegally staying third-country nationals, regardless of the Member State which carries out the return procedure.[4] While the common standards set out by the Returns Directive reflect on a number of occasions a draconian policy towards migrants, they can, as will be seen below, act as a limit to further criminalisation of migration by providing clear limits to Member State enforcement action.

Negotiations leading to the adoption of the Directive have proven to be controversial, in view of the different views of the EU institutions involved as regards the content of the Directive and the significant potential consequences of the Directive for the protection of fundamental rights (see Baldaccini 2009a, pp. 114–138; Acosta 2009). At the heart of the Directive lies Chapter II, which is entitled 'Termination of Illegal Stay' and contains detailed provisions on the return

[2] Article 1.

[3] The Hague Programme: Strengthening Freedom, Security and Justice in the European Union, OJ C53/1, 3.3.2005, Paragraph 1.6.4. See also recital 2 in the Preamble of the returns Directive.

[4] COM(2005) 391 final, Brussels, 1.9.2005.

decision, voluntary departure and removal, detention and the relevant safeguards. There are two main areas which underline the criminalisation of migration in the Returns Directive: the combination of a return decision with a re-entry ban and allowing Member States to detain migrants pending their return. A very broadly worded re-entry ban is set out in Article 11 of the Directive, according to which such a ban is compulsory if no period for voluntary departure has been granted or if the obligation to return has not been complied with—but Member States may also impose such a ban in other cases (Returns Directive, Art. 11(1)). The length of such a ban is also prohibitive and arguably disproportionate—it will in principle not exceed 5 years, but this time limit is not absolute—it can exceed 5 years if the third-country national represents a serious threat to public policy, public security or national security (Returns Directive, Art. 11(2)). There is a relaxation of the ban under certain conditions for victims of trafficking who co-operate with the authorities under Directive 2004/81/EC (Returns Directive, Art. 11(3)) and an obligation to apply the provisions on the re-entry ban without prejudice to the right of international protection under EU asylum law (Returns Directive, Art. 11(5)). As regards immigrant detention, the key provision signalling the criminalisation of migration is Article 15 of the Directive, which confirms detention as an accepted means of enforcing the return of irregular migrants.

However, it must be noted that the Returns Directive places Member States' detention powers under a series of limits. Detention is allowed only for the purposes of removal[5] and only if other sufficient but less coercive measures cannot be applied effectively in a specific case (Returns Directive, Art. 15(1)). Most importantly, any detention shall be for as short a period as possible and 'only maintained as long as removal arrangements are in progress and executed with due diligence' (Returns Directive, Art. 15(1)). The requirement for the existence of a link between detention and a prospect of removal is confirmed by Article 15(4) of the Directive, according to which when it appears that a reasonable prospect of removal no longer exists for legal or other considerations or the conditions laid down in Article 15 (1) of the Directive no longer exist, detention ceases to be justified and the person concerned shall be released immediately. These limits to Member States' power to detain are watered down significantly by the length of detention allowed by the Directive. According to Article 15(5), detention will be maintained for as long a period as the conditions laid down in Article 15(1) are fulfilled and it is necessary to ensure successful removal for a period which may not exceed 6 months. The Directive allows Member States to extend this period for a limited period not exceeding a further 12 months in accordance with national law in cases where

[5] According to Article 15(1) of the Directive, Member States may only keep in detention a third-country national who is the subject of return procedures in order to prepare the return and/or carry out the removal process—in particular when

(a) there is a risk of absconding or
(b) the third-country national concerned avoids or hampers the preparation of return or the removal process.

regardless of all their reasonable efforts the removal operation is likely to last longer owing to a lack of co-operation by the third-country national concerned or delays in obtaining the necessary documentation from third countries (Returns Directive, art. 15(6)). The Returns Directive allows thus Member States to detain immigrants for the sole purpose of removal for a period up to 18 months.[6] The limits that this lengthy period of detention places upon the proportionality requirement for detention have been noted (Cornelisse 2012, pp. 207–228), and the approach of the Directive on the length of detention has been heavily criticised (Baldaccini 2009b, pp. 1–17).[7] However, as will be seen below, the clear link between detention and a prospect of removal and Member States' diligence in this context on the one hand and the setting out of maximum—albeit lengthy—periods of detention by the Directive on the other have proven to be instrumental towards the limitation of national criminalisation practices by the Court of Justice.

3 Immigration Detention, the Returns Directive and National Criminal Law: The Interplay Between the Returns Directive and National Criminal Sanctions for Immigration Offences

While as seen above the Returns Directive has espoused a broad criminalisation approach as regards permitting Member States to impose lengthy periods of immigration detention in the returns procedure, recent national initiatives have compounded and intensified such criminalisation. Unlike EU law in the field, a number of EU Member States have proceeded to criminalise irregular entry and stay *per se*: criminalisation here extends beyond the confines of immigration detention for return purposes and includes the introduction of criminal offences and sanctions at national level for irregular entry and stay, as well as at instances for failure to comply with the return procedure. This draconian approach to irregular migration at national level has now been subject to the intervention of the Court of Justice of the European Union on a number of occasions, with national courts requesting the Luxembourg Court to rule on the compatibility of national criminal law with EU law, and in particular with the Returns Directive. The Court of Justice has thus far ruled on three different scenarios involving criminal sanctions for

[6] The Directive has attempted to introduce common standards in a highly diverse field, with some Member States having established clearly determined and limited periods of detention under their national law, while others not having laid down any maximum time limit for pre-removal detention in their national law—see European Union Agency for Fundamental Rights (2011), pp. 31–36.

[7] As Baldaccini eloquently notes, this is an extremely long period for depriving irregular migrants of their liberty for the sole reason of facilitating their removal and preventing them from absconding in the meantime.

irregular migration at national level: on the compatibility of national legislation criminalising failure to comply with the returns process with the Returns Directive, on the compatibility of national legislation criminalising irregular stay by imposing the penalty of imprisonment with the Returns Directive and on the compatibility of national legislation criminalising irregular stay by imposing a fine, expulsion or detention with the Returns Directive. This section will map the Court's case law in the field and highlight the protective function of EU law (and the Returns Directive in particular) in placing limits in criminalisation and immigration detention at national level.

3.1 The Compatibility of National Legislation Criminalising Failure to Comply with the Returns Process with the Returns Directive: The Case of El Dridi

In the case of *El Dridi*,[8] the Court of Justice examined a preliminary reference request made by the Corte d'Appello di Trento involving a question on the compatibility of the Returns Directive, and in particular Articles 15 and 16 thereof, with Italian legislation imposing a sentence of imprisonment for the offence of failure to comply with a returns order. The Court based its answer on two main premises: on the requirement to interpret the Returns Directive in the light of fundamental rights and on the requirement for national law to be interpreted as ensuring the effectiveness of EU law, and of the Returns Directive in particular. As regards the first aspect of the Court's reasoning (respect of fundamental rights), the Court confirmed a restrictive interpretation of the coercive provisions of the Directive based on the Directive's objective to establish an effective removal and repatriation policy, based on common standards, for persons to be returned in a humane manner and with full respect for their fundamental rights and also their dignity (*El Dridi*, para. 31). Member States can depart from the common standards and procedures established by the Directive only as provided for therein (*El Dridi*, para. 32). In any case, although Article 4(3) of the Directive allows Member States to adopt or maintain provisions that are more favourable than Directive 2008/115 to illegally staying third-country nationals provided that such provisions are compatible with it, that directive does not allow those States to apply stricter standards in the area that it governs (*El Dridi*, para. 33).

The Court linked the requirement to respect fundamental rights with the high level of harmonisation provided by the Returns Directive. The latter sets out specifically the procedure to be applied by each Member State for returning illegally staying third-country nationals and fixes the order in which the various, successive stages of that procedure should take place (*El Dridi*, para. 34). It is only in particular circumstances, such as where there is a risk of absconding, that

[8] Case C-61/11 PPU, *Hassen El Dridi, alias Karim Soufi*, [2011] ECR I-03015.

Member States may, first, require the addressee of a return decision to report regularly to the authorities, deposit an adequate financial guarantee, submit documents or stay at a certain place or, second, grant a period shorter than 7 days for voluntary departure or even refrain from granting such a period (*El Dridi*, para. 37). In the latter situation, but also where the obligation to return has not been complied with within the period for voluntary departure, Article 8(1) and (4) of Directive 2008/115 provides that, in order to ensure effective return procedures, those provisions require the Member State which has issued a return decision against an illegally staying third-country national to carry out the removal by taking all necessary measures, including, where appropriate, coercive measures, 'in a proportionate manner and with due respect for, inter alia, fundamental rights' (*El Dridi*, para. 38), following from recital 16 in the Preamble to the Directive and from the wording of Article 15(1) that the Member States must carry out the removal *using the least coercive measures possible*. It is only where, *in the light of an assessment of each specific situation*, the enforcement of the return decision in the form of removal risks being compromised by the conduct of the person concerned that the Member States may deprive that person of his liberty and detain him (*El Dridi*, para. 39, emphasis added). Articles 15 and 16 of the Directive place strict limits on detention (*El Dridi*, para. 40).

In the light of the above considerations, the Court of Justice confirmed that the return procedure established by the Directive corresponds to a *gradation* of the measures to be taken in order to enforce the return decision, a gradation which goes from the measure which allows the person concerned the most liberty, namely granting a period for his voluntary departure, to measures which restrict that liberty the most, namely detention in a specialised facility (see Mitsilegas 2012, pp. 87–114). The principle of proportionality must be observed throughout those stages (*El Dridi*, para. 41, emphasis added). Even the use of the latter measure, which is the most serious constraining measure allowed under the directive under a forced removal procedure, is strictly regulated, inter alia *in order to ensure observance of the fundamental rights of the third-country nationals concerned* (*El Dridi*, para. 42, emphasis added).[9] Compliance with proportionality and fundamental rights is the basis for assessing whether the common rules introduced by the Returns Directive preclude national legislation from imposing custodial sentences for failure to comply with removal proceedings in the case of *El Dridi* (*El Dridi*, para. 44).

As regards the second premise of the Court's reasoning—the assessment of the compatibility of national criminal law with the Directive—the Court began by granting a certain degree of freedom to Member States to adopt national criminal law aimed inter alia at dissuading those nationals from remaining illegally on those States' territory. However, this freedom arises only if it is clear that the coercive measures Member States may adopt in implementing the Returns Directive have not led to the expected result being attained, namely the removal of the third-

[9] See also the references to relevant human rights instruments and case law in para. 43.

country national against whom they were issued (*El Dridi*, para. 52). The Court went on to limit Member States' freedom further. By evoking settled case law in the field,[10] the Court reiterated its finding that although in principle criminal legislation and the rules of criminal procedure are matters for which the Member States are responsible, this branch of the law may nevertheless be affected by European Union law (*El Dridi*, para. 53). While neither the legal basis of the Directive (or its Lisbon successor) nor the Directive itself precludes the Member States from having competence in criminal matters in the area of irregular immigration and irregular stays, they must adjust their legislation in that area in order to ensure compliance with European Union law (*El Dridi*, para. 54). The Court based the limits on the power of Member States to adopt criminal law upon the principles of effectiveness and loyal co-operation (*El Dridi*, paras. 55–56).

Applying these principles to the specific case before it, the Court found that Member States may not, in order to remedy the failure of coercive measures adopted to carry out removals under Article 8(4) of the Returns Directive (measures which are subject to the principle of proportionality), provide for a custodial sentence *on the sole ground* that a third-country national continues to stay illegally on the territory of a Member State after an order to leave the national territory was notified to him and the period granted in that order has expired; rather, they must pursue their efforts to enforce the return decision, which continues to produce its effects (*El Dridi*, paras. 57–58, emphasis added). Such a custodial sentence risks jeopardising the attainment of the objective pursued by that Directive, namely the establishment of an effective policy of removal and repatriation of illegally staying third-country nationals as it is liable to frustrate the application of the measures referred to in Article 8(1) of Directive 2008/115 and delay the enforcement of the return decision (*El Dridi*, para. 59). The Returns Directive, and in particular Articles 15 and 16 thereof, must thus be interpreted as precluding a Member State's legislation, such as that at issue in the main proceedings, which provides for a sentence of imprisonment to be imposed on an illegally staying third-country national on the sole ground that he remains, without valid grounds, on the territory of that State, contrary to an order to leave that territory within a given period (*El Dridi*, para. 62).

[10] Case 203/80 *Casati* [1981] ECR 2595; Case 186/87 *Cowan* [1989] ECR 195; and Case C-226/97 *Lemmens* [1998] ECR I-3711. For an analysis of the limits placed by European Union law on the powers of Member States to criminalise, see Mitsilegas (2009), para. 53.

3.2 *The Compatibility of National Legislation Criminalising Irregular Stay by Imposing the Penalty of Imprisonment with the Returns Directive:* The Case of Achughbabian

The extent to which European Union law places limits on the power of EU Member States to criminalise migration was tested again post-*El Dridi* in the case of *Achughbabian.*[11] The judgment was in response to a reference for a preliminary ruling from the Cour d'Appel de Paris and concerned the compatibility of French law criminalising migration with EU law. The case differs from *El Dridi* in that it concerns the criminalisation and imposition of criminal sanctions by French law for irregular entry or residence *per se and prima facie unrelated to a returns procedure.* In *Achughbabian*, the Court confirmed that Member States retain a degree of sovereignty in adopting criminal sanctions for the breach of immigration law: the Returns Directive is not designed to harmonise in their entirety the national rules on the stay of foreign nationals (note the use by the Court of the term 'stay' and not 'residence' here) and thus does not preclude the law of a Member State from classifying an illegal stay as an offence and laying down penal sanctions to deter and prevent such an infringement of the national rules on residence (*Achughbabian*, para. 28). Neither does the Directive (which concerns only the adoption of return decisions and the implementation of those decisions) preclude a third-country national being placed in detention with a view to determining whether or not his stay is lawful (*Achughbabian*, paras. 29–30).

However, the above findings do not mean that national action to criminalise or detain third-country nationals necessarily falls outside the scope of the Returns Directive. Firstly, the Court states that national authorities are required, in order to prevent the objective of the Returns Directive from being undermined, to act with diligence and take a position without delay on the legality or otherwise of the stay of the person concerned. The finding that the stay is illegal will lead in principle, according to the Returns Directive, to a return decision (*Achughbabian*, para. 31). Detention is thus inextricably linked with the outcome of the return of the third-country national concerned. Secondly, and notwithstanding state power to criminalise or detain along the lines set out above, it needs to be examined whether the Returns Directive precludes the criminalisation of irregular entry or residence under French law *in so far as it is capable of leading to an imprisonment in the course of the return procedure* governed by the said Directive (*Achughbabian*, para. 32, emphasis added). In that respect, the Court reiterated its ruling in *El Dridi* that Member States cannot apply criminal legislation capable of imperilling the realisation of the aims pursued by the said Directive, thus depriving it of its effectiveness (*Achughbabian*, para. 33). The Court thus envisages the possibility that

[11] Case C-329/11, *Alexandre Achughbabian v Préfet du Val-de-Marne*, judgment of 6 December 2011.

national law criminalising irregular entry or residence is assessed in the light of the Returns Directive.

Having concluded that national law criminalising irregular entry or stay may be assessed in the light of the Returns Directive, the Court found that in the present case the situation of the applicant in the main proceedings fell indeed within that referred to in Article 8(1) of that Directive (*Achughbabian*, paras. 34–36). It is clear to the Court that the imposition and implementation of a sentence of imprisonment during the course of the return procedure provided for by the Returns Directive does not contribute to the realisation of the removal which that procedure pursues, namely the physical transportation of the person concerned outside the Member State concerned and that such a sentence does not therefore constitute a 'measure' or a 'coercive measure' within the meaning of Article 8 of the Directive (*Achughbabian*, para. 37). The Court went on to highlight the differences between national criminalisation and the system put forward by the Returns Directive: it is undisputed that the national legislation at issue in the main proceedings, in that it provides for a term of imprisonment for any third-country national aged over 18 years who stays in France illegally after the expiry of a period of 3 months from his entry into French territory, is capable of leading to an imprisonment whereas, following the common standards and procedures set out in Articles 6, 8, 15 and 16 of the Returns Directive, such a third-country national must, as a matter of priority, be made the subject matter of a return procedure and may, as regards deprivation of liberty, be subject at most to placing in detention (*Achughbabian*, para. 38). National legislation such as that at issue in the main proceedings is, consequently, likely to thwart the application of the common standards and procedures established by the Returns Directive and delay the return, thereby, like the legislation at issue in *El Dridi*, undermining the effectiveness of the said Directive (*Achughbabian*, para. 39).

Linking the criminalisation of irregular stay with the return of the third-country national enabled the Court to apply *El Dridi* in this case, which prima facie involved the criminalisation of irregular stay *per se*. A key factor in the Court's reasoning was the self-standing nature of criminalisation. The Court noted that in the particular case there was nothing in the evidence before the Court to suggest that Mr Achughbabian has committed any offence other than that consisting in staying illegally on French territory. The situation of the applicant in the main proceedings could not therefore be removed from the scope of the Returns Directive, as Article 2 (2)(b) of the latter clearly cannot, without depriving that Directive of its purpose and binding effect, be interpreted as making it lawful for Member States not to apply the common standards and procedures set out by the said Directive to third-country nationals who have committed only the offence of illegal staying (*Achughbabian*, para. 41). The finding of the applicability of the Returns Directive led the Court to apply its *El Dridi* reasoning and stress that the principles of effectiveness and loyal co-operation must be respected in order to ensure the objectives of the Returns Directive, in particular that return must take place as soon as possible (*Achughbabian*, paras. 43–45). That would clearly not be the case if, after establishing that a third-country national is staying illegally, the Member

State were to preface the implementation of the return decision, or even the adoption of that decision, with a criminal prosecution followed, in appropriate cases, by a term of imprisonment. Such a step would delay the removal and does not appear among the justifications for a postponement of removal referred to in Article 9 of the Returns Directive (*Achughbabian*, para. 45). However, that does not exclude the possibility of Member States adopting or maintaining provisions, which may be of a criminal nature, governing, in compliance with the principles of the said Directive and its objective, the situation in which coercive measures have not enabled the removal of an illegally staying third-country national to take place (*Achughbabian*, para. 46).[12]

3.3 The Compatibility of National Legislation Criminalising Irregular Stay by Imposing a Fine with the Returns Directive: The Case of Sagor

The case of *Sagor*[13] concerned a reference to a preliminary ruling from the Tribunale di Rovigo in Italy on the compatibility of Returns Directive with national law which penalises illegal stay by third-country nationals by means of a fine which may be replaced by an order for expulsion or home detention. Unlike *Achughbabian*, where the Court was asked to rule on the compatibility of the Directive with national law criminalising irregular stay by the imposition of custodial sentences, *Sagor* addressed the question of the compatibility of the Returns Directive with alternative forms of criminalisation, i.e. the imposition of fines which may be replaced by an expulsion order or home detention. The Court reiterated its finding in *Achughbabian* that in principle the Returns Directive does not preclude the criminalisation of illegal stay by Member States (*Sagor*, para. 31) but qualified this statement by reiterating its finding in both *Achughbabian* and *El Dridi* that Member States may not apply criminal law rules which are liable to undermine the application of the common standards and procedures established by the Returns Directive and thus to deprive it of its effectiveness (*Sagor*, para. 32). The Court proceeded by distinguishing criminalisation leading to imprisonment from criminalisation under the facts of the present case leading to a fine or to an expulsion order. According to the Court, legislation which provides for a criminal prosecution which can lead to a fine for which an expulsion order may be substituted *has markedly different effects* from those of legislation providing for a criminal prosecution which may lead to a term of imprisonment during the course of the return procedure (*Sagor*, para. 34, emphasis added). The key factor here is the impact of such criminalisation on the functioning of the Returns Directive: according to the Court, the possibility that *a criminal prosecution as prescribed*

[12] See also the reference to *El Dridi*, paragraphs 52 and 60.

[13] Case C-430/11.

by the Italian legislation under review may lead to a fine is not liable to impede the return procedure established by the Returns Directive—the imposition of a fine does not in any way prevent a return decision from being made and implemented in full compliance with the conditions set out in Articles 6 to 8 of the Directive, nor does it undermine the common standards relating to deprivation of liberty set out in Articles 15 and 16 of the Directive (*Sagor*, para. 36). Moreover, the option given to the criminal court of replacing the fine with an expulsion order accompanied by an entry ban of at least 5 years is also not, in itself, prohibited by the Directive, which does not preclude the decision imposing the obligation to return from being taken—in certain circumstances as determined by the Member State concerned—in the form of a criminal judgment (*Sagor*, paras. 37–39). The Court noted in this context that Article 7(4) of the Directive allows the Member States to refrain from granting a period for voluntary departure, *in particular where there is a risk that the person concerned may abscond* in order to avoid the return procedure (*Sagor*, para. 41, emphasis added).[14] The discourse of risk enabled the Court here to adopt a harsh interpretation of the Returns Directive as regards the process of return, privileging automatic enforced removal over voluntary return.

However, the Court did apply its findings on the link between imprisonment and the effectiveness of the Returns Directive on the imposition by national law of a fine for which a home detention order may be substituted. The Court reiterated its finding in *Achughbabian* that it follows both from the duty of loyalty of the Member States and from the requirements of effectiveness referred to in the Directive that the obligation imposed on the Member States by Article 8 of that Directive to carry out the removal must be fulfilled as soon as possible (*Sagor*, para. 43). According to the Court, the imposition and enforcement of a home detention order during the course of the return procedure provided for by the Directive clearly do not contribute to the achievement of the removal which that procedure pursues, namely the physical transportation of the relevant individual out of the Member State concerned. Such an order does not therefore constitute a 'measure' or a 'coercive measure' within the meaning of Article 8 of the Returns Directive (*Sagor*, para. 44). The Court added that the home detention order is liable to delay, and thus to impede, the measures, such as deportation and forced return by air, which can be used to achieve removal. Such a risk of undermining the return procedure is present in particular where the applicable legislation does not provide that the enforcement of a home detention order imposed on an illegally staying third-country national must come to an end as soon as it is possible to effect that person's removal (*Sagor*, para. 45). The Returns Directive thus precludes national legislation which allows illegal stays by third-country nationals to be penalised by means of a home detention order without guaranteeing that the enforcement of that order must come to an end as soon as the physical transportation of the individual concerned out of that Member State is possible. The Directive's aim of speedy return thus prevails upon national criminalisation, which may take the form of home detention.

[14] But the Court added that such assessment must be done on an individual basis.

3.4 *The Compatibility of National Criminal Sanctions with the Returns Directive in the Context of the Imposition of Re-entry Bans:* Filev and Osmani

In its recent ruling in *Filev* and *Osmani*,[15] the Court examined the compatibility with the Returns Directive of German legislation imposing criminal sanctions for irregular entry following the imposition of an entry ban of unlimited duration predating the Directive. In the case of *Osmani*, an additional element has been that initial removal has been a consequence of a criminal conviction for drug trafficking (*Osmani*, paras. 15–18). The referring Court made clear that Mr Filev did not appear to pose a serious threat to public policy, public security or national security within the meaning of Article 11(2) of the Returns Directive (*Osmani*, para. 21). The Court was called to answer two questions concerning the compatibility of national criminal law with the Directive. The first question involves the compatibility of the imposition of national criminal sanctions for breach of an entry ban. Following its classic effectiveness reasoning in *El Dridi* and *Achughbabian*, the Court reiterated that Member States may not apply criminal legislation capable of imperilling the achievement of the objectives pursued by the Directive, thus depriving it of its effectiveness (*Osmani*, para. 36). The application of this reasoning in the present case led to the conclusion that a Member State may not impose criminal sanctions for breach of an entry ban falling within the scope of the Returns Directive if the continuation of the effects of that ban does not comply with Article 11(2) of the Directive (*Osmani*, para. 37). Moreover, Article 11(2) of the Directive precludes a continuation of the effects of entry bans of unlimited length made before the date on which the Directive became applicable, beyond the maximum length of entry ban laid down in that provision, except where those entry bans were made against third-country nationals constituting a serious threat to public order, public security or national security. As mentioned by the referring Court, Mr Filev did not appear to constitute such threat.

The Court was also called upon to answer a second question, on a different aspect of the relationship between the Returns Directive and national criminal law. The referring Court asked whether an expulsion order which predates by 5 years or more (i.e., the maximum period of the entry ban) the period between the date on which the Directive should have been implemented and the date on which it was actually implemented may subsequently be used as a basis for criminal proceedings, where that order was based on a criminal sanction within the meaning of Article 2(2)(b) of the Directive (*Osmani*, para. 46). Article 2(2)(b) allows Member States to decide not to apply the Directive to third-country nationals who are the subject of, inter alia, return as a criminal law sanction or as a consequence of a criminal law sanction in accordance with the provisions of national law (*Osmani*, para. 40). This question is of relevance as regards Mr Osmani, whose conviction for

[15] Case C-297/12, judgment of 19 September 2013.

drug trafficking framed him as a high-risk third-country national. The Court accepted that the Directive will not apply to third-country nationals referred to in Article 2(2)(b) in cases where Member States use the discretion conferred to them by this provision at the latest upon expiry of the period for implementing the Returns Directive (*Osmani*, para. 52). By contrast, if Member States have not made use of such discretion after the expiry of the implementation deadline, in particular because of the fact that they have not yet implemented the Directive in national law, they may no longer restrict the scope of the persons covered by the Directive (*Osmani*, para. 53). According to the Court, allowing Member States to use their discretion after the implementation deadline against a third-country national such as Mr Osmani in the present case *who could already directly rely* on the relevant provisions of the Returns Directive would be to worsen that person's situation (*Osmani*, para. 55, emphasis added). Member States can thus not exclude third-country nationals, whatever the risk they pose, from the scope of the Returns Directive and the protection it may offer if they do not loyally enforce EU law. European constitutional law, as reflected in the duty of loyal co-operation as far as Member States are concerned and the principle of direct effect as far as the affected individual is concerned, has come here to the rescue of a presumably in the eyes of the German authorities high-risk third-country national.

3.5 Commentary: The Returns Directive as a Limit to Immigrant Detention Following the Criminalisation of Migration at National Level

In all three cases analysed above, the Returns Directive places limits on domestic law criminalising immigration, and in particular national criminal law imposing sentences of imprisonment for immigration offences. While the Court has distinguished between criminalisation leading to detention from non-detention options, immigrant detention resulting from a national criminal prosecution without regard to the objectives of the Returns Directive is incompatible with EU law. A key element to the Court's reasoning is the tenuous link between detention and the achievement of the objectives of the Returns Directive: in all three cases, the Court has taken the view that detention may frustrate the returns process. Detention which is not linked to a speedy removal process or backed up by Member States' due diligence or is compliant with proportionality and fundamental rights is incompatible with EU law. While the Court was careful, in particular in its post-*El Dridi* case law, to leave Member States a degree of freedom in their domestic policy choices to criminalise migration, it has also sent a very strong signal against the symbolic criminalisation of migration. There needs to be a close link between criminalisation leading to detention and the achievement of the objectives of the Returns Directive (Mitsilegas 2012). Imprisonment for its own sake or as an end in itself is incompatible with EU law as it is not designed to lead to the eventual return of irregular migrants in accordance with proportionality and fundamental rights. At the same time, non-compliance with fundamental EU law principles such as loyal co-operation and the triggering of direct effect limit the criminal enforcement powers of Member States even in cases involving third-country nationals which may be perceived as high risk. In this manner, and for all its shortcomings, the Returns Directive—interpreted in the light of EU constitutional law—may act as a limit to the criminalisation and detention of migrants under national law.

4 Detention in the Context of the Implementation of the Returns Directive by Member States

A further opportunity for the Court of Justice to clarify the relationship between immigration detention and EU law has arisen in the context of litigation concerning the implementation of the Returns Directive. A key ruling in this context has been the Court's judgment in *Kadzoev*.[16] The case concerned the prolonged detention in Bulgaria of Mr Kadzoev, who was eventually declared by the Bulgarian authorities to be a stateless person. According to the order for reference, the help centre for survivors of torture, the office of the United Nations High Commissioner for Refugees and Amnesty International, found it credible that Mr Kadzoev was the victim of torture and inhuman and degrading treatment in his country of origin. Moreover, and despite the efforts of the Bulgarian authorities, several non-governmental organisations and Mr Kadzoev himself to find a safe third country which could receive him, no agreement was reached, and he had not as yet obtained any travel documents (*Kadzoev*, paras. 22–24). The reference by the Administrativen sad Sofia-grad has led to the Court of Justice clarifying a number of aspects of the Returns Directive related to immigration detention. Foremost, the Court confirmed that the period of detention completed by the person concerned during the procedure in which the lawfulness of the removal decision is the subject of judicial review must be taken into account for calculating the maximum duration of detention laid down in Article 15(5) and (6) of the Returns Directive. The Court held that, if it were otherwise, the duration of detention for the purpose of removal could vary, sometimes considerably, from case to case within a Member State or from one Member State to another because of the particular features and circumstances peculiar to national judicial procedures, which would run counter to the objective pursued by Article 15(5) and (6) of the Returns Directive, *namely to ensure a maximum duration of detention common to the Member States* (*Kadzoev*, paras. 53–54, emphasis added). The Court distinguished the maximum period of detention from the situation concerning suspensive appeals in asylum law, stating that the maximum periods laid down in Article 15(5) and (6) of the Returns Directive *serve the purpose of limiting the deprivation of a person's liberty*

[16] C-357/09 PPU, *Said Shamilovich Kadzoev (Huchbarov)*.

(*Kadzoev*, para. 56, emphasis added). This maximum detention limit also applies when the affected individual was deemed to be high risk by state authorities. The referring Court asked whether Article 15(4) and (6) of the Returns Directive allows the person concerned not to be released immediately, even though the maximum period of detention provided for by that Directive has expired, on the grounds that he is not in possession of valid documents, his conduct is aggressive and he has no means of supporting himself and no accommodation or means supplied by the Member State for that purpose (*Kadzoev*, para. 68). To this the Court reiterated that Article 15(6) of the Returns Directive in no case authorises the maximum period defined in that provision to be exceeded and that the possibility of detaining a person on grounds of public order and public safety cannot be based on the Directive (*Kadzoev*, paras. 69–70).

The Court stressed further the requirement for immigration detention under the Returns Directive to be linked with a reasonable prospect of removal. According to the Court, it is clear that, where the maximum duration of detention provided for in Article 15(6) of the Directive has been reached, the question whether there is no longer a 'reasonable prospect of removal' within the meaning of Article 15(4) does not arise. In such a case, the person concerned must in any event be released immediately. Article 15(4) of the Directive can thus only apply if the maximum periods of detention laid down in Article 15(5) and (6) of the Directive have not expired (*Kadzoev*, paras. 60–61). The Court added that under Article 15(4) of the Returns Directive, detention ceases to be justified and the person concerned must be released immediately when it appears that, for legal or other considerations, a reasonable prospect of removal no longer exists (*Kadzoev*, para. 63). As is apparent from Article 15(1) and (5) of the Directive, the detention of a person for the purpose of removal *may only be maintained as long as the removal arrangements are in progress and must be executed with due diligence, provided that it is necessary to ensure successful removal* (*Kadzoev*, para. 64, emphasis added). It must therefore be apparent, at the time of the national court's review of the lawfulness of detention, that a real prospect exists that the removal can be carried out successfully, having regard to the periods laid down in Article 15(5) and (6) of the Directive, for it to be possible to consider that there is a 'reasonable prospect of removal' within the meaning of Article 15(4) of that Directive (*Kadzoev*, para. 65). A reasonable prospect of removal does not exist where it appears unlikely that the person concerned will be admitted to a third country, having regard to those periods (*Kadzoev*, para. 66).

Kadzoev is an important judgment as it confirms the limits of detention under the Returns Directive and reiterates the key principles which govern its interpretation. As regards the length of detention, the Court links the achievement of a high level of harmonisation via the adoption of common standards with the imposition of a non-negotiable, maximum duration of immigration detention for the purposes of the Directive. Member States are prohibited by EU law to extend immigration detention beyond the time limits set out by the Returns Directive, even in cases where the individual under detention is deemed to be a risk to public order. This restrictive interpretation is inextricably linked with the teleological interpretation espoused by the Court in relation to the objectives of the Directive. In *Kadzoev*, the Court stresses that detention can be justified only if there is a reasonable prospect of removal and if Member States exercise due diligence in relation to the returns procedure. As in its case law in the *El Dridi* type cases analysed above, the Court emphasises again here that detention is only justified if it serves the key objective of the Returns Directive, which is the removal of irregular migrants. What *Kadzoev* also confirms is that the requirements of the existence of a reasonable prospect of removal and of the exercise of due diligence by States exist throughout the returns process and underpin the legality of immigrant detention. This has been confirmed recently by the European Court on Human Rights in its ruling on *Amie v Bulgaria.*[17] The Court avoided to rule specifically on the compatibility of domestic law with the Returns Directive and the maximum detention periods prescribed therein (*Amie v Bulgaria*, paras. 74–75). However, the Court found a breach of Article 5(1) (f) ECHR as it found that the grounds for the first applicant's detention—action taken with a view to his deportation—did not remain valid for the whole period of his detention due to *the lack of a realistic prospect of his expulsion and the domestic authorities' failure to conduct the proceedings with due diligence* (*Amie v Bulgaria*, para. 79). The Court also confirmed that the length of detention should not exceed that reasonably required for the purpose pursued (*Amie v Bulgaria*, para. 72).[18]

If *Kadzoev* can be read as a judgment setting limits to risk-based immigration detention, the Court's approach to risk in the context of immigration detention appears to be more nuanced in its more recent ruling in *Arslan.*[19] The case involved a request for a preliminary ruling by the Czech Supreme Administrative Court in proceedings between Mr Arslan, a Turkish national arrested and detained in the Czech Republic with a view to his administrative removal who during his detention has made an application for international protection, and the Czech police. Mr Arslan's detention was extended notwithstanding his lodging of an asylum application as it was deemed that the extension was necessary for preparing for the enforcement of the decision to remove him in view of the fact that the asylum procedure was still ongoing and it was not possible to enforce the removal decision while the asylum application was being considered. The Czech authorities also stated that the application for international protection had been made with the intention of hindering enforcement of the removal decision (*Arslan*, para. 25). In the light of the above facts, the Czech Court asked the Luxembourg Court whether the Returns Directive does not apply to a third-country national who has lodged an application for international protection within the meaning of the asylum procedures Directive and whether, if the Returns Directive does not apply, the detention

---

[17] Application No 58149/08.

[18] The Court noted that a similar point was recently made by the ECJ in relation to Article 15 of the Returns Directive. It should, however, be pointed out that unlike that provision Article 5(1) (f) ECHR does not lay down maximum time limits: the question whether the length of deportation proceedings could affect the lawfulness of detention under this provision thus depends solely on the particular circumstances of each case.

[19] Case C-534/11, judgment of 30 May 2013.

of a foreigner for the purpose of return must be terminated if he applies for international protection and there are no other reasons to keep him in detention.

The Luxembourg Court appeared to concur in principle with the referring Court in finding that the Returns Directive does not apply to a third-country national who has applied for international protection within the meaning of the asylum procedures Directive during the period from the making of the application to the adoption of the decision at first instance on that application or until the outcome of any action brought against that decision is known (*Arslan*, paras. 40–49). However, this prima facie exclusion of the applicability of the Returns Directive does not result in an unqualified protection of the asylum seeker from detention. In answering the second question, the Court of Justice—rather than applying directly the Returns Directive—used this Directive in order to interpret European asylum law. The Court noted that European asylum law (and in particular Article 7(3) of the reception conditions Directive and Article 18 of the asylum procedures Directive) allows Member States to confine an applicant to a particular place in accordance with their national law (*Arslan*, paras. 53/54, respectively). The Court further noted that neither the reception conditions nor the procedures Directive carries out currently a harmonisation of the grounds on which the detention of asylum seekers may be ordered—therefore, for the time being it is for Member States to establish, in full compliance with their obligations under international and EU law, the grounds on which an asylum seeker may be detained or kept in detention (*Arslan*, paras. 55–56). According to the Court:

> *As regards a situation such as that at issue in the main proceedings, in which, firstly, the third-country national was detained on the basis of Article 15 of Directive 2008/115 on the ground that his conduct gave rise to the concern that, if not detained, he would abscond and frustrate his removal, and, secondly, the application for asylum seems to have been made with the sole intention of delaying or even jeopardising enforcement of the return decision taken against him, such circumstances can indeed justify that national being kept in detention* even after an application for asylum has been made (*Arslan*, para. 57, emphasis added)

The Court has thus combined the limited harmonisation in European asylum law with the use of the Returns Directive, interpreted in a highly securitised, risk-based approach, in order to justify Member Sates' discretion to detain asylum seekers for extensive periods of time. The Court justified this approach further by arguing that a national provision which allows, in such circumstances, the detention of an asylum seeker is compatible with Article 18(1) of the asylum procedures Directive, since that detention does not result from the making of the application for asylum but from circumstances characterising the individual behaviour of the applicant before and during the making of that application (*Arslan*, para. 58). Detention under Article 15 of the Returns Directive acts thus as a factor justifying the detention of asylum seekers under European asylum law, based on the pre-supposition that the asylum seeker in question is a high-risk individual. The objectives of the Returns Directive (the effective return of third-country nationals) are used here not to protect third-country nationals but to extend detention under this risk-based approach (*Arslan*, para. 60). However, this approach sits uneasily with the Court's constant finding that detention for the purposes of removal governed by the Returns Directive and detention of asylum seekers under the reception and procedures Directives and national law fall under different legal rules (*Arslan*, para. 52; *Kadzoev*, para. 45). It also results in the criminalisation of asylum seekers, by allowing their extensive detention under national law which is interpreted in the light of the Returns Directive, which provides a high degree of harmonisation on enforcement. Immigration enforcement law is thus also applied in asylum law, although the objectives and scope of these two areas of law are markedly different. This approach, which is based heavily on the acceptance by the Court of governmental perceptions of risk, leads to clearly disproportionate outcomes for the asylum seekers involved. In the case of *Arslan*, the Court's ruling means that the effects of detention are intensified rather than alleviated by the fact that the third-country national in question has lodged an asylum application.

Another recent judgment which is informed by a restrictive, law enforcement approach is the Court's ruling in *M.G.*[20] In this case, the Court of Justice was asked to examine the impact of a breach of the rights of the defence by a decision by a national authority to prolong detention to the actual detention decision. The Court found that irregularities in the exercise of the rights of the defendant do not trigger automatically the release of the third-country national in detention (*M.G.*, para. 39). It is for the national judge to ascertain whether such irregularity could lead to a different result for the third-country national (*M.G.*, para. 40). According to the Court, not recognising a margin of appreciation in this context to the national judge and ruling that any violation of rights would lead automatically to the annulment of the decision prolonging detention would risk to undermine the effectiveness of the Returns Directive (*M.G.*, para. 41). The Court added that coercive measures taken under the Directive are subject not only to the principle of proportionality but also to the principle of effectiveness (*M.G.*, para. 42) and reiterated that the return of irregularly staying third-country nationals is a priority for Member States under the Directive (*M.G.*, para. 44). In this manner, the principle of effectiveness is used here by the Court to strengthen coercive action by the state under the Returns Directive and to nuance the protection of fundamental rights. The Court has thus used effectiveness in the field of procedural law in a markedly different manner to its approach in the *El Dridi* type cases involving criminalisation under substantive national criminal law. The ruling in *M.G.* is also another nod of the Court in favour of state sovereignty in the field of immigration control, most notably by stressing the discretion that national authorities, including courts, have in assessing aspects of the compliance of implementing action with the Returns Directive and EU constitutional law more broadly.

[20] Case C-383/13 PPU, *M.G. and N.R. v Staatsecretaris van Veligheid en Justitie*, judgment of 10 September 2013.

5 Conclusion

The adoption of the Returns Directive has been perceived as yet another reflection of the phenomenon of the criminalisation of migration in Europe. This assessment is largely justified in view of the choice of the EU legislator to maximise detention by allowing Member States to detain irregular migrants for a period up to 18 months. However, this chapter has demonstrated that the inclusion of immigrant detention provisions within the framework of European Union law and the efforts to achieve a high level of harmonisation in the field via the adoption of common standards have also contributed to the development of clear limits and protective safeguards as regards immigration detention. In particular, the introduction of a harmonised legal framework on returns at EU level has triggered the application of the general principles of European Union law: domestic law and practice on returns must thus be implemented and interpreted not only in compliance with the provisions and the general objectives of the Returns Directive but also in compliance with EU constitutional law, including human rights law. This 'federalisation' of the returns process in Europe has led to the development of a series of safeguards in the case law of the Court of Justice of the European Union. These safeguards are applicable at two levels: at the level of assessing the criminalisation of migration and immigrant detention in Member States in the light of the Returns Directive and at the level of the interpretation of the provisions of the Returns Directive *per se* in the process of its implementation by Member States. In both cases, the Court has rejected legislation and practices leading to symbolic criminalisation and detention of migrants (on the symbolic function of immigrant detention, see Cornelisse 2010, pp. 101–122/115) and has challenged the view prevalent in a number of Member States that immigration detention is an end in itself (on the use of detention by governments as an end in itself, see Wilsher 2011, p. 334). The Court has placed national implementation of the Returns Directive firmly within the scope of the fundamental principles of EU constitutional law. The Court further developed a teleological interpretation of the provisions of the Returns Directive, based on the need to ensure both the effectiveness of Union law and the protection of fundamental rights. This interpretation has resulted to immigrant detention being justified only if it is linked to a reasonable prospect of removal and only if it can be ascertained that Member States operate with due diligence in order to achieve the return of the affected third-country nationals. These important EU law safeguards, which apply throughout the removal process, are also increasingly permeating the case law of the European Court of Human Rights. Having said that, the Court's case law on the Returns Directive thus far should not be seen as shielding totally migrants from national criminalisation efforts: as demonstrated in the more recent judgment in *Arslan*, the Court of Justice has attempted to nuance somewhat its interpretation of the Directive in the light of persistent national law enforcement rhetoric. Further nuances to procedural protection can be discerned in the recent Court's ruling in *M.G.* The inevitable future challenges which will arise related to the Returns Directive will provide the European courts with further opportunities to develop their interpretation of the relationship between immigration detention and return. In the European Union legal order, the interpretation of the Returns Directive in the light of the Charter of Fundamental Rights and general principles of Union law, including legality and proportionality, will be crucial in this context.

References

Acosta D (2009) The good, the bad and the ugly in EU migration law: is the European parliament becoming bad and ugly? (The Adoption of Directive 2008/15: The Returns Directive). Eur J Migr Law 1(1):19–39

Baldaccini A (2009a) The EU directive on return: principles and protests. Refug Surv Q 28 (4):114–138

Baldaccini A (2009b) The return and removal of irregular migrants under EU law: an analysis of the returns directive. Eur J Migr Law 11(1):1–17

Cornelisse G (2010) Immigration detention and the territoriality of universal rights. In: De Genova N, Peutz N (eds) The deportation regime. Sovereignty, space, and the freedom of movement. Duke University Press, Durham, pp 101–122, 115

Cornelisse G (2012) Detention of foreigners. In: Guild E, Minderhoud P (eds) The first decade of EU migration and asylum law. Nijhoff, Leiden, pp 207–228 at 223

European Union Agency for Fundamental Rights (2011) Detention of third-country nationals in return procedures. Fundamental Rights Agnecy, Vienna

Mitsilegas V (2009) EU criminal law (chapter 2, para 53). Hart, Oxford

Mitsilegas V (2012) The changing landscape of the criminalisation of migration in Europe. The protective function of European Union Law. In: Guia M, Van der Woude M, Van der Leun J (eds) Social control and justice. Crimmigration in an age of fear. Eleven International Publishing, The Hague, pp 87–114

Wilsher D (2011) Immigration detention. Law, history, politics. Cambridge University Press, Cambridge, p 334

Immigration Detention and Non-removability Before the European Court of Human Rights

Marloes Anne Vrolijk

Abstract In this paper, case law of the European Court of Human Rights (ECtHR) is analysed to explore if repeated immigration detention amounts to a violation of fundamental human rights. This case law is compared to similar cases before other international human rights bodies. Finally, the paper recommends possible ways to address the problem of repeated immigration detention. Overall, this paper concludes that the jurisprudence of the ECtHR does not adequately clarify the situation and recommends turning to other disciplines to provide potential remedies.

1 Introduction

This paper examines repeated immigration detention in the European Union (EU). Repeated immigration detention is the successive use of pre-removal immigration detention for *non-removable* irregular immigrants. This practice resembles a tension which runs throughout international immigration law, namely the sovereign right of states to regulate migration versus the human rights of the migrants.[1]

This paper is a recapitulation of a master thesis which was written from May 2012 until July 2012 for the completion of a Master of Laws (cum laude) in Public International Law at Utrecht University, the Netherlands (2011–2012). The full thesis includes, amongst others, more detailed analyses of cases, a thicker description of international jurisprudence and a schematic table of the considered jurisprudence. When interested in receiving the full thesis, do not hesitate to contact me.

[1] Benhabib (2004), p. 47; Cornelisse (2010), pp. 113–125; Goodwin-Gill n/a.

M.A. Vrolijk (✉)
Utrecht University, Utrecht, The Netherlands
e-mail: marloesvrolijk@hotmail.com

M.J. Guia et al. (eds.), *Immigration Detention, Risk and Human Rights*,
DOI 10.1007/978-3-319-24690-1_4

The use of pre-removal immigration detention lies within the sovereign management of migration in the European Union Member States.[2] This is an administrative detention, and thus the immigrants deprived of their liberty in immigration detention are not detained as a result of a criminal conviction but with the view upon their removal.[3] While immigration detention as part of the removal process has generally been expanding,[4] so has the study of it. International organisations,[5] an international coalition,[6] research groups[7] and a human rights organisation[8] have all addressed the topic, particularly related to the length of detention.[9] Research shows that the longer the immigration detention lasts, the less likely it is that the immigrant detainee is *removed.*[10]

Non-removable irregular immigrants, including difficult to be removed or temporarily non-removable people, do not have legal status and do not want to or cannot be sent back to a country of origin.[11] As a result, these people find themselves in legal limbo.[12] Reactions to non-removability vary strongly from state to state.[13] The issue of non-removability generally remains unanswered within

---

[2] Returns Directive (2008), Art. 15 (with respect to the European Union); Cornelisse (2010), p. 1 (all European Union Member States include the possibility to resort to immigration detention in national legislation).

[3] van Kalmthout et al. (2007), p. 50.

[4] Fialho (2012), p. 2 (with respect to the United States of America); Leerkes and Broeders (2010), p. 830 (with respect to Europe, the United States of America and Australia).

[5] a.o. Human Rights Council (2009); Council of Europe (2010).

[6] The International Detention Coalition is a coalition of more than 250 non-governmental organisations and individuals advocating more respect for the human rights of immigrant detainees. See: International Detention Coalition n/a, Sect. About Us.

[7] The Global Detention Product is an interdisciplinary research centre concerned with mapping the use of immigration detention and the role the administrative measure plays in response to migration. See: Global Detention Project n/a, Sect. About the Global Detention Project: Aims, Origins, Staff.

[8] a.o. Amnesty International (2009b), Human Rights Watch (2010) (for a focus upon immigration detention in the USA), Amnesty International (2008) (concerning immigration detention in the Netherlands), Equal Rights Trust (2009) (focusing upon stateless persons in immigration detention worldwide).

[9] International Law Commission (2010), pp. 117–123; the ILC notes in its Draft Articles relating to the Expulsion of Immigrants, including a Draft Article on immigration detention, that it cannot be denied that the length of detention has an impact upon the conditions of the detention. See: *Ibid.*, p. 117.

[10] van Kalmthout et al. (2005), pp. 95–98.

[11] In this paper, the term irregular immigrant will be used to describe the group of people who are residing in a State without the proper documentation. This term is used in sake of neutrality and in line with the recommendations of the Council of Europe (CoE). Other used terms to refer to this group of people include undocumented migrants, unauthorised immigrants and illegals. See: Council of Europe Parliamentary Assembly (2006), para. 7.

[12] European Union Fundamental Rights Agency (2011), p. 29.

[13] *Ibid.*, p. 34.

domestic and supranational legislation.[14] Still, the manner in which states treat their citizens and non-citizens is an aspect of public international law due to international human rights law.[15]

This paper links the elements of pre-removal immigration detention and non-removability through focusing upon repeated immigration detention in the EU. Indefinite immigration detention is described as a limitless, potentially permanent, deprivation of an individual's liberty for purposes related to immigration.[16] In the EU, a legal time limit for immigration detention ostensibly prevents indefinite immigration detention.[17] In this paper it is argued that indefinite detention comes about with repeated detention.[18] Administrative detention can be functioning as a 'revolving door' where the to-be-removed immigrants cannot leave.[19] Overall, repeated immigration detention in the EU indicates that (temporarily) non-removable people remain part of a removal process that includes the use of pre-removal immigration detention.

Since the problem of non-removability remains unresolved,[20] the jurisprudence before the European Court of Human Rights (ECtHR), a leading court for the protection of constitutional or convention rights, is studied. The research question addressed in this paper is: how is repeated immigration detention dealt with by the ECtHR? In order to answer this question, this paper examines the ECtHR's broader treatment of non-removability in combination with immigration detention. Furthermore, the repeated use of immigration detention is examined through the lens of the European Convention of Human Rights (ECHR) and international human rights.

Immigration detention is foremost linked to non-removability through describing the repeated use of immigration detention in the EU. Additionally, various cases are selected and analysed from the ECtHR. The analysed cases all contain a link with non-removability and immigration detention because applicants are non-removable or difficult to be removed immigrants or the case raises related issues, such as grounds for immigration detention and length of detention. Building upon the cases, questions are raised about the lawfulness of repeated immigration detention. Additionally, the manner the Court treats the cases concerning immigration detention and non-removability is compared to international and regional jurisprudence about the issues of immigration detention and non-removability. This includes judgments and opinions of the International Court of Justice, the Human Rights Committee, the Court of Justice of the European Union, the

---

[14] Arcarazo (2011), pp. 8/16 (with respect to the EU); Fialho (2012), p. 2 (with respect to the USA).

[15] Lambert (2006).

[16] Zadvydas v. Davis 2001.

[17] Returns Directive (2008), Art. 15(5).

[18] United Nations High Commissioner for Refugees (1997), para. 2; United Nations High Commissioner for Refugees (2011), p. 60, para. 147 (regarding statelessness in the Netherlands); European Union Fundamental Rights Agency (2011), p. 27; Leerkes and Broeders (2010), p. 831.

[19] Leerkes and Broeders (2010), p. 831.

[20] Arcarazo (2011), pp. 8/16 (with respect to the EU); Fialho (2012), p. 2 (with respect to the USA).

Inter-American Court of Human Rights and the International Law Commission.[21] Finally, recommendations are made for addressing non-removability from a human rights perspective.

2 Non-removability and Immigration Detention

2.1 Non-removable Irregular Migrants

Non-removable irregular migrants are defined in terms of trying to enter a country, not being accepted and unable or unwilling to be returned to another country. It also covers immigrants in removal proceedings who cannot leave.[22] Various causes of non-removability are recognised. The International Organization for Migration (IOM) refers to a study from 2004 in which *lack of willingness of migrants* is considered the main hindering factor for return out of immigration detention.[23] Additionally, according to the European Union Fundamental Rights Agency (FRA) the reasons for non-removability beyond those within the migrant's personal control can be categorised in three groups:[24] human rights law safeguards which might hinder removal,[25] practical and technical reasons preventing removal[26] and state decisions not to return certain migrants on grounds which do not fall within the previous categories, such as public interests considerations.[27]

In the EU, the Directive on Common Standards and Procedures in Member States for Returning Illegally Staying Third Country Nationals (Returns Directive) has been in force since December 24th, 2010,[28] with the objective to create common arrangements and rules in the EU regarding, amongst others, return, removal and detention.[29] The Returns Directive does not make explicit what the legal status is of those people who cannot be removed.[30] Nor does it illustrate how to deal with or end situations of legal limbo.[31] Thus, the question of what to do with the people who are not desired but cannot be sent back remains unanswered.[32]

---

[21] Statute of the International Court of Justice (1945), Art. 38(1)d.

[22] Arcarazo (2011), p. 7; European Union Fundamental Rights Agency (2011), p. 27.

[23] Kox (2011), p. 10; van Kalmthout et al. (2005), p. xviii.

[24] European Union Fundamental Rights Agency (2011), pp. 29–30.

[25] This is, amongst others, addressed by the ECtHR in *Boultif v. Switzerland* and *Üner v. the Netherlands*. See: European Union Fundamental Rights Agency (2011), pp. 30–31.

[26] European Union Fundamental Rights Agency (2011), pp. 29–30.

[27] *Ibid.*

[28] Zwaan (2011), p. 1.

[29] Arcarazo (2011), pp. 8/16 (with respect to the EU); Fialho (2012), p. 2 (with respect to the USA).

[30] Arcarazo (2011), pp. 8/16.

[31] European Union Fundamental Rights Agency (2011), p. 29.

[32] Arcarazo (2011), p. 16.

2.2 *Immigration Detention*

Immigration detention is an administrative measure used for migration-related issues. It is not a measure of the penal system, and immigration detainees are deprived of their liberty not as a result of a criminal conviction but in order to prevent entrance into a country or ensure departure.[33] Immigration detention knows various forms, including border detention upon arrival and pre-removal immigration detention.[34] This paper mainly focuses on pre-removal immigration detention, concerning irregular migrants who are not legally entitled to stay in the country they are residing in and are awaiting removal to their home country.[35] When considering the link with non-removability, various phenomena of the removal process become relevant such as indefinite administrative detention and repeated immigration detention. In the USA, indefinite administrative immigration detention has been recorded[36] and criticised[37] and is still warned for since no time limit for all forms of immigration detention exists.[38] Fialho argues that such a time limit should be set for all forms of immigration detention in the USA in order to comply with international law standards.[39] She warns that even if such a time limit exists for all forms of immigration detention in the USA, there is a danger for non-removability issues still showing themselves in the form of repeated immigration detention.[40] I consider that this is exactly what is occurring in the EU.

3 Repeated Immigration Detention in the European Union

The repeated use of immigration detention can be described as a series of administrative detentions following each other. If an irregular migrant is repeatedly detained in immigration detention, a first immigration detention did not achieve the purpose of removal in the allowed maximum time of detention or there was no further view upon removal and the immigrant detainee is released. Still, this individual keeps an irregular status and can be re-arrested with the view upon removal and subsequently released and re-arrested continuously. This practice is

[33] van Kalmthout et al. (2007), p. 50.

[34] Cornelisse (2010), pp. 1–2.

[35] van Kalmthout et al. (2007), p. 50.

[36] Siskin (2012), p. 6.

[37] Global Detention Project (2010), p. 12; Inter-American Commission on Human Rights (2010), p. 83; Fialho (2012), p. 2.

[38] Fialho (2012), p. 22.

[39] *Ibid.*, pp. 28–30.

[40] Fialho (2012), p. 30.

also referred to as *re-detention*[41] or *revolving-door* immigration detention.[42] Cornelisse states that even though the legislation of most EU Member States includes maximum time limits upon immigration detention, released immigrant detainees cannot always leave the country and are re-apprehended and re-detained.[43] Within the different Member States of the EU, possibilities for non-citizens to be re-detained in immigration detention differ.

In some countries, non-citizens are safeguarded from repeated immigration detention. In Austria, national law provides a safeguard for repeated immigration detention through setting a 2-year time period in which a non-citizen can be detained for 6–10 months. If this time limit is exceeded, the non-citizen cannot be detained anymore within these 2 years, unless non-removability is caused by the non-citizen himself or herself.[44] Moreover, the non-citizens have the right to get a free certificate indicating how much time is already spent in immigration detention.[45]

In other countries, there are no such explicit safeguards from repeated immigration detention. For instance, in Malta repeated immigration detention is explicitly addressed and allowed in the national legislation.[46] Without consulting the Immigration Appeals Board, the Principal Immigration Officer can re-detain a non-citizen in immigration detention if there are no current procedures under the Refugees Act and the Officer considers that there is a *reasonable prospect of removal*.[47]

Moreover, in Belgium repeated immigration detention can occur because the various times spent in immigration detention are not considered to provide a cumulative total length of detention. To begin with, a new detention decision is ordered every time there is objection to an attempted deportation.[48] The Committee on Civil Liberties, Justice and Home Affairs of the European Parliament committee concluded after visiting Belgian immigration detention centres that despite the officially determined maximum length, the detention can remain limitless in practice because a new time limit starts when a person appeals against his or her deportation.[49] Additionally, the Committee criticises that the statistics provide an inaccurate overview of the maximum lengths which people are spending in

---

[41] Fialho (2012), pp. 15/30.

[42] Leerkes and Broeders (2010), p. 831.

[43] Cornelisse (2010), p. 18.

[44] Federal Act on the Exercise of Aliens' Police (2006), Art. 80(4); European Union Fundamental Rights Agency (2010), p. 47.

[45] Federal Act on the Exercise of Aliens' Police (2006), Art. 81(3); European Union Fundamental Rights Agency (2010), p. 47.

[46] Immigration Act 1970, Art. 25(A)(12).

[47] European Union Fundamental Rights Agency (2010), p. 48.

[48] *Ibid.*

[49] Committee on Civil Liberties, Justice and Home Affairs (2007), p. 3.

immigration detention.[50] Each time an immigrant detainee is transferred to another detention facility, the counted time in immigration detention starts anew.[51]

With respect to the Netherlands, the Committee for the Prevention of Torture (CPT) reports, after its last country visit to the Netherlands in October 2011, that several sources indicate that immigrants were at times re-arrested after being released from immigration detention and having spent the maximum period of time there.[52] The CPT requests the Dutch authorities to comment on this point.[53] Additionally, the United Nations High Commissioner for Refugees (UNHCR) criticises that the Netherlands is amongst the countries where a formalised determination procedure for stateless people is missing.[54] The UNHCR discusses in a study to the situation of stateless people in the Netherlands that, without a procedure for determining statelessness, some people are not able to get a legal resident status and run the risk to be repeatedly detained in immigration detention.[55] The UNHCR describes the detention of stateless people in immigration detention in the Netherlands as very common and lengthy.[56] Moreover, the UNHCR expresses its concerns over the repetitiveness of the process of detention in which the stateless people find themselves.[57] Finally, with respect to the Netherlands, and similarly as in Belgium, no statistics are kept of the repeated use of immigration detention.

With respect to immigration detention practices in Italy, the United Nations Working Group on Arbitrary Detention concludes that many of the immigrant detainees were detained two, three or four times.[58] These people would have spent the nationally allowed 60-day period in immigration detention, could not be removed, were released and additionally re-detained. The Working Group concludes that authorities would not take the situation of non-removables and the resulting possibility of pointless immigration detention properly into consideration.[59]

Concerning Greece, Akritidou, Antonopoulo and Pitsela describe how a group of immigrants whose deportation is considered infeasible is released from immigration detention after the legal time limit of 3 months expired. These immigrants are released and ordered to leave the country within 30 days. After this period, it is

---

[50] *Ibid.*, pp. 3–4.

[51] European Union Fundamental Rights Agency (2010), p. 48.

[52] European Committee for the Prevention of Torture and Inhuman and Degrading Treatment or Punishment (2012), para. 54.

[53] *Ibid.*, p. 62.

[54] United Nations High Commissioner for Refugees (2011), p. 1.

[55] *Ibid.*, p. 2.

[56] *Ibid.*, p. 2, para. 13.

[57] *Ibid.*

[58] Human Rights Council (2009), para. 81.

[59] *Ibid.*

possible that these immigrants are re-detained for a new period of 3 months.[60] They conclude that as a result, there are many immigrants repeatedly going out and coming in of immigration detention.[61]

In two EU countries, the issue of repetitive immigration detention has been explicitly considered to be unlawful at a national level.[62] First of all, in Portugal the National Supreme Court decided in 2007 that it is against the law to detain a non-citizen in an immigration detention facility if this individual has already spent the maximum period of immigration detention in another facility.[63] Second, in Greece the national Ombudsman communicated in 2008 that successive deportation orders, including successive detention decisions, are not in accordance with the law.[64]

Various bodies, such as the UNHCR and the FRA,[65] describe and criticise the repeated use of immigration detention and reaffirm the presence of non-removable people or people who are difficult to be removed in immigration detention.[66] Moreover, the FRA reasons that in countries where non-removed irregular migrants are tolerated but do not get an official recognition of this status, the non-removed irregular migrants are not protected from being rearrested and detained in an arbitrary manner[67], and thus can experience repeated immigration detention.

In academia the phenomenon is explored and criticised as well. Cornelisse refers to the practice of repeated immigration detention and reasons that the situation is not regulated by legal provisions which limit the length of detention. She additionally criticises that repeated instances of immigration detention do not show in the statistics of duration of detention since the repeated instances of immigration detention are not recorded.[68] Leerkes and Broeders describe this repeated process of pre-removal immigration detention as a result of an act they call *cobbling*. *Cobbling* refers to the act of releasing immigrants from immigration detention if expulsion is not realised into life without a legal status. Additionally, they describe

[60] Akritidou et al. (2007), pp. 418–419.

[61] *Ibid.*, p. 419.

[62] European Union Fundamental Rights Agency (2010), p. 47.

[63] *Ibid.*, p. 47 (referring to the Case: 07P2836, [2007] Supreme Court of Portugal (Supremo Tribunal de Justiça) http://www.dgsi.pt/jstj.nsf/954f0ce6ad9dd8b980256b5f003fa814/5d58a7ea0581ce80802573640058fee7?OpenDocument. Accessed 3 August 2012).

[64] European Union Fundamental Rights Agency (2010), p. 47 (referring to Press release (2008, 7 January) Successive deportation in a 'legal vacuum': Actions of the Greek Ombudsman to stop successive deportations of aliens. www.synigoros.gr (in Greek). Accessed 3 August 2012).

[65] The European Union Fundamental Rights Agency (FRA) is an advisory body of the European Union which was established in 2007 by a legal act of the European Union. The FRA collects evidence regarding fundamental rights of people living in the EU. See: European Union Fundamental Rights Agency (n/a), Sect. About the FRA.

[66] United Nations High Commissioner for Refugees (2011), p. 60, para. 147; European Union Fundamental Rights Agency (2011), p. 27.

[67] *Ibid.*, p. 35.

[68] *Ibid.*, p. 18.

that such *cobbled* detainees are often re-detained when continuing illegal residence and conclude that the immigration detention system could become a *revolving door* for these immigrants.[69]

4 Repeated Immigration Detention and Human Rights

Article 5 of the ECHR addresses the right to liberty and security of person.[70] It includes the possibility to resort to immigration detention as a lawful form of liberty deprivation.[71] Additionally, the Returns Directive includes in Article 15(5) and (6) that immigration detention in the EU knows a formal time limit of 18 months.[72] At an international level, the International Covenant on Civil and Political Rights (ICCPR) includes the protection against arbitrary liberty deprivation in Article 9 (1).[73] This Article is not violated if detention is applied consistently with a procedure established by law.[74] The Human Rights Committee (HRC) elaborates that this Article is applicable to deprivations of liberty in light of the immigration process.[75]

5 Repeated Immigration Detention Before the European Court of Human Rights

The ECtHR explicitly considers repeated immigration detention in *John v. Greece*. The repeated use of immigration detention was considered in violation of Article 5 (1) of the ECHR.[76] Since only one case raises the issue of repeated immigration detention before the ECtHR, general trends from the case law applied to cases concerning non-removable immigrants and immigration detention are addressed. These include one of the earliest immigration detention cases raising the issue of non-removability (*Chahal v. United Kingdom* in 1996), a case brought before the court by a stateless applicant (*Auad v. Bulgaria* in 2011) and a case addressing a non-citizen held in various types of immigration detention (*Longa Yonkeu v. Latvia* in 2011). Consequently, the general principles following from these cases are applied to repeated immigration detention.

[69] Leerkes and Broeders (2010), p. 831.

[70] Convention for the Protection of Human Rights and Fundamental Freedoms (European Convention on Human Rights) 1950, Art. 5(1)(f).

[71] *Ibid.*

[72] Returns Directive (2008), Art. 15(5).

[73] International Covenant on Civil and Political Rights (1966), Art. 9(1).

[74] *Ibid.*

[75] Human Rights Committee (1982), para. 1.

[76] John v. Greece 2007, para. 33.

6 The Necessity of Immigration Detention

The ECtHR reasons that the grounds for immigration detention do not have to be *reasonably considered necessary* with respect to, amongst others, risk of fleeing or committing an offence. It is not relevant if the underlying decision for the immigration detention is justified by national or Convention law.[77] This is a recurring theme in the case law of the ECtHR and was primarily raised in *Chahal*[78] in 1996. In this case, the immigration detention for 6 years caused debate among the Judges but was not considered in breach of Article 5(1). Moreover, the *reasonable considered necessary* principle is addressed in *Conka*[79] in 2002 and was reassured in *Soldatenko v. Ukraine*[80] in 2008 and *Auad*[81] in 2011. In these cases, this aspect is raised as the first general principle, in the section of the Courts' assessment of the alleged violation of Article 5(1).

The Court does not address the aspect of necessity in *Longa Yonka v. Latvia* in 2011 but goes straight into discussing the *quality of law* requirement. Additionally, in *John v. Greece*, the case which explicitly raises the repeated use of immigration detention, the Court does not raise the *reasonable considered necessary* aspect but contrastingly reasons that Article 5(1) has to be interpreted narrowly.

The International Commission of Jurists states that when applying Article 5(1)(f) in relation to detention preventing unauthorised entry, the ECtHR finds that there is no need to prove that the immigration detention is reasonable, necessary or proportionate.[82] They argue that this approach is in contrast with 5(1)(b), (d) and (e), which acquire that necessity and proportionality must be assessed in each individual case and detention should be a last resort measure.[83]

In relation to pre-removal immigration detention, the International Commission of Jurists holds that due to the terms used in Article 5(1)(f) the scrutiny applied to this type of detention is narrower than in comparison with other types of detention.[84] They consider that other human rights conventions, such as the ICCPR, do not apply such a narrow scrutiny to administrative immigration detention cases.[85] The International Commission of Jurists is critical that undertaken activities in order to realise deportation can solely justify pre-removal immigration detention while other factors do not have to be proven.[86]

[77] Bleichrodt (2006), p. 481.

[78] Chahal v. The United Kingdom 1996, para. 112.

[79] Conka v. Belgium 2002, para. 38.

[80] Soldatenko v. Ukraine 2008, para. 109.

[81] Auad v. Bulgaria 2011, para. 128.

[82] International Commission of Jurists (2011), p. 152.

[83] *Ibid.*

[84] *Ibid.*, p. 157.

[85] *Ibid.*

[86] *Ibid.*

Cornelisse states that the ECtHR has problems in defining safeguards for immigration detainees who, according to her research, enjoy a protection of human rights below the standard level.[87] She identifies the root of the problem in the ECtHR's perspective that immigration detention would be a necessary element of a country's sovereign right to control the territory.[88]

Overall, the ECtHR's immigration detention precedent shows that Article 5(1)(f) provides a surprisingly low level of protection from arbitrary detention. Thus, immigrant detainees enjoy less protection from infringements upon fundamental human rights compared to other detainees.

7 The Quality of Law Scrutiny

As a second principle, the Court generally considers whether the detention was lawful with respect to the purposes of Article 5(1)(f).[89] In doing so, the Court considers if a legal procedure, as Article 5 requires, has been followed and considers adherence to the substantive and procedural rules.[90]

According to the ECtHR, the legal procedure allowing immigration detention according to domestic law has to be in conformity with the general principles expressed or implied in the ECHR.[91] The Court emphasises that in cases of deprivation of liberty, general legal principles should be adhered to.[92] Thus, Article 5(1) also refers to the *quality of the law* standard, which requests that the application of lawful liberty deprivation is accessible, precise and foreseeable.[93] The *quality of law* standard is addressed, amongst others, in *Soldatenko v. Ukraine* in 2008 and in *Longa Yonkeu v. Latvia*.[94] Moreover, in *John v. Greece* the Court reasons that each deprivation of liberty has to be *in accordance with the law* and thus should be in line with the procedural and substantive norms which are included in Article 5 of the ECHR.[95] Costello considers that due to this *quality of law* standard, there is room to incorporate new legal standards or norms into the conception of *in accordance with the law* applied by the ECtHR.[96]

---

[87] Cornelisse (2010), p. 310.

[88] *Ibid.*

[89] Soldatenko v. Ukraine 2008, para. 109.

[90] *Ibid.*, para. 110.

[91] *Ibid.*, para. 111.

[92] *Ibid.*, para. 109 (referring to Khudoyorov v. Russia 2005, Ječius v. Lithuania 2000, Baranowski v. Poland 2000 and Amuur v. France 1996).

[93] *Ibid.*, para. 111.

[94] Longa Yonkeu v. Latvia 2011, para. 120.

[95] John v. Greece 2007, para. 28.

[96] Costello (2012), p. 278.

8 Due Diligence and Action Taken with a View to Deportation

In *Auad*, which raises the issue of non-removability since the applicant is stateless, the Court considers the detention to be in violation of Article 5(1). Proceedings with a view to deportation do not meet the requirements of due diligence.[97] The Court explicitly notices that uncertainty regarding the origin of the non-citizen to be removed can hamper due diligence and considers that legal certainty has to be applied in such cases.[98] The Court notices that due diligence can only be established when considering the facts of the case and thus applies a case-by-case analysis.[99] The ECtHR refers in *John v. Greece* to the need to respect the substantive safeguards to a repeated instance of immigration detention when applying Article 5 (1) properly.[100] Nevertheless, this is not repeated as a general trend throughout the case law.

9 Sending a Refugee in Orbit

A related notion to repeated immigration detention is the repeated attempt to expel an irregular migrant to a country without being granted entrance to that particular country.[101] This is known as *sending a refugee in orbit* and was already discussed in 1980.[102] Spijkerboer and Vermeulen refer to two cases when stating that repeated failed attempts of removal to various countries can violate the prohibition upon non-human and degrading treatment or behaviour as spelled out in Article 3 of the ECHR. In *Manitu Giama v. Belgium* in 1980[103] and *Z. v. the Netherlands* in 1984,[104] the European Commission of Human Rights (ECommHR)[105] considered that repeated deportations of a person of whom no identity or nationality was known could amount to a violation of Article 3 of the ECtHR.[106]

[97] Auad v. Bulgaria 2011, pp. 131–135.

[98] *Ibid.*, para. 133.

[99] *Ibid.*, para. 131 (referring to Chahal, A. and Others v. the United Kingdom, Mikolenko v. Estonia, Raza).

[100] John v. Greece 2007, para. 28.

[101] Spijkerboer and Vermeulen (2005), p. 106; United Nations High Commissioner for Refugees (2011), pp. 37/60, para. 147.

[102] Spijkerboer and Vermeulen (2005), p. 106.

[103] Manitu Giama v. Belgium 1980, pp. 73–94.

[104] Z. v. the Netherlands 1984, p. 150, para. 1.

[105] The European Commission functioned from 1953 to 1988 alongside the European Court of Human Rights. See: Lawson (2009).

[106] Z. v. the Netherlands 1984, para. 31.

Likewise, Mandal states that repeated attempts at expulsion to a country which is not guaranteed to admit the individual may amount to inhuman or degrading treatment under Article 7 of the ICCPR.[107] Additionally, the UNHCR claims that the repetitive process of detention of non-removable people may amount to treatment prohibited by the same Article.[108]

Considering the prohibition on *sending a refugee in orbit* and recognising the similarities of the futile repetitiveness of repeated immigration detention and the *sending of a refugee in orbit*, I question if the repetitive immigration detention of individuals who are non-removable or difficult to be removed would account for 'cruel or inhuman treatment' as prohibited by the ECHR and the ICCPR. After all, the sole purpose of the administrative immigration detention should be return or preparation for return to a country of origin.[109]

Overall, it shows from the case law before the ECtHR that it is reasoned that the detention itself does not have to be *reasonably considered necessary* and no actual case-by-case analysis is required. Following, it is explored if repeated immigration detention is a theme within international jurisprudence as well and if so, how the ECtHR's reasoning compares to the reasoning of the international bodies. Again, textual law does not address the issue of repeated immigration detention, but jurisprudence does and is therefore elaborated upon.

10 Repeated Immigration Detention in the International Jurisprudence

Various international bodies deal with immigration detention cases and address the aspects of the necessity of immigration detention in order to validate its non-arbitrariness. Principally, at a regional level the case law of the Court of Justice of the European Union (CJEU) is considered. Additionally, for a regional comparison the Supreme Court of the United States of America (SCOTUS) is elaborated upon. The international jurisprudence of the Human Rights Committee (HRC), the Inter-American Court of Human Rights (IACtHR) and the International Court of Justice (ICJ) are explored. Finally, the writings of the International Law Commission (ILC) are elaborated upon as well.

The Court of Justice of the European Union (CJEU) addressed two cases concerning pre-removal immigration detention. The first case called *Saïd*

---

[107] United Nations High Commissioner for Refugees (2011), p. 37, para. 81 (quoting UNHCR consultant Mandal R (2010) Discussion Paper no. 4: What Status Should Stateless Persons Have at the 109 National Level? Discussion papers series for the establishment of a UNHCR Handbook on the Determination of Statelessness, p. 20).

[108] *Ibid.*, p. 60, para. 147.

[109] Returns Directive (2008), Art. 15.

Shamilovich Kadzoev v. Direktsia 'Migratsia' pri Ministerstvo na vatreshnite raboti[110] from 2009 concerns the immigration detention of a declared stateless person for a period of 34 months.[111] In this case, the Court clarifies, amongst others, that the notion of a reasonable prospect of removal, which is included in the Returns Directive, is not applicable if the maximum period of time in immigration detention has been exceeded.[112] The CJEU's second ruling regarding the legality of pre-deportation immigration detention is *El Dridi*, decided in 2011.[113] The Court decides against the criminalisation of irregular stay in this case.[114]

In the United States of America, the Supreme Court of the United States (SCOTUS) has dealt with several cases raising issues of indefinite immigration detention.[115] Due to the similar root causes of indefinite and repeated immigration detention, the conclusions of the Court are of relevance to the present discussion. The SCOTUS safeguarded constitutional rights for immigrant detainees in *Zadvydas v. Davis* in 2001, addressing the constitutionality of indefinite immigration detention.[116] In this case, the Court took a judicial activist role by reading in an implicit time limit into the statute allowing post-removal immigration detention and thus hindering the occurrence of indefinite immigration detention.[117] On the one hand, the Court did not apply this time limit to pre-removal immigration detention.[118] On the other hand, the Court did safeguard immigrant detainees in immigration detention upon admittance from indefinite immigration detention by applying the time limit set in its earlier jurisprudence to this group as well.[119] Thus, the time limit safeguarding immigrant detainees from indefinite immigration detention is not applied to all types of immigration detention; this is criticised since indefinite immigration detention is considered constitutionally doubtful for all types of immigration detention since *Zadvydas v. Davis* was decided in 2001.[120]

At an international level, the Human Rights Committee (HRC) reasons in *A. v. Australia* in 1997 that resort to immigration detention should be necessary when

[110] Saïd Shamilovich Kadzoev v. Direktsia 'Migratsia' pri Ministerstvo na vatreshnite raboti is a reference to the ECJ from the Bulgarian 'Sofia City Administrative Court' to give a preliminary ruling concerning a declared stateless person residing in immigration detention. See: Saïd Shamilovich Kadzoev v. Direktsia 'Migratsia' pri Ministerstvo na vatreshnite raboti 2009, para. 1-2/22.

[111] Costello (2012), p. 264.

[112] Saïd Shamilovich Kadzoev v. Direktsia 'Migratsia' pri Ministerstvo na vatreshnite raboti 2009, paras. 59–62.

[113] Costello (2012), p. 295.

[114] El-Dridi (2011), paras. 25/58/59.

[115] Clark v. Martinez 2005; Demore v. Kim 2003; Zadvydas v. Davis 2001; United States ex rel. Knauff v. Shaughnessy 1950.

[116] Zadvydas v. Davis 2001.

[117] *Ibid.*, p. 9.

[118] *Demore v. Kim* 2003, p. 20.

[119] *Clark v. Martinez* 2005, pp. 2-3/5.

[120] Fialho (2012).

considering each circumstance of the case.[121] The case concerned the prolonged detention upon arrival of an asylum seeker and the continuous detention for 4 years in various immigration detention facilities.[122] Additionally, the HRC considers in this case that arbitrariness does not purely equal unlawfulness but includes elements such as inappropriateness and injustice.[123] Moreover, the Committee reasons in *Danyal Shafiq v. Australia* in 2002 concerning a *de facto* stateless person spending 7 years in immigration detention[124] that apart from being necessary, the detention should be proportionate in relation to the goals which are aimed to be achieved.[125] The Committee considers the lengthy immigration detention in *Shafiq* to be arbitrary and in violation of Article 9(1) of the ICCPR.[126] The HRC finds that individual circumstances justifying detention must be established on a case-by-case basis to establish if the detention is arbitrary or not. This follows from *Samba Jalloh v. the Netherlands* in 2002[127] and *C. v. Australia* in 2002.[128]

The Inter-American Court of Human Rights (IACtHR) holds in the immigration detention case of *Vélez Loor v. Panama* in 2010 that detention not only has to be a necessity but even essential in order to realise the intended purpose.[129] Moreover, the International Court of Justice (ICJ) addresses necessity in relation to length of detention. In the case of *Republic of Guinea v. Democratic Republic of the Congo* in 2010, the ICJ considers that the immigration detention of the Guinean national *Ahmadou Sadio Diallo* is arbitrary because authorities did not consider if it was necessary to detain the immigrant.[130]

Another factor is the requirement that alternatives should be used or considered before resorting to immigration detention.[131] Firstly, the HRC considers the detention in *Bakhtiyari* arbitrary because no alternatives were considered.[132] Secondly, the IACtHR finds that detention should only be used if no less restrictive measures are available which could achieve the same end.[133] Finally, the HRC requests a

---

[121] A. v. Australia 1997, para. 9.4.

[122] *Ibid.*, para. 9.3.

[123] *Ibid.*, para. 9.3; C. v. Australia 2002, para. 8.2; Samba Jalloh v. the Netherlands 2002, para. 8.2.

[124] Applicant is stateless since he has no birth certificate from Bangladesh, and the Bangladesh mission to Australia does not recognise him as citizen of Bangladesh due to the omission of a birth certificate. See: Danyal Shafiq v. Australia 2006, para. 2.2.

[125] Danyal Shafiq v. Australia 2006, para. 7.2.

[126] *Ibid.*

[127] Samba Jalloh v. the Netherlands 2002, para. 8.2.

[128] C. v. Australia 2002, para. 8.2.

[129] Vélez Loor v. Panama 2010, para. 167.

[130] Republic of Guinea v. Democratic Republic of the Congo 2010, para. 82.

[131] Ali Aqsar Bakhtiyari and Roqiha Bakhtiyari v. Australia 2003, para. 9.3 (referring to A. v. Australia and C. v. Australia); Vélez Loor v. Panama (2010), para. 166; Samba Jalloh v. the Netherlands 2002, para. 8.2; C. v. Australia 2002, para. 8.2.

[132] Ali Aqsar Bakhtiyari and Roqiha Bakhtiyari v. Australia 2003, para. 9.3 (referring to A. v. Australia and C. v. Australia).

[133] Vélez Loor v. Panama 2010, para. 166.

case-by-case analysis to establish if the detention is arbitrary or not.[134] The ICJ applies a similar individual analysis,[135] and so does the IACtHR.[136] The *Diallo* case before the ICJ raises an aspect of repetitive immigration detention, and the ICJ reasons that the *cumulative* amount of the various detentions should not have exceeded the maximum allowed length of immigration detention.[137] This is an indication that repeated immigration detention might cumulatively be interpreted in accordance with international law.

Additionally, the International Law Commission (ILC), which was created in order to promote the development and codification of international law,[138] has focused since 2004 on the issue of *expulsion of non-citizens*.[139] The ILC drafted a draft article concerning the interaction between conditions in and of immigration detention and the universal human rights of the irregular immigrants who are detained or expelled.[140] The ILC includes in its draft article that immigration detention should only last as long as *reasonably considered necessary* to realise removal.[141] Costello concludes that it would be appropriate if the ECtHR would follow the jurisprudence of the HRC and adhere to the norms of the EU law and thus apply necessity and proportionality requirements to immigration detention.[142] The International Commission of Jurists states that the HRC does not apply the same narrow scrutiny as the ECtHR regarding detention pending removal.[143] Additionally, Cornelisse criticises this aspect of the ECtHR and describes immigration detention cases as *blind spots* of the ECtHR.[144]

Thus, all international courts offer the protection of necessity. The HRC and the IACtHR protect necessity the strongest since these bodies reason that the detention has to be necessary from the initial moment that the immigration detention commences. Thus, especially when considering these bodies, there is a clear difference with the ECtHR, which rejects the *reasonable considered necessary* test. Costello describes how in the immigration detention case law the ECtHR takes a more modest role compared to the CJEU. Moreover, she criticises that the HRC offers a stronger protection for immigrant detainees than the ECtHR. She reasons that

[134] Samba Jalloh v. the Netherlands 2002, para. 8.2; C. v. Australia 2002, para. 8.2.

[135] Republic of Guinea v. Democratic Republic of the Congo 2010, para. 82.

[136] Vélez Loor v. Panama 2010, para. 166.

[137] Republic of Guinea v. Democratic Republic of the Congo 2010, para. 79.

[138] Shaw (2008), p. 121.

[139] ILC (2010).

[140] ILC (2010), pp. 122–123.

[141] International Law Commission (2010), pp. 122–123.

[142] *Ibid.*, p. 287.

[143] International Commission of Jurists (2011), p. 157.

[144] Costello (2012), pp. 308–312.

failures at both the national and regional levels are made if the regional system offers protection lower than the internationally lower limit set by the ICCPR.[145]

Overall, it shows that the standards and safeguards applied to immigration detention cases by international bodies are generally higher than those which the ECtHR applies. This is especially clear when considering that the ECtHR applies that the immigration detention does not have to be *reasonably considered necessary* and no individual case analysis is needed, while other human rights bodies, the CJEU and the IACtHR in particular, consider that immigration detention has to be necessary in order not to become arbitrary.

11 The Lawfulness of Repeated Immigration Detention

In first instance, it seems that non-removable or difficult to be removed irregular migrants are not safeguarded from repeated immigration detention through an application of the ECHR. After all, the general trends in the case law show that the need to resort to detention is not analysed on a case-by-case basis. Moreover, immigration detention does not have to be *reasonably considered necessary*, while other forms of detention under the ECHR do.

Still, when actually being detained, immigrant detainees will find that the Court applies more safeguards to a reasonable length of detention. It requests the adherence to good faith and procedural and substantive norms in order for the detention not to be considered arbitrary. This follows from the case law which shows that the manner in which the detention is executed does have to adhere to fundamental principles of international human rights law, including due diligence requirements. This is applied in immigration detention cases such as *Auad*, concerning a stateless applicant, and *John*, with respect to repeated immigration detention in which the length of the immigration detention has to be proportional to the ends sought and the authority has to act with due diligence. Additionally, as a second general principle a *quality of law* standard is applied to the immigration detention cases.[146] The *quality of law* standard safeguards detainees from arbitrariness and obliges authorities to adhere to procedural and substantive norms applicable to immigration detention.

With respect to this second principle, and the case-by-case analysis, the early findings of the ECommHR become relevant. This body reasoned that the repeated attempt to expel a person could amount to a violation of Article 3 of the Convention if the individual cooperated,[147] while they considered Article 3 irrelevant if the

---

[145] Costello (2012), p. 267.

[146] Longa Yonkeu v. Lativa 2011, para. 120; Soldatenko v. Ukraine 2008, paras. 109–111; John v. Greece 2007, para. 28.

[147] Manitu Giama v. Belgium 1980, para. 13.

individual refused cooperation.[148] These findings are also in line with the Draft Article the ILC proposed with respect to immigration detention, stating that the detention should end when the failure to send an individual back is not accountable to the immigrant detainee.[149]

Overall, it is likely that the ECtHR will not find the repeated use of immigration detention *ipso facto* in violation of the Convention due to the lack of the *reasonable considered necessary* scrutiny and the neglect of a case-by-case analysis. Still, the Court generally applies a second principle which includes the consideration of the case by itself and the application of the *quality of law* standard. The Court is more likely to conclude after applying this second general principle that in specific cases of repeated immigration detention, a violation of the Convention occurred.

Turning to the international jurisprudence, the HRC and the IACtHR apply a principle of necessity for justifying resort to detention, and the ICJ and the CJEU require necessity for the execution of the measure. Therefore, it is plausible that repeated immigration detention will be considered in violation of the relevant international human rights provisions, including the prohibition to arbitrary detention and the right to liberty and security of person.

12 Solutions to Repeated Immigration Detention

The EU statistics concerning immigration detention are at times unclear.[150] National statistics, such as in the Netherlands and in Belgium, do not show if repetitive detentions occur. The number of times an immigrant detainee is administratively detained is simply not registered. Cornelisse states that the repeated instances of immigration detention are not recorded and not apparent from statistics concerning duration of detention.[151] The United Nations Working Group on Arbitrary Detention addresses this issue with respect to immigration detention practices in Italy where the repeated detention of one irregular immigrant appears in the statistics as several irregular immigrants detained for a short period of time. The Working Group concludes that due to this distorted representation in statistics, the cases of repeated instances of immigration detention even lower the number of the official overall average time spent in immigration detention and the amount of irregular immigrants detained in immigration detention.[152] Thus, first and foremost, even before addressing the substantive possible solutions, it is of high importance that the statistics regarding the repeated use of immigration detention are properly kept.

[148] Z. v. the Netherlands 1984, p. 145.

[149] International Law Commission (2010), p. 123.

[150] Cornelisse (2010), p. 7.

[151] *Ibid.*, p. 18.

[152] Human Rights Council (2009), para. 81.

13 Preventing Repeated Immigration Detention

The FRA reasons that an upper time limit for time possibly spent in immigration detention is meaningless if the immigrants can be repeatedly detained after release.[153] The FRA proposes to set a time frame in which detentions may cumulatively not exceed the legal time limit of immigration detention in order to solve this.[154] Such a construction already exists in Austria.[155] Similarly, Fialho suggests that in the USA next to the general time limit of 6 months to immigration detention, a maximum overall period of 12 months in immigration detention within any 5-year period should be set as a second ceiling.[156]

Another means to prevent the repeated use of immigration detention is application of the necessity and proportionality requirements.[157] If the ECtHR does not change the current standards and continues to reason that immigration detention does not have to be *reasonably considered necessary*, the resort to detention knows a lower threshold than the safeguards during the actual application of the detention, and the possible repeated aspect of immigration detention is not prevented. Thus, if the safeguard for irregular migrants who risk to be repeatedly detained in immigration detention will not change from the onset, the repeated use of immigration detention will not decrease.

14 Stateless People in Immigration Detention

The immigration detention of stateless people showed a recurring issue in the case law relating to immigration detention and non-removability before human right bodies. This is in line with the UNHCR's perception of statelessness as a global problem[158] and the UN Secretary General's affirmation of this perception.[159] Thus, the queries resulting from non-removability in combination with immigration detention would already be decreased if at least for the group of *de jure* and *de facto* stateless people it is ensured that they do not end up in immigration detention as long as they remain stateless. The United Nations Secretary General reasons that a prerequisite to protect the rights of stateless people would be a formalised procedure in order to determine statelessness and through which stateless individuals can claim protection, including due process safeguards.[160] An official

[153] European Union Fundamental Rights Agency (2010), p. 47.

[154] *Ibid.*

[155] Federal Act on the Exercise of Aliens' Police (2006), Art. 80(4).

[156] Fialho (2012), p. 30.

[157] Costello (2012), p. 287.

[158] United Nations High Commissioner for Refugees (1997), para. 2.

[159] United Nations Secretary-General (2011), p. 6.

[160] *Ibid.*

determination of *de jure* and *de facto* statelessness would help to keep these people out of immigration detention.

15 Alternatives to Immigration Detention

The application of the requirements of necessity and proportionality would also lead to a presumption against immigration detention and enhance the use of alternatives for immigration detention.[161] The Returns Directive requires that before resorting to detention, less coercive measures should be considered and thus detention is a last resort.[162] In the international jurisprudence, the HRC interprets the prohibition of arbitrary detention to include the need to consider or use alternatives to immigration detention.[163] The International Detention Coalition (IDC) has been studying alternatives to immigration detention and developed a *Community Assessment and Placement model*.[164] This model argues for a presumption against immigration detention, the use of immigration law enforcement through non-custodial measure combined with the effective support of individuals in the community and the use of immigration detention only as a last resort.[165] Moreover, the Vera Institute researched alternatives for immigration detention in the USA such as supervised release which would serve the same purpose as detention.[166] Other bodies and organisations such as Amnesty International and the Jesuit Refugee Research Service have studied alternatives to immigration detention as well.[167]

16 Situation of Non-removable Immigrants

Altogether it shows that the repeated use of immigration detention is an expression of the underlying problem that no answer is provided to the presence of non-removable people living in a legal limbo in a state where they are not desired. In line with Arcarazo's criticism that the Returns Directive does not address the

[161] Costello (2012), p. 287.

[162] Returns Directive (2008), Art. 15(1).

[163] Ali Aqsar Bakhtiyari and Roqiha Bakhtiyari v. Australia 2003, para. 9.3 (referring to A. v. Australia and C. v. Australia); C. v. Australia 2002, para. 8.2.

[164] International Detention Coalition (2011); Office of the High Commission for Human Rights' United Nations High Commission for Refugees (2011).

[165] Sampson et al. (2011).

[166] *Ibid.*; Fialho (2012), p. 20.

[167] Jesuit Refugee Service Europe (2011), Amnesty International (2009a) (general report), Amnesty International (2011) (concerning the Netherlands specifically).

question of what to do with those immigrants who cannot be removed,[168] the case law similarly leaves this question unanswered. The FRA identifies three policy responses to non-removed irregular migrants, namely de facto toleration, formal toleration or the granting of a residence permit.[169] Costello criticises that the question of how to respond to non-removability is not adequately answered, identifies that there is no identified solution beyond the level of the national state and considers that emphasis should be put upon proper political and judicial developments at the national level.[170]

17 Conclusion

Repeated immigration detention in the EU shows that non-removable or difficult to be removed people are made part of a removal process which includes the use of administrative immigration detention. Since the situation of non-removability is not addressed in domestic and supranational legislation, it has been studied how the ECtHR deals with cases raising this issue.

The ECtHR has only dealt with one case raising repeated immigration detention, where they found a violation of the right to liberty and security of person.[171] When considering the other case law before the ECtHR addressing non-removability and immigration detention, several general trends in the jurisprudence are identified. First of all, the ECtHR considers that the detention itself does not to have to be *reasonably considered necessary* and no actual case-by-case analysis is required to justify the immigration detention.[172] Due to this trend, it is likely that the ECtHR will not find the repeated use of immigration detention *ipso facto* in violation of the Convention. This trend in the Court's jurisprudence is criticised, especially because a more narrow scrutiny is applied to other forms of detention such as criminal detentions.[173] Second, the Court generally applies a second principle to the immigration detention cases, according to which the case is considered by itself, and the *quality of law* requirement is applied.[174] Moreover, in the most striking cases combining immigration detention and non-removability, an explicit scrutiny of adherence to due diligence is applied by the ECtHR.[175] Thus, if it is clear that the

[168] Arcarazo (2011), pp. 8/16.

[169] European Union Fundamental Rights Agency (2011), p. 334.

[170] Costello (2012), p. 303.

[171] John v. Greece 2007, para. 33.

[172] Chahal v. The United Kingdom 1996, para. 112; Conka v. Belgium 2002, para. 38; Soldatenko v. Ukraine 2008, para. 109; Auad v. Bulgaria 2011, para. 128.

[173] Cornelisse (2010), pp. 277–308; Costello (2012).

[174] Longa Yonkeu v. Lativa 2011, para. 120; Soldatenko v. Ukraine 2008, paras. 109–111; John v. Greece 2007, para. 28.

[175] Auad v. Bulgaria 2011, paras. 131–135; John v. Greece 2007, para. 28.

detention was applied without a reasonable view upon removal, the ECtHR could conclude that in specific cases addressing repeated immigration detention, a violation of the Convention occurred.

Turning to the international jurisprudence, the HRC and the IACtHR apply a principle of necessity for the resort to detention, and the ICJ and the CJEU require necessity for the execution of the measure. Therefore, it is very likely that repeated immigration detention will be considered by these international bodies as being in violation of the relevant international human rights provisions, including the prohibition to arbitrary detention and the right to liberty and security of person.

Turning to solutions to repeated immigration detention, it is foremost concluded that statistics have to be kept properly in order to register the repeated use of immigration detention. Various sources show that this is not occurring properly at the moment. Additionally, in order to prevent the repeated use of immigration detention apart from an upper time limit of immigration detention, a set time frame in which this time limit cumulates is suggested. After all, an upper time limit of detention without a time frame in which this applies shows meaningless since the repeated use of immigration detention is not prevented.

Throughout the literature and case law, it also shows that *de facto* stateless people end up in pre-removal immigration detention. A formal recognition of *de jure* and a (temporary) recognition of *de facto* statelessness would already exclude this group of people from the complexities regarding non-removability and immigration detention. Addressing the deeper causes of indefinite immigration detention and the repeated use of immigration detention, it is suggested that when applying the principles of necessity and proportionality the use of alternatives to immigration detention is enhanced. The ECtHR does not apply these principles, but other international bodies do. A presumption against immigration detention and the application of immigration detention as a last resort will reduce the instances of repeated immigration detention since it requires a narrower scrutiny before using the measure.

References

Books and Contributions in Edited Volumes

Akritidou M, Antonopoulo A, Pitsela A (2007) Greece. In: van Kalmthout A, Hofstee-van der Meulen F, Dünkel F (eds) Foreigners in European prisons, vol 1. Wolf Legal Publishers, Nijmegen, pp 393–423

Arcarazo D (2011) The returns directive: possible limits and interpretations. In: Zwaan K (ed) Returns directive: central themes, problems, issues and implementation in selected Member States. Wolf Legal Publishers, Nijmegen, pp 7–24

Benhabib S (2004) The right of others: aliens, residents and citizens. Cambridge University Press, Cambridge

Bleichrodt E (2006) Right to liberty and security of person (Article 5). In: van Dijk P, van Hoof F, van Rijn A, Zwaak L (eds) Theory and practise of the European Convention on Human Rights. Intersentia, Antwerpen

Cornelisse G (2010) Immigration detention and human rights: rethinking territorial sovereignty. Martinus Nijhoff, Leiden

Lawson R (2009) The European Convention on Human Rights. In: Krause C, Scheinin M (eds) International protection of human rights: a textbook. Gummerus Printing Abo Akademi University, Abo, pp 423–462

Shaw M (2008) International law. Cambridge University Press, New York

Spijkerboer T, Vermeulen B (2005) Vluchtelingenrecht. Ars Aequi Libri, Nijmegen

van Kalmthout A, Graft A, Hansen L, Hadrouk M (2005) Terugkeermogelijkheden van Vreemdelingen in de Vreemdelingenbewaring. Wolf Legal Publishers, Nijmegen

van Kalmthout A, Hofstee-van der Meulen F, Dünkel F (2007) Foreigners in European prisons, vol 1. Wolf Legal Publishers, Nijmegen

Zwaan K (2011) Introduction. In: Zwaan K (ed) Returns directive: central themes, problems, issues and implementation in selected Member States. Wolf Legal Publishers, Nijmegen

Journal Articles

Costello C (2012) Human rights and the elusive universal subject: immigration detention under international human rights and EU law. Indiana J Global Leg Stud 19(10):257–303

Fialho C (2012) Rethinking pre-removal immigration detention in the United States: lessons from Europe and proposals for reform. Refugee Surv Q 31:69–100

Leerkes A, Broeders D (2010) Formal and informal functions of administrative immigration detention: a case of mixed motives? Br J Criminol 50:830–850

Case Law and Treaties

A. v. Australia (1997) Comm. No. 560/1993 (U.N. Doc. CCPR/C/59/D/560/1993). Human Rights Committee

Ali Aqsar Bakhtiyari and Roqiha Bakhtiyari v. Australia (2003) Comm. No. 1069/2002 (U.N. Doc. CCPR/C/79/D/1069/2002). Human Rights Committee

Auad v. Bulgaria (2011) App. No. 46390/10. EctHR

C. v. Australia (2002) Comm. No. 900/1999 (U.N. Doc. CCPR/C/76/D/900/1999). Human Rights Committee

Chahal v. The United Kingdom (1996). App. No. 22414/93. ECtHR

Clark v. Martinez (2005) 543 U.S. SCOTUS

Conka v. Belgium (2002) App. No. 51564/99. ECtHR

Convention for the Protection of Human Rights and Fundamental Freedoms (European Convention on Human Rights) 1950

Danyal Shafiq v. Australia (2006) Comm. No. 1324/2004 (U.N. Doc. CCPR/C/88/D/1324/2004). Human Rights Committee

Demore v. Kim (2003) 538 U.S. SCOTUS

El-Dridi (2011) Case C-61/11. ECR

Federal Act on the Exercise of Aliens' Police (2006) The Issue of Documents for Aliens and the Granting of Entry Permits (2005 Aliens' Police Act). http://www.unhcr.org/refworld/docid/46adc4932.html. Accessed 3 August 2012

Longa Yonkeu v. Latvia (2011) App. No. 57229/09. ECtHR
International Covenant on Civil and Political Rights (1966)
Immigration and Nationality Act (1952) http://www.uscis.gov. Accessed 3 August 2012
John v. Greece (2007), App. No. 199/05. ECtHR (only available in French)
Manitu Giama v. Belgium (1980) App. No. 7612/76. Decisions and Reports (21). ECommHR
Republic of Guinea v. Democratic Republic of the Congo (2010). ICJ
Returns Directive: Directive 2008/115/EC of the European Parliament and of the Council of 16 December 2008 on common standards and procedures in Member States for returning illegally staying third-country nationals (2008) Official Journal of the European Union: 98–107
Saïd Shamilovich Kadzoev v. Direktsia 'Migratsia' pri Ministerstvo na vatreshnite raboti (2009) Case C-357/09. ECR
Samba Jalloh v. the Netherlands (2002) Comm. No. 794/1998 (U.N. Doc. CCPR/C/74/D/794/1998). Human Rights Committee
Soldatenko v. Ukraine (2008) App. No. 2440/07. ECtHR
Statute of the International Court of Justice (1945)
United States ex rel. Knauff v. Shaughnessy (1950) 345 U.S. 544
Vélez Loor v. Panama (2010). IACtHR
Z. v. the Netherlands (1984) App. No. 10400/83. Decisions and Reports (38). ECommHR
Zadvydas v. Davis (2001) 533 U.S. SCOTUS

Reports, Webpages and Miscellaneous Sources

Amnesty International (2008) The Netherlands: the Detention of Irregular Migrants and Asylum-Seekers. http://www.amnesty.nl/sites/default/files/public/rap_nederland_vreemdelingendetentie_0.pdf. Accessed 2 August 2012
Amnesty International (2009a) Irregular Migrants and Asylum-Seekers: Alternatives to Immigration Detention. http://www.amnesty.org/en/library/asset/POL33/001/2009/en/08b817ac-d5ae-4d47-a55c-20c36f7338cf/pol330012009en.pdf. Accessed 7 August 2012
Amnesty International (2009b) Jailed Without Justice: Immigration Detention in the USA. http://www.amnestyusa.org/pdfs/JailedWithoutJustice.pdf. Accessed 2 August 2012
Amnesty International (2011) Vreemdelingendetentie in Nederland: Het Moet en Kan Anders. http://www.amnesty.nl/sites/default/files/public/1110_vreemdelingendet.pdf. Accessed 7 August 2012
Committee on Civil Liberties, Justice and Home Affairs (2007) Report on a visit to closed detention centres for asylum seekers and immigrants in Belgium (European Parliament Doc. PE404.456v01-00) http://www.europarl.europa.eu/meetdocs/2004_2009/documents/pv/714/714008/714008en.pdf. Accessed 7 August 2012
Council of Europe (2010) The Detention of Asylum Seekers and Irregular Migrants in Europe (Parliamentary Assembly, Resolution 1707). http://www.unhcr.org/refworld/docid/4b6bec802.html. Accessed 2 August 2012
Council of Europe Parliamentary Assembly (2006) Human Rights of Irregular Migrants (Resolution 1509)
Equal Rights Trust (2009) Unravelling Anomaly Detention; Detention, Discrimination and the Protection Needs of Stateless Persons. http://www.equalrightstrust.org/ertdocumentbank/UNRAVELLING%20ANOMALY%20small%20file.pdf. Accessed 22 July 2012
European Committee for the Prevention of Torture and Inhuman and Degrading Treatment or Punishment (2012) Report to the Government of the Netherlands on the visit to the Netherlands carried out by the CPT from 10 to 21 October 2011. http://www.cpt.coe.int/documents/nld/2012-21-inf-eng.pdf. Accessed 9 August 2012

European Union Fundamental Rights Agency (n/a) European Union Fundamental Rights Agency: Helping to make fundamental rights a reality for everyone in the European Union. http://fra.europa.eu/fraWebsite/about_fra/about_fra_en.htm. Accessed 6 May 2012
European Union Fundamental Rights Agency (2010) Detention of Third Country Nationals in Return Procedures. http://fra.europa.eu/fraWebsite/attachments/detention-third-country-nationals-report-092010_en.pdf. Accessed 7 August 2012
European Union Fundamental Rights Agency (2011) Fundamental Rights of Migrants in an Irregular Status in the European Union. http://fra.europa.eu/fraWebsite/attachments/FRA_2011_Migrants_in_an_irregular_situation_EN.pdf. Accessed 4 August 2012
Global Detention Project (n/a) Global Detention Project: Mapping the Use of Detention in Response to Growing Global Migration. www.globaldetentionproject.org/. Accessed 1 August 2012
Global Detention Project (2010) Immigration and Detention and the Law: U.S. Policy and Legal Framework. http://www.globaldetentionproject.org/fileadmin/docs/US_Legal_Profile.pdf. Accessed 1 August 2012
Goodwin-Gill G (n/a) International Migration Law. United Nations Audiovisual Library of International Law. http://untreaty.un.org/cod/avl/ls/Goodwin-Gill_IML_video_1.html. Accessed 18 June 2012
Human Rights Committee (1982) General Comment no. 8: Right to Liberty and Security of Person (Art. 9). Sixteenth session CCPR
Human Rights Council (2009) Promotion and Protection of all Human Rights, Civil, Political, Economic, Social and Cultural Rights, Including the Right to Development (Report of the Working Group on Arbitrary Detention, UN Doc. A/HCR/10/21/Add.5)
Human Rights Watch (2010) Costly and Unfair; Flaws in US Immigration Detention Policy. http://www.hrw.org/sites/default/files/reports/usimmigration0510webwcover.pdf. Accessed 2 August 2012
Inter-American Commission on Human Rights (2010) Report on Immigration in the United States; Detention and Due Process. http://www.oas.org/en/iachr/migrants/docs/pdf/Migrants2011.pdf. Accessed 7 August 2012
International Commission of Jurist (2011) Migration and International Human Rights Law, Practitioners Guide No. 6. http://www.icj.org/dwn/img_prd/PGNo6-ElectronicDistribution1.pdf. Accessed 11 August 2012
International Detention Coalition (n/a), International Detention Coalition: Human Rights for detained refugees asylum seekers and migrants. www.idcoalition.org. Accessed 1 August 2012
International Detention Coalition (2011) There Are Alternatives to Prevent Unnecessary Immigration Detention. http://idcoalition.org/cap/. Accessed 7 August 2012
International Law Commission (2010) Sixth Report on the Expulsion of Aliens; by Mr. Maurice Kamto, Special Rapporteur (doc. A/CN.4/625)
Jesuit Refugee Service Europe (2011) From Deprivation to Liberty: Alternatives to Detention in Belgium, Germany and the United Kingdom. http://jrseuropefromdeprivationtoliberty20122011.pdf/. Accessed 7 August 2012
Kox M (2011) Leaving Detention? A Study on the Influence of Immigration Detention on Migrant's Decision Making Processes Regarding Return, International Organization for Migration Publication
Lambert H (2006) The Position of Aliens in Relation to the European Convention on Human Rights. Council of Europe Publication, Strasbourg
Office of the High Commission for Human Rights/United Nations High Commission for Refugees (2011) Global Roundtable on Alternative to Detention of Asylum-Seekers, Refugees, Migrants and Stateless. http://www.unhcr.org/4dde23ab9.pdf. Accessed 7 August 2012
Sampson R, Mitchell G, Bowring L (2011) There Are Alternatives: A Handbook for Preventing Unnecessary Immigration Detention. International Detention Coalition Publication, Melbourne. http://massivefishball.com/IDC_Handbook.pdf. Accessed 7 August 2012

Siskin A (2012) Immigration-Related Detention: Current Legislative Issues. Congressional Research Service Publication

United Nations High Commissioner for Refugees (1997) Brief on Statelessness and Detention Issues. http://www.unhcr.org/refworld/docid/4410638fc.html. Accessed 3 May 2012

United Nations High Commissioner for Refugees (2011) Staatloosheid in Nederland. http://www.unhcr.nl/unhcr-in-nederland/campagnes/staatloosheid.html. Accessed 12 July 2012 (report is currently not available online)

United Nations Secretary-General (2011) Guidance Note of the Secretary General: The United Nations and Statelessness. http://www.unhcr.org/refworld/docid/4e11d5092.html. Accessed 4 May 2012

Immigration Detention: An Instrument in the Fight Against Illegal Immigration or a Tool for Its Management?

Galina Cornelisse

Abstract This contribution argues that immigration detention's distinctly territorial logic needs to be fully accounted for in any attempt to understand the contemporary use of this instrument. As such, penal approaches to the study of detention policies need to be complemented and informed by constitutional and transnational legal scholarship, not only so that we can fully grasp the distinctiveness of immigration detention but also in order to be able to formulate adequate legal responses to this measure. This chapter substantiates these claims by taking a look at the case law of both the European Court of Human Rights (ECtHR) and the Court of Justice of the EU (CJEU) concerning the detention of irregular migrants.

1 Introduction

Over the past two decades, immigration detention has evolved from an issue that received little scholarly or public attention to a subject of intense academic debate and considerable public discussion. Whereas early academic writings focused mostly on the alleged exceptional nature of immigration detention, more recent scholarship has tried to make sense of that measure by the use of the paradigm of *crimmigration*, denoting a process in which states increasingly rely on the logic and tools of criminal policing to govern international human mobility. In this contribution, I will argue that immigration detention's distinctly *territorial logic* needs to be fully accounted for in any attempt to understand the use of detention in immigration policies. As such, penal approaches to the study of detention policies need to be complemented and informed by constitutional and transnational legal scholarship, not only so that we can fully grasp the distinctiveness of immigration detention but also in order to be able to formulate adequate legal responses to this measure. This chapter substantiates these claims by taking a look at the case law of both the European Court of Human Rights (ECtHR) and the Court of Justice of the EU (CJEU) concerning the detention of irregular migrants. Although the CJEU has only relatively recently began to address immigration detention (in the context of

G. Cornelisse (✉)
Department of Transnational Legal studies, Faculty of Law, Free University, Amsterdam, The Netherlands
e-mail: g.n.cornelisse@vu.nl

M.J. Guia et al. (eds.), *Immigration Detention, Risk and Human Rights*,
DOI 10.1007/978-3-319-24690-1_5

the Returns Directive), we will see that it is less susceptible to the logic of territorial sovereignty than the ECtHR has so far been in its case law on immigration detention. The case law by the CJEU is also pertinent to our subject because it has explicitly addressed the relationship between on the one hand *administrative forms of immigration control* and the *governing of migration by the means of criminal laws* on the other hand.

The chapter is structured as follows. In Sect. 2, I will set the stage by briefly addressing penological approaches to the study of immigration detention. The distinctly territorial logic of immigration detention is further elaborated upon in Sect. 3, with particular attention to the way in which this logic has impacted upon the legal control of immigration detention by the ECtHR. Section 4 will focus on the case law of the CJEU in this area and pay particular attention to (1) differences with the ECtHR case law and (2) the way it has addressed the relationship between administrative forms of immigration control and its penal counterpart. The chapter concludes with some remarks regarding opportunities to pose legal challenges to contemporary practices of immigration detention in the EU.

Before continuing, a preliminary remark remains to be made: this chapter does not address the detention laws and policies of a particular country but rather takes a more general approach by which contemporary tendencies that can be witnessed throughout the EU are explained and contextualised against the background of international and European legal norms. Notwithstanding the European focus of the chapter, as regards those parts that discuss the theory of immigration detention, I have also made use of literature that seeks to shed light on the situation in other parts of the world.

2 Immigration Detention and the New Penology

As already mentioned above, the increase in the use of immigration detention by liberal democracies over the last 20 years has been accompanied by a steadily growing academic interest. Not surprisingly, a large part of the research in the legal studies stems from criminological roots, and it has tended to view the growing use of immigration detention as part of a general tendency in contemporary societies towards risk minimisation and societal control, and in which unwanted migrants are seen as a "dangerous" group that needs to be identified and managed by the use of measures from the criminal justice system, such as "police, penalties and prisons" (Welch 2002, p. 23; see also Schuster 2005). In order to explain the growth in immigration prisons, several authors have pointed to the emergence of the *New Penology*, a concept embracing both the theory and practice of punishing, and supposedly entailing a novel way of controlling and responding to crime and deviant behaviour (Simon 1998; Welch 2000). The New Penology differs from traditional penology in that it focuses on "categories of potential and actual offenders rather than on individuals, and on managerial aims rather than rehabilitation or transformation of the offender" (Easton and Piper 2008, p. 21; see also

Welch 2000, p. 74).[1] As a result, enforcement and coercion are no longer primarily directed at the individual but focus unevenly across categories of specific populations, whose potential for risk is assessed by means of actuarial policies and technological tools and contained by increased reliance on imprisonment (see also Bauman 2000).

It is inherent in the very paradigm of the New Penology that it encompasses forms of social control which fall outside the traditional sphere of criminal law enforcement, and as such it is not surprising that a link has been made between the New Penology and contemporary tools of immigration law enforcement (Feeley and Simon 1992; Miller 2003, 2005). Indeed, the increasing criminalisation of "illegal" stay, the setting up of annual quota to be achieved for deportation and the steep increase in the use of technological tools in order to "combat" illegal migration can be seen as reflecting the contemporary rise of so-called actuarial justice in a risk-obsessed society. With regard to immigration detention in particular, it has been argued that this practice reflects a "globalizing culture of control" driven by "perceptions of difference and putative threat" (Schuster and Welch 2005, p. 347; see also Bauman 1998). The way in which the detention of "illegal" migrants resonates with the contemporary political "management of risk" has also been emphasised by authors who claim that immigration detention has primarily become an instrument to "assuage public fears concerning supposed 'risks' and potential dangers to 'security'" (Malloch and Stanley 2005).

Undeniably, the everyday practice of immigration detention in the EU Member States fits these observations: immigration detention is a large-scale instrument—almost punitive in character—that explicitly targets categories of persons, leaving ever less scope for the consideration of the individual circumstances of each and every case. This holds true not only for the decision by the executive to resort to detention, but it often also applies to the way in which the judiciary assesses its legitimacy. Thus, for a long time, the highest administrative court in the Netherlands argued that the fact that someone is detained on grounds which are applicable to nearly every applicant for asylum does not mean that these grounds in themselves are not enough to justify the use of detention in an individual case (Administrative Division of the Council of State, 22 January 2008). The inexorable result of such a line of reasoning is that it is no longer the specific situation of the individual that is decisive for the application of a particularly coercive form of social control. Instead, depriving the individual of his or her liberty is seen as legitimate merely because he or she is designated as belonging to a specific group, a mechanism that is even more explicitly at work in countries that have mandatory detention provisions for certain nationalities. The discourse of "efficiency, management and control" even seemed to have found its way to the ECtHR. In the case of *Saadi*, the Grand Chamber did not deem the detention of an asylum seeker for reasons of mere "administrative convenience" to be in violation of the right to personal liberty, even if the decision to detain Mr Saadi, a Kurdish asylum seeker from Northern

[1] On the "New Penology" in general, see Feeley and Simon (1992).

Iraq, was primarily based on his nationality (*Saadi v. United Kingdom*, 29 January 2008, Appl. No. 13229/03, para. 24). Decisive for its judgment were "the difficult administrative problems" with which the national state concerned was confronted as a result of "an escalating flow of huge numbers of asylum seekers" (*Saadi v. United Kingdom*, 29 January 2008, Appl. No. 13229/03, para. 80).

Approaches that draw on the paradigm of the New Penology to explain the institutionalisation of immigration detention in contemporary liberal democracies are valuable because they encourage a critical stance towards this practice in light of important constitutional principles. More specifically, as its proponents argue that deprivation of liberty as a means of immigration law enforcement is increasingly based on an instrumental order that almost exclusively targets categories, they urge us to engage in a thorough investigation of this practice from the perspective of the rights of the *individual*. However, any approach that emphasises the "new" also runs a risk of losing sight of lines of continuity. Thus, it can be convincingly argued that there are important similarities between the practice of immigration detention in contemporary societies and other coercive forms of social control and mechanisms of exclusion in the history of the modern state, such as the large-scale incarceration of vagrants in seventeenth-century Europe, and the use of internment camps in twentieth-century Europe to deal with refugees and stateless people. To begin with the first example, during the seventeenth and eighteenth centuries, the poor laws of medieval Europe (the local logic of which seems at present to be reconstituted on a global, international scale through immigration policies) were replaced by regulations which provided for the confinement of the poor, the homeless and the mentally ill (Foucault 1967, p. 48). Underlying the detention of these groups was a "fear of pauperism, with its dangerous, fluid, elusive sociality, impossible to control or utilise" (Walters 2002, p. 286). The spatial confinement of people that belonged to a category that was perceived as a threat to the upcoming nation-state was paired by a wish to correct and discipline the concerned individuals. This rationale of "rehabilitation" had been absent in measures that were previously used to deal with the socially undesirable, and which consisted in banishment from cities or provinces, measures that would evidently not work in a *national* state. A second significant historical comparison is to be found in the internment camps which were set up for the stateless and refugees that fled totalitarian regimes during the thirties in Europe. Towards the end of the Second World War, millions of refugees and displaced people were kept in these camps, scattered all over Europe, and many of the former work and concentration camps in Germany were used as "assembly centres" for those people after the war had ended (Malkki 1995, p. 499). Liisa Malkki writes that these camps were a device of power as they provided for the spatial concentration and ordering of people: a "standardized, generalizable technology of power in the management of mass displacement" (Malkki 1995, p. 498). The internment camps were a response to the assumed threat of the stateless and the refugees to the unity of the state and the overall order of the state system. Hence, just as the Great Confinement had been three centuries before, the internment of these peoples was ultimately an instrument to deal with groups that were seen as a threat to the particular political order of that moment.

Surely, there have been many more instances of spatial confinement over the course of history that explicitly targeted categories of people—as opposed to individuals. But far from carrying out an in-depth historical analysis of measures of confinement, I wanted to touch briefly upon two of them here in order to highlight that important similarities exist between historical forms of spatial confinement and contemporary immigration detention. These measures are also similar in that they seem to fall to some extent outside the normal framework of political and legal accountability. Thus, Michel Foucault has written about the Great Confinement as being characterised by "jurisdiction without appeal" and carried out by means of "writs of execution against which nothing can prevail" (Foucault 1967, p. 40). Comparable forms of exceptionalism are evident in Hannah Arendt's account of the internment camps, where individuals that had lost the protection of their countries of origin were forced to live "outside the jurisdiction of the law" (Arendt 1976, pp. 284/287). Similarly, the contemporary practice of immigration detention, depriving persons from their liberty merely because they have allegedly breached the state's territorial sovereignty, certainly gives the impression of being a practice which is outside the usual legal framework of constitutional democracies.

The exceptional nature of the use of confinement in immigration policy feeds directly into the second point that needs to be made regarding penal approaches to the study of immigration detention: it is crucial to be aware of the fact that immigration detention cannot be reduced to a mere punitive measure. Thus, even if contemporary developments undeniably bear witness to an uneasy blurring of the line between criminal law and immigration policies, we need to pay attention to the distinctiveness of the context in which immigration detention takes place, one that differs profoundly from the purely domestic, national context within which criminal law enforcement is principally carried out. Immigration law enforcement is particular because the legal framework within which it takes place is determined by the relationship between the individual, the nation-state and territory in a global system of sovereign, territorial nation-states, a relationship that will be addressed in more detail below. Perhaps it is precisely in the nature of the perceived threat that we find the difference between penal sanctions as expressed in criminal law, which are a response of behaviour that is seen as presenting a danger to a given *social* order, and those forms of coercion and control that are meant to deal with threats to a particular *political* order. As such, recent developments that point at the normalisation of certain forms of exceptionalism in the field of criminal law may indicate a disturbing confusion with regard to the distinction between state and society, but there is nothing novel in states resorting to exceptionalism when dealing with phenomena that they see as a threat to their sovereignty or to the stability of the sovereign state system as a whole, as evidenced by the historical forms of spatial confinement discussed above. At present, EU Member States predominantly perceive (undocumented) immigration as a phenomenon that upsets the existing order, based on territoriality. The implications of this way of perceiving the relationship between territorial sovereignty and human mobility are exemplified in the legal regulation of immigration detention, as will be discussed in the section below.

3 International Law, Territorial Sovereignty and Immigration Detention

Above, I already briefly alluded to the case of *Saadi*, in which the ECtHR did not deem the detention of an asylum seeker which was purely based on administrative grounds in violation of Article 5 ECHR, the provision safeguarding the right to personal liberty. It is noteworthy that seven judges wrote in a dissenting opinion to the judgment that they "fail[ed] to see what value or higher interest can justify the notion that [. . .] fundamental guarantees of individual liberty in a State governed by the rule of law cannot or should not apply to the detention of asylum seekers" (see *Saadi*, Joint Partly Dissenting Opinion of Judges Rozakis, Tulkens, Kovler, Hajiyev, Spielmann and Hirvelä). Here I will delve a little deeper into the ECtHR case law regarding immigration detention, as it exemplifies the importance of fully engaging with the territorial logic underlying immigration detention.

Long before *Saadi* was decided, it was known that the ECtHR does not subject the detention of irregular migrants in the context of their deportation proceedings to the same scrutiny as other forms of detention and, for that matter, other interferences by states with the fundamental rights of individuals. Thus, in its case law on detention *outside* the immigration context, the ECtHR has repeatedly stressed the fundamental nature of the right to personal liberty in the following terms:

> Detention is such a serious measure that it is justified only as a last resort, where other, less serious measures have been considered and found insufficient to safeguard the individual or public interest which might require that the person concerned be detained. That means that it does not suffice that the deprivation of liberty is executed in conformity with national law but it must also be necessary in the circumstances. (*Witold Litwa v Poland*, 4 April 2000, para. 78. See also *Varbanov v. Bulgaria*, 5 October 2000, para. 46.)

However, in the case of *Chahal*, the ECtHR explicitly diverged from this approach if the detention concerned unwanted foreigners in the context of their deportation proceedings:

> Article 5 does not demand that the detention of a person against whom action is being taken with a view to deportation be reasonably considered necessary, for example to prevent his committing an offence or fleeing (*Chahal v United Kingdom*, 15 November 1996, para. 69).

This approach to the right to liberty in the immigration context (which is not called for on the basis of the text of Article 5!) does not only diverge from the way in which conflicts between the public interest and the individual's right to personal liberty are usually dealt with, but it is also at odds with the general way of human rights adjudication. When called upon to resolve conflicts between human rights and competing public interests, judges have to reconcile the special status of such rights with the legitimate power of the state to set limits—under certain conditions—to their exercise. They usually do this by reviewing the proportionality of the interferences. As such, the proportionality principle plays a fundamental role in constitutional adjudication: it safeguards the special status of human rights by ensuring that they are not *simply* traded away for other social gains but that any interference is suitable and necessary and does not burden the individual disproportionately (Greer 2004, p. 412; McHarg 1999, p. 672). However, according to the ECtHR, a detained immigrant does *not* have the right to contest the proportionality of the interference with his personal liberty, "unlike other Convention issues, for example under Article 8 (2) of the Convention" (*Batalov v. Lithuania*, 15 November 2005).

Notwithstanding its explicitness about the fact that immigration detainees derive a lesser degree of protection than other categories of detainees under the ECHR, the ECtHR fails to make explicit the reasons for this difference. In *Saadi*, the ECtHR may have come closest to an explanation by classifying immigration detention a "necessary adjunct" to an "undeniably sovereign right" (*Saadi*, para. 94)—a remark worth contextualising. Contemporary political and legal discourse portrays the right to control the entry and stay of non-nationals as inherent in the state's sovereign claims over its territory, and the ECtHR is no exception in this regard (see, amongst many others, *Amuur v. France*, 25 June 1996, para. 43; *Abdulaziz, Cabales and Balkandali v. United Kingdom*, 28 May 1985, paras. 67–68). The link between immigration and notions of territorial sovereignty is most explicit in populist discourse, which adopts the rhetoric of "threat" and "invasion" to address problems associated with migration. But more mainstream approaches by policymakers and judiciaries also base the right of the modern state to exclude on the notion of territorial sovereignty and the "integrity of national borders". Such a view seems to be largely inspired by the notion of inviolability of territorial boundaries in classic international law, which is a discourse almost exclusively about the rights and duties of states towards each other, and in which the interests of the individual as such did not feature (Cornelisse 2010). An approach to the right to regulate human mobility that is so deeply embedded in a legal discourse in which the sanctity of territorial boundaries is paramount could only come about as a result of a perception in which individuals' relationships to territory are static and in which each and every one of them belongs to a certain, clearly demarcated piece of the earth: the state (Hindess 2000, p. 1486). According to this way of thinking, international migration poses a problem to the global system based on territory and the political system of the territorial state, which therefore needs to be prevented and contained by the use of violent dissuasive measures (Düvell 2004, p. 9). The circle is complete if the judiciary that is supposed to assess the legitimacy of these dissuasive measures (such as detention) in its adjudication reverts to the discourse of classical international law, in which sovereign state interest is central, territorial integrity paramount and the interests of the individual remain largely inarticulable.

The contemporary portrayal of immigration as impinging first and foremost on the "territorial integrity" of states thus facilitates so-called exceptionalism. Nevertheless, it should be noted that it has not managed to overpower the consideration of *all* individual rights that are at stake in the enforcement of migration control. Thus, the ECtHR has established the requirement that immigration detention needs to be "closely connected" to its purpose of preventing unauthorised entry or deportation. In a recent case, the ECtHR even appeared to carry out a concealed proportionality test under this requirement: the relationship between detention and purpose was deemed absent in the case of detention of a seriously ill person because the authorities had failed to consider *other less serious measures* (*Yoh-Ekale Mwanje v Belgium*, 20 December 2001, para. 124). This recent tendency towards more fully fledged protection of individual rights seems to have progressed furthest in the case of detention of migrant children. According to the ECtHR, the detention of children, if it fails to take full account of their *personal circumstances* and is not a *measure of last resort*, is not lawful under the ECtHR (*Popov v France*, 19 January 2012, para. 119). Noteworthy in the context of this chapter is the observation of the ECtHR that immigration control is fundamentally different from criminal law enforcement—and as such it has ruled also that the place for and conditions of immigration detention should be appropriate, considering that "the measure is applicable not to those who have committed criminal offences" (*Saadi*, para. 74; see also *Rashed v. Czech Republic*, 27 November 2008). Along the same lines, it has condemned deprivations of liberty that were based on deception on the part of the authorities, observing that the use of certain stratagems could be justified when it came to the arrest of criminals, but not in the case of rejected asylum seekers (*Čonka v. Belgium*, 5 February 2002, paras. 40–42). It remains to be seen how it will keep this distinction in place in a case where immigration detention and the criminalisation of illegal stay coincide. That such a case will eventually reach the ECtHR is to be expected in view of the growing tendency to criminalise irregular stay by the EU Member States.

4 Immigration Detention in a Transnational Setting: The Returns Directive and the CJEU

This section deals with the case law by the CJEU on immigration detention, and we will see that EU law generally requires national states to bring forward more adequate justifications for the use of detention in immigration procedures than they have so far been required to do under Article 5 ECHR. It should be noted that the CJEU's engagement in this area is relatively recent and results from the adoption of the Returns Directive in 2008, the instrument harmonising Member States legislation concerning the return of irregular migrants. Before going into the way in which the CJEU has interpreted those provisions of the directive dealing with detention in the context of removal proceedings, I will sketch a brief overview of EU policymaking in this field and the Returns Directive in general.

4.1 EU Law and Policymaking in the Field of Return

As the Preamble of the Returns Directive reiterates, the Tampere European Council of 1999 stressed the importance of a comprehensive approach with regard to a common immigration and asylum policy. Such an approach was to be composed of three parts: the creation of a common asylum system, a legal immigration policy and the fight against illegal immigration (Tampere European Council of 15 and 16 October 1999, Presidency Conclusions). With regard to the latter, the EU has a clear aim "to prevent and control existing pressures deriving of irregular migration" which is presented as "a pre-condition for a credible legal migration and mobility policy".[2] In the particular context of control, the EU has always regarded an effective return policy as an integral and vital component of "a coherent approach to reducing irregular migration" evidenced by the creation of a legal basis at Amsterdam for the adoption of European legislation on the "repatriation of illegal residents".[3] Accordingly, the Hague Programme, adopted by the European Council in 2004, called for the establishment of an "effective removal and repatriation policy based on common standards for persons to be returned in a humane manner and with full respect for their human rights and dignity" (Council of the European Union, 8 December 2004, p. 22). As a direct result, a Commission proposal in September 2005 marked the beginning of a long process of negotiation over a common set of standards for return procedures, first within the Council and second between the Council and Parliament. After almost 3 years, a final draft of the Returns Directive was approved by the Parliament in June 2008 and had to be implemented in the national legislation of the Member States by 24 December 2010. According to the Commission, the directive is an instrument that does not only envisage the approximation of norms and practices of Member States but that also contributes to the *intensification* of the efforts by the EU to return third-country nationals that stay illegally on its territory.[4]

The directive itself is applicable to all third-country nationals who do not or do not longer fulfil the conditions for entry, stay or residence in a Member State (Article 2). The system of return that the directive establishes is straightforward: Member States are obliged to issue a return decision against any third-country national that stays illegally on their territory (Article 6(1)).[5] If, on humanitarian grounds, they do not want to take such a decision they must regularise the stay of the third-country national (Article 6(4)). This logic is based upon the wish to establish a "credible and clear" policy on irregular migration which has only two possible responses to that phenomenon: return or regularisation. As a rule, the return decision should provide for a period of 7 days during which the third-country national can depart voluntary. However, if there is a risk of absconding or if an application for a legal stay has been dismissed as manifestly unfounded or

[2] Communication from the Commission to the European Parliament and the Council, 4th Annual Report on Immigration and Asylum (2012) COM(2013) 422 final.

[3] Article 63 paragraph 3 under b EC Treaty, now Article 79 paragraph 1 under c TFEU.

[4] Commission Staff Working Document on the fulfillment of the 29 measures for reinforcing the protection of the external borders and combating illegal immigration adopted at the Justice and Home Affairs Council Meeting, held in Brussels on 25 and 26 February 2010, SEC(2010) 1480 final.

[5] Note that there are some exceptions to this obligation in 6 (2)–(5).

fraudulent or if the person concerned poses a risk to public policy, public security or national security, the Member State may choose not to grant a period for voluntary departure (Article 7(1)–(4)). If no period of voluntary departure has been granted, or—in case it has been granted—the third-country national has not departed within that period, Member States may enforce the return decision: i.e., take the necessary measures in order to remove the third-country national (Article 8).[6]

4.2 Detention According to the Returns Directive

Chapter IV of the directive regulates detention for the purpose of removal. In Article 15 (1), Member States are authorised to detain a third-country national who is the subject of return procedures in order to prepare the return and/or carry out the removal process, unless "*other sufficient but less coercive measures* can be applied effectively in a specific case". In this context, it is appropriate to highlight that the Preamble to the directive stipulates that "the use of detention [. . .] should be limited and *subject to the principle of proportionality* with regard to the means used and objectives pursued". Furthermore, it emphasises that "detention is justified only to prepare the return or carry out the removal process and if the application of *less coercive measures* would not be sufficient". According to the first paragraph of Article 15, detention can be applied in particular if there is a risk of absconding or when the third-country national avoids or hampers return or removal. In addition, the same provision requires that detention shall last for as short a period as possible and only maintained as long as removal arrangements are in progress and executed with due diligence. The second paragraph of Article 15 prescribes a speedy judicial review of the lawfulness of the detention if the measure has been ordered by administrative authorities, either *ex officio* or upon the request of the third-country national concerned. Article 18 of the directive provides a possibility to derogate from the requirement of speediness when an exceptionally large number of third-country nationals to be returned would result in an unforeseen heavy burden on Member States' administrative or judicial staff.

According to Article 15(4), detention is no longer justified if there is no reasonable prospect of removal for legal or other reasons or if the conditions in Article 15(1) are no longer satisfied. In that case, the third-country national should be released immediately. Article 15(4) limits the duration of the detention to a maximum period of 6 months. As a rule, this period may not be extended, except for a limited period not exceeding a further 12 months in cases where removal is likely to last longer because the third-country national refuses to co-operate or because of delays in obtaining the necessary documents from third countries. The remaining

[6] In these cases, return decisions will be coupled with an entry ban, a decision prohibiting entry and stay in the territory of the Member States during a specified period, generally not longer than 5 years (Article 11 and Article 1).

provisions of Chapter IV regulate the conditions of detention and pay specific attention to the situation of vulnerable persons, (unaccompanied) minors and families. Article 16 deserves special mention in so far as it echoes the requirement in the ECtHR case law that the place and conditions of immigration detention should reflect the fact that the measure does not target persons convicted of criminal offences: it stipulates that detention shall take place as a rule in specialised detention facilities. Where this is not possible and a Member State is obliged to resort to prison accommodation, the third-country nationals in detention shall be kept separated from *ordinary prisoners*.

4.3 CJEU Case Law on Immigration Detention

Since 2009, national judges have referred a number of questions concerning the interpretation of the Returns Directive. A large amount of these questions concerned the way in which the system set up by the Returns Directive relates to the criminalisation of irregular stay, either by means of a fine or spatial confinement in the form of a prison sentence or house arrest. The other cases decided by the CJEU have centred more narrowly on the application of Article 15 on detention and have addressed the relationship between the Returns Directive and those instruments of European asylum law that regulate the detention of asylum seekers. Until now, the CJEU has rendered five judgments on the Returns Directive—the other cases referred for a preliminary ruling were decided by an order as they raised questions that had already been answered by the CJEU or were inadmissible. I shall first discuss the judgments that focused specifically on the requirements for lawful detention and addressed the relationship with the EU *acquis* on asylum and the detention of asylum seekers. Thereafter, I will deal with the cases that concern questions related to the criminalisation of irregular entry or stay.

The first case concerning the Returns Directive ever brought before the ECJEU was the case of *Kadzoev* (Case C-357/09). Kadzoev was an asylum seeker from Chechen who had been detained for 34 months by Bulgaria in the context of his deportation proceedings. The national judge referred several questions to the CJEU, regarding *inter alia* the maximum duration and the grounds for detention, as well as the question whether asylum seekers could be detained under the directive. The CJEU stressed that one of the objectives of the directive consists in ensuring that detention for the purpose of removal does not exceed the maximum periods stipulated therein. Extending the maximum duration of immigration detention as laid down by the directive is not permissible *under any circumstances*. Accordingly, once that period has expired, the person concerned has to be released immediately (*Kadzoev*, paras. 49–57). The CJEU unambiguously held that detention on grounds of public order and public safety (the referring judge had listed the absence of valid documents, aggressive conduct and insufficient means of subsistence) can *never* be based on the Returns Directive (*Kadzoev*, paras. 68–71). As such, the judgment in *Kadzoev* is important, not in the least in view of the increasing "informal functions" that immigration detention supposedly acquires in the EU. Thus, it has been argued that there is a growing tendency according to which states use immigration detention "to relieve public order disturbances that are associated with immigrant pauperism" (Leerkes and Broeders 2010). Previously informal functions may even become formalised, if we are to take seriously the response by the Dutch government to recent critique on its extensive use of immigration detention: it has replied that it wants to work towards a policy in which detention will only be resorted to in cases of criminally convicted migrants or migrants that in any other way disturb public order.[7] The pursuing of "informal functions" is to a certain extent also prevented by the requirement that detention is only justified as long as a "reasonable prospect of removal" exists. The CJEU clarified this concept in *Kadzoev* by equating it to a "real prospect that removal can be carried out successfully" within the permissible period of detention (*Kadzoev*, para. 68). Such a prospect is absent if it is unlikely that the third-country national will be admitted to a third country within the maximum period for detention (*Kadzoev*, paras. 66–67).

In the third place, the judgement in *Kadzoev* addressed the question whether *asylum seekers* could be detained under the Returns Directive. The CJEU ruled that someone who has applied for asylum in a Member State cannot be regarded as someone who is staying illegally on the territory of that Member State until his application has been rejected, or a decision ending his right to stay has been issued. Accordingly, the detention of asylum seekers could not be based upon the Returns Directive but would have to be based upon and be in conformity with EU asylum law, more particularly the Reception Conditions Directive and the Procedures Directive.[8] However, the precise implications of these legal instruments for the lawful detention of asylum seekers were not addressed until more than 3 years later in *Arslan*, a case referred by a Czech judge asking the CJEU for clarification of the personal scope of the Returns Directive (Case C-534/11).

Arslan is significant, not so much because the CJEU reaffirmed the ruling in *Kadzoev* according to which asylum seekers cannot be detained under the Returns Directive but because it sets out in considerable detail the requirements that EU law sets for the detention of asylum seekers. Arslan had been detained after he had been arrested as an irregular immigrant, and he applied for asylum whilst in detention. The CJEU noted that neither the Procedures Directive nor the Reception Conditions Directive carries out a harmonisation of the grounds for the detention of asylum seekers. Therefore, "it is for Member States to establish, in full compliance with their obligations arising from both international law and European Union law, the grounds on which an asylum seeker may be detained or kept in detention".

[7] See http://www.volkskrant.nl/vk/nl/2686/Binnenland/article/detail/3461165/2013/06/19/Alleen-nog-cel-voor-criminele-en-agressieve-asielzoekers.dhtml.

[8] Council Directive 2003/9/EC of 27 January 2003 laying down minimum standards for the reception of asylum seekers; and Council Directive 2005/85/EC of 1 December 2005 on minimum standards on procedures in Member States for granting and withdrawing refugee status. See paras. 40–48 of the judgment.

According to the CJEU, a third-country national *can* be held in detention under the Reception Conditions Directives and the Procedures Directives if he had been previously detained under the Returns Directive because his behaviour had indicated that he would be likely to abscond and if his application for asylum seemed to have been predominantly motivated by the wish to postpone or obstruct the deportation procedures (*Arslan*, para. 57). However, the CJEU then unmistakably introduces the requirement that such detention should be proportionate by ruling that the detention of an asylum seeker in such a situation would only be justified "after an assessment on a case-by-case basis of all the relevant circumstances" and if "it is *objectively necessary* to maintain detention to prevent the person concerned from permanently evading his return" (*Arslan*, paras. 58–59/63). Accordingly *Arslan* signals a cautious but distinctive departure from the logic underlying the ECtHR case law as exemplified by *Saadi*. It is perhaps not surprising that the discursive predominance of territorial sovereignty cannot be found in the case law by the CJEU on the rights of immigrants: it is well known that in its case law on family reunification concerning third-country nationals it has destabilised national exclusionary powers by requiring from national authorities to bring forward more convincing justifications for the decision to deport third-country nationals or to refuse them entry than mere references to a sovereign right to control the entry and residence of foreign nationals.[9] It could be argued that the very position of the CJEU as a supranational court which has from the very beginning shown little deference for sovereign prerogatives over national territory (not only when addressing human mobility but also in judgments covering a range of areas such as environmental protection and free movement of goods) makes it less susceptible to the way in which traditional legal discourse has tended to obliterate most individual interests from view whenever the exercise of state power is based upon its territorial sovereignty.

The other three judgments on the Returns Directive concern the relationship between the system of return that the Returns Directive establishes on the one hand on and national laws criminalising irregular stay on the other hand. The first of these cases was *El Dridi*, a case concerning an immigrant who had entered Italy illegally (Case C-61/11 PPU). A removal order was issued against him, and when it transpired that he had not complied with that order, he was sentenced to one year's imprisonment. The Italian judge that had to deal with his appeal against the sentence asked the CJEU if Italian penal law on this point violated the directive. The judgment by the CJEU is makes clear that the system of enforcement that the directive establishes is based on a step-by-step approach, in which "Member States must carry out the removal using the least coercive measures possible." Member States may deprive a person of his liberty *only* if it appears in his particular case that the enforcement of the return decision risks being compromised by the conduct of

[9] See, amongst others, Case-60/00, Carpenter; Case C-459/99, *MRAX*; Case C-503/03, *Commission* v. *Spain*; Case C-127/08, *Metock*; and Case C-578/08, *Chakroun*. See also Case C-43/09, *Zambrano*.

the person concerned. The CJEU further underlined the importance of abiding by the principle of proportionality during *each phase* of the return and removal procedure (*El Dridi*, paras. 34–41).

With specific regard to criminal sanctions as a response to not complying with a return decision, it held that, although in principle criminal legislation is a matter for which the Member States are responsible, they may not apply criminal law rules which are liable to deprive the directive of its effectiveness (*El Dridi*, paras. 53–55). It concluded that Member States may not provide for a custodial sentence on the sole ground that a third-country national continues to stay illegally on the territory of a Member State after an order to leave the national territory was notified to him and the period granted in that order has expired; rather, they must pursue their efforts to enforce the return decision in the ways that the directive provides. A prison sentence, due to its "conditions and methods of application", would, in the eyes of the CJEU, delay the enforcement of the return decision (*El Dridi*, paras. 58–59). As such it would undermine the objective pursued by the directive, namely, the establishment of an effective return policy. However, the CJEU added that Member States had the possibility to adopt legislation regulating "the situation in which coercive measures had not resulted in the removal of persons staying illegally on their territory" (*El Dridi*, para. 60). This statement, which seemed to raise more questions than it answered, was elaborated upon in *Achughbabian*, a judgment that was rendered by the CJEU a few months after it had decided *El Dridi* (Case C-329/11).

In *Achughbabian*, the referring judge had asked the CJEU whether the Returns Directive precludes national legislation which provides for the imposition of a sentence of imprisonment on a third-country national on the sole ground of his illegal entry or stay. The CJEU reaffirmed its ruling in *El Dridi* by stating that such legislation is "likely to thwart the application of the common standards and procedures established by the directive" (*Achughbabian*, para. 39). Accordingly, such legislation is not permitted, a conclusion which followed from its reasoning in *El Dridi*. However, the CJEU clarified its position with regard to the remaining competence of Member States to adopt criminal legislation with regard to illegal residence: it ruled that the directive does not preclude penal sanctions being imposed on migrants illegally staying in the territory of a Member State if two conditions are satisfied: (1) the return procedure established by directive has been applied to these immigrants; and (2) there is not any justified ground for non-return (*Achughbabian*, para. 48). It highlighted that the application of penal sanctions would have to comply fully with fundamental rights, particularly those guaranteed by the ECHR (*Achughbabian*, para. 49). The case of *Sagor* finally, concerned the question whether national legislation that penalises illegal stay by means of a fine, which may be replaced by an order for expulsion or home detention would be precluded by the directive. The CJEU ruled that criminal prosecution which may lead to a fine is "not liable to impede the return procedure" and as such is not precluded by EU law (*Achughbabian*, para. 36). However, with regard to home detention, it reiterated its reasoning in *Achughbabian* to the extent that such deprivation of liberty is liable to undermine an effective return policy. However, it did not exclude the possibility of home detention completely, for example if it would be guaranteed that such detention comes to an end as soon as the physical transportation of the individual concerned out of that Member State is possible (*Achughbabian*, para. 45).

We may summarise the case law as follows: the CJEU attaches decisive weight to the principle of proportionality with regard to each and every step of the return procedure, and it strongly insists on its application with regard to detention. Criminal sanctions are not prohibited by the directive—also because the EU does not have exclusive competence in the field of irregular migration. However, the directive poses significant limits to Member States' freedom in this regard: imprisonment as a criminal sanction is only permitted after the step-by-step approach provided by the directive has been exhausted and when the failure to return is not justifiable. An effective return policy *always* overrides criminal law enforcement—if such enforcement is the response to mere illegal entry or residence. Together with the fact that immigration detention may never be based on public order considerations, EU law as such precludes national legislation that serves symbolic ("we are not a soft touch") or informal functions of immigration detention.

5 Conclusions

I have argued that it is crucial to engage with the territorial logic underlying immigration detention, not only so that we fully understand this measure but also in order to subject it to effective legal challenge. In this regard, increasing transnational regulation, such as through the EU Returns Directive, may present opportunities that were absent when immigration detention was merely regulated by national or international law. Although contemporary political discourse, according to which deportation and detention are not considered as merely one of many conceivable responses to illegal immigration, but singular and inevitable, is to a certain extent reproduced in directive, which obliges national states to issue return decisions in the case of illegal immigrants, it also has the potential to disrupt some aspects of contemporary state practice through the applicability of general principles of EU law, according to which "decisions taken under the directive should be adopted on a case-by-case basis and based on objective criteria, implying that consideration should go beyond the mere fact of an illegal stay" (Preamble, para. 8). The case law of the CJEU shows how EU law can be used to counter some of the more troubling aspects of contemporary immigration detention, such as its use for public order or symbolic purposes, and its categorical use without regard to the specific circumstances of each and every case. Thus, its recent judgment in *Arslan* has clear implications for the lawfulness of the way in which a country such as the Netherlands routinely detains asylum seekers that arrive at the international airport. Opportunities for contestation are not absent from the ECtHR case law, but even a superficial analysis of *Saadi* makes clear that this latter court also *affirms* the logic according to which the safeguarding of territorial sovereignty justifies a certain degree of exceptionalism. In addition to the CJEU's relative insusceptibility to this logic, it is also important to draw attention to the ways in which EU law may more generally provide opportunities for strategic litigation: as every national judge may refer questions for a preliminary ruling to the CJEU, it is possible to circumvent domestic courts' hierarchy where, at least in the field of immigration, highest courts have tended to be more protective of sovereign state interest.

I will wrap up this contribution with some final remarks with regard to the criminalisation of migration—captured in the term *crimmigration*. The tendency to criminalise unwanted human mobility is deplorable, not only for its symbolic connotations but also in that it has a very damaging effect on the real life of individuals. As such, it is worth to point out the inconsistency of the EU Member States: they defend a firm stance against illegal immigration by arguing that the policies to fight it are partly resorted to in order to protect irregular migrants from exploitation and abuse, but they simultaneously marginalise these people further by criminalising them. However, if regarded from a perspective that takes into account how the legal regulation of human mobility since the beginning of the twentieth century has been bound up with the most absolute conceptions of sovereign power, the shadows of which are still very much visible in international and domestic laws, there may be some reason to be cautiously optimistic, at least with regard to long-term developments. Criminalisation of migration could signify a shift away from exceptionalism, and it may possibly be a sign that the way in which we perceive the relationship between the nation state and human mobility across borders is becoming normalised, regulated by more "mainstream" legal discourses. Thus, according to well-established ECtHR case law, the due process guarantees contained in Article 6 do not apply to immigration procedures, but such a view can of course not be maintained when irregular migration has become a criminal offence. Similarly, CJEU case law, by allowing penal sanctions in the form of imprisonment *only* after Member States have applied the return procedure and when there is "no justified ground for non-return", raises interesting questions regarding who should bear the burden of proof in these criminal procedures, especially with regard to the question why deportation has not been achieved during the return procedure, and, perhaps even more poignantly, with regard to establishing criminal intent.[10] Penal sanctions in the form of imprisonment as a response to unwanted human mobility could thus mean that the *very power to exclude* becomes measurable, accountable and contestable, something which it has until now barely ever been.[11] Yet whether that will be of much help to the irregular migrants who find themselves in the Europe of today is a question that should be of concern to us all.

[10] I thank Marie-Benedicte Dembour for pointing out this last aspect to me during an interesting discussion at the VU in June 2013.

[11] Paraphrasing the words of Simon (1998, p. 597).

References

Arendt H (1976) The origins of totalitarianism. Harcourt Brace and Company, San Diego
Bauman Z (1998) Globalization: the human consequences. Columbia University Press, New York
Bauman Z (2000) Social issues of law and order. British J Criminol 40:205–221
Cornelisse G (2010) A new articulation of human rights, or why the European Court of Human Rights should think beyond Westphalian sovereignty. In: Dembour K (ed) Are human rights for migrants? Critical reflections on the status of irregular migrants in Europe and the United States. Routledge, Abingdon
Council of the European Union, *Presidency Conclusions of the Brussels European Council, 4 and 5 November 2004,* 8 December 2004.
Düvell F (2004) Illegal immigration: what to do about it. Working Paper Working Group Migration-Mobility-Minorities-Membership. EUI/RSCAS, Florence
Easton S, Piper C (2008) Sentencing and punishment: the quest for justice. Oxford University Press, Oxford
Feeley M, Simon J (1992) The new penology: notes on the emerging strategy of corrections and its implications. Criminology 30:449–474
Foucault M (1967) Madness and civilization: a history of insanity in the age of reason. Tavistock Publications, London
Greer S (2004) 'Balancing' and the European Court of Human Rights: a contribution to the Habermas-Alexy debate. Cambridge Law J 63:412–434
Hindess B (2000) Citizenship in the international management of populations. Am Behav Sci 43:1486–1497
Leerkes A, Broeders A (2010) A case of mixed motives? Formal and informal functions of administrative immigration detention. Br J Criminol 50:830–850
Malkki LH (1995) Refugees and exiles: from "Refugee Studies" to the national order of things. Annu Rev Anthropol 24:495–523
Malloch MS, Stanley E (2005) The detention of asylum seekers in the UK: representing risk, managing the dangerous. Punishment Soc 53:53–71
McHarg A (1999) Reconciling human rights and the public interest: conceptual problems and doctrinal uncertainty in the jurisprudence of the European Court of Human Rights. Mod Law Rev 62:671–696
Miller TA (2003) Citizenship & severity: recent immigration reforms and the new penology. Georget Immigr Law J 17:611–666
Miller TA (2005) Blurring the boundaries between immigration and crime control after September 11th. Boston Coll Third World Law J 25:81–124
Schuster L (2005) A sledgehammer to crack a nut: deportation, detention and dispersal in Europe. Soc Policy Adm 39:600–621
Schuster L, Welch M (2005) Detention of asylum seekers in the US, UK, France, Germany, and Italy: a critical view of the globalizing culture of control. Crim Justice 5:331–355
Simon J (1998) Refugees in a carceral age: the rebirth of immigration prisons in the United States. Public Cult 10:577–607
Walters W (2002) Deportation, expulsion, and the international police of aliens. Citizenship Stud 6:256–292
Welch M (2000) The role of the immigration and naturalization service in the prison industrial complex. Soc Justice 27:73–88
Welch M (2002) Detained: immigration law and the expanding I.N.S. jail complex. Temple University Press, Philadelphia

Trapped Between Administrative Detention, Imprisonment, and Freedom-in-Limbo

Dr. Charles Gosme

Abstract Recent decades have witnessed the increasing criminalisation of irregular migration in the European Union (EU). A notable move in many EU states has been the transformation of illegal entry and stay of third-country nationals (TCNs) into a crime, involving possible imprisonment. The Court of Justice of the EU (CJEU) paved the way for the partial decriminalisation of illegal stay in the 2011 *El Dridi* and *Achughbabian* rulings. In these rulings, the CJEU interpreted the EU Directive on the return of illegally staying TCNs (Return Directive) as prohibiting member state legislation which provides for a sentence of imprisonment to be imposed on irregular migrants on the sole ground of their illegal stay. Irregular migrants may only be imprisoned if they have been subjected to every stage of a return procedure and if they have no justified ground for non-return. Academic focus has mainly been on the positive ramifications of these rulings for irregular migrants. While the two rulings laudably restricted member states' ability to imprison TCNs for the offence of illegal stay, these rulings also shined a spotlight on an already very vulnerable category of irregular migrants in many EU states. In this chapter, I offer to take a closer and more specific look at the *residual* category of irregular migrants that the CJEU singled out as permissible targets for imprisonment. I examine who makes up this *residual* category of irregular migrants, the multiple forms of exclusion that they experience in certain member states, the impact of the CJEU rulings on their exclusionary plight, as well as the functions of this plight.

1 Introduction

Recent decades have witnessed the increasing criminalisation of irregular migration in the European Union (EU). A notable move in many EU states has been the transformation of illegal entry and stay of third-country nationals (TCNs) into a crime, involving possible imprisonment. In those states, imprisonment serves to reinforce the arsenal of repressive measures that are already used against irregular migrants. These measures include socio-economic exclusion and coercive removal

Dr. C. Gosme (✉)
The Sciences Po Law School, Paris, France
e-mail: charles.gosme@sciencespo.fr

M.J. Guia et al. (eds.), *Immigration Detention, Risk and Human Rights*,
DOI 10.1007/978-3-319-24690-1_6

procedures. I use the terms irregular migrant and illegally staying TCN as synonyms.

The Court of Justice of the EU (CJEU) paved the way for the partial decriminalisation of illegal stay in the 2011 *El Dridi* and *Achughbabian* rulings. In these rulings, the CJEU interpreted the EU Directive on the return of illegally staying TCNs (Return Directive) as prohibiting member state legislation which provides for a sentence of imprisonment to be imposed on irregular migrants on the sole ground of their illegal stay. EU member states have since then been prohibited under EU law from imprisoning irregular migrants for the mere offence of illegal stay. Following the CJEU's interpretation of the Return Directive, irregular migrants, whose only criminal offence is that of illegal stay, may only be imprisoned if they have been subjected to every coercive measure to remove them by their host member state (including placement in administrative detention for the maximum period pending removal). Irregular migrants may also be imprisoned if they have committed a criminal offence unrelated to illegal stay, as member states may exclude them from the scope of the Return Directive.

The general impact and economy of these rulings have been thoroughly analysed in case comments and academic articles. Focus has mainly been on the positive ramifications of these rulings for migrants. For example, Mitsilegas (2013) has stressed the "protective function" of EU law, arguing that "the Court managed to use EU law … in order to protect third-country nationals from extensive criminalisation in Member States" (Mitsilegas 2013, p. 110). While the two rulings have laudably restricted states' ability to imprison TCNs for the offence of illegal stay, these rulings also shined a spotlight on an already very vulnerable category of irregular migrants in many EU states. In this article, I offer to take a closer and more specific look at the *residual* category of irregular migrants that the CJEU singled out as permissible targets for imprisonment.

In Sect. 2, I explain that this *residual* category is made up of irregular migrants who are not removable due to practical obstacles, who have been administratively detained (pending removal) for the maximum period under national law, and who are deemed responsible for the practical obstacles to their removal (due to non-cooperation on their part). They are what I describe as non-cooperative exhausted returnees. Their existence is particularly precarious and exclusionary, in comparison with other irregular migrants who are not removable by EU member states. This makes it all the more important to further explore their singling out by the CJEU.

In Sect. 3, building on Alessandro De Giorgi's notion of the selectivity and intensity of the criminalisation and control of irregular migrants in Europe, I argue that the CJEU rulings actually confirmed (and legally entrenched) a policy trend in several EU member states to limit the general criminalisation of irregular migrants and to intensify control and criminalisation against select groups of irregular migrants, namely those who did not cooperate with their return procedures (and who today fall under the CJEU's *residual* category). In EU states that criminalise irregular migrants, individuals who find themselves within the *residual* category of irregular migrants face the risk of being bounced around between three exclusionary spaces: prison, administrative detention, and freedom-in-limbo. I use a French case study to illustrate the entrapment of the *residual* category that took place before the CJEU rulings, and which continues in the aftermath of the rulings.

In Sect. 4, building on Juliet Stumpf's seminal crimmigration article (Stumpf 2006), I argue that the three exclusionary spaces perform similar functions to one another in their converging use against the *residual* category of irregular migrants. They namely perform functions of deterrence and enhanced removability, which I examine before concluding in Sect. 5 on how the *residual* category has become the focus of state contempt and wrath in certain EU member states in what can be framed as a struggle between states and non-cooperative exhausted returnees. I seek to provide some conceptual insight on this struggle. My conclusion includes some words on the legal and policy reforms that defenders of irregular migrants should seek with regard to irregular migrants who end up, or risk ending up, in the *residual* category.

2 The Residual Category of Irregular Migrants

I turn now to an explanation of how the *residual* category was derived. I begin by looking at the tension between various levels and types of sanctions against illegal stay that were at play (Sect. 2.1), at how the CJEU resolved that tension through its partial decriminalisation of illegal stay (Sect. 2.2), and end with a detailed explanation of who falls under the criminalisable *residual* category of irregular migrants (Sect. 2.3). I provide an illustration of a migrant I interviewed who recently fell under this category.

2.1 Tension Between EU Immigration Sanctions and National Criminal Sanctions

Illegally staying TCNs can broadly be subjected to three types of sanctions in most EU member states: immigration, criminal, and collateral. The CJEU rulings touch upon the nexus between immigration and criminal sanctions. Illegal stay is met with several sanctions because it is a violation of EU immigration law, national immigration laws, and/or national criminal laws.

There is firstly an immigration sanction of return, set out under EU and national laws, which was optional under EU law until the 2008 Return Directive made it mandatory.[1] Return measures must now be issued against irregular migrants unless

[1] Before: ECJ, Cases C-261/08 and C-348/08, *Zurita Garcia* [2009] ECR I-10143. After: Article 6 of Directive 2008/115/EC of the European Parliament and of the Council of 16 December 2008 on the return of illegally staying third-country nationals, OJ 2008 L 348/98.

states decide to regularise their status. While return should as a matter of principle be voluntary, there are many grounds in the Directive which member states can rely on to enforce removal and to do so coercively. During the course of a return procedure, there are also many circumstances under which the Return Directive allows state authorities to administratively detain irregular migrants when removal is not immediately possible.

There are secondly criminal sanctions, in the form of fines and imprisonment, which are set out not under EU law but under national legal systems. In recent years, an increasing number of EU member states have introduced national legislative provisions that allow prison sentences to be imposed on the ground of illegal stay and grounds related to illegal stay (European Union Agency for Fundamental Rights 2011, pp. 42–44). A distinction needs to be made between imprisonment, which corresponds to criminal detention, and administrative detention, which is a form of detention that exists under immigration powers.

There are lastly collateral sanctions. Irregular migrants suffer from a strong discriminatory function that is attached to the legal/illegal immigration dichotomy in EU and national laws and policies. In the EU, a *fair treatment* goal has been reserved for legally resident TCNs since the first freedom, security and justice (FSJ) multi-annual programme was adopted in 1999. The *fair treatment* goal reserves a quantitative and qualitative set of socio-economic rights, far beyond the core set of rights possessed by all individuals, for legal residents. While all individuals within EU jurisdiction possess a core set of human rights, irregular migrants may be excluded from many rights (e.g. social security rights) and be denied access to another set of rights (e.g. comprehensive health care rights). Most EU member states make full use of these exclusionary possibilities (European Union Agency for Fundamental Rights 2011, pp. 42–44). This exclusion can be described as a group of "collateral sanctions"[2] attached to the violation of illegal stay, the collateral sanction being the indefinite exclusion from *legal residence rights* which leads to extensive societal discrimination.

The buildup to the two CJEU rulings revealed a growing tension between the EU immigration sanction of return, on the one hand, and the national criminal sanction of imprisonment for the offence of illegal stay, on the other. The effective return of irregular migrants has become one of the central goals of EU immigration and asylum law and policy, in order to promote and protect the integrity of the system. EU legislation was adopted with the aim of making the return of irregular migrants more effective; this legislation was the 2008 Return Directive. This Directive set out detailed standards with regard to the stages that EU member states are obliged to follow in order to ensure the effective return of apprehended irregular migrants. In 2012, the European Commission set out a long-term policy goal to ensure the effective removal of 75 % of apprehended irregular migrants, a percentage far higher than the current one (Directorate-General Home Affairs 2012, p. 6). The

[2] Notion borrowed from the following article and used in a slightly modified manner from Stumpf (2006), pp. 404–405.

problem is that the imprisonment of irregular migrants for nationally defined offences of illegal stay had the potential to thwart the effective return of irregular migrants set out under the Return Directive. When irregular migrants are in prison, they are not in the process of being removed.

2.2 The CJEU's Partial Decriminalisation of Illegal Stay

In 2011, the CJEU's *El Dridi* and *Achughbabian* rulings paved the way for the partial decriminalisation of illegal stay.[3] These cases concerned irregular migrants in EU states (respectively Italy and France) who were subjected to return measures. Following their lack of compliance with these return measures, they were later imprisoned for nationally defined criminal offences related to illegal stay. In the *El Dridi* case, the irregular migrant was convicted and sentenced to one year of imprisonment. In the *Achughbabian* case, the irregular migrant was simply subjected to police custody on suspicion of having committed an offence punishable by imprisonment, that offence being the crime of illegal stay. But Mr *Achughbabian* was not prosecuted for the crime of illegal stay, as police custody was only used for the purpose of preparing removal procedures. The issue in both cases was whether national legislation, which provided the possibility of imposing a prison sentence for the sole offence of illegal stay (or offences related to illegal stay), was compatible with the Return Directive, which set standards for an effective EU return policy.

The CJEU interpreted the Return Directive as prohibiting member state legislation from providing a sentence of imprisonment on the *sole* ground of illegal stay. It ruled that imprisonment for the offence of illegal stay may only be imposed on illegally staying TCNs who have been subjected to every stage of the removal process as set out under the Directive and who have no valid grounds to remain. The Return Directive sets out successive stages for the enforcement of return measures, administrative detention being the ultimate coercive stage for enforcing a return measure. The CJEU made it clear that imprisonment for the sole crime of illegal stay may only be imposed on individuals who have been released from administrative detention following expiry of the maximum period during which they can be held and for whom there is no justified ground for non-return. It might also implicitly concern individuals who have been effectively removed as a result of a return procedure and who have re-entered the EU in violation of a re-entry ban. However, this chapter only focuses on the explicit category of persons mentioned by the CJEU, which consists of illegally staying TCNs who have not been removed despite all attempts to coercively remove them. The dominant and explicit rationale

[3] CJEU, Case C-61/11, *PPU El Dridi, alias Karim Soufi* [2011] ECR I-03015; CJEU, Case C-329/11, *Alexandre Achughbabian v. Préfet du Val-de-Marne* [2011] ECR I-0000.

behind these rulings was that of promoting an effective EU return policy.[4] Priority was to be given to the European immigration sanction of removal over the national criminal sanction of imprisonment.

The CJEU's case law on the relationship between the Return Directive and national criminal legislation did not end with these two rulings. Several have followed and many are pending. However, its interpretation of the Return Directive with regard to imprisonment for the offence of illegal stay remains unchanged. In the *Sagor*[5] and *Mbaye*[6] cases, the CJEU examined the compatibility of fines and home detention orders (as national criminal sanctions) with the Return Directive. In the pending case of *Da Silva*,[7] the CJEU shall deliver a ruling on the compatibility of imprisonment for the offence of illegal *entry* (as opposed to illegal *stay*) with the Return Directive. This chapter focuses solely on the issue of imprisonment for the offence of illegal stay and not on the closely related issues raised in the cases that followed the *El Dridi* and *Achughbabian* rulings.

2.3 A Residual Category of Irregular Migrants: Non-cooperative Exhausted Returnees

In the *El Dridi* and *Achughbabian* rulings, the CJEU singled out a *residual* category of irregular migrants who can be subjected to prison sentences under national laws for criminal offences related to illegal stay. They are what I describe as non-cooperative exhausted returnees, notions that I define and develop below. The rulings principally set out two criteria to determine whether an irregular migrant may be imprisoned for the criminal offence of illegal stay; that is, whether an irregular migrant falls under the criminalisable *residual* category. There is firstly a clear criterion that requires member states to have administratively detained an irregular migrant for the maximum period under national law. There is secondly a criterion that the irregular migrant must have no justified ground for non-return. The first criterion requires that the irregular migrant be an exhausted returnee, which means that he/she is not removable due to exhaustion of the return procedure. The second criterion is that the exhausted returnee be non-removable on practical grounds due to non-cooperation with the return procedure. I turn now to an explanation of these criteria and notions (Sects. 2.3.1 and 2.3.2). I end with an example of a migrant who recently endured such categorisation (Sect. 2.3.3).

[4] For more on the rationale and principle of effectiveness, see Mitsilegas (2013), pp. 107–109.

[5] CJEU, Case C-430/11, *Sagor* [2012].

[6] CJEU, Case-522/11, *Mbaye* [2013].

[7] CJEU, Case 189/13, *Da Silva* (pending).

2.3.1 The First Criterion: The Irregular Migrant Must Be an Exhausted Returnee

The *residual* category concerns non-removable irregular migrants who find themselves in a position of exhausted removal. This is a position irregular migrants find themselves in when return procedures against them are exhausted due to expiry of the maximum period during which they can be held in administrative detention pending removal.

Hundreds of thousands of illegally staying TCNs who are apprehended by EU member state authorities turn out to not be removable despite the issue of return measures against them. In 2009, Eurostat data estimates suggest that out of 594,610 orders to leave the territory of an EU-27 member state, 341,820 were not effectively carried out.[8] Over the years, the number of orders to leave has slightly decreased, but the proportions of returns that ensued have remained very similar. In 2012, 276,965 out of 483,640 orders to leave were not carried out.[9] Thus, in 2009 and 2012, the majority of return measures were never carried out, which suggests that most illegally staying TCNs in the EU were not removable. According to the European Commission, preliminary figures for 2013 confirm this trend (European Commission 2014, p. 3). Obstacles to removal may be broadly divided into three groups: legal, practical, and policy obstacles. Persons may not be removable on legal grounds (e.g. protection from removal on a range of human rights grounds). Persons may not be removable on practical grounds (e.g. due to difficulties in ascertaining the identity of returnees or to the lack of cooperation of countries of origin). Lastly, non-removability may be on policy grounds (e.g. policy-defined humanitarian protection from removal). Eurostat does not provide more detailed data with regard to the types of obstacle to removal.

When illegally staying TCNs cannot be removed, things can principally go one of three ways depending on the precise obstacle to removal (legal, practical, etc.). Their status might be regularised, their removal might be postponed or they might be subjected to administrative detention pending removal. If administrative detention does not lead to removal before expiry of the maximum period during which they can be held, those concerned are released in a position of exhausted removal. So persons who are impossible to remove in the long run might end up in a position of postponed removal or exhausted removal, or their status might be regularised if they are lucky.

The Return Directive allows member states to administratively detain irregular migrants for 6 months, and up to 18 months in exceptional cases, as long as there is

---

[8] Based on data extracted from Eurostat Population Database. Enforcement of Immigration Legislation. http://epp.eurostat.ec.europa.eu/portal/page/portal/eurostat/home/. Accessed 31 Jan 2014.

[9] Ibid.

a reasonable prospect of removal.[10] Although the Return Directive sets the maximum period of permissible detention at 18 months, national maximum periods vary from a few weeks in some member states to the full 18 months in others. In many of the states with maximum periods that are inferior to 18 months, irregular migrants can be subjected to repeated placements in administrative detention. However, under EU law, they may only be subjected to repeated and successive placements in administrative detention for a cumulative period of 18 months.

In order to fall under the CJEU's residual category, irregular migrants need only have been administratively detained once for the maximum period under national law, even if they are subsequently subjected to repeated placements in administrative detention. In France, for example, the national maximum period of administrative detention is 45 days. The Comité inter mouvements auprès des évacués (Cimade, NGO) has reported numerous cases of TCNs who have been placed in administrative detention 15 times, one individual having been placed 27 times (Assfam et al. 2011, p. 60). Even though many irregular migrants can be repeatedly placed in administrative detention for the full 45 days, only one 45-day placement suffices for them to fall under the Court's *residual* category.

Europe-wide, exhausted returnees are a very vulnerable group of irregular migrants from a socio-legal point of view. The Return Directive sets out standards on the formal status and human rights of irregular migrants whose removal is *postponed (as opposed to exhausted)*. It requires member states to "ensure that the following principles are taken into account as far as possible":[11] family unity, emergency healthcare, and access of minors to the basic education system. It also requires member states to provide postponed returnees with written certification of postponement of their removal so as to protect them from repeated apprehensions. These standards on the status and rights of postponed returnees are very thin and weakly phrased, but their position is at least addressed in hard law. Neither the Return Directive nor any other piece of EU legislation contains standards with regard to the formal status and rights of exhausted returnees.

2.3.2 The Second Criterion: The Irregular Migrant's Non-removability Must Be on Practical Grounds and due to Non-cooperation

Although the CJEU's *residual* category of irregular migrants only concerns irregular migrants who are exhausted returnees, these exhausted returnees must additionally have *no justified ground for non-return*. It is not enough for irregular migrants to have been released from administrative detention following expiry of

[10] Article 15 of Directive 2008/115/EC of the European Parliament and of the Council on the return of illegally staying third-country nationals [2008] OJ L 348/98.

[11] Article 14 of Directive 2008/115/EC of the European Parliament and of the Council on the return of illegally staying third-country nationals [2008] OJ L 348/98.

the maximum period. Their continued presence must not be justified on any valid ground.

Rosa Raffaelli has commented that the concept of a "justified ground for non-return... is quite vague" (Raffaelli 2012, p. 11) and was not clearly defined by the CJEU. This concept would seem to protect persons who cannot be removed for legal reasons (e.g. human rights protection from removal), who cannot be removed for policy-based reasons (e.g. humanitarian reasons), as well as persons who cannot be removed for practical reasons that are beyond their control. Rosa Raffaelli expressed a similar view when she hypothesised that the CJEU "meant it to refer not only to those third-country nationals whose expulsion is prohibited by international law (e.g. in accordance with the principle of *non refoulement),* but also to those whose return has proven impossible for reasons outside their control" (Raffaelli 2012, p. 11).

This leaves only one group of non-removable irregular migrants within the confines of the *residual* category, those not removable for practical reasons within their control. Non-removability on practical grounds does not automatically correspond to an unjustified ground for non-return. However, practical non-removability may amount to an unjustified ground for non-return if the practical obstacle is due to the irregular migrant's actions or omissions. Irregular migrants might be non-cooperative if they hide their identity documents, destroy them, refuse to disclose their identity and/or country of origin, refuse to be accompanied to their country of origin's embassy in order to obtain travel documentation, or refuse to board a plane or some other type of transport.

Beyond academic speculation, this is how French authorities interpreted the CJEU's concept of an unjustified ground for non-return (Ministère de l'Intérieur 2013). The Court of Justice's residual category of irregular migrants therefore includes non-cooperative exhausted returnees. They are persons who are not removable on practical grounds, who have been administratively detained for the maximum period under national law, and whose practical non-removability is due to non-cooperation with their return procedure.

The Return Directive clearly sets out privileged targets of administrative detention, especially prolonged detention. Privileged targets are irregular migrants who might otherwise abscond if not placed in detention, as well as migrants who delay or hamper the return process. Prolonged detention targets non-cooperative detainees, along with those who are not removed due to "delays in obtaining the necessary documentation from third countries".[12] When responsibility for practical non-removability lies with the third country, there would presumably be a justified ground for non-return upon exhaustion of removal. When responsibility for practical non-removability lies with the irregular migrant, there would presumably not be a justified ground for non-return upon exhaustion of removal.

[12] Article 15 (6) (b) of Directive 2008/115/EC of the European Parliament and of the Council of 16 December 2008 on the return of illegally staying third-country nationals, OJ 2008 L 348/98.

2.3.3 Illustration of a Migrant Who Fell Under the CJEU's Residual Category of Irregular Migrants in France

I recently interviewed Mr S.I., a 36-year-old man from Bangladesh who fell under the *residual* category of irregular migrants in France.[13] He entered France without authorisation in 2013, well after the CJEU delivered its two rulings. He was apprehended and placed in administrative detention for the maximum period under French law (which is 45 days). He applied for asylum from the administrative detention centre, but his application was swiftly rejected through a fast-track asylum procedure. The asylum application provided him with legal protection from removal, but the rejection of his asylum application propelled him back into a position of illegal stay without any legal protection from removal. During his time in administrative detention, he was handcuffed and escorted to an airport on two occasions, each time with a one-way ticket to Bangladesh. He refused to board the plane both times. Before being escorted the second time, police officers warned him that he would face 3 months in prison if he refused to embark on a flight to his country. They exerted a lot of pressure on him, but he resisted because of the bigger problems that he faced in Bangladesh. Upon expiry of the maximum period during which Mr S.I. could be held, he was not released but was sent to a police station where he was held in police custody in order to await prosecution for refusing to board a plane. He spent one night in police custody and was released the next day because a decision was made to not prosecute him.

Mr S.I. was an exhausted returnee who was not removable for a practical reason; that practical reason was his refusal to cooperate with the return procedure on two occasions by refusing to embark on flights to Bangladesh. He was lucky because as I show below in a case study on France, many non-cooperative exhausted returnees are sent to prison.

3 Residual Category Potentially Trapped in-Between Administrative Detention, Imprisonment, and Freedom-in-Limbo

The CJEU's rulings reflected (and legally entrenched) a policy trend in numerous EU member states, which was to decrease imprisonment of irregular migrants on the sole ground of their illegal stay and to reserve imprisonment for irregular

[13] Interview with Mr S.I. (France terre d'asile, Paris, France, 10 July 2013). This interview took place within the framework of wider empirical research that I carried out for the NGO France terre d'asile on the deterrent effect of administrative detention in France on irregular migrants. It was a qualitative research project based on semi-structured interviews with a purposive sample of irregular migrants. The final report will be published in Summer of 2014. Preliminary results of the research were presented at a conference on 23 January 2014: http://www.france-terre-asile.org/lagenda-de-pierre-henry/item/9254-experience-et-effets-dissuasifs-de-la-retention-en-france.

migrants who either had committed other criminal offences or were non-cooperative with their return procedures. This trend could be described as a recent intensification and increasing selectiveness of control and criminalisation of irregular migrants (Sect. 3.1). In certain of these member states, non-cooperative exhausted returnees were already singled out for criminalisation and bounced around between three exclusionary spaces: administrative detention, imprisonment, and freedom-in-limbo (Sect. 3.2). In these states, the position of non-cooperative exhausted returnees has remained intact in the aftermath of the rulings delivered in 2011, since the CJEU singled them out as the sole permissible targets of imprisonment for offences related to illegal stay. I use a French case study to illustrate the entrapment[14] of non-cooperative exhausted returnees between the three exclusionary spaces, an entrapment that took place before the rulings in France and that remains intact in the aftermath of the rulings.

3.1 How the CJEU Rulings Confirmed a Trend in Certain EU Member States: The Intensification and Increasing Selectiveness of Control and Criminalisation Against the Residual Category of Irregular Migrants

Illegal entry and stay are not criminal offences in all EU member states. Even in states where they are criminal offences, imprisonment is not always a possibility. They are, however, prison-worthy criminal offences in a slight majority of member states (European Union Agency for Fundamental Rights 2011, p. 43; European Commission 2014, pp. 24–25). In EU countries where illegal entry or stay are prison-worthy offences, there are often additional prison-worthy offences of non-cooperation with return procedures. In these countries, an important number of *non-cooperative* persons have long been bounced around between three exclusionary spaces: administrative detention, prison, and freedom-in-limbo. This has been the case in France. Prime targets of these non-cooperation offences are exhausted returnees. Many are sent from administrative detention to prison upon expiry of the maximum period during which they can be held in administrative detention. The CJEU's *El Dridi* and *Achughbabian* rulings improved the right to liberty of a large number of illegally staying TCNs by prohibiting imprisonment on the sole ground of illegal stay. However, by singling out non-cooperative exhausted returnees as the sole permissible targets of imprisonment for offences related to illegal stay, these rulings correspondingly shined a spotlight on an already highly vulnerable group of irregular migrants in countries that criminalise illegal stay.

The CJEU's singling out of non-cooperative exhausted returnees matched a trend in certain EU member states that impose prison sentences for the offence of

[14] The word *entrapment* is not used here in the legal sense of luring an individual into committing a crime. It is used to describe the state of being caught in a trap.

illegal stay and for non-cooperation offences. This trend was to decrease prosecutions for the general offence of illegal stay and focus such prosecutions on irregular migrants who did not cooperate with authorities in ensuring the success of their removal. Several countries had developed particularly repressive practices towards those deemed to not be cooperating with their removal procedures. This was, for example, the case in France, and also in other EU countries such as Germany and the UK. But while this trend of singling out non-cooperative irregular migrants for criminalisation already existed in several EU states, it was a policy that was not set in the stone of hard law. Prior to the CJEU rulings, these EU states focused the tool of imprisonment on a select group of irregular migrants, but they also had the discretionary power to continue criminalising the totality of irregular migrants. This power was taken away from them by the CJEU rulings, and to that extent, these rulings were protective of irregular migrants. However, they also legitimised and reinforced the practice of singling out non-cooperative irregular migrants for criminalisation.

In these countries, non-cooperative exhausted returnees have not just been privileged targets of imprisonment. They have also tended to be privileged targets of exclusion from both security of residence and legal residence rights. At a general level, all non-removable persons who are excluded from legal residence find themselves in a legal limbo of protracted toleration or illegality of stay. However, persons who are not removable on practical grounds—and especially those deemed to not be cooperative—have generally suffered from greater socio-economic exclusion in comparison with other non-removable persons.[15]

The CJEU's crystallisation of this trend suggests that the control and criminalisation of irregular migrants in Europe has become more selective in recent years. Alessandro De Giorgi has noted that over the past decades, irregular migrants were already victims of the "selectivity . . . (and) intensity" (De Giorgi 2010, p. 154) of penal practices in Europe. Irregular migrants in Europe have been particularly affected and targeted due to the multifarious crimes linked to their immigration status and to crimes which their immigration status compels them to commit. When talking about the selective control and criminalisation of irregular migrants, Alessandro De Giorgi has explained that their "limited access to civil, social, and political rights, hyper-incarceration, and the constant threat of deportation contribute to the creation of a grey area of legal vulnerability" (De Giorgi 2010, p. 159), as well as their "subordinate inclusion" (De Giorgi 2010, p. 159) in the lowest levels and darkest corners of European economies.

Although irregular migrants as a whole have experienced what Alessandro De Giorgi has described as selective and intense control and criminalisation, the CJEU's rulings confirmed a more recent trend of further intensification and selectiveness of control and criminalisation against the *residual* category of irregular

[15] For example, see information on Germany and the UK in: European Migration Network, Ad-hoc Query on Practices followed concerning Third Country Nationals whose compulsory removal is impossible. Compilation produced on 14 April 2010, pp. 7–8 and 14–15.

migrants. This trend has shielded a large number of irregular migrants from imprisonment for offences related to their illegal stay, but it has also intensified the exclusionary nightmare of all those left out by the protective side of this trend. It has reduced the legal vulnerability of most irregular migrants and amplified the legal vulnerability of a small group of irregular migrants.

I turn now to a French case study on non-cooperative exhausted returnees who have been bounced around between administrative detention, imprisonment, and freedom-in-limbo.

3.2 French Case Study on Non-cooperative Exhausted Returnees' Entrapment Between Administrative Detention, Imprisonment, and Freedom-in-Limbo

In France, a small but significant number of irregular migrants who cannot be removed on practical grounds find themselves trapped between administrative detention, imprisonment, and freedom-in-limbo. These individuals are non-cooperative exhausted returnees and persons who have committed criminal offences that are not immigration related. The focus here is on non-cooperative exhausted returnees. There are Cimade reports with documented narratives of individuals who have experienced entrapment between administrative detention, imprisonment, and freedom-in-limbo. I restate one of these narratives at the end of this case study. This is the narrative of M.J. Before relaying M.J.'s story, I examine how non-cooperative exhausted returnees can end up in such a position of entrapment.

This portrait serves to highlight the position of many non-cooperative exhausted returnees before the 2011 *El Dridi* and *Achughbabian* rulings, which remains unchanged in the aftermath of these rulings. I first provide contextual legal background on the administrative detention and imprisonment of irregular migrants in France and the impact of the 2011 rulings on French law (Sect. 3.2.1). I move on to examine the law and data relating to exhausted returnees who have been bounced around between administrative detention, imprisonment, and freedom-in-limbo (Sect. 3.2.2). I end with the narrative of M.J. as a practical illustration of the entrapment endured by the CJEU's *residual* category of irregular migrants in France (Sect. 3.2.3).

3.2.1 The Administrative Detention and Imprisonment of Irregular Migrants in France

I provide a contextual overview of French law relating to the imprisonment and administrative detention of irregular migrants.

3.2.1.1 The Imprisonment of Irregular Migrants in France

Until 31 December 2012, illegal stay was a free-standing criminal offence under French law.[16] This possibility dated back to 1938. It is no longer a criminal offence due to a post-*Achughbabian* reform. Non-cooperation on the part of irregular migrants with their return procedures is currently, and has long been, a criminal offence under French law, punishable by a prison sentence and a fine.[17] Non-cooperation offences target individuals who obstruct their removal procedures either by refusing to exit or by refusing to cooperate with state authorities in obtaining the necessary documentation for removal. Quantitative data is limited on the number of prosecutions and convictions for the sole offence of illegal stay over the past decades, as well as for offences of non-cooperation with return procedures. The data that is available provides figures on the number of persons imprisoned for a principal offence related to illegal stay without specifying the existence of other criminal offences. What this data does tell us is that there has been a decrease in the number of persons imprisoned for a principal offence related to illegal stay over the past two decades. The number of imprisoned irregular migrants peaked in 1993; an estimated 9641 irregular migrants were incarcerated for a principal offence related to illegal stay that year (Le Contrôleur général des lieux de privation de liberté 2010, p. 265). In 2001, an estimated 2850 irregular migrants were incarcerated for a principal offence related to illegal stay (Le Contrôleur général des lieux de privation de liberté 2010, p. 265). The number of yearly incarcerations for a principal offence related to illegal stay has remained relatively stable since 2001.

The overall decrease in the number of persons imprisoned for a principal offence related to illegal stay is partly due to a shift in policy. Circulars[18] adopted by competent ministries in 2006 and 2011 specified that imprisonment on the sole ground of illegal stay was to be avoided; the new priority was to *effectively remove* irregular migrants from France. These circulars, however, strongly encouraged the prosecution of non-cooperative irregular migrants, as well as irregular migrants who had committed other criminal offences. Non-cooperation offences correspond to a wide range of actions and omissions that can take place at various stages of a

[16] Code de l'entrée et du séjour des étrangers et du droit d'asile (Code on the Entry and Residence of Foreigners and on the Right of Asylum), former Article L.621-1. Illegal entry, on the other hand, has long been and continues to be a criminal offence: Code de l'entrée et du séjour des étrangers et du droit d'asile (Code on the Entry and Residence of Foreigners and on the Right of Asylum, consolidated version on 24 January 2014), Article L.621-2.

[17] Ibid, Article L. 624.

[18] Ministère de la Justice, Circulaire relative aux conditions de l'interpellation d'un étranger en situation irrégulière, garde à vue de l'étranger en situation irrégulière, réponse pénales. CRIM 2006 05 E1/21-02-2006; Ministre de la Justice et des Libertés, Portée de l'arrêt de la Cour de Justice de l'Union européenne (CJUE) "Achughbabian" du 6 décembre 2011 portant sur la compatibilité de l'article L.621-1 du CESEDA avec la directive 2008/115/CE dite "directive retour". 11-04-C39, 13 décembre 2011.

return procedure. They range from absconding upon written notification of a return measure to non-cooperation with authorities following placement in administrative detention. Detained irregular migrants might be deemed non-cooperative if they, for example, hide or destroy their identity documents; refuse to disclose their identity and/or country of origin; refuse to be accompanied to their country of origin's embassy in order to obtain travel documentation; or refuse to embark on transportation to their country of origin.

A shift therefore occurred in French public policy before the CJEU delivered its two rulings in 2011. Prosecutions for offences related to illegal stay increasingly focused on non-cooperative irregular migrants as opposed to the totality of irregular migrants. To that extent, the CJEU's rulings confirmed a trend in France. However, the rulings set that trend in the stone of hard law (not mere policy guidelines) and pushed it further. In the aftermath of the 2011 rulings, non-cooperation with return procedures is no longer sufficient for French authorities to imprison irregular migrants. Non-cooperation offences, like the general offence of illegal stay, may only lead to imprisonment when non-cooperative irregular migrants have been administratively detained for the maximum period under French law (which is 45 days). The majority of administratively detained irregular migrants are released from detention before the expiry of the maximum period; this is largely the result of NGO and judicial activism (Ravignan 2010). The CJEU's maximum-period criterion is therefore a constraint for states like France that wish to imprison non-cooperative irregular migrants. Prior to the CJEU rulings, placement in administrative detention for the maximum period was not a prerequisite for the successful prosecution and conviction of irregular migrants for non-cooperation offences.

3.2.1.2 The Administrative Detention of Irregular Migrants in France

Irregular migrants can be placed in administrative detention if an enforceable return measure has been issued against them. The maximum period of administrative detention in France is quite short in comparison with the maximum period in other EU member states (it is 45 days). This period used to be shorter (32 days) and was increased after the entry into force of the EU Return Directive. Placement in administrative detention is for an initial period of 5 days, which can be prolonged for an extra 20 days and prolonged a second time for another 20 days. Administrative authorities may only lawfully prolong detention following judicial oversight. Exhausted returnees in France are irregular migrants who have been continuously detained for the maximum 45-day period. There are no limits under French law on the number of times an irregular migrant can be placed in administrative detention, the only limit coming from EU law, which sets out an absolute maximum of 18 months.

Eurostat estimates suggest that there were respectively 88,565, 76,590, and 83,440 TCNs who were ordered to leave *mainland* France in 2009, 2010, and

2011.[19] They also suggest that only 18,400, 17,045, and 20,425 returned following an order to leave in 2009, 2010, and 2011. The overwhelming majority of these migrants were thus never returned. There are no precise figures on the number of placements in administrative detention following an order to leave. According to NGO reports, there were respectively at least 50,000, 60,282, and 51,385 administratively detained irregular migrants in *mainland and overseas France* in 2009, 2010, and 2011 (Assfam et al. 2011, p. 9; Assfam et al. 2012, p. 9). Thus, a large proportion of irregular migrants ordered to leave are subjected to administrative detention in France.

3.2.2 From One Exclusionary Space to Another

I now turn to examine the law and data relating to exhausted returnees' entrapment between the three exclusionary spaces. My analysis examines movement from administrative detention to prison, from prison to administrative detention, from both to freedom-in-limbo, and from freedom-in-limbo back to either prison or administrative detention.

3.2.2.1 From Administrative Detention to Prison

When the maximum period of administrative detention is reached for irregular migrants, French authorities might have one of two choices. They might release them or criminally prosecute them under a non-cooperation offence. Governmental statistics are lacking on the fates of administratively detained irregular migrants who have been detained for the maximum period. However, French NGOs have in recent years gathered quantitative data on the fates of numerous detainees.

In 2010, the Cimade and other NGOs found that out of a sample of 24,018 administrative detainees, 13,333 were released and freed (55.5 %), whereas 10,004 were effectively removed from France (41.7 %) (Assfam et al. 2011, p. 13). Amongst those who were released, only 2803 were released following expiry of the maximum period of administrative detention (11 % of the 24,018 detainees). Amongst those who were neither removed nor released, at least *634 were placed in police custody and prosecuted for a non-cooperation offence* (2.6 % of the 24,018 detainees) (Assfam et al. 2011, p. 13). Data provided by the same NGOs in 2011 and 2012 show similar proportions of administrative detainees who were released, removed, and imprisoned (Assfam et al. 2012, p. 11; Assfam et al. 2013, p. 13). The percentage of administrative detainees who were released upon expiry of the maximum period and the percentage of those sent to prison are both small but far from insignificant.

---

[19] Eurostat Population Database, Enforcement of Immigration Legislation. http://epp.eurostat.ec.europa.eu/portal/page/portal/eurostat/home/. Accessed 27 Jan 2013.

In August of 2013, a legal adviser in a French administrative detention centre informed me that there was an increasing number of prosecutions of exhausted returnees for non-cooperation offences.[20] These exhausted returnees are systematically held in police custody pending their trial. The legal adviser specified that the increase was post CJEU rulings, which suggests that more non-cooperative exhausted returnees are prosecuted for non-cooperation offences and potentially sent to prison.

3.2.2.2 From Prison to Administrative Detention

I now turn to estimates on the number of irregular migrants sent from prison to administrative detention centres. The Cimade and other NGOs recently suggested that exhausted returnees were often bounced around between administrative detention and prison as a form of state harassment that aimed to deter non-cooperation (Assfam et al. 2012, p. 273). These NGOs estimated that at least 1070 irregular migrants prisoners were sent to administrative detention centres in 2010 (Assfam et al. 2011, p. 60). Exhausted returnees likely represent an important percentage of the 1070 prisoners sent to administrative detention in 2010, as it is known that at least 634 exhausted returnees were sent to prison in 2010. However, an important percentage of these 1070 prisoners were probably made up of individuals being sent to administrative detention for the first time. Irregular migrant prisoners are not all exhausted returnees. Thousands of irregular migrants are imprisoned every year, either for a principal offence related to illegal stay or for a principal offence unrelated to illegal stay (Secrétariat Général du Ministère de la Justice 2012, p. 199).

A horrible feature of several prisons in France is the practice of telling irregular migrant prisoners that they have a 50 % chance of being escorted to an administrative detention centre upon expiry of their prison sentence. In these prisons, irregular migrant prisoners have to deal with uncertainty over whether they will be freed or sent to administrative detention upon expiry of their prison sentence. Such is the practice in France's largest prison at Fleury Mérogis.[21]

3.2.2.3 Release from Prison and/or Administrative Detention in the Worst Form of Legal Limbo

Exhausted returnees, if not sent to prison, and ex-prisoners, if not sent to administrative detention centres, are simply released. In such cases, they are often released in the worst form of legal limbo. Chances of seeing their status regularised or their

[20] Discussion via email with Mr A.B., Legal Adviser at France terre d'asile's Department of Assistance for Detained Foreigners, 1 August 2013.

[21] I am aware of these practices as I provided voluntary legal aid there in 2010.

removal formally postponed are very thin. This is especially the case for exhausted returnees who have been subjected to a period of imprisonment as regularisation mechanisms and programmes tend to exclude ex-prisoners (Baldwin-Edwards and Kraler 2009, pp. 33/35). Further, regularisation and postponement mechanisms are geared towards illegally staying TCNs who cannot be removed on legal or policy grounds (as opposed to those who cannot be removed on practical grounds) (European Union Agency for Fundamental Rights 2011, p. 33; Ramboll and Eurasylum 2013, p. 165). This is a sorry state of affairs for exhausted returnees who are usually not removable for practical reasons.

If release from administrative detention is not followed by regularisation of status or formal postponement of removal, those concerned are left in a limbo of exhausted removal. Some might argue that being in such a limbo is preferable to being in prison or administrative detention. However, as examined in Sect. 2.3.1 of this chapter, exhausted returnees have the weakest status and rights of all non-removable irregular migrants. They live in permanent fear of future administrative detention or imprisonment on the ground of their illegal stay. They often have to go into hiding because of the informal nature of their status, they have virtually no socio-economic entitlements as most of these entitlements are tied to some kind of immigration status, and they are also deterred from exercising the few rights they have due to the risk and fear of being apprehended and sent to either administrative detention or prison.

3.2.2.4 From Freedom-in-Limbo to Prison or Back into Administrative Detention

When exhausted returnees are released and granted freedom, I have explained that this is a limbo-like freedom. It is characterised by exclusion from numerous socio-economic rights and benefits. But more frighteningly, exhausted returnees face the palpable prospect of being either imprisoned or placed once again in an administrative detention centre. The CJEU's 2011 rulings allow member states to imprison non-cooperative exhausted returnees. These rulings do not require member states to prosecute these exhausted returnees immediately following expiry of the maximum period of administrative detention. Exhausted returnees can be released from administrative detention and imprisoned at some later stage if they are arrested and found to have no justified ground for non-return. This situation is expressly covered in French legislation[22] and would appear to be compatible with the Return Directive as interpreted by the CJEU. While French NGOs have in recent years provided estimates on the number of irregular migrants sent directly from administrative detention to prison, estimates are not available on the number of exhausted

[22] Code de l'entrée et du séjour des étrangers et du droit d'asile (Code on the Entry and Residence of Foreigners and on the Right of Asylum, consolidated version on 24 January 2014), Article 624-1, para. 1.

returnees sent to prison long after their release from administrative detention. The latter are swallowed up in overall figures on prosecutions and convictions for offences related to illegal stay. As seen earlier, there are thousands of individuals who are prosecuted every year for a principal offence related to illegal stay.

Freed exhausted returnees do not just face the prospect of imprisonment. They can also be subjected to repeated placements in administrative detention. The maximum period during which irregular migrants can be placed in administrative detention is 45 days in France. But this maximum period only applies to one placement in administrative detention. French law sets no explicit limit on the number of times an irregular migrant can be placed in administrative detention. The only limit on repeated placements in administrative detention comes from the Return Directive, as interpreted by the CJEU in *Kadzoev*,[23] which prohibits repeated placements in administrative detention that add up to an overall period of more than 18 months. For as long as exhausted returnees have not been administratively detained for a cumulative period of 18 months, they are *temporarily* exhausted returnees and not *definitively* exhausted returnees. The Cimade and its partner NGOs' yearly reports on administrative detention in France are ripe with narratives of irregular migrants who have experienced multiple placements in administrative detention. One of these reports states that numerous irregular migrants have suffered 15 placements in detention; one irregular migrant was reported to have experienced 27 placements (Assfam et al. 2011, p. 60).

To illustrate the constant fear of apprehension and detention that is experienced during periods of freedom-in-limbo in France, I turn now to the narrative of an exhausted returnee whom I recently interviewed.[24] Mr F.S., a 30-year-old man from Mali, has experienced multiple apprehensions and placements in police custody over the past decade, all linked to his illegal stay. He was placed in administrative detention on four occasions. The first placement in administrative detention lasted for the maximum period under national law. The subsequent placements in administrative detention ended before expiry of the maximum period due to procedural irregularities surrounding his apprehension. He was never imprisoned for the offence of illegal stay nor for the offence of non-cooperation with his return procedure but easily could have been. He was nearly deported during his second placement in administrative detention. He was placed on a flight to Mali but resisted and screamed on the plane. Passengers protested and he was escorted off the plane. The refusal to embark on a plane is sufficient to be prosecuted and convicted for not cooperating with a return procedure. He could easily have been sent to prison. But he wasn't. Nonetheless, being bounced around between administrative detention and freedom-in-limbo has tainted his periods of freedom with a gut-wrenching fear of apprehension and detention. He told me that he was terrified of being apprehended once again and placed a fifth time in administrative detention, that

[23] ECJ, Case C-357/09, *PPU Kadzoev* [2009] ECR I-11189.

[24] Interview with Mr F.S. (France terre d'asile, Paris, France on 17 July 2013). This interview took place within the research framework discussed in footnote 13.

he did not know if would be able to go through it again. This fear of apprehension and renewed placement in detention has led to various health problems, including chronic insomnia. He has survived all these years, thanks to illegal work carried out on various construction sites. He told me that his irregular status allowed his various employers to coerce him into carrying tasks and working under conditions that he would otherwise never have accepted. Mr F.S. was not bounced around between administrative detention, imprisonment, and freedom-in-limbo. I turn now to the story of M.J., documented by an NGO, who was trapped between these three exclusionary spaces in France.

3.2.3 Narrative Reported by the Cimade of a Third-Country National Bounced Around Between the Three Exclusionary Spaces

The Cimade's report on administrative detention in 2007 (La Cimade 2008, p. 9) contains a narrative of a non-removable TCN who experienced entrapment between administrative detention, imprisonment, and freedom-in-limbo. It is the story of M. J., the son of a Moroccan mother and Algerian father, who was raised by neither parent and possessed neither of his parents' nationalities. Before summarising his ordeal, it is important to specify that at the time of these events the maximum period of administrative detention under French law was 32 days, not the current 45 days. M.J.'s story took place before the 2011 rulings, but it is the prototype story of irregular migrants who were singled out by the CJEU as permissible targets of imprisonment. Stories like his persist to this day in the aftermath of the two rulings.

M.J. first experienced administrative detention in Toulouse for 17 days in 2006, following which he was released. He was thus released before expiry of the maximum 32-day period. A few months later, he was re-apprehended and administratively detained again. After having been detained for 32 days this time around, he was successfully returned to Algeria. However, lacking the necessary documentation in Algeria, he was held in the basement of a police station in Algiers for 45 days. French police officers escorted him back to France (Marseille), where he was sent to prison for 3 months. Upon release, he was sent to an administrative detention centre for 17 days. He was then prosecuted, convicted, and sentenced to 3 months' imprisonment. Upon release, he experienced 2 months of freedom-in-limbo, which ended when he was placed in a new removal procedure and yet another administrative detention centre. He was eventually released, then apprehended and administratively detained, and finally released again!

Would M.J.'s entrapment be any different today in the aftermath of the CJEU's two rulings? No. Under the post-*Achughbabian* state of EU law, the imprisonment of irregular migrants on grounds related to illegal stay may take place after they have been subjected to every stage of a coercive removal procedure and if they have no justified ground for non-return. M.J. was subjected to the maximum period of administrative detention, was returned to Algeria, but was escorted back to France due to the lack of necessary documentation. M.J.'s position clearly falls under the CJEU's *residual* category of irregular migrants who can be imprisoned as long as his non-removal can be attributed to his non-cooperation. Even if he hadn't been detained for the maximum period, the fact that he was administratively detained and removed would probably suffice as he was subjected to every stage of a coercive removal procedure and effectively removed, even if only for a short period of time. The entrapment endured by M.J. and many others begs the question of what functions are performed by this entrapment. What are the functions of the three exclusionary spaces in their use against non-cooperative exhausted returnees?

4 Converging Functions of These Three Exclusionary Spaces

Stumpf (2006) has noted the increasing convergence between immigration and criminal laws in the American legal system and a parallel convergence of harsh ideological motivations behind immigration and criminal sanctions. These are motivations of retribution, deterrence, incapacitation, etc. Building upon Juliet Stumpf's convergence-of-motivations idea, I argue that administrative detention, imprisonment, *and freedom-in-limbo* may all be viewed as sanctions and that they may be seen to perform similar functions under EU law and member states' national laws. All three are forms of membership exclusion that internally segregate individuals concerned within society. Administrative detention and imprisonment segregate through physical seclusion from society. Freedom-in-limbo does not correspond to physical seclusion but corresponds to extensive societal alienation and discrimination outside detention.

Deportation, imprisonment, and exclusion from regularisation/toleration are all forms of membership exclusion. Stumpf explains that "a decision to exclude in criminal law results in segregation within our society through incarceration, while exclusion in immigration law results in separation from our society through expulsion from the national territory" (Stumpf 2006, p. 397). Imprisonment of an irregular migrant internally segregates that individual, whereas deportation rids society of the individual. Much like imprisonment, both administrative detention and exclusion from legal residence internally segregate irregular migrants. All three internally exclude them from membership in various ways. Administrative detention corresponds to physical confinement of irregular migrants, usually in order to ensure their removal. Exclusion from legal residence rights corresponds to extensive societal discrimination of irregular migrants in their relationships with both public and private actors in order to punish and deter their violations of immigration rules.

Exclusion from legal residence has two sides, a formal side and a substantive side. Starting with the substantive, exclusion from substantive rights reserved for legal residents is a collateral sanction attached to illegal residency. Stumpf has used this idea of "collateral" (Stumpf 2006, pp. 404–405) sanction to describe the post-incarceration exclusion of ex-offenders from a range of social and political rights.

This idea of *collateral* sanctions can also be used to describe the situation of exhausted returnees who are deprived of most socio-economic rights and benefits following release from administrative detention, as punishment for both their illegal residency and persistent non-removability. There is a slight difference because collateral sanctions against ex-offenders who are citizens deprive those citizens of rights they held before, whereas the collateral sanctions I talk about here deprive illegal residents of rights they did not necessarily ever hold.

The formal side of exclusion from legal residence relates to immigration status. The status of exhausted returnees is rarely regularised. They are rarely provided with formal protection from future enforcement of removal, which would otherwise offer them some sort of toleration status (akin to a postponed-removal status). At best, they have a written certificate of release from detention and, at worse, nothing at all. They are left hanging with the threat of future apprehension and detention, as well as imprisonment in countries that provide for that possibility.

I argue that administrative detention, imprisonment, and freedom-in-limbo may be perceived as performing similar functions to one another that essentially serve to protect territorial sovereignty, the "integrity" (Guild 2010, p. 8; Rosenblum 2010, p. 2) of immigration and asylum systems, and the goals of those systems (namely socio-economic and security goals).[25] These converging functions become apparent when the three exclusionary tools are used against persons who fall under the CJEU's *residual* category. There are namely formal or informal functions of retribution, deterrence, enhanced removability (which is closely related to deterrence), and expressing the power of the State. Functions that might apply to at least one of the three spaces are selective regularisation, curbing public expenditure, and incapacitation. In this chapter, I focus only on the twin functions of deterrence and enhanced removability. I do not argue that all EU institutional actors assign these functions to all the exclusionary spaces but that certain of the actors behind the current state of EU law may assign such functions. I refer to elements of the Return Directive, institutional discussions surrounding the Return Directive, certain national legal systems, interviews I conducted with exhausted returnees, and more generally of institutional discussions at EU level. I now provide a brief explanation of the functions of deterrence and enhanced removability (Sect. 4.1) before examining how they apply to the administrative detention (Sect. 4.2), imprisonment (Sect. 4.3), and freedom-in-limbo (Sect. 4.4) of non-cooperative exhausted returnees.

[25] This builds on William Walters' analysis of the evolving motivations behind the power of deportation (Walters 2002, pp. 276–280).

4.1 Functions of Deterrence and Enhanced Removability

A core, dominant, and explicit motivation behind the variety of sanctions imposed on irregular migrants is deterrence of irregular migration. The aim is to deter irregular migrants from remaining, and potential irregular migration candidates from giving it a go, by sending a signal (Rodier and Saint-Saëns 2007, p. 6) on the harsh consequences that may await apprehended irregular migrants in the EU.

With regard to the CJEU's *residual* category of irregular migrants, the variety of sanctions may perform a very specific deterrent function. Repeated or prolonged administrative detention, imprisonment, and freedom-in-limbo all serve to deter the *residual* category of irregular migrants from deliberately frustrating efforts to remove them. In situations where irregular migrants are responsible for their practical non-removability, the three exclusionary spaces may serve to discourage non-cooperative behaviour. They may correspondingly serve to encourage cooperation with removal procedures, in order to ensure the long-term failure of non-cooperative strategies, or to nurture a desire to self-repatriate. The deterrent function is thus allied with a function of enhancing removability that relies on the physically and psychologically alienating and exclusionary effects of detention and freedom-in-limbo. Removability is enhanced by the three exclusionary spaces through the gradual erosion of the will, desire, or capacity to obstruct removal, as well as the ability to live a dignified life in the EU.

4.2 Prolonged and/or Repeated Placements in Administrative Detention

Under the Return Directive, non-cooperative individuals are explicit targets of administrative detention, especially of prolonged 18-month detention. A specific deterrent function was mentioned in institutional negotiations on the European Commission's Return Directive proposal. Certain member state delegations in an early Council Working Party meeting displayed considerable hostility towards the setting of a maximum period of administrative detention.[26] These delegations suggested that a maximum period might encourage non-cooperative behaviour on the part of detained irregular migrants; the hope of future release from detention was seen as a potential incentive for non-cooperation. Prolonged detention would therefore seem to perform a function of specifically deterring non-cooperative behaviour. Practices of subjecting irregular migrants to repeated placements in detention are presumably motivated by the same desire to deter non-cooperative behaviour. Such practices of repeated placements in detention are common in countries like France that have shorter maximum periods of administrative

[26] Council doc. 13934/06, 18 October 2006, p. 3.

detention than other European countries. Although a deterrent function is assigned to administrative detention by many institutional actors, Alice Edwards has noted that "there is no empirical evidence that the prospect of being detained deters irregular migration" (Edwards 2011, p. 1)[27] on a global scale.

4.3 The Imposition and/or Threat of Imprisonment

The imposition—or threat—of a sentence of imprisonment on grounds related to illegal stay performs a general deterrent function. If illegal stay can be met with the harsh consequence of imprisonment, this may be believed to generally deter violations by TCNs of rules relating to entry and residence, thus protecting the integrity of overall immigration systems. In the *Achughbabian* ruling, the CJEU made a direct reference to this general deterrent motivation when it stated that the Return Directive "does not preclude the law of a Member State from classifying an illegal stay as an offence and laying down penal sanctions to deter and prevent such an infringement of the national rules on residence".[28] States that provided written observations in the *Achughbabian* case went as far as dramatically stating that deterrence of illegal stay was entirely reliant on the threat of imprisonment.[29]

But imprisonment on the sole ground of illegal stay is no longer permissible since the CJEU delivered its two rulings in 2011. Imprisonment for offences related to illegal stay may now only be imposed on a *residual* group of irregular migrants, which might be seen as diminishing the general deterrent function of criminalising illegal stay. The 2011 rulings interpreted the Return Directive as only allowing member states to impose prison sentences on irregular migrants who have been subjected to every stage of a coercive removal procedure and who have no justified ground for non-return. The ultimate goal of the Return Directive, according to the CJEU, is to ensure the effective return of irregular migrants, and national criminal laws must not thwart this objective. If removal procedures, and the administrative detention that is often resorted to, do not lead to the ultimate objective of removal, it is only then that imprisonment might play a role in securing future removal through specific deterrence of non-cooperative behaviour.

The deterrent function of imprisonment is thus a very specific one in its use against non-cooperative exhausted returnees as it is allied with a function of enhancing removability. The threat of a sentence of imprisonment may serve to

[27] Also see: Robinson and Segrott (2002); Thielemann (2004). In the empirical research that I carried out for France terre d'asile, mentioned above in footnote 13, administrative detention in France was found to have little-to-no deterrent effect on our sample of irregular migrants. This research will be published in Summer of 2014.

[28] CJEU, Case C-329/11, *Alexandre Achughbabian v. Préfet du Val-de-Marne* [2011] ECR I-0000, para. 28.

[29] CJEU, Case C-329/11, *Alexandre Achughbabian v. Préfet du Val-de-Marne* [2011] ECR I-0000, para. 47; Commission Nationale Consultative des Droits de l'Homme (2004), p. 20.

specifically deter irregular migrants in administrative detention centres from deliberately hampering/delaying their removal. The actual imprisonment of non-cooperative exhausted returnees may serve to encourage them to cooperate with authorities when released from prison and sent back to an administrative detention centre. The aim is to break down the practical obstacles to removability that are caused by non-cooperative behaviour. The CJEU in *El Dridi* commented that states may adopt "criminal law measures, aimed inter alia at dissuading those nationals from remaining illegally on those States' territory".[30]

I turn to practices and narratives in two EU countries to illustrate the deterrent/removability function behind the imprisonment of non-cooperative exhaustive returnees. These countries are France and the United Kingdom (UK). France is bound by the Return Directive (and thus the *El Dridi* and *Achughbabian* rulings); the UK is not as a result of a Treaty opt-out. In France, the maximum period of administrative detention is 45 days. The UK does not have an explicit maximum period, which means that irregular migrants can theoretically be indefinitely detained. However, limits do exist in the UK on the duration of administrative detention, namely through the requirement that there be a *reasonable prospect of removal*. For the purposes of this chapter, exhausted returnees in France are irregular migrants who have been administratively detained for the maximum 45-day period; exhausted returnees in the UK are irregular migrants whose administrative detention has reached an end due to the lack of a realistic prospect of removal.

In both countries, illegal stay and non-cooperation with removal procedures are criminal offences punishable by imprisonment (even though the general offence of illegal stay in France was repealed on 31 December 2012; what remains are specific offences of illegal entry).[31] State authorities in both the UK and France, prior to the 2011 rulings, had already explicitly made policy choices to limit prosecutions for offences related to illegal stay. Prosecutions were to be reserved for specific groups of irregular migrants, namely those that had committed other crimes and more

---

[30] CJEU, Case C-61/11, *PPU El Dridi, alias Karim Soufi* [2011] ECR I-03015, para. 52.

[31] With regard to France, see: Code de l'entrée et du séjour des étrangers et du droit d'asile (Code on the Entry and Residence of Foreigners and on the Right of Asylum, consolidated version on 24 January 2014), Articles L621-2 and L624.

With regard to the UK, see: Immigration Act 1971, Section 24; Asylum and Immigration (Treatment of Claimants, etc.) Act 2004, Section 35. In the UK, the offence of illegal stay is fragmented into various offences that are described as *illegal entry and similar offences*.

importantly those that were non-cooperative with return procedures.[32] These policy choices reflected a prioritising of removal whereby irregular migrants were generally to be subjected to removal procedures instead of imprisonment; irregular migrants who successfully hampered their removal procedures were to be prosecuted and possibly imprisoned in order to deter continued hampering of removal.

In France, the Cimade and other NGOs have noted that exhausted returnees who are sent to prison (for non-cooperation with removal procedures) tend to systematically be sent back to administrative detention upon expiry of their prison sentences (Assfam et al. 2011, p. 60). Imprisonment would therefore appear to serve as a very harsh incentive for exhausted returnees to cooperate with authorities when placed back in administrative detention after their time in prison. These NGOs have further reported that police officers often try to coerce administrative detainees into cooperating with removal procedures. In Sect. 2.3.3 of this chapter, the narrative of Mr S.I. provides a perfect illustration of the manner in which police officers have used the threat of imprisonment as an incentive to cooperate with return procedures.

In the UK, policy documents[33] and case law have highlighted the deterrent/removal motivation behind the imprisonment of actual and potential exhausted returnees. It is an offence, under section 35 of the Asylum and Immigration (Treatment of Claimants, etc.) Act of 2004, for irregular migrants to deliberately not comply with removal procedures against them (e.g. by refusing to comply with the documentation process). A UK case which provides an excellent illustration of this offence and of its function is the *Rostami* case.[34] Feridon Rostami, an Iranian national who unsuccessfully applied for asylum, was subjected to several periods of imprisonment and administrative detention for almost 3 years. He consistently refused to cooperate with state authorities in preparing his return to Iran and attempted to kill himself on numerous occasions. During his time in administrative detention, Mr Rostami was frequently threatened by state authorities with possible imprisonment in the event of non-cooperation. Immigration authorities interviewed

---

[32] With regard to the UK, see: UK Legal Services Commission (2010) Simple cautions for foreign national offenders: pilot policy statement. http://ftp.legalservices.gov.uk/Simple_cautions_for_foreign_national_offenders_pilot_-_policy_statement.pdf. Accessed Oct 2011; The Law Society (2013) Conditional cautions for foreign national offenders. http://www.lawsociety.org.uk/advice/articles/conditional-cautions-for-foreign-national-offenders/. Accessed 30 Jun 2014.

With regard to France, see: Ministère de la Justice, Circulaire relative aux conditions de l'interpellation d'un étranger en situation irrégulière, garde à vue de l'étranger en situation irrégulière, réponse pénales. CRIM 2006 05 E1/21-02-2006; Ministre de la Justice et des Libertés, "Portée de l'arrêt de la Cour de Justice de l'Union européenne (CJUE) "Achughbabian" du 6 décembre 2011 portant sur la compatibilité de l'article L.621-1 du CESEDA avec la directive 2008/115/CE dite "directive retour". 11-04-C39 13 décembre 2011.

[33] UK Legal Services Commission (2010) Simple cautions for foreign national offenders: pilot policy statement. http://ftp.legalservices.gov.uk/Simple_cautions_for_foreign_national_offenders_pilot_-_policy_statement.pdf. Accessed Oct 2011; The Law Society (2013) Conditional cautions for foreign national offenders. http://www.lawsociety.org.uk/advice/articles/conditional-cautions-for-foreign-national-offenders/. Last accessed 30 Jun 2014.

[34] *R (on the application of Feridon Rostami) v SSHD* [2009] EWHC 2094 (QB).

him "to see if he (was) ... now prepared to comply with the documentation process"[35] and to warn him "that he could face up to two years in prison".[36] His responses included "Do it"[37] and "Prison is better than Iran".[38] The threats of imprisonment led to actual imprisonment on several occasions, and Mr Rostami was indeed bounced around between prison and administrative detention.

4.4 Freedom-in-Limbo

When non-cooperative exhausted returnees are freed from administrative detention or prison, excluding them from legal residence may be perceived as a manner of deterring them from remaining and from not cooperating with state authorities. If illegally staying TCNs cannot be removed through coercive removal as a result of non-cooperative behaviour, they can be encouraged to leave through a highly precarious and alienating sort of freedom.

Some EU member state actors have been very explicit about the deterrent objective behind the exclusion of non-cooperative irregular migrants from legal residence and the rights reserved for legal residents. For example, in response to the European Commission consultation on a Community Return policy in 2002, the Swedish state explained that when faced with a failed return procedure against an "alien ... the only sanctions we can use to persuade the alien to cooperate in obtaining adequate documents for return, are to make restrictions in the allowances, the social benefits" (Eriksson 2002, page 3). In a 2006 Council Working Party meeting relating to the European Commission's Return Directive proposal, British and Maltese delegations[39] also stressed the importance of preserving the deterrent effect of deportation on non-removable persons by not providing them with a secure status.

I now turn to German law and policy to further illustrate the deterrent motivation that can exist behind laws regulating the limbo positions of non-cooperative irregular migrants. In Germany, persons who are released from administrative detention, including those released due to the expiry of the maximum period of detention, are usually granted a postponed-removal status which takes the form of a toleration certificate. Holders of this certificate are entitled to a minimum set of benefits for accommodation facilities, food, other items of daily need, and medical treatment. However, a distinction is made between cooperative and non-cooperative persons who hold this toleration certificate. According to the European Migration Network's (EMN) German Contact Point, persons who

[35] *R (on the application of Feridon Rostami) v SSHD* [2009] EWHC 2094 (QB), para. 36.
[36] *R (on the application of Feridon Rostami) v SSHD* [2009] EWHC 2094 (QB), para. 38.
[37] *R (on the application of Feridon Rostami) v SSHD* [2009] EWHC 2094 (QB), para. 48.
[38] *R (on the application of Feridon Rostami) v SSHD* [2009] EWHC 2094 (QB), para. 38.
[39] Council doc. 13025/06, 16 October 2006, p. 7, footnote 6.

"have not influenced the duration of their stay through an abuse of legal rights … will, after the expiry of 48 months, receive higher benefits commensurate to the general rules and regulations governing social welfare benefits", possible authorisation to take up employment "after a one year waiting period" (European Migration Network 2010, pp. 7–8), and may be granted a residence permit after 18 months. Persons "who do not cooperate … in order to obtain a temporary suspension of deportation" (European Migration Network 2010, pp. 7–8) are excluded from eligibility for these extra socio-economic benefits, from prospects of regularisation, and they also run the risk of criminal prosecution for not cooperating with state authorities. The rationale behind this exclusion is to deter the intentional delaying or hampering of removal.

5 Conclusion: EU States Versus Non-cooperative Exhausted Returnees

This chapter has sought to highlight the plight of the CJEU's *residual* category of irregular migrants in several EU states, namely in France. I do not wish to cast a dark shadow over the CJEU's rulings, which attracted widespread acclaim from academics, migrant-friendly NGOs, and lawyer associations. Instead, I wish to draw attention to those left out by the CJEU's protective ruling. Every time the CJEU has angered member states by limiting their sovereignty over specific categories of migrants, states have reacted by unleashing their sovereign fury on migrants in the cracks left open by the CJEU. I highlighted that some member states, long before the CJEU's rulings, were already moving away from imposing prison sentences on the sole ground of illegal stay and trying to gear the tool of imprisonment towards non-cooperative irregular migrants. In some of the states examined in this chapter, many persons falling under the CJEU's *residual* category were/are trapped between administrative detention, imprisonment, and freedom-in-limbo, which represent three spaces of exclusion from societal membership that perform similar functions to one another. The CJEU's *El Dridi* and *Achughbabian* rulings have shined a spotlight on non-cooperative exhausted returnees by prohibiting the imprisonment of all other irregular migrants on the ground of their illegal stay. This spotlight might make their already-terrible plight even worse; this requires attention from defenders of irregular migrants in the EU who already lobby for the complete decriminalisation of illegal stay.

Legal or policy changes should be sought by defenders of irregular migrants in order to limit or prohibit repeated placements of irregular migrants in administrative detention; provide irregular migrants who are released from administrative detention, for reasons other than postponement of their removal, with a legal status or formal toleration status (akin to a postponed-removal status) and a decent set of rights attached, at least after a certain period of time; restrict or prohibit the imprisonment of irregular migrants for offences of illegal stay and non-cooperation with return procedures, even in situations where they have been administratively detained for the maximum period and have no justified ground for non-return.

The notion of states versus immigrants is extremely palpable when analysing the struggle between exhausted returnees and EU member states. Non-cooperative exhausted returnees are often treated as the least "desirable"[40] category of non-removable persons. The weak grounds of their non-removability (practical as opposed to legal) and their actual or presumed resistance to removal make them targets of state contempt and wrath. This state wrath manifests itself in several EU countries through the entrapment of such persons between the three exclusionary spaces of administrative detention, prison, and freedom-in-limbo. They are branded as system *abusers*. An illustration of contempt can be found in the *Rostami* case examined above in Sect. 4.3, which concerned an Iranian national who was bounced around between administrative detention and prison. Before one of the numerous courts that convicted and sentenced him to imprisonment on non-cooperation grounds, a Recorder described him as "an experienced and knowledgeable evader of the immigration laws of this country [who has] done everything [he] can to frustrate [his] removal from this country".[41] He was perceived by this Recorder as an abuser of non-removability strategies, and prison was seen as a tool for deterring him from continued abuse of the system. This portrait of him as a cunning abuser very clearly corresponds to a biased and short-sighted state-centric view, in light of the fact that he tried to kill himself on numerous occasions and that he openly stated he would rather spend his life in a UK prison than return to Iran.

An important role is assigned by states here to the agency of those concerned. The motivations and strategies of migrants are "highly varied and dynamic, and thus highly resistant to generalisation" (Collinson 2009, p. 3). Not all non-removable TCNs could be described as pursuing a strategy of non-removability. Regarding TCNs for whom non-removability is a deliberate strategy, non-removability opportunities correspond to one group of factors that sit alongside many other factors (e.g. work opportunities in formal and informal economies, familial networks, etc.)

According to Collinson (2009, p. 8), the strategies of individuals who migrate from a poorer to a richer country can broadly be divided into survival strategies and accumulative strategies. Migration as a survival strategy concerns individuals or households whose agency is restricted to coping. Migration as an accumulation strategy concerns individuals with greater financial leeway and whose agency can be directed towards more specific goals of financial accumulation. It is in this light that non-removability opportunities can be viewed as part of a wider strategy of either survival or capital accumulation. This allows us to move away from the state-centric angle of abuse to an understanding of non-removability strategies as smaller

---

[40] For an interesting analysis of the issue of deportability and desirability in the UK context, see: Paoletti (2010).

[41] *R (on the application of Feridon Rostami) v SSHD* [2009] EWHC 2094 (QB), para. 52.

parts of broader strategies. It also allows critical light to be shed on notions of abuse. Non-removability strategies do not have to be perceived as an abuse of immigration control but can be perceived as a strategy for surviving or for accumulating capital. Further, broad strategies are not always about economic survival or accumulation. Refugees, and other categories of maltreated persons or persons at risk of maltreatment, are concerned not just with economic survival but also with avoiding physical harm or death, which is more of a push factor. Families who face separation due to EU and national immigration laws may use non-removability as part of a broader strategy of family unity, whether through the exercise of the human right to family unity or by default through strategies of practical obstruction of removal (e.g. by hiding identity documents).

When non-removability is viewed as part of a broader strategy, it could be perceived as a TCN's claim to emplacement in a host state. EU member state immigration policies rest on the foundations of an international legal order, territorially divided into nation-states, which allocates the emplacement of individuals in accordance with their nationality and entitles states to emplace or displace non-nationals. It, therefore, entitles EU member states to determine the "emplacement" or "misplacement"[42] of TCNs within their countries. Strategies for curtailing state claims of misplacement may be looked at as competing claims of emplacement under what could be described as a European heteropia. Lindahl (2004, pp. 471–472) uses this concept of countervailing claims to emplacement and misplacement with regard to squatters in a building who transgress private property rights, "laying claim to a place for which there is no place in the legal order" (Lindahl 2004, p. 471). The parallels are strong because concepts of private property ownership and nation-state territorial sovereignty share an exclusionary trait with regard to place (Kostakopoulou 2004, p. 41).

The international legal order's allocation of populations exists within a context characterised by strong socio-economic disparities, as well as other complex dynamics, between and within nation-states. Strategising TCNs could be perceived as contesting their misplacement under the international legal order's allocation of populations into territorially divided nation-states in a complex and imperfect world. To quote the Swedish's State's response to the 2002 Consultation on a Community Return Policy, the "issue is where a person really belongs" (Eriksson 2002, p. 2), and that issue is what lies at the centre of the battle between EU member states and non-cooperative exhausted returnees.

[42] These concepts were borrowed from an article by Lindahl (2004).

References

Assfam, Forum Réfugiés, France terre d'asile, la Cimade, l'Ordre de Malte (2011) Centres et locaux de rétention administrative: rapport 2010. http://www.lacimade.org/publications/57. Last accessed 30 June 2014

Assfam, Forum Réfugiés, France terre d'asile, la Cimade, l'Ordre de Malte (2012) Centres et locaux de rétention administrative: rapport 2011. http://www.lacimade.org/publications/70. Last accessed 30 June 2014

Assfam, Forum Réfugiés, France terre d'asile, la Cimade, l'Ordre de Malte (2013) Centres et locaux de rétention administrative: rapport 2012. http://www.lacimade.org/publications/83. Accessed 30 June 2014

Baldwin-Edwards M, Kraler A (2009) REGINE regularisations in Europe: study on practices in the area of regularisation of illegally staying third-country nationals in the Member States of the EU. ICMPD, Vienna. http://research.icmpd.org/fileadmin/Research-Website/Project_material/REGINE/Regine_report_january_2009_en.pdf. Accessed 30 June 2014

Collinson S (2009) The political economy of migration processes: an agenda for migration research and analysis. International Migration Institute Working Paper 12

Commission Nationale Consultative des Droits de l'Homme (2004) Etude sur les étrangers détenus (propositions). http://www.cncdh.fr/sites/default/files/04.11.18_etude_sur_les_etrangers_detenus.pdf. Accessed 30 June 2014

De Giorgi A (2010) Immigration control, post-Fordism, and less eligibility: a materialist critique of the criminalization of immigration across Europe. Punishment Soc 12:147

Directorate-General Home Affairs (2012) Management Plan. European Commission

Edwards A (2011) Back to basics: the right to liberty and security of person and 'alternatives to detention' of refugees, asylum-seekers, stateless persons and other migrants. Legal and Protection Policy Research Series. http://www.refworld.org/docid/4dc935fd2.html. Accessed 30 June 2014

Eriksson KI (2002) Removal – enforcement of return decisions: paper prepared for the European Commission hearing on a community return policy on illegal residents. http://ec.europa.eu/dgs/home-affairs/what-is-new/public-consultation/2002/pdf/contributions/sweden_en.pdf. Last accessed 30 June 2014

European Commission, Communication to the Council and the European Parliament on EU Return Policy COM (2014) 199 final

European Migration Network (2010) Ad-hoc query on practices followed concerning Third Country Nationals whose compulsory removal is impossible. Compilation produced on 14 April 2010

European Union Agency for Fundamental Rights (2011) Fundamental rights of migrants in an irregular situation in the European Union: comparative report. Publications Office of the European Union, Luxembourg

Guild E (2010) Criminalisation of migration in Europe: human rights implications. CommDH/IssuePaper

Kostakopoulou T (2004) Irregular migration and migration theory: making state authorisation less relevant. In: Bogusz B, Cholewinski R, Cygan A, Szyszczak E (eds) Irregular migration and human rights: theoretical, European and international perspectives. Martinus Nijhoff, Leiden

La Cimade (2008) Centres et locaux de rétention administrative: rapport 2007. http://www.lacimade.org/publications/16. Accessed 30 June 2014

Le Contrôleur général des lieux de privation de liberté (2010) Rapport d'activité 2009. Editions Dalloz, Paris

Lindahl H (2004) Finding a place for freedom, security and justice: the European Union's claim to territorial unity. Eur Law Rev 29(4):461

Ministère de l'Intérieur (2013) Circulaire n° NORINTK1300159C

Mitsilegas V (2013) The changing landscape of the criminalisation of migration in Europe: the protective function of European Union law. In: Guia MJ, Van Der Woude M, Van Der Leun J (eds) Social control and justice: crimmigration in the age of fear. Eleven International Publishing, The Netherlands

Paoletti E (2010) Deportation, non-deportability and ideas of membership. Refugee Studies Centre Working Paper No 65

Raffaelli R (2012) Case note: the Achughbabian case. Impact of the return directive on national criminal legislation. Diritto Penale Contemporaneo. http://papers.ssrn.com/sol3/papers.cfm?abstract_id=1998324. Accessed 30 June 2014

Ramboll, Eurasylum (2013) Study on the situation of third-country nationals pending return/removal in the EU Member States and the Schengen Associated Countries: Annex 1 – Country Reports. Study commissioned by the European Commission. http://ec.europa.eu/dgs/home-affairs/e-library/documents/policies/immigration/return-readmission/docs/11032013_sudy_report_on_immigration_return-removal_annex_1_en.pdf. Accessed 30 June 2014

Ravignan A (2010) La Cimade, grain de sable dans la machine à expulser. Alternatives économiques 9(294):48

Robinson V, Segrott J (2002) Understanding the decision-making of asylum seekers. Home Office Research Study 243, Home Office Research, Development and Statistics Directorate. http://www.irr.org.uk/pdf/understand_asylum_decision.pdf. Accessed 30 June 2014

Rodier C, Saint-Saëns I (2007) Contrôler et filtrer: les camps au service des politiques migratoires de l'Europe. In: Caloz-Tshopp MC, Chetail V (eds) Mondialisation, Migrations, Droits de l'homme. Bruylant, Bruxelles

Rosenblum MR (2010) Immigration legalization in the United States and European Union: policy goals and program design. Migration Policy Institute Brief. http://www.migrationpolicy.org/pubs/legalization-policydesign.pdf. Accessed 30 June 2014

Secrétariat Général du Ministère de la Justice (2012) Annuaire statistique de la Justice: Edition 2011–2012. La Documentation française – Direction de l'information légale et administrative, Paris

Stumpf J (2006) The crimmigration crisis: immigrants, crime and sovereign power. Am Univ Law Rev 56:367

Thielemann E (2004) Why Asylum policy harmonisation undermines refugee burden-sharing. Eur J Migration Law 6:47

Walters W (2002) Deportation, expulsion, and the international police of aliens. Citizenship Stud 6 (3):265

Immunity from Criminal Prosecution and Consular Assistance to the Foreign Detainee According the International Human Rights Law

Larissa Leite

Abstract The present paper addresses immunity from prosecution and consular assistance granted to the detainee as two legal concepts that ensure the foreign individual a differentiated treatment that is more beneficial than the one received by a national citizen of any given State—as opposed to what is generally the case in foreigners legislation. With the purpose of analysing where these rules are presently heading, this paper turns to the major cases where the subject was debated internationally and concludes that the enforcement of International Human Rights Law has given way to a narrowing of jurisdictional immunity and, on the other hand, to the enhancement of consular assistance granted to the foreign detainee. On a final note, this paper explores how these issues have been addressed by Brazilian courts, evidencing a certain improvement on some fronts despite the continuity of a conservative line of thought in many instances.

1 Introduction

Being "the most traditional chapter of International Private Law",[1] foreigners legislation is sometimes perceived as a simple and secure set of rules and concepts, even though it occupies a central role in many sensitive debates concerning law and international relations in the present.

However, being tied to the States' sovereignty and to the regulation enforced by each country, the attribution of nationality continues to create problems as to

[1] Soares (2004), p. 170.

L. Leite (✉)
Protection Coordination of the Reference Centre for Refugees, Caritas Arquidiocesana de São Paulo, UNHCR, São Paulo, Brazil

University de São Paulo, São Paulo, Brazil
e-mail: larissagleite@gmail.com

M.J. Guia et al. (eds.), *Immigration Detention, Risk and Human Rights*,
DOI 10.1007/978-3-319-24690-1_7

plurinationality and statelessness, despite several attempts to define international standards on this matter.[2] The urgency of new types of armed conflicts (internal or international) and the triggering of new flows of refugees, transnational criminality and the increased mobility of people, as well as other phenomena emanating from globalisation, pose new challenges to foreign nationals legislation, which, furthermore, needs to overcome the difficulties posed by traditional concepts.

All these issues challenge the Foreigner Law, but amongst all them the most difficult discussion laid down one basic dilemma: is a differentiated treatment, merely based on the nationality of the individual, legitimated under international human rights law?

International human rights have weakened the protections that a nation-state has traditionally afforded to citizens. This has occurred in large part because human right in theory at least protects the individual regardless of citizenship and national boundaries. As will be argued, this applies to diplomatic protection....[3]

The purpose of this paper is to analyse rules of criminal procedure involving consular assistance (included in the Vienna Convention on Consular Relations—VCCR—from 1963), personal inviolabilities and immunity from prosecution (included in the VCCR, in the Vienna Convention on Diplomatic Relations—VCDR, from 1961, and in other sources of international law). This theme challenges the privileged treatment of foreign nationals and thus attracts attention from international human rights law scholars.

In the second section the approach will address the Brazilian case, which is currently undergoing a review and debate process as to the rights of foreign nationals.

In the following sections, these institutions will be analysed through the lens of its traditional configuration and through the lens of its subordination to human rights principles.

2 On Inviolability and Immunity from Criminal Prosecution

2.1 On Immunities in General

Historically, the duties exercised by a *nuncio*, by ambassadors and by other representatives of a sovereign State in a foreign territory were protected by immunity. International law developed the concept of immunity to apply to

[2] Hague Convention of Nationality (1930), Convention on the Nationality of Married Woman (1358); United Nations Convention Relating to the Status of Stateless Persons (1954), UN Convention for the Reduction of Statelessness cases (1961), European Convention on Nationality (1997).

[3] Cançado Trindade (1984), pp. 123 and 165.

representatives of a foreign State. Such immunity (here presented in a simplified manner) is reinforced by international customary law and treaties, such as the VCCR, the VCDR, the Havana Convention on Diplomatic Officers, the Convention on Private International Law (Bustamante Code), the Convention on Special Missions, the Convention on the Representation of States in International Organizations and the Convention on Immunities of States and their Property. They establish, in a very detailed form, the immunity granted to foreign States and their official representatives, or governmental representatives, before national legal and judicial systems, involving civil, administrative, criminal and tributary matters, and they impose on the host State the duty to protect them even during armed conflicts.

In their current configuration, immunities and inviolabilities can be conventional or customary, *intuito personae* or *intuito materiae*, absolute or relative, regarding jurisdiction on execution, and involving people, locations or objects (such as diplomatic mission location and diplomatic bags).

As I argue, these immunities and inviolabilities are controversial since they may affect the enforcement of individual rights in the host country and grant impunity for acts committed abroad.

2.2 Personal Inviolability and Immunity from Prosecution: Concepts and Fundamentals

Personal inviolability and immunity from prosecution are an exception to the control exerted by the criminal authorities of any given State based on the status held by a certain individual, which prevents his arrest and the prosecution for any criminal offence he has committed.

The first hypothesis involves head of State immunity, based on his close association to sovereignty. This immunity has a *ratione personae* and a *ratione materiae* character, not only temporally (during the time in office) but overall official acts performed. Head of State immunity is provided for in the Convention on Private International Law from 1928 (Bustamante Code), which reinforced international customary law and, according to Articles 296 to 301, provides for exemption from criminal jurisdiction by another State, to diplomatic or foreign officers who are present in its territory in a military operation, to navy ships and military aircraft and even to merchant ships and aircraft in the same situation.

Another example can be found in Article 14 of the Havana Convention on Diplomatic Officers (1928), declaring that these officers are inviolate as to their person, private residence and property. Moreover, the Convention on the Representation of the States in their Relations with International Organizations of a Universal Character (1975) provides immunity from prosecution to, for instance, certain members of the United Nations and their agencies (such as ILO, UNESCO or FAO).

Equally significant are the rules included in the Vienna Conventions of 1961 and 1963, on Diplomatic and Consular Relations, which provide immunities and privileges to foreign State officers, according to three traditional categories: the inviolability of the person and residence, immunity from civil and criminal prosecution and tax exemption.[4] The present study concerns personal inviolability and immunity from criminal prosecution.

In the Vienna Convention on Diplomatic Relations (VCDR), Articles 29, 31, 32, 37, 38, 40 and 41 establish that the diplomatic officer exercising his duties in a State other than the sending one, his family (forming part of his household) and the technical and administrative staff in mission (together with accompanying family members) are inviolable and cannot be subjected to any form of arrest by the authorities of the receiving country or any third State crossed to take up or return to the diplomatic mission post. They are equally immune to criminal jurisdiction in the above-mentioned countries, and this immunity (despite being absolute) may be waived by the sending country (as was the case with a third secretary from the Embassy of Zambia, in London,[5] and with the Consul General of El Salvador, in Brazil[6]). The sending State is responsible for the investigation of any crime committed by a diplomatic officer or technician and by any member of the administrative staff in mission (as well as accompanying family members in the receiving country), whether or not such acts pertain to the exercise of his diplomatic activity. If the diplomatic agent is a national or a permanent resident in the receiving State, immunity from prosecution will only include "official acts performed in the exercise of his functions" (CVRD, Art. 38).

The same applies to career consular officials, who are only partially inviolable and liable to arrest, for aggravated felonies and pursuant to a decision by the competent authority, or even "in execution of a judicial decision of final effect" (Vienna Convention on Consular Relations—VCCR, Arts. 41 e 43). The immunity and inviolability of the consular officer also stand against third countries that he is forced to cross when performing his duties and can equally be waived by the sending State (VCCR, Arts. 45 e 54). The VCCR also dictates that if any criminal proceedings are issued against a (honorary or career) consular officer, they "shall be conducted with the respect due to him" and, unless he is under arrest or detained, "in a manner which will hamper the exercise of consular functions as little as possible" (Arts. 41-3 e 63).

The justification of personal inviolabilities and immunities has changed throughout history with the development of international relations. Theories of extraterritoriality, the representative character and functional needs can be recognised as the most important factors to change.

---

[4] Accioly (2009), p. 557.

[5] Lima (2002), pp. 53–54.

[6] This hypothesis is described in the ruling by the Superior Court of Justice of Brazil, HC 149.481/DF.

According to the first (which probably goes back to the sixteenth century), the immunity of foreign officers was based on the premise that, despite being physically present in a foreign territory, they still "belonged" to their States of origin and, for that reason, they could only be subjected to their domestic legal systems. This premise is based on the idea that the location of the diplomatic or consular mission does not belong to the territory of the receiving country but is instead an extension of the sending State territory. However, the "extension of exemption" held by this doctrine is not compatible with the relevant provisions of the VCCR. Both the location of the mission and the diplomatic officer are, under certain conditions, subject to the jurisdiction of the receiving State.[7]

The explanation of privileges and immunities based on the theory of the representative character, on the other hand, focuses on the submission of the diplomatic officer to the authority of the sending sovereign State, which places the former exclusively under the laws and jurisdiction of the latter, who would become the offended party if any offence was directed against its representative.

However, although some monarchies and the VCCR still consider the ambassador a representative of his sovereign State, this idea is outdated, as evidenced in the Preamble text of the Havana Convention, which states that "diplomatic officers do not in any case represent the person of the Chief of State but only their Government".

Consequently, in present times, the existence of immunities and privileges attached to diplomatic officers is justified with the functional need criterion, which demystifies the space of the mission and the image of the foreign officer. The general functional design of diplomatic privileges and immunities was also contained in the preambles of the VCDR and the VCCR.

Recently, this concept has been reasserted more restrictively, as an exception to the rule of territorial jurisdiction and based on the need to protect the communication between the State and the officer acting as its representative in a foreign territory, to the extent that this protection is also an instrument to the enforcement of other rights. Therefore, this chapter will examine the contested terrain between immunity and personal inviolability from prosecution on the one hand and individual human rights on the other.

2.3 Subordination to International Human Rights Law

Personal inviolability and, above all, jurisdictional immunity have been questioned as to their validity and relevance. During the 1980s, the abuse of diplomatic prerogatives instigated strong reactions, particularly in Anglo-Saxon countries,[8] and gave way to several proposals suggesting the limitation of privileges. The solution,

---

[7] Lima (2002), p. 42.

[8] Lima (2002), p. 30.

in most countries, involved administrative control measures over accreditations, the number of diplomatic and consular staff and diplomatic bags.

However, the biggest challenge in the immunities and inviolabilities area, besides the strong public reaction to the registered abuses, was the internationalisation of human rights, defined by the Nuremberg trials following the Second World War.

The Neuremberg trials triggered the development of an international criminal system, a system capable of ensuring the prosecution of serious human rights violations and the international accountability of individuals, marking an important expansion of human rights on an international level.[9] This is where the notion that every State is responsible for punishing such violations, as one of its functional duties,[10] was born.

On the other end of this international punitive duty ascribed to the States is the idea of ownership of the individual under international law, where he is not only entitled to rights and protection but also accountable for serious violations to human rights.

The issue of personal immunities and inviolabilities in international law began to be examined since a great number of traditional international crimes involved acts committed by individuals holding a State position or using the State framework. The protection granted by these immunities to such individuals would represent (if they had not been discussed and minimised) a real obstacle to the enforcement of international criminal law in one of its most significant examples.

Following the model of the Nuremberg trials and Tokyo trials in the 1990s, the issue of immunity was lifted (in several conventional instruments) by international courts specialised in prosecuting serious violations to human rights.[11] In the International Criminal Court, the *Gadaafi* and *Bashir* cases are two primary examples of (acting) head of State prosecution, despite the closing of the first case owing to Gadaafi's death, in Libya. In reality, the controversy involving the lifting of immunities on a conventional level is minimal.

The same, however, does not happen in the criminal jurisdiction sphere. Not to be confused with extraterritoriality of national jurisdiction, the idea that every State has the power to prosecute and bring to trial international crimes regardless of the relationship between the facts and its territory, sovereignty or national citizens, universal jurisdiction has been justified by the absence of a "prohibitive rule in international law concerning the exercise of a *universal repressive jurisdiction*" along with the obligation to "extradite or prosecute", imposed by conventions

[9] Cançado Trindade (1991), p. 1.

[10] Carvalho Ramos (2008), p. 614.

[11] Letter from the International Military Court for Nuremberg, 1945, Arts. 7 and 12; Letter from the International Military Court for the Far East—Tokyo Court, 1946, Art. 6; Statute of the International Tribunal for the Former Yugoslavia, 1993, Art. 7; Statute of the International Tribunal for Rwanda, 1994, Art. 6; Statute of the International Criminal Court, 1991, Art. 27.

dealing with the protection of human rights, such as the Geneva Convention, 1949, and the Convention against Torture.[12]

The most emblematic case involving a national court in universal jurisdiction against a head of State (usually covered by customary immunity) was the prosecution of Pinochet by the Judiciary of Spain (involving an extradition request issued to England), for crimes committed during the Chilean dictatorship. Being a subject matter immunity (and, therefore, an absolute immunity), the lifting of the exception from criminal prosecution was justified by the House of Lords with the statement that the intensity of the violation to fundamental human rights would rule out the investigated actions as functional actions, to the extent that these actions could never be committed in the name of the State. In another paradigmatic case, the Judiciary of France prosecuted Muamar Gaddafi for attacking a UTA commercial flight, in 1989, considering that the suspension of the immunity enjoyed by the former head of State of Libya was mandatory, even though the prosecution did not involve war crimes, crimes against humanity or crimes against peace.

The existence of a universal repressive jurisdiction is strongly advocated by many international human rights law jurists, as a fundamental mechanism to effectively prevent and prosecute serious human rights violations. Even after the Rome Statute entered into force and 10 years after the creation of the International Criminal Court (where great hope was placed), its very limited capacity as to the number of reviewed cases has triggered calls for renovation amongst universal jurisdiction advocates.

Nevertheless, even its advocates recognise the lack of agreement surrounding a number of issues, such as the risk of destabilising international relations, the lack of impartiality during the trial, as well as a "threat to impose the law of the strongest in the international field" and the existence of "selectivity and double standards" that can express "parallel political interests on the part of certain States, as they assume the role of human rights defenders in third countries, through universal criminal prosecution". Moreover, the lack of solutions for questions involving the "discrepancy between the State of nationality of the accused and the State performing the arrest as to an accurate definition of crimes against humanity"[13] calls for a certain caution regarding the generalisation and a loose declaration of a universal jurisdiction in international law.

Illustrating this issue, the *Yerodia case* trial held in the International Court of Justice (few months before the Rome Statute entered into force) signals an important episode in international law. Based on national law, which provided for the prosecution of international crimes and asserted universal jurisdiction, even *in absentia*, the Judiciary of Belgium issued an arrest warrant against the acting Foreign Minister committed in the Congolese territory and against non-Belgian citizens.

---

[12] Perrone-Moisés (2012), pp. 71–72.

[13] Carvalho Ramos (1999), p. 112.

In its petition to the International Court of Justice, Congo based its claim on the violation of its sovereignty, on the immunity enjoyed by its Foreign Minister and on the fact that Belgium could not exercise a pure universal jurisdiction. Despite the detrimental nature of the last argument, the Court focused solely on the first underlying theme adopted by Congo in its final allegations. In conclusion, the arrest warrant was considered illegal, precisely for being issued against an officer covered by subject matter immunity.

This ruling was heavily criticised and viewed as the "most expressive legal setback after the Nuremberg logic" since, in the beginning of the twenty-first century, it ruled "for the complete preservation of immunity from criminal prosecution of a Foreign Minister as a fundamental requirement for the exercise of his duties", highlighting "the greater importance held by immunity as the essence of diplomatic logic of sovereignty" and superimposing "the traditional *jus gentium* over the judiciary logic inspired by Nuremberg".[14]

Moreover, the criticism involving the *Yerodia case* focused precisely on the silence surrounding the universal jurisdiction issue—whose final and express deliberation would have represented a most crucial step for international criminal law.

The ruling in the *Yerodia case* is frequently cited as counteracting the tendency to lift immunities when dealing with serious violations to human rights (the so-called *core crimes*).

2.4 On Personal Inviolability and Jurisdictional Immunities in Brazilian Jurisprudence

The issue of personal inviolability and immunity to criminal prosecution apparently has not had many opportunities to manifest itself in Brazil—which can be partially explained by the construction of a certain invisibility around the theme during the military dictatorship (when certain events took place, such as the abduction of the Ambassador of the United States, as described in the *Habeas Corpus* appeal trial no. 49183 in the Brazilian Supreme Federal Court[15]).

[14] LAFER, Celso, *in* Perrone-Moisés (2012), p. XVI.

[15] Despite being unrelated to the main purpose of this paper, it is important to note that when dealing with the other types of State immunities, the jurisprudence of the Brazilian Superior and Federal Regional Courts has revealed a somewhat shy stand as to the development of the matter on an international level, prevailing a favourable position towards the concept of absolute immunity. Amongst the most recurring topics, we can highlight the following:

a) immunity from accountability for acts committed by another State in times of war, acts considered *jure imperii* (STJ, RO 72/RJ, RO 66/RJ e REsp 436.711; TRF-4, AC 2001.04.01.044284-8);
b) on the responsibility for improper billing for consular services, considered to be equally protected by consular immunity (TRF-3, AC 0031093–58.2001.4.03.6100);

Historically, in the jurisprudence of Brazilian Superior Courts and Regional Federal Courts, the debate surrounding immunity from criminal prosecution has solely focused on its recognition or not, that is, on the strict compliance with the norms and distinctions established by the VCDR and the VCCR (which the country has signed).

In this sense, in the Appeal and *Habeas Corpus* 34029 trial, the Supreme Federal Court lifted the immunity of the non-officers in diplomatic mission, for being composed by Brazilian nationals; the same happened in two *Habeas Corpus* (HC 55014 and HC 129.189) and three other *Habeas Corpus* Appeals (RHC 49183, RHC 372 and RHC 372), reaffirming the conventional rule that the Honorary Consul enjoys immunity from criminal jurisdiction when the facts concern acts committed during the exercise of this duty.[16]

The Superior Court of Justice, on the other hand, in *Habeas Corpus* trial 149.481 (HC 2009.01.00.045158-6 in the Regional Federal Court of the first Region) recognised the lifting of immunity granted to the General Consul of El Salvador based on the waiver manifested by the sending country, in a perfect subordination of the facts to the dispositions of the VCCR.

However, being a signatory of the Rome Statute, Brazil received an international cooperation request dispatched by the International Criminal Court, concerning the issuing of an arrest warrant against the president of Sudan, Omar Al Bashir. Although it is still in progress, the manifestation of the presidency—in the opening order—holds the deliberations that bring the Judiciary of Brazil closer to the contemporary debates surrounding immunity from criminal prosecution.

In this decision, besides providing for the necessary arrangements to process the petition, Minister Celso de Mello (who acted through the presidency of the SFC—and not as a reporter of the facts) put into context the request to carry out the arrest warrant issued by the ICC within the combat against impunity involving serious violations to human rights and set forth other considerations, whose clear purpose was to lay down the debate points that needed to be addressed by the following reporting minister.

Amongst these, he indicated the theme of immunity as one of the issues that gave way to a conflict between the content of the Rome Statute and the domestic law.[17]

---

c) on tributary responsibility, with an oscillating interpretation (STJ, RO49/RJ; TRF1 AC 2001.01.00.036122-9/DF e AC 2005.34.00.036894-2/DF);
d) immunity from accountability for labour issues involving States and international organizations, with an interpretation that alternates between relative and absolute theories as to jurisdictional immunity but prevailing the absolute theory regarding immunity from enforcement (STF, RE 222368 AgR e AI 139671 AgR; STJ, RO 26/RJ)—on immunity from labour enforcement, Bill 3276/2012 and 245/2011 by the House of Representatives are currently being processed. Equally important was the vote cast by Min. Francisco Rezek in ApCiv 9696 by the SFC.

[16] The same theme is under trial by the Regional Federal Court of the first Region in ACR 91.01.04099-5/BA.

[17] **The theme** herein **addressed prompts a number of observations** involving the International Criminal Court **and** the Statute of Rome, **especially** considering the **several objections** raised by notable scholars, **and summarized as follows** by MARCOS ALEXANDRE

Accordingly, the Minister referred to Bill no 4.038/2008 by the House of Representatives (which tries to differentiate the system dealing with common crimes from that dealing with the crimes of genocide, war, against humanity and against the administration of the International Criminal Court), indicating it as a solution to the observed inconsistencies between the Statute and domestic law.

After further commenting on the nature of the TPI and its subsidiary position in relation to national jurisdictions, he returned to the theme of immunities, to declare as follows:

> **It is important to emphasize**, moreover, **bearing in mind** the perspective of the **authorship** of the crime **submitted** to the jurisdiction of the International Criminal Court, **that the Statute of Rome subjugates**, to the abovementioned judiciary jurisdiction, **any** person **involved** in the practice of crimes of genocide, war, against humanity **or** aggression, **regardless** of his official capacity (**Article** 27). **Indeed**, the Statute of Rome **thus proclaims the absolute irrelevance** of the official capacity **of the author** accused of the submitted crimes, according to the aforementioned multilateral convention, to the jurisdictional **and** competent sphere of the International Criminal Court.
>
> **This means**, **according to** what is provided for in the Statute of Rome **in Article 27**, **that the political status** of the Head of State, **as is the case** under review, **does not qualify** as a an **exclusion** factor from criminal accountability **nor** as a legitimating factor for the reduction of the sentence of the officer **connected** with the crimes of genocide, against humanity, war **and** aggression.
>
> **It is important to notice**, at this point, **that the clause** stating the "*irrelevance of the official capacity*" held by the author of the aforementioned crimes, **provided for** in Article 27 of the Statute of Rome, **highlights one of the most** expressive issues, **considering** the pertinence of **the so called** *sovereign immunity* of national States **representatives** (**such as** Heads of State **and** Government, Government Ministers **and** members of the National Congress).
>
> **Let us remember**, in that regard, **that the International Court of Justice** – **the main** judicial body of the United Nations (...) -, **in a trial** held in 14/02/2002, **concerning the issuing**, by a Belgian magistrate, **of an arrest warrant** for the Congolese Foreign Minister, **at the time** in full exercise of his duties, **reasserting the old dogma** of international customary law, **ruled** that the arrest warrant **and** its corresponding "*international circulation*" **were in violation** of the international law, **for disrespecting** the personal inviolability **and** immunity from criminal prosecution **enjoyed** by the involved foreign authority, **contradicting** the Judiciary of Belgium **domestic** legislation.
>
> **It occurs**, however, as was **previously** mentioned, that, **according** to the Statute of Rome, and **for the purpose** of "*persecutio criminis*", **the political status** of the **officer is irrelevant**, and **the so called** "*sovereign immunity*" **or** "*crown immunity*" **does not**

COELHO ZILLI, MARIA THEREZA ROCHA DE ASSIS MOURA e CLEUNICE VALENTIM BASTOS PITOMBO (**"Anotações sobre o Seminário Internacional: a implementação do Estatuto de Roma no direito interno e outras questões de direito penal internacional"**, '*in*' Boletim IBCCRIM, Ano 12, n° 139/2-3, jun/2004): '***In Brazil****, who signed* ***and*** *ratified the Statute,* ***inquiries have turned to the possible unconstitutionality of the rules*** *concerning, primarily:* ***i) the exceptions*** *to the principle of the* res judicata*;* ***ii) the lifting*** *of immunities and prerogatives provided for in internal legislation;* ***iii) the imprescriptibility*** *of international crimes;* ***iv) the possibility*** *of delivering national citizens for trial* ***before*** *the International Criminal Court;* ***v) the provision*** *involving life imprisonment;* ***vi) the lack*** *of criminal sanctions imposed on international crimes* (**highlighted**).

stand before the International Criminal Court, **even if the case involves** a Head of State **or** Government, **as expressly stated** in **Article 27** of that multilateral convention (...). **That is** the reason why **Article 27** of the Statute of Rome **has raised** controversy, **namely** because there are those who, **evoking** the *Westphalia model*, **enforced** since 1648, **support** the **absolute character** theory of State sovereignty (**which makes** the exercise of the International Criminal Court jurisdiction **unfeasible**), **opposing** not only those who **ascribe** a relative weight **to the notion** of State Sovereignty, **but most of all justify** the aforementioned conventional clause (**Article** 27) **with the**, presently **reinforced** in art. 4, **item** II, of our Constitution, "*prevalence of human rights*" **idea**, **being worthy of mention**, at this point, **the observations** made by CARLOS EDUARDO ADRIANO JAPIASSÚ ("**O Direito Penal Internacional**", p. 115/116, item n. 4.3, 2009, Del Rey): '***It is important to note that the crimes that fall under the jurisdiction of the International Criminal Court are****, generally speaking,* ***perpetrated by individuals occupying*** *a State position.* ***Consequently, the rule imposed by Article 27*** *of the Statute of Rome* ***prevents*** *the use of privileges* ***and*** *immunities* ***enjoyed*** *by these individuals, granted by internal legislation,* ***as shield to avoid accountability*** *for international crimes.* ***On a final note,*** *we believe that* ***the prevalence of the human rights principle****, provided for in Article 4°, II, of the Federal Constitution,* ***'implies restrictions to the immunities',*** *usually enjoyed by officers in the exercise of their functional activity, when charged with violations to human rights,* ***not interfering****, therefore,* ***with article 27*** *of the Statute of Rome.*

Accordingly, on the one hand, we can praise the Minister for trying to emphasise human rights, which justify the conventional standard (Art. 27 in the Rome Statute) and lift immunity from prosecution for crimes within its jurisdiction. The fact that these deliberations were included in an order, whose sole purpose was to determine the processing of an international cooperation request, reveals a concern towards the theme and an attempt to seize this rare opportunity to make a stand as to the view of our Supreme Court on the subordination of immunities from criminal prosecution according human rights law.

On the other hand, however, we cannot help but notice with a certain unease how insistently the Minister resumes traditional arguments that are favourable to these immunities, such as the reference to the *Yerodia case* and the debates involving the respect for State sovereignty. After all, such arguments have no power to dismiss compliance with a conventional norm that Brazil endorsed by ratifying the Treaty of Rome.

Notwithstanding, it must be recognised that, given the invisibility of the theme of jurisdictional immunity in the Brazilian jurisprudence, the ruling by Minister Celso de Mello in petition 4625 (currently under the rapporteurship of Minister Rosa Weber) is extremely relevant and worthy of respect, for stressing the "irrelevance of the official quality" held by the accused in the practice of crimes subject to the jurisdiction of the International Criminal Court.

3 On Consular Assistance

3.1 General Considerations

In the context of international relations law, a second theme is relevant for the analysis of human rights universalism. It concerns the institution of consular assistance to the foreign detainee, under pre-trial custody or serving a sentence, as provided for in Art. 36 of the VCCR,[18] where we can easily read the imposition of a duty on the receiving State, primarily, to inform the foreign citizen subject to detention that he has a right to communicate with his consular representation. Moreover, when the arrested individual manifests interest, that same State is responsible—according to its competent authority in the criminal sphere—for enabling, as quickly as possible, the abovementioned communication, allowing it freely and including visitations.

Even though the literal content of Article 36 of the VCCR emphasises the assistance granted to the foreign detainee in order to protect the running and the exercise of consular activities, the instrument also provides for the protection of individuals in a particularly vulnerable position. Moreover, as opposed to what happens with immunities from criminal prosecution, the incidence rate of this international instrument is high in the context of domestic laws and international law—having been submitted three times to the analysis of the International Court of Justice.

[18] ARTICLE 36.° **Communication and Contact with Nationals of the Sending State**

1. With a view to facilitating the exercise of consular functions relating to nationals of the sending State:
   a) consular officers shall be free to communicate with nationals of the sending State and to have access to them. Nationals of the sending State shall have the same freedom with respect to communication with and access to consular officers of the sending State;
   b) if he so requests, the competent authorities of the receiving State shall, without delay, inform the consular post of the sending State if, within its consular district, a national of that State is arrested or committed to prison or to custody pending trial or is detained in any other manner. Any communication addressed to the consular post by the person arrested, in prison, custody or detention shall also be forwarded by the said authorities without delay. The said authorities shall inform the person concerned without delay of his rights under this sub-paragraph;
   c) consular officers shall have the right to visit a national of the sending State who is in prison, custody or detention, to converse and correspond with him and to arrange for his legal representation. They shall also have the right to visit any national of the sending State who is in prison, custody or detention in their district in pursuance of a judgment. Nevertheless, consular officers shall refrain from taking action on behalf of a national who is in prison, custody or detention if he expressly opposes such action.
2. The rights referred to in paragraph 1 of this Article shall be exercised in conformity with the laws and regulations of the receiving State, subject to the proviso, however, that the said laws and regulations must enable full effect to be given to the purposes for which the rights accorded under this Article are intended.

In these occasions, which involved the conduct of US criminal authorities, the Court has stressed the character of individual protection granted by consular assistance and, nevertheless, assumed a somewhat traditional position, placing this institution within the scope of consular activities.

In the first case (from 1998), Paraguay submitted a complaint because its national citizen Angel Francisco Breard had been sentenced to death row by US authorities without compliance with Article 36 of the VCCR. After the hearings and given the proximity of the execution date, the Court filed with the United States a request to suspend the execution of Breard until final deliberation. This request, however, was not implemented, and Paraguay was forced to give up its claim.

The second case (from 1999) concerned a death penalty conviction as well and led to the non-compliance for the enforcement order issued by the International Court of Justice, who solicited the suspension of the sentenced execution. In this case, however, Germany, which argued the non-compliance with Article 36 of the VCCR towards the brothers Karl and Walter La Grand, maintained its claim. As such, the Court was able to rule on the merit of the claim and dismiss the arguments offered by the defendant (which included a statement asserting that US authorities did not know that the LaGrand brothers were German citizens), declaring that the US violated its duty imposed by Art. 36 of the VCCR to inform Germany, even if the accused brothers did not express the wish to resort to consular assistance or if, in case they did, the assistance was not effectively provided by their consular representation. "In the meantime, the Court thought it unnecessary to consider the additional arguments presented by Germany, to the extent that the law derived from article 36 (1) in the 1963 Convention concerned not only individual rights but human rights".[19]

The third case involving this issue was presented before the International Court of Justice in 2003 and filed by Mexico against the sentencing of 52 Mexican citizens to death row by US authorities (again, without respecting the rule of consular assistance).[20] In the initial application of the *Avena case*, the plaintiff country further argued that the right to consular assistance represents an important due process trait in criminal accusations involving foreign nationals—constituting a human right.

The Court failed to address this argument more than once, despite having reaffirmed the position expressed in the LaGrand case, in that Art. 36 of the VCCR represents a "regime designed to facilitate the implementation of the system of consular protection" and that the right to information concerning the assistance to the foreign detainee is, in itself, an obligation imposed on the receiving State, regardless of the posture subsequently adopted by the foreign national or by the consular representation of his country of origin.

---

[19] Sala (2009), p. 99. *The same author notes that US authorities admitted that they did not comply with their international obligation, having offered a formal apology.*

[20] Both regarding informing the accused as to their right to communication and allowing consular officers to maintain contact and provide consular assistance to their national citizens.

Moreover, the Court deliberated that this obligation should be carried out "without delay" and that this choice of words, adopted in the conventional text, meant that the first authority to be informed of the foreign citizen detention should comply with the provisions in Article 36. In conclusion, it determined the review and the reassessment of the sentences pronounced by US judicial authorities, particularly in three cases that had already exhausted all stages of internal procedures.

Even though the 52 Mexican citizens had not yet been executed when the sentence was delivered by the International Court of Justice, and even though the ruling involved an individual assessment of each situation, the US domestic handling of the process lacked homogeneity, which led, in several cases, to the enforcement of the death penalty without the order of the Court being carried out.[21]

3.2 *Subordination to the International Human Rights Law*

After the impact and the regrettable events that followed the ruling by the International Court of Justice, the theme of consular assistance was finally associated and integrated in international human rights law. This happened with Advisory Opinion no. 16 issued by the Inter-American Court of Human Rights—which, triggered by Mexico, made a peremptory statement on the need to incorporate the right to consular assistance in the content of the relevant legal process.[22] The following passage of the Advisory Opinion is quite emblematic:

> 1. That article 36 of the Vienna Convention on Consular Relations recognizes the individual rights of the foreign detainee, including the right to information concerning consular assistance, and assigns corresponding duties to the host State.
> 2. That article 36 (. . .) concerns the protection of the rights assigned to the national citizen of the sending State and is included in the international human rights law.
> 3. That the formulation "without delay" (. . .) means that the State must comply with its duty of informing the detainee of his rights in the moment of his arrest and, in any case, before he makes his first statement before the authorities.
> 4. That the compliance with the rights of the individual provided for in article 36 (. . .) is not subject to the protests of the sending State. (. . .)
> 6. That the individual right to information provided for in article 36.1.b) (. . .) allows practical effects, in specific cases, concerning the right to due process of law provided in article 14 of the International Covenant on Civil and Political Rights; and that this provision establishes minimum guarantees that can be expanded in light of other international instruments, such as the Vienna Convention on Consular Relations, which expand the scope of the protection granted to individuals.

[21] Sala (2009), p. 100.

[22] In this point, the ruling included a disagreement expressed by Judge Oliver Jackman, according to whom it would be unwise to abstractly expand the content of the due process, given that the concepts of relevance, proportionality and opportunity of these fundamental tools are equally necessary to the development of a balanced criminal process.

7. That the neglect to comply with the right to information ascribed to the foreign detainee, recognized in article 36.1.b) (...), affects the guarantees of the due process and, in these circumstances, the imposition of the death penalty constitutes a violation to the right not to be "arbitrarily" deprived of life", according to the relevant provisions of the treaties on human rights (...), encompassing the juridical consequences of such violation, i.e., those relating to the responsibility of the State and the duty to make full reparation.
8. That the international provisions concerning the protection of human rights in the American States, including the rights provided for in article 36.1.b) (...), must be respected by the American States parties in their respective conventions, regardless of their federal or unitary structures.

To reach these conclusions, the Court addressed and dismissed the traditional idea that the VCCR encompassed State laws. Moreover, it stressed that the interpretation of treaties is evolutionary and should be contextualised not only in its inception but also in the moment of its enforcement—which, at present, is permeated by the universal promotion of human rights.

Probably considering the excuses presented by the United States in the LaGrand and Avena cases, the Court openly stated that the arresting State is responsible for inquiring about the nationality of the arrested individuals, whose notification (concerning the right to consular assistance) is to be carried out in the moment of the arrest.

As was emphasised by Judge Antônio Augusto Cançado Trindade in his concurring vote, Advisory Opinion no. 16 was significantly important, both for its content and for the number of States and international organisations involved.[23]

One of the consequences of this subordination of consular assistance to the grammar of human rights, through Inter-American Court of Human Rights Advisory Opinion no. 16, was felt in a number of American States, where the States of California and Texas adopted subsequent measures for the enforcement of Art. 36 of the VCCR.[24]

3.3 *Interpreting the Right to Consular Assistance in Brazil*

As was already mentioned, because it refers to the imprisonment of common foreign citizens (as opposed to diplomatic, consular or governmental officers), the issue of consular assistance is more noticeable and frequent in the routine of a country than immunity to criminal jurisdiction. Following this rule, Brazil reveals a higher number of rulings and official documents on the matter, including a reaction to Inter-American Court of Human Rights Advisory Opinion no. 16.

---

[23] United States of Mexico, Costa Rica, El Salvador, Guatemala, Honduras, Paraguay, Dominican Republic, United States of America, Inter-American Commission, Amnesty International, MCDPHR, Human Rights Watch/Americas y CEJIL, International Human Rights Law Institute of DePaul University College of Law, Death Penalty Focus de California, Minnesota Advocates for Human Rights.

[24] Sala (2009), p. 48.

With this in mind, we can quote Recommendation n° 38/2001-MPF/PR/SP/SOTC/PRDC, issued by initiative of the State Attorney André de Carvalho Ramos, and Dispatch n° 045/2002-COGER/DPF, from the Federal Police, intended to regulate the actions of federal agents in compliance with Art. 36 of the VCCR as to the arrest of foreign nationals.

Similar initiatives can be found statewide, as expressed in an Ordinance issued by the Civilian Police of the Mato Grosso State (DGPC/SEJUSP/MS N° 080/2009) and by a State Law in Rio de Janeiro (n° 1301, de 03/05/1988, defining the procedures to be adopted by police authorities, in compliance with the rights and guarantees of the prisoner in the moment of arrest).

Besides, the integration of every authority involved in the enforcement of consular assistance has been pursued, as seen in a recent Seminar on Foreign Detainees (held in the city of São Paulo), attended by representatives from the state and the federal sphere, police forces, magistracies, public defenders, as well as the Public Ministry, besides the Foreign Nationals Department from the Ministry of Justice, the National Justice Council, private defenders and consular representatives.

In our analysis of the Brazilian jurisprudential position, we can also observe a positive effect emanating from the interpretation of consular assistance through the lens of the international human rights law, despite a number of strict rulings that do not take into account the parameters established by the International Court of Justice.

In the last group of rulings, it is important to mention the simplistic approach adopted in court rulings by the Federal Regional Courts of the third (HC 2008.03.00.037136-9, ApCrim 92.03.36987-2) and fourth Regions (HC N° 0004456-92.2010.404.0000/PR), endorsing compliance with Art. 36 of the VCCR merely from a documentary record of the communication issued to the consular representation, concerning the arrest of one of its nationals. These rulings do not only declare the sufficiency of this functional statement (given the full faith and credit of the employee); they also exclude any concern for the right of expression of interest held by the detainee as to this communication.

Contradicting the readings of the International Court of Justice and the Inter-American Court of Human Rights, which held that non-compliance with consular assistance does not provide for an effective assistance to the foreign detainee, the Federal Regional Court of the first Region (2007.32.00.008656-6) shows an example of a questionable interpretation, by which it dismissed the invalidity of criminal proceedings for lack of evidence as to the damage sustained by the accused for non-compliance with Art. 36 of the VCCR.

Conversely, the Supreme Federal Court has already, to date, at least issued two rulings based on the interpretation of consular assistance according to the international human rights law.

In **Extradition n° 954**, requested by Italy against a Belgian citizen, Minister Joaquim Barbosa ordered the arrest of the individual in his opening order (01/02/2005), and later (in an order dated from 24/05/2005), considering that the State Prosecutor saw no need to communicate the arrest to the Consulate of Belgium, he voiced a number of thoughts concerning the nature of human rights on which the institution of consular assistance was raised, although he mentioned the rulings of the International Court of Justice (which, as was already seen, has no statements on the matter). Afterwards, he addressed the specific nature of the case in hand, ultimately stating that the right provided for in Art. 36 of the VCCR prevails in all forms of foreign nationals' detention—being therefore applicable in arrest cases while processing extradition requests. From the entire content of this ruling, we highlight the following passage:

In a latter case, when assessing the request for extradition **Ext 1126** issued by Germany, Minister Celso de Mello, from the Supreme Federal Court, also reasserted the "essentiality" of the "consular notification" to ensure "any foreign national under arrest, the possibility of receiving consular assistance from his own country, thus enabling the full exercise of all his rights and privileges that comprise the constitutional due process clause". As observed in Extradition 945, in the vote cast by Minister Celso de Melo we can also find reference to the content of the rulings held by the International Court of Justice and the Advisory Opinion issued by the Inter-American Court of Human Rights, as a basis for the enforcement of the *due process of law* according to the VCCR rule.

4 Conclusion

The analysis of immunity from criminal jurisdiction and the right of the foreign national detainee to consular assistance illustrates how the international legal order, under customary and conventional sources, provides rules that, in a number of exceptional circumstances, dictate that States grant a different and privileged treatment to foreign nationals.

Originally, those concepts are based on the sovereignty of states, on both the diplomatic and consular activities, including on the protection provided by the assistance of the arrested foreigner. Its existence should be related to the freedom of exercise of the representation of the State abroad. Despite being closely connected to the concept of nationality and to a consequent resistance to the universal promotion of human rights protection, immunity from criminal jurisdiction and consular assistance have been subject to an extensive degree of interpretation under the lens of the International Human Rights Law. This process, however, does not steer the two rules in the same direction, and, contrary to what a more unsuspecting analysis might assume, it does not enhance the privileged treatment assigned to the foreign national, when compared to a national citizen.

As seen in the first section, the subordination of immunity from prosecution to human rights principles did not lead to its reassurance as a mechanism that protects the individual against international law. The issue was viewed within the context of individuals who were victims of serious violations to human rights, which demand a greater level of protection from international law. Thus, the interpretation through the lens of human rights results in a significant restriction of immunity from prosecution.

In the opposite sense, the second section stressed that the vulnerable position occupied by any individual under any form of imprisonment outside his national territory highlights the crucial role held by consular assistance, as a compensation mechanism to this vulnerability. This is why its content and scope were expanded under the interpretation based on international human rights law, which recognised in consular assistance a fundamental tool to an adequate development of the legal process.

Our analysis to the national interpretation given to immunity from criminal jurisdiction and consular assistance, on a final note, suggests a maturation process in Brazilian courts, despite the existence of rulings both deserving of criticism and praise.

References

Accioly H (2009) Tratado de Direito Internacional Público, 3rd edn. Quartier Latin, São Paulo

Cançado Trindade AA (1984) O esgotamento de recursos internos no Direito Internacional. Editora Universidade de Brasília, Brasília

Cançado Trindade AA (1991) A Proteção Internacional dos Direitos Humanos. Fundamentos Jurídicos e Instrumentos Básicos. Saraiva, São Paulo

Carvalho Ramos A (1999) O caso Pinochet: passado, presente e futuro da persecução criminal internacional. Revista Brasileira de Ciências Criminais 7(25):106–114

Carvalho Ramos A (2008) Direito dos Estrangeiros no Brasil: imigração, Direito de Ingresso e os Direitos dos Estrangeiros em situação irregular. In: Sarmento D, Ikawa D, Piovesan F (coord.) Igualdade, diferença e direitos humanos. Lúmen Juris, Rio de Janeiro

Carvalho Ramos A (2008) Direitos humanos e responsabilidade internacional. In: Direito CAM et al (coord.) Novas perspectivas do Direito Internacional Contemporâneo. Estudos em homenagem ao Professor Celso D. de Albuquerque Mello. Renovar, Rio de Janeiro

Lima SEM (2002) Privilégios e Imunidades Diplomáticos. Fundação Alexandre de Gusmão, Brasília

Perrone-Moisés C (2012) Direito Internacional Penal. Imunidades e Anistias. Manole, Barueri

Sala MG (2009) Assistência consular a presos estrangeiros nos Estados Unidos: o caso do México. Universidade de São Paulo. http://www.teses.usp.br/teses/disponiveis/84/84131/tde-27062011-092712/pt-br.php

Soares GFS (2004) Os Direitos Humanos e a proteção dos estrangeiros. Revista de Informação Legislativa 41(162)

Understanding Immigration Detention in the UK and Europe

Elspeth Guild

Abstract In a number of European states there appears to be substantial use of administrative detention against foreigners. In the UK, for example, at any given time there are likely to be between 2000 and 3000 foreigners in immigration detention. In total, the number of persons passing through immigration detention annually accounts for between 26,000 and 28,000 persons (figures for 2009–2011). In this chapter, I will examine the practice of detention in the UK with regard to the legal framework in Europe.

1 Introduction

The administrative detention of foreigners in Europe has become a matter of increasing concern to parts of civil society at least since the 1980s. The non-governmental organization Migreurop began collecting and publishing information on detention centres for foreigners in Europe in the early 2000s and currently updates and publishes a map of detention centres across Europe, the Middle East and North Africa.[1] The Global Detention Project, based at the Institute of Graduate Studies, Geneva, began mapping immigrant detention worldwide in 2006. The Jesuit Refugee Service, established in 1980, has a special project on immigration detention which includes detailed information on the national laws on European states which permit detention, detention practices and human rights challenges.[2] There has been sustained questioning of immigration detention by the academic community in Europe as well, with trenchant critiques of its existence and justification (Mitsilegas 2012; Bigo 2007; Krause 2008). Yet, from all available information, immigration detention continues to be used by European states. Using the UK as an example, I will examine why immigration detention is so enduring and

[1] Migreurop observatoire des frontiers, *Detention des Migrants* http://www.migreurop.org/?lang=fr. Accessed 1 Aug 2013.

[2] http://www.detention-in-europe.org/. Accessed 1 August 2013.

E. Guild (✉)
Queen Mary University, London, UK

Radboud University, Nijmegen, Netherlands
e-mail: elspeth.guild@conflits.org

M.J. Guia et al. (eds.), *Immigration Detention, Risk and Human Rights*,
DOI 10.1007/978-3-319-24690-1_8

how it fits into the European human rights framework. The longer history of the development of immigration detention in the UK has been admirably analysed by Wilsher elsewhere, I will not repeat his work here (Wilsher 2011).

2 What Is Immigration Detention?

Immigration detention is the state authorities' act of deprivation of liberty of persons exclusively on the basis of the fact that they are not citizens of the state. States deprive people of their liberty for a number of reasons. The most common is in the context of criminal proceedings, either as a pre-trial measure or as part of the penalty which follows conviction of a criminal offence. There are other circumstances where state authorities engage in detention of people, for instance, under mental health powers where people are assessed as being a risk to themselves or others. A comprehensive list of the grounds on which European states may lawfully deprive a person of their liberty is contained in Article 5 European Convention on Human Rights (see Annex 1). Immigration detention comes within the category of deprivation of liberty permitted by Article 5(1)(f) in order to prevent a person effecting an unauthorised entry into the country or of a person against whom action is being taken with a view to deportation. As citizens always have a right, guaranteed by international law, to enter their country of nationality, it is primarily foreigners who can seek to effect an unauthorised entry into a state and only foreigners against whom deportation or expulsion proceedings can be taken. It is imaginable that a citizen might seek to effect an unauthorised entry into his or her state, for instance by failing to make use of authorised border crossing points during their working hours, and instead entering by little boats at night into small harbors. However, in such a case what may be unauthorised is the way in which the citizen has accessed the territory of his or her state, not the fact that he or she has accessed the state's territory at all. Where the person is a foreigner, that is to say the national of some other country (or a stateless person), unauthorised entry has quite a different meaning. As in most cases, the individual's presence is dependent on a positive decision by the state authorities; failing to seek or obtain such a positive decision results in the individual being classifiable in the category of persons seeking to enter the state unlawfully (Costello 2012).

Immigration detention can take place in many different types of venues, from police stations to specialised detention centres run by private sector actors (as in the UK). In some European countries, places where immigration detention takes place are called reception centres and there is a differentiation between those places where people can leave the premises though they may be required to return at specific times and hours (usually they are required to sleep in the centre) and other closed centres. However, even in the so-called open centres, so long as the individual is under an obligation established by state authorities that he or she must spend a substantial part of his or her time at the centre, there will be a deprivation of liberty which is central to the legal concept of detention (Cornelisse 2010). The individual is no longer able to go about his or her business but must remain in the allocated place. One of the characteristics of immigration detention is that it is open ended. It is not subject to a time limit established by a court in advance. While this detention may be subject to a presumption in favour of bail or release (as is required by the EU Returns Directive 2008/115) and in many countries is subject to a maximum duration (in the Returns Directive this is limited to 18 months in total) (Mincheva 2010), in other countries such as the UK there is no maximum to its duration.

3 What Are the Reasons for Using Immigration Detention?

Article 5(1)(f) ECHR provides that the detention of foreigners is only lawful if its purpose is to prevent an unauthorised entry or for the purposes of deportation or expulsion (the two terms are used synonymously here). However, these grounds for immigration detention cover a wide range of secondary reasons which state authorities use to justify immigration detention. For example, the UK authorities most commonly detain foreigners for the purposes of removing them, even where their actual removal may be some time in the distance and the necessary formalities such as the acquisition of valid passports or laissez passer documents have not been fulfilled. Foreigners may also be detained for the purpose of establishing their identity, where state authorities do not believe the documents which the individual has presented are either genuine or belong in fact to the individual. Circumstances also exist where individuals have no documents at all. If the state authorities believe that the foreigner will not comply with any conditions which may be applied to his or her entry onto the territory, they may choose to detain him or her. Additionally, where the state authorities consider that there is a risk that the foreigner may harm him or herself or the public, he or she may be the subject of a detention decision. Further, where the foreigner seeks asylum from the state authorities he or she may be detained for administrative purposes (Mole and Meredith 2010).

Thus, while Article 5(1)(f) ECHR seems to place rather stringent conditions on immigration detention, in fact state authorities are able to mount a wide variety of grounds to justify their decisions to detain some foreigners. According to the UK statistical agency, in 2012 over 30 million foreigners arrived in the UK (Office for National Statistics 2012). For the EU, these are over 180 million foreigners per year entering and exiting the territory.[3] Of those persons only a statistically insignificant number will be detained, which brings us to the next question, who are these people who are detained?

[3] One off-data collection effort by the Council in 2009 which only measured movement of people into and out of the EU as a whole during 1 week (31 August–6 September 2009) revealed that there were 2,130,256 entries and exits by non-visa third country nationals and 1,464,660 entries and exits by visa nationals. This indicates that there are probably more than 182 million entries and exits by third country nationals into and out of the EU annually.

4 Who Is Detained?

Exact numbers of foreigners detained in the EU are not easily or indeed available at all. There is no authority which is responsible for collecting this data. While the EU agency FRONTEX is responsible for collecting and publishing data on the number of persons refused admission to the EU and expelled from its territory, detention statistics are not published by it. From UK statistical information, it appears that between 26,000 and 30,000 people are subject to immigration detention in that country, which is considered to be one with among the largest networks of immigration detention facilities in Europe (Silverman and Hajela 2012). At any given time, there are about 2500 people in immigration detention in the UK.[4] Taking the figures of the end of the third quarter, 2013, in the UK a total of 7093 people passed through immigration detention. Of those, 4166 were removed from the UK (this means deported or expelled), 30 were given permission to enter the UK and 2459 were granted temporary admission or released temporarily into the UK (which means released from immigration detention but not formally given permission to enter the UK).[5] The chances of ending up in immigration detention are not equal depending on the nationality of the person or his or her gender. Starting with the first criteria, nationality, the picture of immigration detention for the first quarter 2013 in the UK is the following:

Africa: 1421,
Americas (North and South): 574,
Asia: 3770,
Europe: 902,
Middle East: 366,
Oceania: 17,
Other: 23.

Taking individual nationalities where over 300 persons were in immigration detention in this quarter, the picture looks like this:

Afghans: 346,
Bangladeshis: 437,
Indians: 905,
Nigerians: 483,
Pakistanis: 1152.

Of those in detention over the period 6040 were men and 1053 were women. Thirty-eight children were in detention, twenty-nine of whom were seeking asylum. For the adults, the division between those seeking asylum and those who were not was fairly equal (3508 for the former and 3547 for the later), though a more detailed

[4] https://www.gov.uk/government/publications/immigration-statistics-january-to-march-2013: table dt_10, visited 1 August 2013.

[5] Ibid.

analysis of the data carried out on earlier statistical information by the Migration Observatory in 2012 indicates that the most common category of immigration detention is people who have sought asylum in the UK at some point in their immigration process (Silverman and Hajela 2012). This means that of people in detention, about half will be in a current asylum procedure. Of the rest, many will have already been through an asylum procedure which was unsuccessful and has been finally concluded. Assuming the correctness of the research of the Migration Observatory indicating that the large majority of those in immigration detention have at some time sought asylum, this means that however these visa nationals first came to the attention of the UK immigration authorities, following them is relatively straightforward. In the context of making an asylum application, the individual must provide very detailed personal information and update the authorities of any changes, including of address. This means that for this group of foreigners, the authorities hold detailed information, including about friends and family or contacts of the individual which information may greatly facilitate finding the person if the authorities wish to do so. For some nationalities, such as Afghans, the vast majority of those in immigration detention were seeking asylum.

All of the nationalities where there were over 300 persons in detention in the first quarter of 2013 are on the UK's mandatory visa list. Thus, either the people in immigration detention arrived with visas which they had obtained abroad and then became the subject of concern by the immigration authorities or they arrived without a visa, clandestinely or with false documents and then came to the attention of the immigration authorities.

If one considers the available information on visits by foreign residents to the UK in 2012 (the latest available information), the UK statistical authorities indicate the following total numbers of visitors (Office for National Statistics 2012) (separate figures for Afghans and Bangladeshis are not immediately available):

Indians: 118,000;
Nigerians: 67,000;
Pakistanis: 15,000.

On the other hand, over one million US citizens visited the UK over the same period, while 91 of these nationals were in immigration detention in the first quarter of 2013. Fourteen Japanese nationals were in detention over the same period, while in the preceding year 130,000 had visited the UK. A total of 464,000 Australians visited the UK in 2012, and 12 were in immigration detention in the first quarter of 2013. If one compares the risk of being in immigration detention with the numbers of nationals of a state who visit the UK, clearly being a Pakistani man means coming within the highest risk category. Each immigration detention decision is taken on the basis of the facts of each individual person. Further, to be lawful detention must be for one of the statutory purposes for which the power is given. The initial statutory power is found in paragraph 16(2) Schedule 2, Immigration Act 1971. This power was enhanced in 2002 by section 62 of the Nationality, Immigration and Asylum Act of that year, which gave the state authorities a free standing power to detain a foreigner wherever the authorities have the power to set removal directions (i.e., directions for deportation or expulsion) (Bosworth 2007). According to UK law, detention can only be lawfully exercised where there is a realistic prospect of removal within a reasonable period. Further, there is a presumption in favour of release and there must be strong grounds for believing that a person will not comply with conditions of release to be justified. All reasonable alternatives to detention must be considered, and each case must be considered on its individual merits, including consideration of the duty to have regard to the need to safeguard and promote the welfare of any children involved, according to the UK authorities' detention and removal guidance (Gov.UK n.d.).

The state authorities' published guidance sets out the factors which must influence a decision to detain, which include the likelihood of the person being removed in a reasonable timescale, any evidence of previous absconding, evidence of a previous failure to comply with conditions of release, any history of attempted breach of immigration laws, previous history of complying with the requirements of immigration law, the person's ties with the UK, the individual's expectations about the outcome of the case, the risk of offending or harm to the public, the age of the person (is he or she a minor under 18), whether the individual has a history of torture or of physical or mental ill health.

Further, the guidance specifies the levels of authority necessary to make different types of immigration detention decisions and requires reviews to take place regularly. In light of the dispassionate, highly regulated and neutral terms of the guidance, it is perhaps surprising that the outcomes in terms of who actually gets detained are so marked.

5 Where Are People Detained?

There are many different types of places of immigration detention. According to the NGO Migreurop, there was, in 2011, capacity to detain in the EU (also including Switzerland and Norway) about 25,000 people at any given time. However, the NGO states that of EU immigration detention centres, it has been able to determine the capacity of 223 establishments out of a total of 351 which have been identified (Migreurop 2012). Places of immigration detention are scattered across the EU and are found in every EU state. Some allow their inmates to leave the premises for periods of time during the day, while others are closed. Immigration detention can also occur in police stations and prisons where it is less visible to those trying to track the phenomenon. In the UK, there are 13 establishments which are dedicated to immigration detention. They are called, respectively, immigration removal centres and short-term holding facilities. There is one pre-departure accommodation centre (The Cedars). Brook House, a removal centre for men, is near Gatwick airport and is run by the private security company G4S. It has capacity for 426 persons. Campsfield House, also a removal centre in Kiddlington, Oxfordshire, is run by GEO Group UK Ltd and has capacity for 216 men. Colnbrook, a removal centre, has a capacity for 420 persons, including some women. It is run by the company SERCO. Dover is a former prison, now a removal centre, still run by the prison service, which has capacity for 316 men. Dungavel, in Scotland, is a mixed facility, a former prison now run by GEO Group UK Ltd capable of housing 217 people. Harmondsworth can house 615 people and is operated by GEO Group, a private company. It can house women as well as men. Haslar began life as an army facility and then was transformed into a detention centre. It has capacity for 160 people and is operated by the company RELIANCE. Lindholme, also a former army facility, is run by G4S and has capacity for 124 people. Morton Hall, a removal centre as well, is a women's facility run by the Home Office itself. It has capacity for 392 women and was a former military facility. Oakington, a removal centre, only houses men (capacity 408) and is run by G4S. Tinsley House can accommodate up to 154 people, men and families. A removal centre, it is run by G4S. Yarl's Wood, also a removal centre, can hold up to 405 persons and is used primarily for women. It is run by Serco. The pre-departure accommodation centre, The Cedars, has capacity for 44 people and is designed to accommodate families with children. It is run by G4S. It was opened following severe criticism over the UK's policy of detaining families with children, which resulted in the closing of Dungavel for the accommodation of children.

All of the UK immigration detention centres have been the subject of reports by HM Chief Inspector of Prisons. While reports in the mid 2000s were very critical of the standards of detention facilities, the more recent reports have been more favourable indicating an improvement in the physical conditions of detention in the UK. However, many shortcomings are still in evidence in the reports. For instance, in the report of an unannounced inspection of Colnbrook Immigration Removal Centre between 28 January and 8 February 2013, the Inspector found that the worst unit was the "cramped and dirty 'first night last night unit' (FNLNU). There was a small separate dormitory for short-stay women detainees but if no space was available there, they were held in inadequate FNLNU alongside men, which is unacceptable" (HM Chief Inspector of Prisons 2013). According to the report, the vast majority of detainees were between the ages of 22 and 39 years. As regards the length of detention, the report states that only 17 % had been held for less than a week. Thirty-three percent had been held between 1 and 4 months. Twelve people had been held there for more than 10 months, with the longest having been in detention there by the time of the inspection for 1079 days (only a few weeks short of 3 years).

The places of immigration detention in the UK are scattered across the country. Most of them are in the countryside, not in cities or towns. Most of the places of detention are run by private companies on contracts from the state. From the reports of HM Chief Inspector of Prisons, it seems that there is quite a lot of change among the contractors with tenders for the operation of detention centres being of fairly short duration (5 years more or less) and changes in the choice of successful tenderers fairly frequent. The impact of such changes remains to be assessed in full. While generally there has been an improvement in the conditions of immigration detention, according to HM Chief Inspector of Prisons over the past 5 years, there are still worrying shortcomings. As the Inspector noted in his report on The

Cedars, the pre-departure centre on which the state authorities have spent much attention, effort and resources in order to satisfy critics of the policy to detain children: 'The circumstances of detention and removal were clearly traumatic for parents and their children but, unlike our consistent finding at Yarl's Wood, the conditions and length of detention at Cedars could not be said to cause distress to children and parents. . .The attractive environment and caring ethos of Cedars contrast with the inevitable fear and uncertainty among families undergoing the removal process to create a sense of dissonance for visitors. It is an exceptional facility and has many practices that should be replicated in other places of detention. However, it is also, when said and done, a place that precedes a traumatic dislocation for children who have, in many cases, been born in this country or been here for much of their lives' (HM Chief Inspector of Prisons 2012).

6 Why Do States Use Immigration Detention?

This question is difficult to answer in the abstract. Mitsilegas has examined how we have seen a convergence of coercive measures in pursuit of immigration and border controls in the EU and the USA following a logic of flanking measures to counter the loss of state control over movement which is inherent in what is generally termed globalization in its wider sense (Mitsilegas 2012). Taking the UK as an example, from the practices of immigration detention it would seem that because there is a wide discretion to state authorities to use such detention and few obstacles in the way of its application, state authorities can see it as a solution to various problems which arise within their immigration and border control practices. While detention of persons in the context of criminal law is subject to much more stringent limitations (and a wider range of actors), state criminal justice authorities have much less opportunity to use criminal detention to resolve problems in the application of criminal justice, for instance delays in trials, suspicions in respect of individuals where prosecutors doubt whether there is sufficient evidence to bring charges, etc. For state authorities responsible for immigration detention, these constraints do not apply. If the authorities are having trouble applying specific rules to various foreigners, they can always fall back on the mechanism of immigration detention. A joint report on the effectiveness and impact of immigration detention by the UK Inspector of Prisons and the Independent Chief Inspector of Borders and Immigration published in December 2012 concludes that as regards compliance with the guidance on when to detain a foreigner, 'both inspectorates have raised concerns that [detention as a last resort] is not always the case and that detention is not always subject to sufficiently rigorous governance' (HM Inspectorate of Prisons and the Independent Chief Inspector of Borders and Immigration 2012, p. 7).

According to FRONTEX, in the first quarter of 2013 EU Member States took 55,285 expulsion decisions (FRONTEX 2013, p. 57). All of those persons against whom an expulsion decision has been taken are within the group of persons whom state authorities may subject to immigration detention in accordance with Article 5 (1)(f) ECHR, provided that the authorities are actually seeking to expel these people. For the same quarter, FRONTEX advises that there were a total of 38,221 effective returns, of which 19,536 were forced returns (FRONTEX 2013, p. 60). This means that there were 17,064 persons present in the EU against whom expulsion decisions had been taken but who had neither left voluntarily nor been the subject of a forced return. These people are eligible for immigration detention according to Article 5(1)(f) ECHR provided that the state is pursuing their departure.

Those persons for whom forced return is envisaged, that is to say those who have not left voluntarily, are among the groups of persons most likely to be subject to immigration detention. This is because the investment of state authorities' time and resources into forced return is high, so being sure that the individual subject to a forced return procedure is available for his or her forced return is a high priority. Thus, the administrative concern to ensure that the forced return proceeds smoothly leads to a heightened concern on the part of state authorities that the individual not have the opportunity to frustrate the forced return by failing to appear at the right place and the appointed time for the expulsion. Immigration detention provides a solution to this concern.

The FRONTEX Annual Report 2012 (FRONTEX 2012) indicates that 39 joint return flights were organised under its auspices in the preceding year; a similar number were organised the year before according to the 2011 Annual Report. The objective of these return flights is to make Member States' expulsion efforts more effective by cooperating regarding the logistics of return. These return flights engage FRONTEX in assisting in chartering planes for expulsion to destinations agreed by a number of Member States. In 2011, the largest number of persons expelled on any one such flight was to Ecuador and Colombia (107 persons) organised with FRONTEX's assistance at the instigation of the Spanish authorities but including only Spain and the Netherlands. The largest number of Member States involved in a joint return operation that year was 11 (Austria, Poland, Malta, Hungary, Czech Republic, Spain, France, Ireland, Norway, Finland and Germany) regarding the expulsion of 54 persons to Nigeria. The operation was instigated by Austria. A moment's reflection on the logistics of this operation indicates the problems and potential human rights issues. A plane had to be chartered for 54 persons, plus their escorts (national authorities charged with ensuring that the persons being expelled do not cause havoc). Either the persons being expelled had to be moved from one state to another (an unlikely scenario on account of a variety of legal constraints) or the plane needed to stop in each of the 11 states to collect people. Given the distances and the time which commercial flights take to fly among these different states, one can only imagine that this was a long flight even before the plane left Europe. The plane may well have needed refueling, and those on board will have needed both food and drink. In view of the fairly small number of people being expelled, the pressure on national authorities to ensure that they had to hand ready for expulsion the number of persons they engaged to put on the plane at the time of the planning of the operation must have been substantial. Such operations are expensive, and if by the time the plane arrives in a state the authorities no longer have anyone available and ready to be expelled to the destination country, undoubtedly this creates inconvenience for all the authorities and actors involved. Thus, the administrative impetus to ensure that at least a number of Nigerians or persons who could be expelled to Nigeria are ready for expulsion and in detention awaiting the plane when it arrived is substantial. As people awaiting detention may become ill and unable to travel or they may lodge a legal challenge to their expulsion or some other impediment to expulsion may arise at the last minute, state authorities no doubt may wish to have a pool of persons available for expulsion under such circumstances in case of mishap with the expulsion of one or more of them. These factors all lead in the direction of the use of detention in order to fulfil administrative needs arising from the changing nature of expulsion and deportation in Europe.

A more problematic allegation regarding the use of immigration detention is that it is used to punish some foreigners for their unauthorised entry and stay in the state. Documentation of this use is not complete. From the cases which have come before the Court of Justice of the European Union regarding the Returns Directive,[6] the facts reveal some Member States using their criminal justice systems to convict foreigners unauthorised on the territory of a criminal offence of such presence and thereby frustrate the objective of expulsion of the individual from the territory. However, in the next section, the facts of the case which came before the European Court of Human Rights (ECtHR) in respect of Malta's policy of mandatory detention of asylum seekers for a period of 14 months (+/−) indicate that immigration detention may also be used in some European states as a form of punishment for unauthorised entry.

7 Is Immigration Detention Consistent with the European Convention on Human Rights?

Costello has undertaken a far-reaching examination of the legality in international human rights law of immigration detention which exposes the problems and lacunae in the international framework and its jurisprudence (Costello 2012). The first requirement which state authorities must satisfy for immigration detention to be lawful is that it must be fully captured in a set of laws. As can be seen from the UK's case, this requirement is not so difficult to fulfil. When the authorities decided that the general power to detain foreigners contained in the Immigration Act 1971 was insufficient, they provided themselves in 2002 with a wider, free standing power contained in law, to carry out immigration detention. This new power also perhaps marks the starting point of an increased interest by the UK authorities in using their detention powers more widely.

[6] E.g., C-61/11 PPU *El Dridi* ECR [2011] I-3015.

Once the legality test has been satisfied, few constraints remain on the state from the European Court of Human Rights' jurisprudence. As Costello points out, in a 1997 judgment,[7] the European Court of Human Rights rejected the test of reasonable necessity as the benchmark for the assessment of the compatibility of immigration detention with the ECHR. However, for immigration detention to be consistent with Article 5(1)(f) ECHR, there must be a reasonable prospect of removal if this is the objective sought by the authorities. If, however, state authorities rely on the second ground of Article 5(1)(f) ECHR—that detention is necessary to prevent an unauthorised entry—the jurisprudence of the ECtHR is less than satisfactory as Costello shows. The leading case, *Saadi v UK*,[8] was something of a disappointment for human rights advocates. It concerned someone who applied for asylum in the UK on arrival, was released but later detained for administrative convenience. The ECtHR accepted the state authorities' argument that even though the man had a pending asylum application (and was eventually recognised as a refugee) his detention under the rubric of preventing an unauthorised entry was still permissible under the ECHR. Although there was a powerful dissenting faction in the ECtHR against the main decision on this point, to date there has not been a change of heart at the ECtHR. The problem with the Saadi judgment is that it justifies all on entry detention, even where the person entering has a right in international refugee law to seek asylum and thus to enter the state during the consideration of the asylum claim (Mole and Meredith 2010).

In July 2013, the ECtHR revisited its jurisprudence on immigration detention but it did not actually take it much further, notwithstanding the compassionate circumstances of the case.[9] While the ECtHR found that the conditions of detention in Malta under which the applicant was held to have breached Article 3 ECHR—the prohibition on inhuman and degrading treatment or punishment—the grounds for finding a breach of Article 5(1)(f) ECHR were more problematic. The facts were as follows: Ms Ahmed arrived from Eritrea in Malta by boat, irregularly on 5 February 2009. She was registered as irregularly present, but she made an asylum application shortly thereafter. Her application was rejected. In May 2009, she escaped from detention and managed to travel as far as the Netherlands irregularly. She applied for asylum there. At this point, she was hoping to get to Sweden as her family had been granted refugee status there and was awaiting resettlement (which occurred on 17 March 2011). However, the Dutch authorities, rather than letting her proceed to Sweden, sent her back to Malta on 11 February 2011, by which time she was 24 years old and 2 months pregnant. On her return to Malta, she was detained for 14½ months before release. She suffered a miscarriage in detention in Malta receiving only rudimentary health care. At the end of her detention in Malta, she was released but not expelled.

[7] *Chahal v. United Kingdom*, application number 22414/93, 23 Eur. H.R. Rep. 413 (1997).

[8] *Saadi v. United Kingdom*, application number 13229/03, 47 Eur. H.R. Rep. 17 (2008).

[9] *Aden Ahmed v Malta* application number 55352/12 judgment: 23 July 2013.

Ms Ahmed complained to the ECtHR that her detention has been arbitrary because her expulsion was not feasible and the length of her detention exceeded what was reasonable for any purpose. The ECtHR found a violation of Article 5 (1) ECHR, but the reasons are somewhat worrying. In the Court's assessment of the case, it reiterated its constant jurisprudence regarding the fundamental human right to liberty. It confirmed that compliance with national law was insufficient, though necessary in itself for immigration detention to be lawful. Additionally, the individual must be protected from arbitrariness. For the purposes of Article 5(1) (f) ECHR, this means that the immigration detention must be carried out in good faith, closely connected to the ground of detention relied upon by the state authorities; the place and conditions of detention must be appropriate; and the length of detention must not exceed what is reasonably required for the purpose pursued.

In applying this reasoning to the facts of the case, the ECtHR held that the Maltese authorities sought to justify the detention of Ms Ahmed on the basis that they were planning to expel or deport her. However, the Court noted that the authorities had submitted no information as to whether they had commenced return procedures at all, 'let alone pursued [them] with diligence' (*Ahmed v Malta*, para. 144). As the Maltese authorities had taken no steps to pursue Ms Ahmed's expulsion, her immigration detention was not permissible under Article 5(1)(f) ECHR. This is something of a pyrrhic victory for Ms Ahmed as undoubtedly although she did not want to be in prison style conditions in detention for 14 months, she did not want to be sent back to Eritrea where she feared for her life. Although the Maltese authorities had been very prompt in refusing her asylum claim, they made no move to expel her back to her country of origin. However horrible it may have been for Ms Ahmed to be in limbo in Malta, it is likely that she would have preferred this to being in most uncertain conditions in Eritrea. Her efforts to get to Sweden to join her family were more likely to be successful from Malta than if she were sent back to Eritrea, though by the time of the judgment, it seems she was still in Malta. The underlying problem of the length of immigration detention was not re-considered by the ECtHR in this judgment.

8 Conclusions

In this chapter, I have examined the developing practice of immigration detention in Europe with specific attention to the UK. Notwithstanding the expense of immigration detention,[10] it is a continuing practice which shows no sign of disappearing in the face of criticism by civil society. The objectives of immigration detention are central to its legality. According to European human rights law, it must be carried out for the purpose of preventing an unauthorised entry into a state or in the pursuit

[10] According to press reports, the UK spends approximately £130 million per year on immigration detention (Johnson 2012).

of expulsion or deportation. When one has regard to the practices of immigration detention, one finds that it is practised against nationals of some countries with much greater frequency than against nationals of others. While in each case an individual decision to detain must be made by state authorities, even so those decisions result in vastly disproportionate immigration detention of nationals of some countries in comparison with those of other countries. This imbalance is not resolved when one takes into consideration the numbers of persons of the nationalities coming to the UK; indeed, it is only pronounced and underscored by such a comparison.

The places where immigration detention takes place are found mainly in the countryside at substantial distances from one another. The centres are run by a variety of private companies with a small number of them in the hands of the state authorities' prison services and one managed by the immigration authorities themselves. While there is oversight by state authorities responsible for prison conditions generally, the conclusion of those authorities is that immigration detention is a practice which creates distress for families and children. This is particularly so in light of the length of detention—some people had been subject to immigration detention for almost 3 years.

The above notwithstanding, as a human rights issue, the practices of immigration detention which have come before the European Court of Human Rights have not been subject to particularly onerous decisions as far as most states are concerned. While some states are condemned for the conditions of immigration detention, the reasonableness of immigration detention has been excluded by the Court itself as a criterion for the assessment of the lawfulness of the detention. Instead, state authorities must only show that they are pursuing deportation or expulsion proceedings against someone whom they are holding in immigration detention for such detention to escape the fault of arbitrariness. Alternatively, where the objective is to prevent an unauthorised entry into the state, state authorities are permitted a very wide range of reasons to subject a person to immigration detention. The fact that the individual has sought international protection at the border does not protect him or her from immigration detention according to the Court's case law. This situation is unsatisfactory. The extent of state authorities' powers to place people in immigration detention and the way in which they are exercised, as discussed in this chapter, reveal a pressing need to visit the jurisprudence of the European Court of Human Rights and to give Article 5(1)(f) ECHR a more purposive interpretation which protects foreigners against what is in effect, in so many cases, arbitrary detention.

Annex 1: Article 5 European Convention on Human Rights

Article 5—Right to liberty and security

1. Everyone has the right to liberty and security of person. No one shall be deprived of his liberty save in the following cases and in accordance with a procedure prescribed by law:

    a. the lawful detention of a person after conviction by a competent court;
    b. the lawful arrest or detention of a person for non-compliance with the lawful order of a court or in order to secure the fulfilment of any obligation prescribed by law;
    c. the lawful arrest or detention of a person effected for the purpose of bringing him before the competent legal authority on reasonable suspicion of having committed an offence or when it is reasonably considered necessary to prevent his committing an offence or fleeing after having done so;
    d. the detention of a minor by lawful order for the purpose of educational supervision or his lawful detention for the purpose of bringing him before the competent legal authority;
    e. the lawful detention of persons for the prevention of the spreading of infectious diseases, of persons of unsound mind, alcoholics or drug addicts or vagrants;
    f. the lawful arrest or detention of a person to prevent his effecting an unauthorised entry into the country or of a person against whom action is being taken with a view to deportation or extradition.

2. Everyone who is arrested shall be informed promptly, in a language which he understands, of the reasons for his arrest and of any charge against him.
3. Everyone arrested or detained in accordance with the provisions of paragraph 1.c of this article shall be brought promptly before a judge or other officer authorised by law to exercise judicial power and shall be entitled to trial within a reasonable time or to release pending trial. Release may be conditioned by guarantees to appear for trial.
4. Everyone who is deprived of his liberty by arrest or detention shall be entitled to take proceedings by which the lawfulness of his detention shall be decided speedily by a court and his release ordered if the detention is not lawful.
5. Everyone who has been the victim of arrest or detention in contravention of the provisions of this article shall have an enforceable right to compensation.

References

Bigo D (2007) Detention of foreigners, states of exception, and the social practices of control of the banopticon. In: Rajaram K, Grundy-Warr C (eds) Borderscapes: hidden geographies and politics at territory's edge. University of Minnesota Press, Minneapolis, pp 3–34

Bosworth M (2007) Immigration detention in Britain. In: Lee M (ed) Human trafficking. Willan, Cullompton, pp 159–177
Cornelisse G (2010) Immigration detention and the territoriality of universal rights. The Deportation Regime. In: De Genova N, Peutz N (eds) Sovereignty, space, and the freedom of movement. Duke University Press, Durham, pp 101–122
Costello C (2012) Human rights and the elusive universal subject: immigration detention under international human rights and EU law. Indiana J Glob Leg Stud 19(1):257–303
FRONTEX (2012) General Report 2012. http://www.frontex.europa.eu/assets/About_Frontex/Governance_documents/Annual_report/2012/EN_General_Report_2012.pdf. Accessed 7 Aug 2014
FRONTEX (2013) Fran Quarterly, Quarter 1 (January–March 2013). http://www.frontex.europa.eu/assets/Publications/Risk_Analysis/FRAN_Q1_2013.pdf. Accessed 7 Aug 2014
Gov.UK (n.d.) Guidance and information on detention and removals for officers dealing with enforcement immigration matters within the UK. http://www.ukba.homeoffice.gov.uk/sitecontent/documents/policyandlaw/enforcement/detentionandremovals/. Accessed 7 Aug 2014
HM Chief Inspector of Prisons (2012) Report on an announced inspection of Cedars Pre-Departure Accommodation. 30 April–25 May 2012
HM Chief Inspector of Prisons (2013) Report on an unannounced inspection of Colnbrook Immigration Removal Centre. 28 January–8 February 2013
HM Inspectorate of Prisons and the Independent Chief Inspector of Borders and Immigration (2012) The effectiveness and impact of immigration detention casework. A joint thematic review by HMInspectorate of Prisons and the Independent Chief Inspector of Borders and Immigration, December 2012. http://www.justice.gov.uk/downloads/publications/inspectorate-reports/hmipris/thematic-reports-and-research-publications/immigration-detention-casework-2012.pdf. Accessed 7 Aug 2014
Johnson W (2012) Immigration detention costs £130 million a year. The Daily Telegraph, 12 December 2012. http://www.telegraph.co.uk/news/uknews/immigration/9737848/Immigration-detention-costs-130-million-a-year.html. Accessed 7 Aug 2014
Krause M (2008) Undocumented migrants an Arendtian perspective. Eur J Polit Theory 7 (3):331–348
Migreurop – Observatoire des Frontières (2012) Atlas des migrants en Europe. http://www.migreurop.org/article2271.html?lang=fr. Accessed 7 Aug 2014
Mincheva E (2010) Case Report on Kadzoev, 30 November 2009. Eur J Migr Law 12(3):361–371
Mitsilegas V (2012) Immigration control in an era of globalization: deflecting foreigners, weakening citizens, strengthening the state. Indiana J Glob Leg Stud 19(1):3–60
Mole N, Meredith C (2010) Asylum and the European Convention on Human Rights. Human Rights Files No. 9. Council of Europe
Office for National Statistics (2012) Travel Trends – Overseas residents' visits to the UK 2008 to 2012. http://www.ons.gov.uk/ons/publications/re-reference-tables.html?edition=tcm%3A77-303829. Accessed 7 Aug 2014
Silverman S, Hajela R (2012) Briefing: immigration detention in the UK. The migration observatory, University of Oxford, 22 May 2012
Wilsher D (2011) Immigration detention: law, history, politics. Cambridge University Press, Cambridge

Women's Immigration Detention in Greece: Gender, Control and Capacity

Mary Bosworth, Andriani Fili, and Sharon Pickering

Abstract Despite sustained media and political interest in Greece as a key site of European border security, there is little academic scholarship about daily life in Greek detention centres. In this article we start to fill this gap, drawing on fieldwork conducted in Athens' Central Holding Centre for immigrants, *Petrou Ralli*, in 2012. This chapter also contributes to feminist criminological accounts of border control that suggest that women and men's experiences diverge in important ways, particularly in relation to experiences of immigration detention. What are women's needs in detention? How do those who work in the detention centre view the women they lock up? What obstacles do detainees face, as women? How do they interpret their experiences? Using testimonies from detainees and the staff who work with them, we unveil the human impact of policies being implemented in response to transnational pressures from Brussels and to more local problems.

The fieldwork for this paper was conducted by Andriani Fili from November 2011 to February 2012, supported by the Oxford University Research Support Fund at the Faculty of Law as well as by the Australian Research Council Future Fellowship of Sharon Pickering. Mary Bosworth would also like to acknowledge funding from the European Research Council, Starter Grant 313362 in writing up the project. Where possible, interviews were digitally recorded and then fully transcribed and translated into English by Andriani Fili. Others were recorded in note form and then translated into English. All interviewees have been anonymised. More information about this ongoing research can be found at www.borderobservatory.org and http://bordercriminologies.law.ox.ac.uk.

M. Bosworth (✉) • A. Fili
Centre for Criminology, University of Oxford, Oxford Uk & Monash University, VIC, Australia
e-mail: mary.bosworth@crim.ox.ac.uk; andriani.fili@crim.ox.ac.uk

S. Pickering
Monash University, Melbourne, VIC, Australia
e-mail: sharon.pickering@monash.edu

M.J. Guia et al. (eds.), *Immigration Detention, Risk and Human Rights*,
DOI 10.1007/978-3-319-24690-1_9

1 Introduction[1]

As states around the world have sought to reduce rates of irregular migration, many have deployed criminal justice agencies and institutions in the name of border control. Such actions have, somewhat belatedly, garnered the attention of criminologists, leading to the development of a vigorous field of inquiry known variously as the 'criminology of mobility' or border criminologies (Aas and Bosworth 2013; *see also, inter alia*, Guia et al. 2012; Leerkes and Broeders 2010; Pratt 2005; Barker 2013; Weber and Pickering 2011; Pickering 2014). As this body of literature has expanded, so too have the sites and methods of analysis in it. While, for the most part, much scholarship has been primarily theoretical or based on secondary and legal analysis (Aas 2011; Welch and Schuster 2005; Bosworth and Guild 2008; Cornelisse 2010), more recently, a handful of criminologists have begun to publish qualitative accounts of the nature and effect of border control (Bosworth 2012, 2014; Fili 2013; Kaufman 2012, 2013; Kaufman and Bosworth 2013; Gerard and Pickering 2012).[2]

This article contributes to that emerging body of work. Starting with a general overview of the Greek immigration system, it turns to focus more narrowly on life for women migrants and detention centre staff inside Athens' Central Holding Centre. Through field notes and testimonies drawn from interviews with 19 female detainees and 10 staff, this article fleshes out our understanding of the relationship between gender and border control. What are women's needs in detention? How do those who work in the detention centre view the women they lock up? What obstacles do detainees face, as women? How do they interpret their experiences?

In asking these kinds of questions, our ambition is twofold. First, we aspire to unveil the human impact of policies being implemented in response to transnational pressures from Brussels and to more local problems. Notwithstanding the legal and geographical significance of Greece to European border security, and the international criticism that Greece has received regarding its responses to irregular flows, we know very little about daily life in Greek detention centres other than what we can glean from reports by NGOs and the government. Greek scholarship has mainly focused on the economic, political and sociocultural changes connected to migration processes and the development of migration policy (*see, inter alia*, Triandafyllidou 2009; Skordas 2002; Triandafyllidou and Veikou 2002; Fakiolas 2003; Vaiou 2003).

Second, we seek to contribute to a feminist body of literature in criminological accounts of border control regarding the salience of gender (*see* also Bosworth and Kellezi 2014; Pickering and Cochrane 2013; Bosworth and Slade 2014). Although traditional accounts of migration paid little attention to gender, more critical

---

[1] Thanks to Brandy Cochrane for editorial assistance.

[2] If we include anthropology, politics and geography, the volume of ethnographic research expands as does the amount of theoretical work on border control (on the former, *see*, for example, Hall 2010, 2012; Mountz 2012; Gill 2009; on the latter, *see* Makaremi 2009; De Genova and Peultz 2010; Fassin 2011).

scholarship on mobility suggests that women and men's experiences diverge in important ways (*see*, for example, Gutierrez-Rodriguez 2010; Yuval-Davis 1997). In Greece, when female migrants have been considered at all, it has primarily been as sex workers or in relation to their male partners (Lazos 1997; Emke-Poulopoulou 2001; Lazaridis 2001). They have rarely been studied in their own right. So far, no academic scholarship exists on their experiences of detention. This article starts to fill that gap.

The research on which this article is based is ongoing, part of a multi-site, transnational research project. Andriani Fili conducted all of the interviews on-site while visiting the detention centre, first as a research officer and then as a member of staff of 'Medical Intervention', an NGO offering social and medical support across a number of detention facilities. Though the stories from *Petrou Ralli*, the Central Holding Facility for irregular migrants in Athens, belong to those who shared them, they resonate with interviews and observations across similar facilities around the world (Bosworth 2012; Bosworth and Kellezi 2014; Grewcock 2011; Hall 2012). As states everywhere pursue border control ever more enthusiastically, it becomes increasingly urgent to bear witness to the human costs of immigration detention and related practices.

2 Immigration Detention and Border Control in Greece

Undocumented migrants can be detained for up to 18 months in Greece in a number of locations, from border guard posts to police stations, at the airport, at the Athens Holding Centre, in purpose-built detention centres, in ad hoc facilities pressed into service and, most recently, in new, so-called closed hospitality centres.[3] Some unlucky individuals might be detained in all of these places, moved from one to another, whereas others languish for months in the same place. After release, nearly all remain vulnerable to further detention, since barely any are given the legal right to remain.[4]

[3] Any expectations of hospitality disappear upon a visit to one of the new 'closed hospitality centres' in Amygdaleza. It is composed of small mobile homes surrounded by high wire and situated in a remote area outside of Athens. The location of the centre makes it particularly difficult for detainees to obtain legal or medical aid, an outcome that appears to have been deliberate, as the young director of the centre revealed: '*we want to deport them and we are going to do it, so do not bother informing them about what they need*' (*see* Johansen 2013, for an account of a short-lived similarly named set of institutions in Norway and their role in enforcing deportation).

[4] Greece has now stopped all regularisation programs for economic immigrants, and accepted asylum applications, though having risen from 0.1 to 3 % recently, are very few compared to the number of requests.

Most immigration detention centres in Greece were established without uniform standards and terms of operation. They are guarded by the police and funded by the Ministry of Interior through the Prefectures.[5] However, there is no statutorily defined public authority responsible for their management. As Amnesty International has commented, the "lack of a Ministerial Decision regarding the framework for management and operation of the current centres causes most of the problems that have arisen in them" (Amnesty International 2010, p. 35), including the lack of activities, recreation and times outdoors (CPT 2010).

Each one is overcrowded. They are also dirty. Detainees find it difficult to access decent healthcare or legal advice. Women and men are often mixed, when they should be kept separate, and children are held alongside adults. Detainees frequently describe an alarming picture of mistreatment, overcrowding and unsanitary conditions. "I can't live in here. This is not a place for humans. This is a place for animals", Anwar from Somalia cried out in the Athens airport detention centre. "I can't stay in here anymore. I'm going to hurt myself or someone else. I'm going crazy in here"; "Look at my clothes, look at me, this is not for us"; "I can't shower here, the toilets are too dirty", others proclaimed.

Human rights organisations routinely describe immigration detention in Greece, especially in the border guard stations, as a human rights emergency. Organisations, from Amnesty to the Council for the Prevention of Torture, highlight deficiencies in the infrastructure, insufficient and unprofessional personnel, as well as ineffective and sometimes unlawful practices (CPT 2010; Amnesty International 2010; Pro Asyl 2007, p. 23; Human Rights Watch 2008). Such criticisms underpin judgments by the European Court of Human Rights (ECHR) which have found Greece guilty for violating Articles 3 and 5 of the European Convention on Human Rights (S.D.,[6] A.A.,[7] Tabesh,[8] M.S.S.,[9] Rahimi,[10] R.U.[11] against Greece) and which have called for an end to transfers of asylum seekers back to Greece under the Dublin II Regulation. Faced with repeated failures on the part of Greek authorities to improve the conditions of immigration detention, the Committee for the Prevention of

[5] The new government wants to pass legislation that will shift responsibility for immigration to the Ministry of Public Protection, i.e. the police will be responsible for the arrest, detention and welfare of immigrants and refugees in Greece.

[6] *S.D. vs. Greece*, 11.06.2009, concerning detention in border guard station, Soufli.

[7] *A.A. vs. Greece*, 22.07.2010, concerning detention conditions in detention centre on Samos island.

[8] *Tabesh vs. Greece*, 26.11.2009.

[9] *M.S.S. vs. Belgium and Greece*, 21.01.2011, concerning detention conditions at the airport detention facility.

[10] *Rahimi vs. Greece*, 05.04.2011, concerning detention conditions on Lesvos island.

[11] *R.U vs. Greece*, 07.06.2011, concerning detention conditions in Soufli.

Torture and Inhuman or Degrading Treatment or Punishment (CPT) issued its first public statement in 2011 addressed to an EU member state, condemning detention conditions in Greece[12] and drawing attention to the failure of this country to 'improve the situation' despite recommendations dating back to 2005.

Nonetheless, Greek immigration detention is expanding. Although Greek Law (3386/2005), 'on the entry, residence and social integration of third-country nationals on Greek territory',[13] makes it quite clear that administrative detention shall only be used in cases of danger for the public order and in view to deportation (Article 76), Greece, in common with many member states of the EU, has been aggressively enlarging its detention capacity (Cornelisse 2010). That it has been doing so under conditions of economic collapse, and in the teeth of vigorous international criticism, is worth exploring.

In part, the timing of the expanding detention estate reflects the broader context of migration. Between 1993 and 2008, for instance, the number of irregular immigrants in Greece quadrupled (Chindea et al. 2008). However, whereas previously much of Greek society was either tolerant or indifferent to this population, since the economic crisis of 2008, matters have changed dramatically. More recently, most discussions of mobility have become marked by a toxic combination of securitisation and racism. Politicians of all stripes, not just members of far-right parties like Golden Dawn,[14] blame irregular migrants for rising crime, urban degradation and widespread economic hardship endured by citizens. In the lead-up to the May and June 2012 national elections, immigration detention and border control more generally became a lightning rod for public opinion, deployed as a cynical political tool to demonstrate the government's determination to salvage Greek national pride.

In a centralised system like Greece, such politics, perhaps inevitably, has been particularly focused on Athens. Following revelations that around 5000 migrants were living in an estimated 500 abandoned buildings in the city, and that more than 2000 other properties occupied by migrants were unfit for human habitation, the Cabinet decided to adopt an action plan for the revitalisation of the city centre.[15]

---

[12] http://www.cpt.coe.int/documents/grc/2011-10-inf-eng.pdf. This is the fifth time the CPT has used this exceptional measure against countries; the first time in Turkey is in 1992 and then again in 1996 and in Russia in 2001, 2003, 2005 for the situation in Chechnya.

[13] For a translation of the law, see http://old.certh.gr/libfiles/PDF/MOBIL-65-Nomos3386_en.pdf.

[14] 'Golden Dawn' (Xrisi Avgi), secured 19 seats in the Parliament in the June 2012 national elections, for a first time in its history. Its programmatic statements included virulent posters promising to 'get rid of the dirt off the city streets' and called for 'Greece only for Greeks'. There is also some evidence that suggests that members of the party belong to groups that organize street patrolling and protect citizens by carrying out violent attacks on migrants. It is estimated that 50 % of police officers voted for this party.

[15] http://government.gov.gr/wp-content/uploads/2011/05/%CE%A3%CF%87%CE%AD%CE%B4%CE%B9%CE%BF-%CE%94%CF%81%CE%AC%CF%83%CE%B7%CF%82-%CE%B3%CE%B9%CE%B1-%CF%84%CE%BF-%CE%9A%CE%AD%CE%BD%CF%84%CF%81%CE%BF-%CF%84%CE%B7%CF%82-%CE%91%CE%B8%CE%AE%CE%BD%CE%B1%CF%82.pdf.

Warning of a "public health time bomb", officials sought to reduce the concentration of irregular migrants in the city centre through daily patrols and police 'sweep operations'. Foreigners are not hard to find:

> All around the city but especially in the centre you can see immigrants pushing trolleys filled with any metal objects they have found in garbage bins. Poverty has visibly increased on the streets of the capital where immigrants can be seen rummaging through garbage cans for food or scraps of metal or glass to sell to garages for some Euros per kilo. The streets there are downhill and due to the weight of the trolleys they sometimes get drifted along on the road risking being run over by cars and buses. Lucky ones have very small cars to transfer everything they find. (Fieldnotes, January, 2012).

Those considered to be irregular are forced to register and may be arrested. Such practices lead directly to the enlargement of the detention population, a connection acknowledged by the government which, in addition to enhanced checks, promised in 2012 to build more detention facilities, manage asylum cases more quickly and expand voluntary return programs.[16] By 2014, then Minister of Public Protection, Mr Chrisochoidis, announced that the state would build 30 new detention centres in 10 Greek prefectures. Officially named 'closed hospitality centres', the facilities will be based on unused military sites, typically apart from urban centres and concomitant sources of assistance. They had a capacity for 30,000 people, with upwards of 15,000 places available in June 2013, a total that not only dwarfs previous numbers in detention but is considerably more than the nation's prison population.[17] In Athens and Korinthos alone, building works are taking place in order to facilitate the detention of 4000 migrants in each centre.[18]

These developments appeared, on the one hand, designed to siphon away voters who were otherwise attracted to the anti-immigrant sentiments of Golden Dawn. Yet they were not implemented solely in response to local ambitions. Partly subsidised by the European Union to the tune of 250 million euro, the origins of the plan appear to have come, as with much Greek border control, from further north.

Even before its current economic problems, Greece was considered a liability for 'fortress Europe'. The country's repeated failure to protect its borders has only heightened political tensions as EU states worried that their own tight job markets cannot handle the tide of irregular migrants pouring into the rest of Europe via Greece. The influx from abroad not only has sustained a backdrop of a wider social unease and anti-immigrant sentiment within Greece but also has led to widespread critique of Greece from EU member states. In June 2012, Greece failed its five-yearly Schengen evaluation due to 'serious shortcomings' in its border management, leading to the possibility that member states may reintroduce internal border

---

[16] http://www.minocp.gov.gr/index.php?option=ozo_content&lang=&perform=view&id=3790&Itemid=513. For an account of the role of 'voluntary return' programmes elsewhere in Europe, *see* Johansen (2013).

[17] Greece's current prison population is estimated at around 12,000 people. The total detention capacity in specialised detention centres at the moment is 2500.

[18] *See*, for instance, Platform for International Cooperation on Undocumented Migrants (2012) http://picum.org/it/attualita/bolletino/38052/.

controls at their own discretion in emergency cases.[19] If this happens, Greece could be effectively isolated from the rest of the Schengen zone. Under these circumstances, irregular migration has become crucial for developing rhetoric surrounding the need for stricter border controls and tougher policies that would at the same time satisfy Greece's EU partners.

Required on the one hand to secure its border with Turkey on behalf of all of Europe and hence effectively deliver a secure external border, Greece must do so, under conditions of financial privation and surging xenophobia. Castigated for contravening the human rights standards expected of EU members, it seems unable to do otherwise than fail. Turning now to the micro politics and lived experiences of immigration detention in Greece, we explore the lived effect of the rapid expansion of penal-inspired responses in light of these competing regional and domestic pressures.

3 Athens Central Holding Facility

Operating since 2005, *Petrou Ralli* is the Central Holding Facility for Aliens in Athens. As such, it was designed to hold detainees for a short period of time (up to 2 weeks) prior to their deportation. Whereas some officials, like Panagiotis, emphasised the particular status of the centre, insisting "this is not a detention centre, it is a special holding facility for migrants (*Eidikoi Xwroi Paramonis Metanastwn*). That's the official name and that's what we offer here" (Principal Officer), in fact, like the holding cells at Athens airport, another site designed for brief stays, women and men languish here in overcrowded, insanitary conditions, for many months at a time (Fili 2013).

Entering *Petrou Ralli*, it is easy to feel overwhelmed by the noise, the smell and the dirt. Walls are painted an institutional light green and yellow. The floors are unwashed. In the men's section, the smell of urine is pervasive. Everywhere, the stench of anxiety is palpable. The iron doors slam, officers shout, detainees speak a confusing mix of languages:

> People who are detained here are either arrested on the street or at their flats following typical raids by the police. This means that they have only the clothes they are wearing. And if they don't have anyone outside who can bring them the clothes, they end up staying with the same clothes for weeks. The smell sometimes is overbearing. (Fieldnotes, January, 2012)

Detainees are housed in a line of cells along a corridor each of which has five cement beds. Due to serious overcrowding, many detainees end up sleeping on the floor. Entry to these rooms is through a barred, locked iron door, affording the detainees no privacy. Most need to ask for permission to use the bathroom. The

[19] http://www.consilium.europa.eu/uedocs/cms_Data/docs/pressdata/en/jha/130761.pdf.

guards allow them out of their cells for 2 hours a day and into the rooftop exercise yard for only 1 hour a week.[20]

Detainees spend little time outside their cells and have nothing to do inside them other than to sit or lie on their beds. The listlessness is patent: "We are not doing anything, nothing. We end up sleeping all the time", Chiora from Georgia complained. For many it is distressing, "I fear I'm going to die here", June from the Dominican Republic protested, "The police don't understand my language and I'm afraid. It's difficult."

Under these conditions, staff and detainees struggle to understand what is happening. Some staff members are critical. "It's much worse than a prison", Alex told us. "It's the trap of temporary detention that doesn't allow us to have the privileges of a prison. They are psychologically distressed here, I would go crazy myself." Others, like Vassilis, a senior police officer, who has served many posts, are more defensive. "In this current economic situation", he claimed, "detention conditions are satisfactory". Any inadequacies could not be held to their account since:

> Most of the time we don't have enough space for the number of immigrants we arrest… Numbers increase constantly. Today we were sent 50 women from the Evros region. The system crashes due to Africans and Asians because you cannot send them back. When you collect from the street, as well as receive women from the border, you end up having a number that you cannot deal with (Vassilis).

Maria, a young officer, who has spent time at the border, agreed; matters were out of their hands. "We are doing a great job here. But no one was prepared for it. The state didn't expect this. My colleagues, they just follow orders. I imagine that if we knew we would have built something appropriate."

Some, however, blame the detainees for having brought their lot upon themselves. In such accounts, staff members draw on familiar narratives around the poor rational choices of migrants and the necessary use of detention as the central plank in deterring these choices. "There are too many immigrants in Athens", Christos, a senior member of the medical personnel at *Petrou Ralli*, asserted. "They have to go back."

If women's choices are considered poorly calculated and in need of correction, the detainees themselves are often viewed as morally and intellectually suspect. They stand accused of sexual promiscuity, instrumentality or naivety; coming to Greece to find a good husband; or working in the sex trade. "They get fooled", Vassilis asserted. "Before they arrive here they are told that they are going to work in houses and such and they end up on the street. They don't know what they are doing and where they are going. Women don't have an idea."

Most detainees in *Petrou Ralli*, as elsewhere, are men. Women constitute around 10 % of the total detained population, a much lower figure than some other European countries (Bosworth and Kellezi 2014). Within the facility, they are sequestered in a row of cells on the third floor, next to the section for

[20] This has now been reduced to once a month due to overcrowding.

unaccompanied minors. Women are separated from men, who are detained on the second floor, but are kept together with their children, in unsanitary conditions, with few clothes or provisions. Staff, aware of the deficiencies, attempts to fill the gaps. "There are many NGOs that help out and of course colleagues. Colleagues help a lot and they have dome many things on their own initiative and they have paid money out of their own pockets", Maria told us. Where possible, mothers are kept together with their children. Beyond the border guard stations and centres, they are, however, separated from their male partners. In *Petrou Ralli*, a number are searching for their boyfriends, unclear where they may be held.

For those who are incarcerated, the meaning of the high walls of *Petrou Ralli*, the metal doors on their rooms and their concrete bunks is clear: "It's a prison, you know." Ana said bitterly, "We can't do anything. We can't move" (Dominican Republic). Staff members were rather less sure. Many recognised the penal in the administrative environment. Vassilis was blunt:

> Look, the official name of this place is 'special centre for hosting foreigners'. But in essence it is a prison. The difference is that we are dealing with administrative issues. We don't have any criminals here. But yes we imprison them.

Others, like Xenia, were less sure:

> I don't know whether I should call this a detention centre or a prison. They stay here for a long time. To begin with it was 3 months, now it is 6 months. It's on the verge of a detention centre and a prison, leaning towards a prison.

Certain staff members were quick to differentiate their job from that of a prison officer. "I don't feel like I work in a prison", a female detention officer called Anastasia confidently asserted. However, the distinction was of cold comfort, she recognised. Unlike prison, "where you end up in... because you have committed a crime [s]ome people don't understand why they are being detained. They can't understand the process of having legal documents." Such lack of clarity, she went on,

> affects my work and how I deal with these women. Women end up being detained here for months under difficult conditions with nothing to do and no one to talk to. It's extremely complicated. Some women stay in here for quite some time and they go crazy. One Nigerian had been here for 6 months and she went crazy and drank the shampoo we give them in a cup and took some pills. We took her to the hospital. You have to stay calm because there is a very thin line dividing sanity from craziness in here.

As in other countries, the slippage between prisons and detention centres is both a defining characteristic of these places of confinement and a particularly productive part of them, offering a shifting justification of a practice that, in a mobile world, otherwise makes little ethical or practical sense (Bosworth 2012, 2013; Hall 2012). Detention centres, particularly in a country like Greece, where the numbers of unauthorised arrivals continue to grow, cannot stem the flow of migration. Instead, their role is largely symbolic, part of a story told by the state about its capacity to govern, an account that, under current circumstances in Greece, must be made ever more urgently even as it rings increasingly hollow.

4 Detainees

Detainees are key to the narrative of state sovereignty. At the time of the research, the three largest groups of female detainees originated from Georgia, Nigeria and Afghanistan. Staff usually differentiated between the women according to national stereotypes. According to Xenia, for instance:

> The Chinese are an extremely disciplined nation. They learn discipline the moment they are born. And these are the women that are the quietest here, you can't hear them, you forget they are here.

She went on:

> Georgians, for example, get along with everyone, they have no issues. Albanians the same. Nigerians form a clique, they are very selective because they face racism because of their color. . .. Ukrainians and Russians hang around together because they are sly and the others don't follow.

Such accounts were also heavily gendered. As Angel-Ajani (2003) found a decade ago, certain women were considered particularly sexualised. Sometimes the blame lay with them; at other times it was attributed to their national culture. "Women", Vassilis asserted, "in their countries are like animals", a view shared by other staff members too. "Women have to be animals", Xenia opined, they must "be uneducated, not knowing what's going on around them, have babies all the time". Anxious not to sound racist, usually the police blame the broader economic and migration context in which Greece finds itself. "I am not racist, ok?" Alex said defensively. "I am not racist. And I believe that nobody is. It's logical and consequential to have some feelings of racism when Greece is full of immigrants."

Women are not only condemned by detention staff as individual failed women, but as emblematic of the cultural failings of entire national and/or ethnic groups. "Women were living in another world where they had no rights", Maria explained, where "they had nothing. . . It's the quality of life. In their countries they might not have anything to eat, they didn't have anything to survive on. . . So when they see us it's different. It's like they know, or maybe they have read, that Greece is something different."

Despite the evident objectification of women by the staff, both female and male, women attempt to assert their own narratives and interpretations of detention. Following the initial shock of being put behind bars, "I was crying and crying", Irema from Georgia angrily highlights the pointlessness and injustice of detention:

> There is no point in keeping us here 3, 4 and 5 months and then give me a paper for one month to ask for political asylum. But even if I get a red card what can I do? If you don't give me a work permit how I work? Always will have problems. And then you, the government, tells me to go and steal, do something bad to survive in Greece. Why do they keep me here then?

Women migrants describe their aspirations for employment and safety, to support their families back in their countries. The Greek immigration detention system, though ignorant about their immediate needs for some recreational activities, "We don't do anything here" (Yasmin, Iraq), "I need books to read" (Liyana, Dominican Republic), "We don't go outside, never" (Amra, Georgia), does not terminate their dreams. For many, detention is just one step in the journey from their country to a better life in Greece or in Europe. Women rarely sound unprepared for their time post release. They plan to go straight away into the already strained Athenian job market.

5 Conclusion

In winter 2012, a UN envoy visited 11 of Greece's detention centres. Headed by François Crepeau, the UN special rapporteur on migrant human rights, the envoy found shocking conditions across the country:

> The Canadian official said he saw infants behind bars at an Athens police station, a group of Afghan children living under an underpass at the port of Patras, and a cramped detention centre near the Greek-Turkish border where newly arrived migrants can be held indefinitely. "Twenty-eight people are held in a small room. The beds are concrete slabs. The toilets are filthy. There is no artificial light. These are shocking places," said Crepeau, who has also visited Tunisia, Turkey and Italy. Most of the Greek detention facilities he visited lacked heating and hot water and the detainees complained about insufficient and poor quality of food, lack of soap and other hygiene products, clothing and blankets (Agence France Press 2012).

Crepeau has urged for a coherent strategy to improve services for migrants, rather than construct more detention centres. In the current political climate, however, his words are unlikely to have much of an effect.

Earlier that same year, the Greek government, funded by allocations from the European External Border Fund worth approximately 10 million euro, began to put in place its most concerted effort thus far to tighten border control. Codenamed Xenios Zeus, it seeks not only to seal the Evros border with Turkey but also to remove irregular immigrants from the centre of Athens and the rest of the country. Immigration detention plays an important role in this plan.

Since the beginning of the operation in August 2012, 65,767 foreign nationals have been brought in for questioning, of whom 4145 have been arrested and detained for not fulfilling the legal residence requirements, and 6012 foreign nationals have been deported.[21] The procedure, criteria and conditions of this police operation appear to rely on perceived ethnicity as much as robust 'intelligence', veering uncomfortably close to discriminatory mass arrests. The outcome for those without papers is poor: administrative detention awaiting deportation, in overcrowded detention facilities either at the Attica Aliens Police Directorate or other temporary detention facilities in Athens or northern Greece. As the number of arrests has dramatically risen, already deplorable detention conditions reach new

[21] http://www.astynomia.gr/index.php?option=ozo_content&lang=%27..%27&perform=view&id=23632&Itemid=1027&lang=.

low standards. As yet, the capacity of detention centres remains small and there are neither sufficient personnel nor enough funds to pay for more.

Contemporary practices of detention and border control in Greece are justified by concerns about European border security as much as they are facilitated by a rise of intolerance and the far right. The practices, facilitated by racialised tropes about dangerous and undeserving 'Others', not only raise questions about the capacity of a democracy for exclusion, but they remind us that border control is related at fundamental levels to beliefs about what it means to be recognised as a person in a world divided by global inequalities. In the words of Judith Butler, "Part of the very problem of contemporary political life is that not everyone counts as a subject" (Butler 2010, p. 31). Those, whose subjecthood we deny, are precarious, existing outside our usual ethical and normative frames and expectations, as well as sometimes outside the law. They are 'ungrievable', expendable, unrecognizable (Kaufman and Bosworth 2013).

By segregating foreigners behind bars, detention centres materially, and metaphorically, excise those within them from the wider Greek community, erasing their subjectivity and refusing them the benefits of shared group membership. In so doing, rather than stemming the flow of racist sentiment, they uphold and amplify it. That they do this, within a human-rights-based framework, is particularly troubling. When asked about the living conditions of Amygdaleza detention centre, Mr Dendias, the Minister of Public Protection, was clear: "We make sure we follow European standards. However, conditions are not ideal, this is not a hotel. The logic is that 'humanely acceptable deficiencies' will force irregulars out of Greece."[22]

References

Aas K (2011) 'Crimmigrant' bodies and bona fide travellers: surveillance, citizenship and global government. Theor Criminol 15(3):331–346

Aas K, Bosworth M (eds) (2013) The borders of punishment: migration, citizenship and social exclusion. Oxford University Press, Oxford

Agence France Press (2012) Migrants in Greece face 'shocking' conditions: UN envoy. 3 December 2012. Available at: http://www.unhcr.org/cgi-bin/texis/vtx/refdaily?pass=463ef21123&id=50bda25d5

Angel-Ajani A (2003) A question of dangerous races? Punishment Soc 5(4):433–448

Barker V (2013) Nordic exceptionalism revisited: explaining the paradox of a janus-faced regime. Theor Criminol 17(1):5–25

Bosworth M (2012) Subjectivity and identity in detention: punishment and society in a global age. Theor Criminol 16(3):123–140

Bosworth M (2013) Can immigration detention be legitimate? In: Aas K, Bosworth M (eds) The borders of punishment: migration, citizenship and social exclusion. Oxford University Press, Oxford, pp 149–165

Bosworth M (2014) Inside immigration detention. Oxford University Press, Oxford

[22] Autopsia, 04/10/2012. http://www.alphatv.gr/Microsites/Autopsia/Shows/04-10-2012.aspx.

Bosworth M, Guild M (2008) Governing through migration control: security and citizenship in Britain. Br J Criminol 48(6):703–719
Bosworth M, Kellezi B (2014) Developing a measure of the quality of life in detention. Prison Serv J 205:10–15
Bosworth M, Slade G (2014) In search of recognition: gender and staff-detainee relations in a British immigration detention centre. Punishment Soc 16(2):169–186
Butler J (2010) Frames of war: when is life grievable? Verso, London
Chindea A, Majkowska-Tomkin M, Mattila H, Pastor I (2008) Migration in Greece: a country profile 2008. International Organization for Migration (IOM), Geneva.
Cornelisse G (2010) Immigration detention and human rights: rethinking territorial sovereignty. Brill, Amsterdam
De Genova N, Peultz N (eds) (2010) The deportation regime: sovereignty, space, and the freedom of movement. Duke University Press, Durham
Emke-Poulopoulou I (2001) Trafficking in women and girls for the sex trade: the case of Greece. Greek Rev Soc Res Special Iss Gender Int Migr Focus Greece 110(A):271–307
Fakiolas R (2003) Regularising undocumented immigrants in Greece: procedures and effects. J Ethn Migr Stud 29(3):535–562
Fassin D (2011) Policing borders, producing boundaries. The governmentality of immigration in dark times. Annu Rev Anthropol 40:213–226
Fili A (2013) The maze of immigration detention in Greece: a case study of the Athens Airport detention facility. Prison Serv J 205:34–38
Gerard A, Pickering S (2012) The crime and punishment of Somali women's extra-legal arrival in Malta. Br J Criminol 52(3):514–533
Gill N (2009) Governmental mobility: the power effects of the movement of detained Asylum seekers around Britain's detention estate. Polit Geogr 28:186–196
Grewcock M (2011) Punishment, deportation and parole: the detention and removal of former prisoners under section 501 *Migration Act* 1958. Aust N Z J Criminol 44(1):56–73
Guia M, Van der Woude M, Van der Leun J (eds) (2012) Social control and justice: crimmigration in the age of fear. Eleven Publishing, Den Haag
Gutierrez-Rodriguez E (2010) Migration, domestic work and affect: a decolonial approach on value and the feminization of labour. Routledge, Abingdon
Hall A (2010) These people could be anyone: fear and contempt (and empathy) in a British immigration removal centre. J Ethn Migr Stud 36(6):881–898
Hall A (2012) Border watch: cultures of immigration, detention and control. Pluto, London
Johansen N (2013) Governing the funnel of expulsion: Agamben, the dynamics of force and minimalist biopolitics. In: Aas K, Bosworth M (eds) The borders of punishment: migration, citizenship and social exclusion. Oxford University Press, Oxford, pp 257–272
Kaufman E (2012) Finding foreigners: race and the politics of memory in British prisons. Popul Space Place 18(6):701–714
Kaufman E (2013) Hubs and Spokes: the transformation of the British prison. In: Aas K, Bosworth M (eds) The borders of punishment: migration, citizenship and social exclusion. Oxford University Press, Oxford
Kaufman E, Bosworth M (2013) Prison and national identity: citizenship, punishment and the sovereign state. In: Scott D (ed) Why prison? Cambridge University Press, Cambridge
Lazaridis G (2001) Trafficking and prostitution. The growing exploitation of migrant women in Greece. Eur J Women's Stud 8(1):67–102
Lazos G (1997) The foreign prostitute in contemporary Greece. Some important social and logical-emotional parameters. In: Dimitriou S (ed) Forms and production mechanisms of social exclusion. Ideokinisi, Athens
Leerkes A, Broeders D (2010) A case of mixed motives? Formal and informal functions of administrative immigration detention. Br J Criminol 50(5):830–850
Makaremi C (2009) Governing borders in France: from extra territorial to humanitarian confinement. Can J Law Soc 24(3):411–432

Mountz A (2012) Seeking asylum: human smuggling at the border. University of Minnesota Press, Minneapolis
Pickering S (ed) (2014) Routledge handbook of migration and crime. Routledge, Abingdon
Pickering S, Cochrane B (2013) Irregular cross deaths and gender: where, how and why women die crossing borders. Theor Criminol 17(1):27–48
Pratt A (2005) Securing borders: detention and deportation in Canada. UBC Press, Vancouver
Skordas A (2002) The new immigration law in Greece: modernization on the wrong track. Eur J Migr Law 4:23–48
Triandafyllidou A (2009) Greek immigration policy at the turn of the 21st century. Lack of political will or purposeful mismanagement? Eur J Migr Law 11:159–177
Triandafyllidou A, Veikou M (2002) The hierarchy of Greekness: ethnic and national identity considerations in Greek immigration policy. Ethnicities 2(2):189–208
Vaiou D (2003) In the interstices of the city: Albanian women in Athens. Espace Popul Soc 3: 373–385
Weber L, Pickering S (2011) Globalisation and borders: death at the global frontier. Palgrave Macmillan, London
Welch M, Schuster L (2005) Detention of asylum seekers in the UK and USA: deciphering noisy and quiet constructions. Punishment Soc 7(4):397–417
Yuval-Davis N (1997) Women, citizenship and difference. Fem Rev 57:4–27

Reports

Amnesty International (2010) Greece: irregular migrants and asylum-seeker routinely detained in substandard conditions. Amnesty International Publications, London
CPT (2010) Report to the Government of Greece on the visit to Greece carried out by the European Committee for the Prevention of Torture and Inhuman or Degrading Treatment or Punishment (CPT) from 17 to 29 September 2009. Strassburg
CPT (2011) Public statement concerning Greece. Strassbourg
Human Rights Watch (2008) Stuck in a revolving door: Iraqis and other asylum seekers and migrants at the Greece/Turkey entrance to the European Union. USA
Pro Asyl (2007) The truth may be bitter but it must be told: the situation of refugees in the Aegean and the practices of the Greek coast guard. Frankfurt a. M. and Athens
Platform for International Cooperation on Undocumented Migrants (2012) http://picum.org/it/attualita/bolletino/38052/

Changing Practices Regarding the Implementation of Entry Bans in Belgian Migration Policy Since 1980

Steven De Ridder and Maartje van der Woude

Abstract In this chapter, we will address the implications of the latest milestone in Belgian migration policy depicting the increasing political interest in managing irregular migration: the implementation of the Return Directive 2008/115/EC. Until 2012, irregular migrants had to represent 'a threat to the public order or national security' under the Foreigners Act of 1980 in order to be eligible for an entry ban (of 10 years). Whereas the number of entry bans remained relatively low over time, this relative leniency was more recently reversed and revived in numbers due to the implementation of the Return Directive 2008/115/EC in the Belgian Foreigners Act. As a result, under the umbrella of representing a "threat to the public order or national security," the possibility to implement both short-term as well as long-term entry bans was eased up. Hence, the legal framework created on the European level gave the Belgian government the opportunity to meet the long-promised political but foremost symbolic goal of strengthening migration policy.

1 Introduction

In the majority of European Member States, including Belgium, people trying to enter or stay on the national territory illegally face a prison sentence and/or a fine (European Union Agency for Fundamental Rights 2011, pp. 42–44).[1] The widespread use of visa regulations, more restrictive requirements over granting a

[1] Belgium, Cyprus, Denmark, Estonia, Finland, France, Germany, Greece, Ireland, Lithuania, Luxembourg, Romania, Sweden, and the United Kingdom impose a prison sentence. Italy uses a fine as punishment. Under certain conditions, irregular entry or residency is considered a crime in Latvia and the Netherlands. Hereafter referred to as "Foreigners Act."

S. De Ridder (✉)
Department of Criminology, Vrije Universiteit Brussel, Brussel, Belgium

Research Group 'Crime & Society' (CRiS), Brussel, Belgium
e-mail: steven.de.ridder@vub.ac.be

M. van der Woude
Department of Criminal Law, Institute of Criminal Law & Criminology at Leiden Law School, Leiden, The Netherlands
e-mail: m.a.h.vanderwoude@law.leidenuniv.nl

M.J. Guia et al. (eds.), *Immigration Detention, Risk and Human Rights*,
DOI 10.1007/978-3-319-24690-1_10

(temporary) residence permit, administrative detention, expulsions and entry bans can be seen as important elements of migration policies' arsenal available in the "fight against illegal migration" (Broeders and Engbersen 2007). The possibility to simultaneously implement penal provisions as well as the numerous administrative measures under migration law (Aliverti 2012, p. 512) perpetuates the *cumulative punitive character* of migration control (van der Leun and De Ridder 2013). Although there is no consensus among the European Member States on the punishment of irregular migration in itself, it has been observed that migration policies have become stricter over the years within "Fortress Europe" (Albrecht 2002), largely contributing to the securitization of migration (Huysmans 2000; van der Woude et al. 2014). In addition to the increasing number of expulsions in Europe, the pace of expulsion procedures is speeding up, resulting in policies of "accelerated removals" (Fekete 2011).

During the nineteenth and the beginning of the twentieth century, Belgium was a rather lenient country in terms of migration law enforcement (Caestecker 2010). This liberal migration policy became politically contested after the economic crisis during the 1930s (De Bock 2008, p. 163). In this respect, the predecessor of the current Act of 15 December 1980 on the entry, stay, settlement, and expulsion of foreign nationals, the Foreigners Act of 28 March 1952, ended the lenient Belgian migration policy. From that moment on, foreign nationals were politically rather viewed as potential threats to the Belgian nation-state (De Bock 2008). The current Foreigners Act should thus be considered as a compromise between strict migration law enforcement on the one hand, while the Act on the other hand also leads to a strengthening of procedural safeguards aimed at protecting migrants against the arbitrary enforcement of the law. However, throughout the 1990s the 1980 Foreigners Act was repeatedly modified. These modifications included the criminalization of several migration law violations as a result of which the Act seemed to reflect an overall stricter stance towards migration and migration control (Foblets and Van den Eeckhout 1999).

At the time the Foreigners Act came into force, imprisonment was the main instrument for managing irregular migration and implementing expulsion measures. Since the late 1980s and the 1990s, closed administrative detention centres have become the main liberty-depriving instrument used in this regard. Belgian Administrations have repeatedly and explicitly promised to intensify the efforts to increase the number of expulsions of irregular migrants. In this respect, they echo the Migration Administration which recommends "a strong and efficient (forced) return policy" (Bergans et al. 2010, p. 89). In recent years, the most fundamental change of the Belgian migration policy with regard to expulsion procedures came about on a legislative level following the implementation of Directive 2008/115/EC of the European Parliament and of the Council of 16 December 2008 on common standards and procedures in Member States for returning illegally staying third-country nationals in Belgian Law.[2] For the first time, "illegal residence," "expulsion," "return" were explicitly defined in article 1 of the Foreigners Act. More importantly, the expulsion procedure and particularly the implementation of entry bans joining expulsion decisions were modified.

This chapter describes the implications following the implementation of the Return Directive and discusses relevant international case law of the ECJ in this respect. *Firstly*, we will present the conditions to legally enter and stay on the Belgian territory and describe the different expulsion measures that the Migration Administration can implement. *Secondly*, we will emphasize the importance of the concept "threat to the public order or national security" in the Foreigners Act and its implications regarding the implementation of entry bans. We will argue that—besides the procedural safeguards that the Return Directive aimed to guarantee—its implementation has mainly strengthened Belgium's migration policy with regard to expulsion procedures and enlarged the implications of being considered a "threat to the public order or national security."

2 Entry and Expulsion as Two Sides of One Coin

2.1 Legal and Illegal Entry and Stay on the Belgian Territory

According to article 2 of the Foreigners Act, legal entry to the Belgian territory is only possible by passing an authorized crossing point whereby the requested (identification, travelling, and/or visa) documents must be submitted. In order to legally reside on the territory after entering, the Foreigners Act foresees different conditions for a short-term stay and long-term stay.

A *short-term stay* is limited to a period of 3 months and requires the granting of a visa, depending on the country of origin. This stay applies to, i.e., tourists, businessmen, and journalists. Within 3 working days after arrival in Belgium, the individual should register with the municipality, except for those who stay in a hotel; EU citizens have until 8 days after entry to register. Non-EU nationals only legally enter the Schengen territory if they have received an entry stamp at the border.

A *long-term stay* exceeds the period of 3 months and can be obtained via different admission procedures within the Foreigners Act: (1) long-term residence status for migrants and their family members, (2) family reunification, (3) immigration of students to study full time in an accredited educational institution, (4) the status of victim of trafficking or smuggling, (5) the status of unaccompanied alien minors, (6) immigration in order to take up employment in Belgium or to follow

[2] Directive 2008/115/EC of the European Parliament and of the Council of 16 December 2008 on common standards and procedures in Member States for returning illegally staying third-country nationals, *Pb. L.* 24 December 2012, 348/98 implemented by the Act of 19 January 2012 modifying the Foreigners Act of 1980, *BS* 17 February 2012, 11.412.

(professional) training, (7) the asylum procedure under the Geneva Convention, and (8) the regularization procedure.

Every violation of these conditions relating to the entry to the territory or the application for short-term or long-term stay in Belgium is considered as illegal entry or stay.

According to article 3 of the Foreigners Act, a person *enters* the territory illegally when the required documents cannot be presented or the purpose of the stay and living conditions in Belgium are not sufficiently demonstrated. According to article 7 of the Foreigners Act, the conditions for illegal *stay* are met when the person:

(1) is residing in the country without the required documents or is overstaying the duration of the residence permit;
(2) is affected by one of the diseases or disabilities listed in the Annex of the Foreigners Act;
(3) is working without authorization;
(4) has to be transferred from Belgium to a country with which Belgium has international relations due to the presence of bound under international conventions or agreements or vice versa.

Some specifications are equally applicable for illegal *entry* and illegal *stay* as well when the person:

(1) has not enough financial resources for the duration of the stay, the return to the country of origin or third country where he is admissible and when he has not legally allowed to earn the necessary funds;
(2) is considered as a threat to Belgium's or other Schengen countries' international relations or a *threat to the public order or national security* or is recorded in the Schengen SIS data system[3] or has returned within the period of an active reentry ban.

The group of irregular migrants thus consists of both those who do not comply with the entry conditions when entering the territory as well as the so-called overstayers as a result of the expiration of their visa or (temporary) residence permit. In many European states, "visa overstaying is the most relevant inflow into irregular residence" (Clandestino 2009, p. 7). This diversity among irregular migrants is also reflected in the definition of "illegal residence" within the Foreigners Act as "the presence on the territory of an irregular migrant who does not or no longer meets the conditions for the entry or stay at the territory."[4]

[3] See Sect. 3 of this chapter.

[4] Art. 1 Act of 19 January 2012 modifying the Foreigners Act of 1980, *BS* 17 February 2012, 11.412.

2.2 *First Criminalization, Afterwards Expulsion*

In Belgium, both illegal border crossing and illegal (over)stay on the territory are criminalized, and breaking the law can result in a prison sentence of 8 days up to 3 months according to article 75 of the Foreigners Act, a fine of 26–200€ or a combination of both sanctions. In addition, repeated violation of these conditions within a period of 3 months is punishable by a prison sentence from 1 month up to 1 year and a fine of 100–1000€. The latter penalty also applies to irregular migrants who do not comply with a Ministerial or Royal Decree of expulsion according to article 76 of the Foreigners Act. According to Bouckaert (2007, p. 39), Belgian Regional Courts do not sentence irregular migrants solely on the basis of violating the entry or stay conditions. Today, irregular migrants can be found in prison as remand prisoners, mentally ill prisoners, or prisoners who are convicted due to criminal law violations. Notwithstanding that several convicted irregular migrants serve an additional sentence due to their illegal status, imprisonment solely on the grounds of migration law violations is scarce.[5] Irregular migrants who have violated the conditions in the Foreigners Act are detained in closed administrative detention centres that were opened during the late 1980s and the 1990s.[6]

Besides the penal provisions and the question whether they are applied, the Foreigners Act enacts different expulsion measures that can be applied depending on where the irregular migrant is geographically apprehended: at the border or on the territory.

2.2.1 Order to Leave the Territory

Irregular migrants apprehended *at the borders* of the Belgian territory without meeting the requirements for legal entry as mentioned in article 3 of the Foreigners Act receive a "bevel tot terugdrijving"[7] from the Migration Administration. This means that the irregular migrant is obliged to return to the territory he left before coming to Belgium.

Irregular migrants apprehended *on Belgian territory* without meeting the requirements for a legal short- or long-term stay enacted in article 7 of the

[5] Lists of convicted irregular migrants prioritized by the Migration Administration for expulsion between 2008 and 2012 ($N = 3.542$) indicate only three cases of convictions for illegal entry to or stay on the Belgian territory: Corr. Leuven, 12 June 2006, LE 55.F1.101284.06; Corr. Leuven, 4 September 2006, LE 55.F1.101286.06; Corr. Leuven, 21 November 2005, 55.L2101049/05. A fourth case consisted of a person who was found in need of medical care at the time of his arrest for violation of a Ministerial Decree.

[6] Closed administrative detention facilities were opened at Melsbroek (1988), Merksplas (1993), Steenokkerzeel (1994), Brugge (1995), Zaventem (1996), and Vottem (1999).

[7] "Bevel tot terugdrijving" can be literally translated in English as "order to refoulement."

Foreigners Act are subjected to an "order to leave the territory."[8] It is the most frequently used expulsion measure by the Migration Administration. It states that the irregular migrant can no longer stay on the Belgian territory or the Schengen area and has to leave within a certain period after the order entered into force.[9] However, since the responsibility to actually leave within the set time frame lies with the irregular migrant himself, many irregular migrants remain illegally on the Belgian territory, leading to a poor enforceability of this specific expulsion measure (Bergans et al. 2010, pp. 88–89).

Following article 11 of the Return Directive, an entry ban of up to 5 years *shall* be implemented along with an "order to leave the territory" "if no period for voluntary departure has been granted, or if the obligation to return has not been complied with. In other cases return decisions *may* be accompanied by an entry ban." In case a third-country national represents a serious threat to public policy, public security, or national security, the entry ban can exceed the period of 5 years.

The Migration Administration has estimated that in 2007, 8763 or 36.6 % out of the 23,938 irregular migrants who received an order to leave the territory had already been imposed the same decision in the past (Bergans et al. 2010, p. 89). Under the current regime, these irregular migrants would be eligible for an entry ban of up to 5 years under article 11 of the Return Directive.

Article 11 §3 of the Return Directive also enables the Member States to use a great deal of discretion with regard to imposing entry bans as they are given the possibility to "refrain from issuing, withdrawing or suspending an entry ban in individual cases for humanitarian reasons" and "may withdraw or suspend an entry ban in individual cases or certain categories of cases of other reasons."

2.2.2 The Combination of an Order to Leave the Territory with Administrative Detention

A stricter variant of the "order to leave the territory" is the "order to leave the territory combined with administrative detention in view of expulsion." Between 2005 and 2013, a minimum of 65.4 % and a maximum of 81.3 % of the irregular migrants who were administratively detained for the first time were deported afterwards.[10] However, this requires the identification of the irregular migrant and the collaboration of the Consulate of his country of origin in order to obtain a

---

[8] Hereafter referred to as "order to leave the territory." Several categories of irregular migrants can receive this decision, i.e., (1) intercepted by the police as illegally staying on the territory, (2) when receiving a negative decision following an application for a residence status, (3) after being eligible for (early) release from prison after having served (partially) the prison sentence ....

[9] The period depends on the Bureau within the Migration Administration that takes the decision. In general, they grant the irregular migrant a period between 7 and 30 days in order to realize by own means his "voluntary" departure.

[10] 2005: 76.3 %; 2006: 81.3 %; 2007: 72.3 %; 2008: 71.4 %; 2009: 65.4 %; 2010: 68.1 %; 2011: 74.7 %; 2012: 78.3 %; 2013: 79.4 % (Migration Administration 2014, p. 175).

travel document (Ellerman 2010; Engbersen and Broeders 2011, p. 879). In case one of these actors is unwilling to collaborate, the expulsion can often not be realized and the Migration Administration will be forced to change its decision to a "plain" "order to leave the territory," which, due to the abovementioned low enforceability of these orders, often leads to a continuation of the illegal stay.

According to the Return Directive, countries have to apply the principles of proportionality and effectiveness and thus implement the least coercive measures possible to enforce an expulsion. With regard to these leading principles of proportionality and effectiveness, the ECJ ruled in the *El Dridi* case vs. Italy that the use of a prison sentence as a consequence of the noncompliance with an order to leave the territory was ruled in opposition with the Return Directive (Mitsilegas 2013) as it would delay the implementation of an expulsion and thereby undermine an efficient expulsion policy and procedure (Weis 2011). However, the *El Dridi* case suggests that a prison sentence cannot be implemented during the period that the person is ordered to leave the country, in Belgium generally between 7 and 30 days, but still can be implemented afterwards. In the *Achughbabian* case vs. France, the ECJ has ruled that a prison sentence can be imposed on a third-country national when all other procedures are in accordance with the Return Directive and in particular when there is a risk of absconding or when the third country national concerned avoids or hampers the preparation of the return or removal process. In the *Sagor* case vs. Italy, however, the ECJ held that according to the Return Directive, detention can only be implemented as long as the Member States guarantee that the expulsion will take place as quickly as possible.

Given the described policy on irregular migration in Belgium above, the question arises how Belgium will comply with the Return Directive and the ECJ rulings in the *El Dridi* case, the *Achughbabian* case, and the *Sagor* case, particularly in cases of noncompliance by irregular migrants with expulsion measures. In this respect, it is important to bear in mind that article 16 of the Return Directive doesn't forbid the punishment of illegal entry or illegal stay on the territory. Although the literature states that few irregular migrants are punished for solely entering or staying on the Belgian territory (Bouckaert 2007), it remains legally enacted and thus the prison sentence *could* be enforced when the judiciary would decide to do so. Considering the ruling in the *El Dridi* case, it seems interesting to mention that once an order to leave the territory is issued, it can always be revoked by the Migration Administration. This would make it legally possible to impose the prison sentence for (repeated) illegal entry to or stay on the Belgian territory enacted in the Foreigners Act of 1980. This would of course require an active collaboration between the Public Prosecutor and the Migration Administration and a sentencing attitude of the Regional Courts in line with the aim of expulsion. After all, as long as sheer punishment isn't implemented in view of expulsion, it doesn't fall within the scope of the Return Directive. However, the legally enacted aims underlying decision making can differ from the daily practices of law enforcement.[11]

3 Threat to the Public Order or National Security

A crucial and central concept within the Foreigners Act is "the threat to the public order or national security." According to article 20 of the Foreigners Act, due to violations of the entry terms or when they are considered a threat to the public order or national security, irregular migrants can receive a Ministerial Decree of Expulsion.[12] This particular type of expulsion measure has always been joined by an entry ban to the Belgian territory for 10 years.[13] At present, this entry ban is applicable in the entire Schengen Area, and the person will be registered in the Schengen Information System (SIS) according to article 96 of the Schengen Agreement.[14] In order to fully understand the implications of the Return Directive for the Belgian practice and decision making on expulsions, it is important to highlight this far-reaching concept.

Whereas the concept "threat to the public order or national security" has a broader scope than just migration law, in this chapter we will consider it as a result of criminal law violations and the implications within migration law enforcement. The main reason is that before the Return Directive was implemented in the

[11] When Belgian correctional judges do implement the prison sentence for illegal entry to or stay on the Belgian territory, in some cases of irregular migrants appearing in court due to criminal law violations, the judicial motivation of the Belgian correctional judges is too limited to conduct an analysis with regard to the rulings of the ECJ and the legal provisions in the Return Directive as it mostly only states that the irregular migrant is in opposition with the Foreigners Act. Whether or not judges take into account the noncompliance of irregular migrants with former orders to leave the country or expulsion measures is thus difficult to ascertain.

[12] Hereafter referred to as "Ministerial Decree." In Dutch translated as "Ministerieel Besluit tot Terugwijzing." Article 20 of the Foreigners Act of 1980 also enacts the possibility to implement a Royal Decree of Expulsion (in Dutch: Koninklijk Besluit tot Uitzetting) to irregular migrants with a long-term residence permit when they represent a threat to the public order or national security.

[13] We use "Ministerial Decree" and "Royal Decree" to differentiate between both measures, and we use the concept "reentry ban" when we refer to all the measures that consist of a prohibition to return to the Schengen area, whether it is an entry ban, a Ministerial Decree, or a Royal Decree.

[14] The police will become aware of the fact the person is considered a threat by one of the countries of the Schengen area once he is intercepted within this area. In addition, applications for a residence permit or a visa will not be possible as long as the decision isn't revoked. Bouckaert (2007, p. 71) notices that due to the signing of the Schengen Agreement, Belgium is obliged to take the necessary measures regarding persons who are a threat to the public order and national security of other countries of the Schengen area. Nevertheless, this is not explicitly enacted in the Foreigners Act as the latter explicitly refers to the public order and national security of the (Belgian) country.

Foreigners Act, it was solely the Bureau Detainees of the Migration Administration[15] that was competent for issuing Ministerial Decrees. Over the last three decades, the number of issued Ministerial Decrees has been relatively low: between 1994 and 2009, the total number of Ministerial Decrees varies between 250 and 400 (Bergans et al. 2010, p. 92). As the Bureau Detainees has the general competence of decision making regarding foreign national prisoners, it makes sense that the decision to issue a Ministerial Decree was the result of convictions following criminal law violations.

3.1 Definition

The Foreigners Act speaks of "public order or national security." However, according to Herreman and De Groot ([1967] in De Ceuster 1982, p. 105), the concepts "public rest" and the "national security/security of the country" are aspects of the broader concept "public order." In some cases, also the (threat to the) public health is mentioned.[16]

The Foreigners Act makes a difference between (1) being accounted to violate,[17] (2) a violation of,[18] and (3) a severe violation[19] of the public order or national security. However, neither the Foreigners Act nor the Parliamentary preparatory documents clearly define under which conditions a person represents a particular threat (De Ceuster 1982, p. 106).

De Ceuster (1982) also emphasizes the facultative character of considering a person as a threat. In this respect, it seems crucial to elucidate that the legislature did not want to connect the implementation of an expulsion to a criminal conviction. The legislature argued that this practice would result in a double punishment and deprives the migrant in possession of a (long-term) residence permit of his right of reintegration after having served a prison sentence. Due to this facultative character, neither the frequency nor the length of the prison sentence nor the time span in which the violations need to occur nor the type of criminal offense is legally defined within the Foreigners Act. Currently, all violations of the Criminal Law can be taken into account by the Migration Administration.[20]

[15] Hereafter referred to as "Bureau Detainees."

[16] I.e., articles 10, 10bis, 11, 43, 46, 61/7.

[17] Art. 3, 3°, art. 11 section 1, art. 15, art. 19, art. 58 section 1 of the Foreigners Act with regard to conditions to enter the Belgian territory and the authorization for settlement.

[18] Art. 7 section 1, 3° and art. 20 section 1 of the Foreigners Act with regard to the order to leave the territory and the Ministerial Decree.

[19] Art. 20 section 2 and art. 21 of the Foreigners Act with regard to the Royal Decree.

[20] In the Parliamentary preparatory documents, the competent Minister did determine that a severe threat to the public order referred to hold-ups, drug trade, sex offences with regard to one's own children, etc. (see De Ceuster 1982, p. 107).

Furthermore, art. 43, 2° of the Foreigners Act states: "the measures taken for reasons of public order or national security must comply with the principle of proportionality and shall be based exclusively on the personal conduct of the individual concerned. Previous criminal convictions shall not automatically provoke these measures [being considered as a threat to the public order or national security]. The conduct of the individual has to constitute an acute, real and sufficiently serious threat to a fundamental interest of society. Motivations that do not relate to an individual case or relate to general preventive reasons cannot be put forward as justifications." A similar reasoning was already stated by the Court of Justice in the case 30/77 *Regina versus Bouchereau* (27 October 1977).

As a clear definition or transparent criteria determining who represents a threat to the public order or national security are not enacted, the discretionary power of the Migration Administration during the decision making is high. In practice, the interpretation is predominantly based on the severity and circumstances of the irregular migrants' criminal law violation. The motivations of the convictions by the Regional Courts often play a crucial role as they allow the Migration Administration to comprehensively describe the elements why the irregular migrant represents a threat.

3.2 Consequences Under the Foreigners Act Following the Return Directive

Since the implementation of the Return Directive in the Foreigners Act in 2012,[21] once an irregular migrant is subjected to an "order to leave the territory," the Migration Administration has also the possibility to implement an entry ban of up to 5 years to all irregular migrants and an entry ban of more than 5 years in case a third-country national represents a serious threat to public policy, public security, or national security (article 11 Return Directive). In comparison to the limited implementation of entry bans in the past following a Ministerial Decree, the Migration Administration now enforces a larger number of entry bans as the Ministerial Decree is no longer the only possibility to implement a reentry ban along with an expulsion measure. According to the European Migration Network, Belgium imposed 3309 entry bans in 2012[22] and 6245 in 2013 (2014, p. 14).[23]

A second crucial observation is that more criminal law violations constitute a threat to the public order or national security and thus trigger an entry ban. Irregular migrants who only committed minor criminal law violations and who would only

[21] Act of 19 January 2012 modifying the Migration Act of 1980, *BS* 17 February 2012, 11.412.

[22] Only from July 1st until the end of the year.

[23] The national report on Belgium mentions different numbers: 3289 entry bans in 2012 and even 9178 entry bans in 2013. See http://www.emnbelgium.be/publication/good-practices-return-and-reintegration-irregular-migrants-belgium-and-eu-emn.

have received an "order to leave the territory" in the past are now subjected to an entry ban of more than 5 years. Notwithstanding article 43, 2°, every criminal conviction *can* invoke measures under the umbrella of "threat to the public order or national security."

Furthermore, the decision making regarding a Ministerial Decree differs significantly from the procedure to implement an entry ban together with an "order to leave the territory." In this respect, lower standards and a higher deal of discretionary power apply to the decision making on entry bans added to an order to leave the territory compared to entry bans joining a Ministerial Decree, the Migration Administration can themselves decide on the implementation of the entry ban, and the burden to prove or motivate with respect to the European Convention of Human Rights is less demanding.

It is also interesting to mention that the types of entry bans being implemented have become more diverse. Initially, the different bureaus of the Migration Administration adopted a rather standardized procedure as only entry bans of 3, 5, or 8 years were implemented. However, jurisprudence of the Council of State and the Council of Alien Law Litigation reminded the Migration Administration of article 74/11 §1 of the Foreigners Act in which the ratio of the Return Directive is absorbed. As a result, the Migration Administration has further differentiated in the implementation of entry bans. Currently, entry bans of 2 years, 3 years, 4 years, 5 years, 6 years, and 8 years are implemented.

4 Conclusion

The presented case of implementation of entry bans in Belgium clearly shows how migration policy has evolved from a rather lenient and limited approach on implementing entry bans towards a standardized implementation of entry bans joining every expulsion measure. The entry ban gives the Belgian Migration Administration additional possibilities to deal with the low enforceability of the "order to leave the territory." In their perspective, more irregular migrants are now being registered in the Schengen Information System and thereby more visible within the Schengen Area. As a result, the increased implementation of entry bans is a clear marker of the Ban-opticon (Bigo 2008). Whether or not the implementation of entry bans will actually resolve the problem of low enforceability of migration policy remains to be seen. However, the symbolical aim of dealing with irregular migration is met (Leerkes and Broeders 2010).

Moreover, whereas before the implementation of the Return Directive irregular migrants had to represent 'a threat to the public order or national security,' currently all expulsion measures are generally joined by an entry ban. In addition, a wider interpretation is given to what behavior can be considered as threatening the public order or national security and there are significantly more entry bans implemented under this umbrella. As a result, via the entry ban, in particular the application of the concept *threat of the public order or national security* has been further embedded within the Foreigners Act and has expanded the discretionary power of the Migration Administration as they can decide themselves on the length of a reentry ban implemented with every "order to leave the territory."

In the spirit of the Return Directive and the leading principles of proportionality and efficiency, affirmed by case law of the ECJ, it seems that the Belgian government has further tightened the legal net around irregular migrants, rather than primarily ameliorating the efficiency of current migration policy.

References

Act of 15 December 1980 on the entry, stay, settlement and expulsion of irregular migrants

Albrecht H-J (2002) Fortress Europe? Controlling illegal immigration. Eur J Crime Crim Law Crim Justice 10(1):1–22

Aliverti A (2012) Exploring the function of criminal law in the policing of foreigners: the decision to prosecute immigration-related offences. Soc Leg Stud 21(4):511–527

Bergans K, Cruysberghs W et al (2010) Het verwijderingsbeleid. In: Foblets MC, Vanheule D (eds) Migratie- en migrantenrecht. Recente ontwikkelingen. Brugge, die Keure, pp 69–197

Bigo D (2008) Globalized (In)Security: the field and the Ban-opticon. In: Bigo D, Tsoukala A (eds) Terror, insecurity and liberty. Illiberal practices of liberal regimes after 9/11. Routledge, Oxon/New York, pp 10–48

Bouckaert S (2007) Documentloze vreemdelingen. Grondrechtenbescherming doorheen de Belgische en internationale rechtspraak vanaf 1985. Maklu, Antwerpen–Apeldoorn

Broeders D, Engbersen G (2007) The fight against illegal migration: identification policies and immigrants' counterstrategies. Am Behav Sci 50(12):1592–1609

Caestecker F (2010) Vluchtelingen en de transformatie van het vreemdelingenbeleid in België (1860–1914). Belgisch Tijdschrift voor Nieuwste Geschiedenis (3):345–381

Clandestino Project (2009) Size and development of irregular migration to the EU. Counting the uncountable: data and trends across Europe. http://irregular-migration.net//typo3_upload/groups/31/4.Background_Information/4.2.Policy_Briefs_EN/ComparativePolicyBrief_SizeOfIrregularMigration_Clandestino_Nov09_2.pdf. Accessed 30 July 2014

De Bock J (2008) De vreemdelingenwet van 28 maart 1952. "L'étranger doit être parfait". BTNG/RBHC:159–200

De Ceuster J (1982) De invulling van de blanco-term "openbare orde" in de verblijfsregeling: het huidige beleid. Tijdschrift voor Vreemdelingenrecht (20):105–112

Ellerman A (2010) Undocumented migrants and resistance in the liberal state. Politics Soc 38 (3):408–429

Engbersen G, Broeders D (2011) Fortress Europe and the Dutch Donjon. Securitization, internal migration policy and irregular migrants' counter moves. In: Truong TD, Gasper D (eds) Transnational migration and human security. The migration-development-security nexus. Springer, Heidelberg

European Migration Network (2014) Good practices in the return and reintegration of irregular migrants: Member States' entry bans policy and use of readmission agreements between Member States and third countries. http://ec.europa.eu/dgs/home-affairs/what-we-do/networks/european_migration_network/reports/docs/emn-studies/emn_study_reentry_bans_and_readmission_agreements_final_december_2014.pdf

European Union Agency for Fundamental Rights (2011) Fundamental rights of migrants in an irregular situation in the European Union. Publications Office of the European Union, Luxembourg

Fekete L (2011) Accelerated removals: the human cost of EU deportation policies. Race Class 52(4):89–97
Foblets M-C, Van den Eeckhout V (1999) Migratiecontrole, sancties en dwangmaatregelen in het Belgische vreemdelingenrecht. Panopticon:420–457
Herreman J, De Groot T (1967) De vreemdelingenreglementering. UGA, Kortrijk-Heule
Huysmans J (2000) The European Union and the securitization of migration. J Common Market Stud 38(5):751–777
Leerkes A, Broeders D (2010) A case of mixed motives? Formal and informal functions of administrative immigration detention. Br J Criminol 50(5):830–850
Migration Administration (2014) Activity report 2013. Migration Administration, Brussel
Mitsilegas V (2013) The changing landscape of the criminalization of migration in Europe. In: Guia M, Van der Woude M, Van der Leun J (eds) Social control and justice: crimmigration in an age of fear. Eleven International Publishers, The Hague
Van Der Leun J, De Ridder S (2013) Het cumulatief punitief karakter van het migratierecht. Orde van de dag. Criminaliteit en samenleving (61):29–36
van der Woude MAH, van der Leun JP, Nijland J (2014) Crimmigration in the Netherlands. Law Soc Inq 39(3):560–579
Weis K (2011) Gevangenisstraf voor negeren uitwijzingsbevel niet conform terugkeerrichtlijn. Juristenkrant 13(229):2

Crimmigration Policies and the *Great Recession*: Analysis of the Spanish Case

José Ángel Brandariz García

Abstract Crimmigration policies, in Spain and elsewhere, have shown a complex interplay between neoliberal and sovereign rationales of control throughout the first decade of the twenty-first century.

However, the analysis of this domain of penal control should be revised in the context of the *Great Recession*. Indeed, in the Spanish case, crimmigration policies have incorporated a set of innovations in recent years. Some of them, such as the readjustment of the deportation system, can be understood from a neoliberal perspective. Others, such as changes in policing, have a more hybrid profile, in which neoliberal features encounter sovereign and neoconservative trends. Therefore, the context of the *Great Recession* requires a new analysis of the hybridization between neoliberal and sovereign devices of control in the area of crimmigration policies.

1 Introduction: Neoliberal and Sovereign Devices of Control

A scholarly body of literature which analyzes the progressive affirmation of neoliberal modes of government and, in particular, of the patterns of control derived from their technologies of power has been consolidated in the last two decades (Dean 2010; Miller and Rose 2008; Rose 1999). A prominent part of that literature bases its analysis on Foucault's concept of *governmentality* and his theory of the *sociétés de sécurité*, developed in the 1978 and 1979 courses at the *Collège de France* (Foucault 2007, 2008). Other scholars have spoken of actuarial devices of control and have drawn attention to the application of the *Law & Economics* theory to the domain of crime and punishment, as developed by the Chicago School of Economics (Harcourt 2007; O'Malley 2010; Simon and Feeley 2003).

There are reasons to believe that in several countries a certain evolution of control policies during the last few decades can be read following the paradigm of government through freedom, or in line with the actuarial rationality of risk

J.Á. Brandariz García (✉)
University of A Coruña, A Coruña, Spain
e-mail: jabrandariz@yahoo.de; branda@udc.es

M.J. Guia et al. (eds.), *Immigration Detention, Risk and Human Rights*,
DOI 10.1007/978-3-319-24690-1_11

management and the economic logic of the *Law & Economics* theory. In effect, "governing through freedom" in this field entails abandoning the project of normalizing subjects as the main goal of punishment. In contrast to this earlier function, control policies shift to aim mainly at managing and distributing risks from a perspective of economic utilitarianism (Dean 2010; Dilts 2008). Furthermore, control policies tend to seek to shape choice, based on the notion that fostering the freedom of individuals is the best way of organizing the social according to a neoliberal mode of government (Razac 2008; Rose 1999). Moreover, the framework of risk management appears to be most useful for the purposes of shaping a pattern of prudential subject, an individual capable of coping with his or her own risks of victimization, e.g., through the policies of situational prevention. This subjective pattern cannot be more consonant with the neoliberal theses of responsibility, individualization, and self-management of freedom (Garland 2003; O'Malley 2004).

On the other hand, the progressive introduction of *New Public Management* theories and practices[1] in the field of control and security policies provides striking evidence of neoliberal penal policies (McLaughlin and Murji 2001; Raine and Willson 1997). Indeed, managerial public policies are grounded on economic concerns regarding the costs of public policies and the limits of public spending. This managerial rationale fosters a broad set of governmental practices, aimed to economize human and financial means, organizing the available resources according to predefined targets, and producing ways of periodically assessing the outcomes of public policies (Mucchielli 2008; Rose 1999).

Yet if anything characterizes current penal and control policies, it is their heterogeneity (Loader and Sparks 2007; Rose 2000). Hence, notwithstanding the prominence achieved by actuarial and economic penal policies during the last decades, these still have to negotiate their coexistence with other penality trends, which do not appear to be entirely coherent with them (Bottoms 1995; O'Malley 2010). A most salient trend in this realm is a neoconservative penal policy, aimed at reinforcing sovereign powers in the field of fighting crime and deviance, shaping a sort of "expressive justice"[2] based on penal severity, governing the fear of crime and disorder, and tackling aliens and dangerous individuals (Garland 2001; Simon 2001; Sparks 2000a).[3]

---

[1] *New public management* (NPM) is an expression which denotes the government policies that since the 1980s have aimed to modernize and allegedly render more efficient the public sector. The basic hypothesis holds that market-oriented management of the public sector will lead to greater cost-efficiency for governments. On the concept of NPM, see Osborne and Gaebler (1992) and Clarke and Newman (1997).

[2] On the concept of "expressive justice," see Tonry (2004), pp. 159 ff.

[3] The level of coherence or contradiction between this neoconservative penality and the neoliberal penal policies of risk management and economic utilitarianism must be further researched. While the majority of the academic literature tends to highlight their inherent contradictions (Easton and Piper 2008; Garland 2001; Sullivan 2001), some authors (Kemshall and Wood 2008; Rose 2000; Sparks 2000b) emphasize their consonance.

This neoconservative penality seems fairly consonant with what Foucault (2007) analyzed as the technology of power of "sovereignty," grounded on law and punishment and focused upon a territory.[4] In contrast to this former pattern, governmentality and the apparatuses of "security" (Foucault 2007) are focused on the task of management and mainly look after a "milieu" of social and economic flows.[5]

2 Neoliberal and Sovereign Devices of Control: The Spanish Case

In order to focus all these analyses on the Spanish case, foremost it may be hypothesized that Spain is arguably not one of the countries which have witnessed the consolidation of a distinctly neoliberal mode of governing control policies (Jiménez Franco 2014). In Spain, control policies and practices have shown the distinctive survival of sovereign or even authoritarian forms of government. There are good reasons for this peculiarity in the Spanish case. Among them are the country's late democratization process, the limited transformation of agencies responsible for security, or the survival of a very prominent phenomenon of political violence in the Basque country.

One piece of evidence of the limited penetration of the neoliberal logic into Spanish security policies is the almost complete absence of measures consistent with the managerial rationale, such as the institutional organization of police profiling, targeted operations, or the structuring of the accountability of agencies responsible for security and control. Another piece of evidence of an authoritarian social government is the fact that Spain has maintained one of the highest prison population rates of the EU-15 during the last decade, while the rates of (registered) crime are among the lowest in the EU (Tables 1 and 2).[6]

While certainly not everything which has happened in Spain in recent years pertaining to control policies can be read from a sovereign perspective, one may find elements which are unambiguously neoliberal. A key example of this is the realm of crimmigration policies.

---

[4] On the Foucaultian concept of "sovereignty," see also Dean (2010) and De Giorgi (2002).

[5] On the concept of apparatuses of "security," see also Bigo (2011), Dilts (2008), and Valverde (2008).

[6] In academic literature, it is highly contested whether high prison population rates are consonant with neoliberal penal trends or if they are, first and foremost, a key feature of a neoconservative penology of harsh punishment. On the former point of view, see O'Malley (2006) and Rose (2000); on the latter perspective, see Garland (2001) and Sullivan (2001). In my opinion, it appears fairly difficult to frame a model of high and rising prison population rates within a pattern of neoliberal penal policies grounded on a principle of economic efficiency, due to the considerable amount of public expenditure that such imprisonment requires.

Table 1 Prison population in major EU countries (September 1st 2013)

Country	Prison population (total amount)	Prison population rate (per 100,000 inhabitants)
France	78,363	119
Germany	67,681	84
Italy	64,835	109
Spain	68,099	146
United Kingdom	93,592	146

Source: Aebi and Delgrande (2015)

Table 2 Crime rates in major EU countries (2012)

Country	Crime rate (offenses per 1000 inhabitants)
France (2009)	56.4
Germany	74.7
Italy	47.5
Spain	48.5
United Kingdom	64.6

Source: Eurostat (http://epp.eurostat.ec.europa.eu)

3 Neoliberalism and Sovereignty in Spanish Crimmigration Policies

During the first decade of this century, Spain experienced a very prominent arrival of migrants, which led to the resident foreign population multiplying by 6 in just 10 years (from 0.92 million in 2000 to 5.74 million in 2010), according to the INE (National Statistics Institute) official data. The governing and control of this phenomenon, characterized by a significant volume of irregular migration,[7] were articulated in accordance with EU legislation through sovereign measures: centres of detention, administrative removals, penal deportations, etc. Not in vain, EU and Spanish crimmigration policies are—at least allegedly—aimed at border control, and borders are still one of the most essential constituents of sovereignty (Huysmans 2006; Weber and Bowling 2004). Crimmigration policies in Spain and all throughout the EU have contributed to strengthen the social cohesion of the national population, to legitimize the symbolic and practical authority of the State and its agencies, to redefine national identities, and to find a useful scapegoat for any sort of threatening social problems (Bosworth and Guild 2008; Tsoukala 2002).

Nonetheless, a relevant body of literature has been developing a less sovereign interpretation of the outcomes of these policies (Brandariz García 2011; Calavita 2005; Mezzadra and Neilson 2013). This literature has pointed out that the Spanish

[7] Carrasco Carpio (2008, pp. 229 ff.) estimates that the amount of irregular migrants in Spain by the middle of the decade was over one million people.

crimmigration policies in these years led less to the exclusion of migrants than to their differential inclusion. This shaped a subordinate and extremely flexible workforce, which served to provide the basis for the significant Spanish economic growth of that decade (Brandariz García 2011, pp. 81 ff.; Calavita 2003, pp. 400 ff.; Romero 2010, pp. 56–57).

3.1 Innovations in the Field of Crimmigration Policies in the Context of the Great Recession

This reading, consistent with a neoliberal framework of risk management and economic utilitarianism in the field of control policies, should be reviewed in the context of the Great Recession. In this frame, one can grasp the complex relationship between sovereign and neoliberal apparatuses of government. In fact, the recession led the Spanish Government to set up innovations in the field of crimmigration policies.

The main perspective of the Spanish Government from the beginning of the crisis has been that migrants are no longer necessary and that it is fairly reasonable to facilitate or even to directly organize the return of a significant number of them. This policy has not had major effects. In fact, the total number of foreigners resident in Spain tended to remain constant since the beginning of the crisis until 2012, as can be seen in Table 3.[8]

The need to adapt the control of migrants to this new phase has been undertaken through various measures—some of them clearly sovereign and exclusive, and others more bound to economic aims and to the management of efficiency. In fact, some innovations introduced in this area in the context of the recession are fairly contradictory.

The first innovation was the relaunch of racist raids in the main Spanish cities, with previously unknown intensity. Since 2008, the press has frequently reported the massive implementation of these raids, which have been criticized not only by NGOs and associations of migrants but even by some police unions (Romero 2010, pp. 100–101). The Spanish Government has always denied the existence of this raiding policy; however, the previous Socialist Government created Circular No. 1/2010, which compelled the arrest of even regular migrants who did not carry with them the residence permit.[9] While data from the results of these raids

[8] The figures of the foreign-born resident population are slightly higher than the numbers of foreign resident population due to nationalization practices. According to INE official data, in 2000 the foreign-born population resident in Spain amounted to 3.6 % of the total population; in 2010, it had risen to 14.0 %, and it slightly dropped to 13.4 % in 2014.

[9] Circular No. 1/2010 was abrogated by the subsequent right-wing Spanish Government in May 2012, through the Circular No. 2/2012, which changed the official interpretation of police powers to stop, search, and arrest migrants. Nonetheless, the practice of police raids against migrants remained untouched and seems to have sidelined the new normative framework (see Bradford et al. 2013; Fernández Rodríguez de Liévana et al. 2013, p. 58).

Table 3 Foreign population in Spain (2000–2013)

Year	Foreign population (total)	Foreign population (percentage of the total population)	Year-on-year evolution (total amount)
2000	0.923 million	2.2 %	+23.3 %
2001	1.370 million	3.3 %	+48.4 %
2002	1.977 million	4.7 %	+44.3 %
2003	2.664 million	6.2 %	+34.7 %
2004	3.034 million	7.0 %	+13.8 %
2005	3.730 million	8.4 %	+22.9 %
2006	4.144 million	9.2 %	+11.0 %
2007	4.519 million	9.9 %	+9.0 %
2008	5.268 million	11.4 %	+16.5 %
2009	5.648 million	12.0 %	+7.2 %
2010	5.747 million	12.2 %	+1.7 %
2011	5.751 million	12.2 %	+0.1 %
2012	5.736 million	12.1 %	−0.3 %
2013	5.546 million	11.8 %	−3.3 %
2014	5.023 million	10.7 %	−9.4 %

Source: INE (*National Statistics Institute*; www.ine.es)

tend to be subject to official secrecy, it is known that 54.7 % of the individuals stopped and searched in Spain from December 2011 to January 2013 were migrants.[10]

This policy could be understood as a sort of revival of the sovereign rationale of control in the context of the recession aimed to legitimize the institutional governing of employment shortages, to ensure social cohesion, and to "prevent" the emergence of xenophobia. However, it is evident that this policy has incorporated neoliberal elements of control. In fact, this raiding policy has incorporated, for the first time in Spain, a task of governmental organization of police profiling. In November 2008, a police union denounced the fact that the Police Commissioner of Madrid had set a monthly quota of arrested irregular migrants, recommending that police officers focus on arresting Moroccan individuals due to the low cost of their deportation. The Spanish Government then denied the existence of these instructions, but the suspicion that these instructions are still active, justified by the aforementioned data, has remained ever since (Amnistía Internacional 2011; Romero 2010, pp. 100–101).

The existence of these instructions and the adoption of police profiling show that the policy of migrant raids in Spanish cities is not only an expression of sovereign control; it also incorporates a neoliberal concern for efficiency (concerning outcomes of police activity).

[10] See *ElDiario.es*, 03/30/2013.

That same impression remains when one looks at the evolution of another prominent domain of crimmigration policies: the deportation regime. It is essential to pay attention to this realm, since the prime purpose of the raids is the detection of irregular migrants in order to arrange for them to be deported.

The Spanish deportation regime has experienced two relevant changes in the context of the recession. On the one hand, there has been a remarkable drop of administrative removals, which sanction the irregular stay in Spain as a mere civil offense.[11] On the other hand, there has been an almost total replacement of administrative removals by criminal deportations, which punish irregular migrants convicted—or accused—of a criminal offense.

In effect, according to Spanish Home Office official data, throughout the decade the number of deportations carried out by the Spanish Government remained at the annual figure of 10,000–14,000. There is no data that enable us to distinguish between administrative removals and criminal deportations until 2008. However, knowing that the figures of criminal deportations imposed by the Spanish courts or executed by the Government during the decade remained quite low (Brandariz García 2011, pp. 85 ff.), it may be stated that the vast majority of the total number of deportations from 2000 to 2007 were administrative removals (Table 4).

This situation changed in 2008. Since then, when the official data began to distinguish between administrative ("nonqualified" in official terms) removals and criminal ("qualified") deportations, the number of removals due to irregular stay began to sharply decrease in the context of the recession. Indeed, *nonqualified* removals dropped from 5687 in 2009 to 1402 in 2013 (Table 5).

However, as was previously mentioned, the total number of deportations has remained fairly stable. The reason for this appears to be that there has been a gradual replacement of administrative removals by criminal deportations (Fernández Bessa 2013; Fernández Rodríguez de Liévana et al. 2013). In 2007, the Spanish Government created within the *Policía Nacional* (National Police) the so-called *Brigada de Expulsión de Delincuentes Extranjeros* (BEDEX, *Brigade for Expulsion of Foreign Criminals*), and since then the deportation of migrants who have committed crimes has become a key element of Spanish immigration control policy. The data is evident: "qualified" (criminal or crime-based) deportations rose from 5564 in 2008 to 9114 in 2011, 8140 in 2012, and 7582 in 2013. This priority is reflected by the breakdown of removals: in 2008, criminal deportations were the 52.4 % of the total number of deportations, and in 2013 this rose to the 84.4 %. Furthermore, the then new right-wing Government declared in April 2012 that its aim was to limit the number of administrative removals and that detention centres should be reserved for migrants with criminal records (Table 6).[12]

[11] In contrast to the legal framework of many EU jurisdictions, such as Germany, France, or Italy (Van Kalmthout et al. 2007), and of the USA (Koulish 2010), in Spain the irregular stay of a foreigner does not constitute a penal offense, but a civil (administrative) one.

[12] See *El Periódico*, 05/01/2012.

Table 4 Number of executed deportations (total and year-on-year evolution)

Year	Deportations (total)	Year-on-year evolution
2002	12,159	
2003	14,104	+15.9 %
2004	11,014	−21.9 %
2005	11,002	−0.1 %
2006	11,567	+5.1 %
2007	9467	−18.1 %
2008	10,616	+12.1 %
2009	13,278	+25 %
2010	11,454	−13.7 %
2011	11,358	−0.8 %
2012	10,130	−10.8 %
2013	8984	−11.3 %

Source: Ministerio del Interior (*Spanish Home Office*; www.interior.gob.es)

Table 5 Evolution of administrative ("nonqualified") removals (total and year-on-year evolution)

Year	Administrative ("nonqualified") removals	Year-on-year evolution
2008	5052	–
2009	5687	+12.6 %
2010	3258	−42.7 %
2011	2244	−31.1 %
2012	2015	−10.2 %
2013	1402	−30.4 %

Source: Ministerio del Interior (*Spanish Home Office*; www.interior.gob.es)

Table 6 Evolution of "qualified" (criminal or crime-based) deportations

Year	"Qualified" deportations	Year-on-year evolution	Percentage of total expulsions
2008	5564	–	52.4 %
2009	7591	+36.4 %	57.2 %
2010	8196	+8.0 %	71.6 %
2011	9114	+11.2 %	80.2 %
2012	8140	−10.6 %	80.4 %
2013	7582	−6.8 %	84.4 %

Source: Ministerio del Interior (*Spanish Home Office*; www.interior.gob.es)

4 Conclusion: The Complex Hybridization of Neoliberal and Sovereign Devices in the Field of Crimmigration Policies

How can this double evolution of the deportation policy be analyzed? First, there could be a sovereign reading, which might emphasize that the Spanish Government has sought to strengthen its legitimacy by announcing that its deportation policy is now focused on delinquent foreigners, rather than on those who are simply irregular migrants.

However, this reading seems inadequate or, at least, incomplete. The interpretation of the evolution of the deportation policy must be made, first and foremost, from a neoliberal perspective. Indeed, that evolution arguably shows a concern regarding the limits of public budgets; hence, the number of administrative removals has to drop because there are not enough resources to significantly increase the number of deportations.[13] Second, that policy seems to assume that it is most appropriate to enforce the penal deportations, since their criminal ground is more solid than the administrative offense of undocumented stay (Fernández Rodríguez de Liévana et al. 2013). Therefore, this evolution shows a concern for improving the efficient use of scarce resources and an actuarial mode of risk management.[14]

Nonetheless, this transformation of the deportation policy is not consistent with what has been happening in the domain of policing. The massive implementation of raids is pointless, whether they have incorporated elements of profiling or not, since administrative removals (due to irregular stay) have been steadily decreasing.

This issue demonstrates that the actuarial and economic rationalization of control policies is not a simple task and that overcoming sovereign trends in the domain of security policies is a slow and controversial process. Not in vain, delinquency, punishment and control policies, no less than borders, (irregular) migration or alienness are densely semiotic social phenomena, riddled with collective passions, emotions, and expectations, and their intrinsically cultural nature does not fit well with the cool semantics of actuarial and economic rationales of control (Garland 1997; Sparks 2000a).

All this leads us to agree with the literature that claims that the field of control policies is shaped in accordance not only with neoliberal guidelines but also with neoconservative trends, generating occasional conflicts between these two logics

---

[13] The aforementioned evolution of the deportation policy and the concern for public expenditure may be also appreciated in the coetaneous evolution of the prison realm. In effect, the Spanish prison population has dropped by 15.0 % between May 2010 and February 2015, according to Spanish Home Office official data. The most striking feature of this recent evolution is its contradiction with the criminal justice system data, since the number of arrested individuals, the number of convicted individuals, and the number of individuals sentenced to prison have risen during the mentioned period.

[14] Nonetheless, the poor official data available in this field leads to certain ambiguities, which require further analysis. In effect, the data provided by the Spanish Home Office are not consistent at all with the ones published by the Fiscalía General del Estado (2014) [Office of the Spanish Attorney General], which accounts for a number of penal deportations far lower than that stated by the Home Office. It may well be the case that a significant amount of the expulsions counted by the Home Office as "qualified" (or criminal) deportations are not formally "criminal" (i.e., enforced by a penal court following a conviction by a criminal offense), but they are the consequence of a criminal conviction or record, even though the sanction is formally an administrative removal. This might allow us to infer that the current Spanish deportation policy seeks efficiency in the use of scarce resources, and also utility of this policy in terms of political currency, by presenting the deported foreigners primarily as dangerous aliens.

(Garland 2001; Monclús Masó 2008; O'Malley 2010). Moreover, at this point we should make mention of the literature on *governmentality* which in recent years has highlighted the argument that neoliberal government through the conduct of freedom is currently complemented by what, in Foucaultian terms, could be called "sovereign" rationales of power (Dean 2007, pp. 108 ff.; Iglesias Skulj 2011, pp. 112 ff.; Mezzadra and Neilson 2013, pp. 167 ff.). This recent literature has qualified the texts on *governmentality* of the 1990s, which exclusively emphasized the centrality of government through freedom.

Furthermore, all this leads us to recall that Foucault (2007) himself pointed out that the different power technologies he analyzed do not replace each other but rather often come into conflict in the same historical time frame.[15] The Spanish experience of the last decade in the field of crimmigration policies demonstrates that devices may coexist of what Foucault calls "power technologies of security" with others that belong to the rationale of the "sovereign societies," and even with neodisciplinary dynamics (Brandariz García 2011, p. 103; Portilla Contreras 2007, p. 41). In effect, while Spanish crimmigration policies throughout the last decade have assumed the lexicon of exclusion and sovereignty, they have actually led to a differential and subordinate inclusion of the migrant population (De Giorgi 2006; Rahola 2010; Sciurba 2009). In this sense, one may claim that crimmigration policies and tools have incorporated elements of normalization. However, unlike disciplinary logic, the normalization here has not been operating as a form of reintegration of each individual. Far from it, the practices of massive stop and search, internment, or deportation of migrants are aimed not at disciplining the particular subject but at normalizing the whole migrant population (Koulish 2010, pp. 67–68; Romero 2010, pp. 57/130–131; Walters 2010, p. 95), in order to subjugate them to the conditions of subordinate inclusion. In sum, both before and after the Great Recession, Spanish crimmigration policies have shaped a far-reaching biopolitical apparatus for the government of migrants' lives (Iglesias Skulj 2011, pp. 212 ff.; Valverde 2008, pp. 211/213–214).[16]

[15] See also Dean (2007), pp. 93 ff/199 ff.; De Giorgi (2002), pp. 96–97/107; Rose (1999), pp. 23–24/234–235.

[16] It should be pointed out that, mirroring the dualism of neoliberal and sovereign control policies, the scholarly literature shows a distinct cleavage in how it analyzes Foucault's concept of biopolitics. On the one hand, some authors (e.g., Agamben 1998 or Esposito 2008) interpret the concept as a derivative of the Reason of State, tying biopolitics to the notion of sovereign exceptionalism. In contrast, another body of literature (e.g., Hardt and Negri 2000 or Rose 1999) understands biopolitics as a paradigm pertaining to the domain of liberal governmentality. On this debate, see Campesi 2011, pp. 179 ff.; Lemke 2011, pp. 34 ff/51 ff.

References

Aebi MF, Delgrande N (2015) Council of Europe Annual Penal Statistics. Space I – Prison Populations. Survey 2013. Council of Europe, Strasbourg

Agamben G (1998) Homo Sacer: sovereign power and bare life. Stanford University Press, Redwood City

Amnistía Internacional (2011) Parad el racismo, no a las personas. Perfiles raciales y control de la inmigración en España

Bigo D (2011) Security: a field left fallow. In: Dillon M, Neal AW (eds) Foucault on politics, security and war. Palgrave MacMillan, Basingstoke, pp 93–114

Bosworth M, Guild M (2008) Governing through migration control: security and citizenship in Britain. Br J Criminol 48:703–719

Bottoms A (1995) The philosophy and politics of punishment and sentencing. In: Clarkson C, Morgan R (eds) The politics of sentencing reform. Clarendon, Oxford, pp 17–49

Bradford B et al (2013) Identificación policial por perfil étnico en España: Informe sobre experiencias y actitudes en relación con las actuaciones policiales. Tirant lo Blanch, Valencia

Brandariz García JA (2011) Sistema penal y control de los migrantes. Gramática del migrante como infractor penal. Granada, Comares

Calavita K (2003) A 'reserve army of delinquents'. The criminalization and economic punishment of immigrants in Spain. Punishment Soc 5:399–413

Calavita K (2005) Immigrants at the margins. Cambridge University Press, Cambridge

Campesi G (2011) Soggetto, disciplina, governo. Mimesis, Sesto San Giovanni

Carrasco Carpio C (2008) Mercado de trabajo e inmigración. In: Izquierdo Escribano A (ed) El modelo de inmigración y los riesgos de exclusión. Foessa, Madrid, pp 213–257

Clarke JH, Newman JE (1997) The managerial state: power, politics and ideology in the remaking of social welfare. Sage, London

De Giorgi A (2002) Il governo dell'eccedenza. Postfordismo e controllo della moltitudine. Ombre corte, Verona

De Giorgi A (2006) Re-thinking the political economy of punishment. Perspectives on post-fordism and penal politics. Ashgate, Aldershot

Dean M (2007) Governing societies. Open University Press, Maidenhead

Dean M (2010) Governmentality. Power and rule in modern society, 2nd edn. Sage, London

Dilts A (2008) Michel Foucault meets Gary Becker: criminality beyond discipline and punish. Carceral Notebooks 4:77–100

Easton S, Piper C (2008) Sentencing and punishment. The quest for justice, 2nd edn. Oxford University Press, Oxford

Esposito R (2008) Bios: biopolitics and philosophy. University of Minnesota Press, Minneapolis

Fernández Bessa C (2013) Il panorama dei Centri di Internamento per Stranieri in Spagna: dal controllo delle frontieri alla gestione della criminalità. Antigone 8(1):68–91

Fernández Rodríguez de Liévana G et al (2013) Qué hacemos con las fronteras. Akal, Madrid

Fiscalía General del Estado (2014) Memoria 2014. Ministerio de Justicia, Madrid

Foucault M (2007) Security, territory, population. Palgrave MacMillan, Basingstoke

Foucault M (2008) The birth of biopolitics. Palgrave MacMillan, Basingstoke

Garland D (1997) 'Governmentality' and the problem of crime: Foucault, criminology, sociology. Theor Criminol 1:173–214

Garland D (2001) The culture of control. Oxford University Press, Oxford

Garland D (2003) The rise of risk. In: Ericson RV, Doyle A (eds) Risk and morality. University of Toronto Press, Toronto, pp 48–86

Harcourt BE (2007) Against prediction. University of Chicago Press, Chicago

Hardt M, Negri A (2000) Empire. Harvard University Press, Cambridge

Huysmans J (2006) The politics of insecurity. Fear, migration and asylum in the EU. Routledge, Abingdon

Iglesias Skulj A (2011) El cambio en el estatuto de la Ley penal y en los mecanismos de control: flujos migratorios y gubernamentalidad neoliberal. Comares, Granada
Jiménez Franco D (2014) La burbuja penal. Mercado, estado y cárcel en la democracia española. Universidad de Zaragoza (unpublished doctoral Dissertation)
Kemshall H, Wood J (2008) Risk and public protection: responding to involuntary and 'taboo' risk. Soc Policy Adm 42:611–629
Koulish R (2010) Immigration and American democracy. Routledge, New York/Abingdon
Lemke T (2011) Biopolitics. New York University Press, New York/London
Loader I, Sparks R (2007) Contemporary landscapes of crime, order and control: governance, risk, and globalization. In: Maguire M, Morgan R, Reiner R (eds) The Oxford handbook of criminology, 4th edn. Oxford University Press, Oxford/New York, pp 78–101
McLaughlin E, Murji K (2001) Lost connections and new directions: neo-liberalism, new public managerialism and the 'modernization' of the British police. In: Stenson K, Sullivan RR (eds) Crime, risk and justice. The politics of crime control in liberal democracies. Willan, Cullompton, pp 104–122
Mezzadra S, Neilson B (2013) Border as method, or, the multiplication of labor. Duke University Press, Durham/London
Miller P, Rose N (2008) Governing the present. Polity, Cambridge
Monclús Masó M (2008) La gestión penal de la inmigración. Del Puerto, Buenos Aires
Mucchielli L (2008) Faire du chiffre: le 'nouveau management de la sécurité'. In: Mucchielli L (ed) La frénésie sécuritaire. La Decouverte, Paris, pp 99–112
O'Malley P (2004) Risk, uncertainty and government. Glasshouse Press, London
O'Malley P (2006) Criminology and risk. In: Mythen G, Walklate S (eds) Beyond the risk society. Open University Press, Maidenhead, pp 43–59
O'Malley P (2010) Crime and risk. Sage, London
Osborne D, Gaebler T (1992) Reinventing government. How the enterpreneurial spirit is transforming the public sector. Addison-Wesley, Boston
Portilla Contreras G (2007) El Derecho Penal entre el cosmopolitismo universalista y el relativismo posmodernista. Tirant lo Blanch, Valencia
Rahola F (2010) La máquina de captura. In: Palidda S et al (eds) Criminalización racista de los migrantes en Europa. Comares, Granada, pp 95–108
Raine JW, Willson MJ (1997) Beyond managerialism in criminal justice. Howard J Crim Justice 36:80–95
Razac O (2008) Avec Foucault. Après Foucault. L'Harmattan, Paris
Romero E (2010) Un deseo apasionado de trabajo más barato y servicial. Migraciones, fronteras y capitalism. Cambalache, Oviedo
Rose N (1999) Powers of freedom. Cambridge University Press, Cambridge
Rose N (2000) Government and control. Br J Criminol 40:321–339
Sciurba A (2009) Campi di forza. Percorsi confinati di migranti in Europa. Ombre corte, Verona
Simon J (2001) 'Entitlement to cruelty': the end of welfare and the punitive mentality in the United States. In: Stenson K, Sullivan RR (eds) Crime, risk and justice. The politics of crime control in liberal democracies. Willan, Cullompton, pp 125–143
Simon J, Feeley MM (2003) The form and limits of the new penology. In: Blomberg TG, Cohen S (eds) Punishment and social control, 2nd edn. Aldine de Gruyter, New York, pp 76–116
Sparks R (2000a) Risk and blame in criminal justice controversies. British press coverage and official discourse on prison security (1993–96). In: Brown M, Pratt J (eds) Dangerous offenders. Punishment and social order. Routledge, London/New York, pp 127–143
Sparks R (2000b) Perspectives on risk and penal politics. In: Hope T, Sparks R (eds) Crime, risk and insecurity. Routledge, London/New York, pp 129–145
Sullivan RR (2001) The schizophrenic state: neo-liberal criminal justice. In: Stenson K, Sullivan RR (eds) Crime, risk and justice. The politics of crime control in liberal democracies. Willan, Cullompton, pp 29–47
Tonry M (2004) Thinking about crime. Oxford University Press, New York

Tsoukala A (2002) Le traitement médiatique de la criminalité étrangère en Europe. Déviance et Société 26:61–82
Valverde M (2008) Beyond *Discipline and Punish*: Foucault's challenge to criminology. Carceral Notebooks 4:201–223
Van Kalmthout A, Hofstee-van der Meulen F, Dünkel F (2007) Comparative overview, conclusions and recommendations. In: Van Kalmthout AM, Hofstee-van der Meulen FB, Dünkel F (eds) Foreigners in European prisons, vol I. Wolf Legal Publishers, Nijmegen, pp 7–88
Walters W (2010) Deportation, expulsion, and the international police of aliens. In: De Genova N, Peutz N (eds) The deportation regime. Duke University Press, Durham/London, pp 69–100
Weber L, Bowling B (2004) Policing migration: a framework for investigating the regulation of global mobility. Policing Secur 14:195–212

"Immigrants as Detainees": Some Reflections Based on Abyssal Thinking and Other Critical Approaches

Katia Cardoso

Abstract Immigration is increasingly considered a security issue. Particularly after 9/11, it became a prominent part of the national and international security agendas. Within this context, in the last years, immigration detention facilities have proliferated in receiving countries.

The main purpose of this chapter is to analyse immigration detention centres in light of the "abyssal thinking" proposal, theorised by the Portuguese sociologist Boaventura de Sousa Santos and other critical approaches on the subject developed by authors such as Giorgio Agamben and Loïc Wacquant, among others.

I argue that immigration detention centres are spaces conducive to human rights violations and places, as Santos states, where "non-citizens" can be treated as "dangerous colonial savages" (Santos, Revista Crítica de Ciências Sociais 78:62, 2007).

1 Introduction

After 9/11, detention practices gained great visibility. A *long durée* analysis leads us to consider that they are "facets of immigration policy which many immigrant communities, [in particular Latino communities], have been intimately acquainted for generations" (Hernández 2008, p. 37). Current detention and deportation practices, which Hernández calls "undue processes", are part of a more comprehensive and continuous context marked by "the stigma of criminal foreignness and illegality" (Hernández 2008, p. 37).

In many countries, there are no clear rules on immigrant detention, which worsens detainees' situation, namely in what concerns "lack of access to the outside world, limited possibilities of challenging detention through the courts, and/or absence of limitations on the duration of detention".[1]

[1] http://www.globaldetentionproject.org/about/about-the-project.html.

K. Cardoso (✉)
Centre for Social Studies, University of Coimbra, Coimbra, Portugal
e-mail: katia@ces.uc.pt

M.J. Guia et al. (eds.), *Immigration Detention, Risk and Human Rights*,
DOI 10.1007/978-3-319-24690-1_12

In 2011, only the United States detained about "429,000 immigrants exposed to myriad abuses—from a lack of adequate medical and mental health care that has caused unnecessary deaths to rape and sexual abuse". Among them were "survivors of torture, asylum seekers, victims of trafficking, families with small children, the elderly, individuals with serious medical and mental health conditions, and lawful permanent residents with longstanding family and community ties".[2]

In recent years, the opening of detention facilities in third countries (see, for instance, Australia or European country cases) contributed to aggravating the "sub-human" conditions that detainees have to face.

Santos states that the "abyssal" cartographical lines that used to demarcate the Old from the New World during colonial times are still alive in the structure of modern occidental thought and remain constitutive of the political and cultural relations held by the contemporary world system" (Santos 2007, p. 3). In other words, there still prevails a stark division between "this side of the line" and "the other side of the line", between "human" and "sub-human, in such a way that human principles don't get compromised by inhuman practices" (Santos 2007, p. 9). Santos uses Guantánamo, literally and metaphorically, as a paradigmatic example of the negation, invisibility and production of inexistence occurring in "the other side of the line". I argue, in this chapter, that immigration detention centres belong to "the other side of the line", in the sense that they are parentheses spaces in what concerns human rights and places where "non-citizens are treated as dangerous colonial savages" (Santos 2007, p. 19).

Agamben compares detention facilities to concentration camps, a kind of "spaces of exception", places "in which the normal order is de facto suspended and in which whether or not atrocities are committed depends not on law but on the civility and ethical sense of the police who temporarily act as sovereign" (Agamben 1998, p. 166). They are places where democratic rights are restricted, supposedly on behalf of their own protection or even enlargement. In sum, they are "sites of exception, where regimes of police prevail over regime of rights" (Fassin 2011, p. 219).

Following these critical approaches, the main purpose of this chapter is to analyse the immigration detention centres, in light of the abyssal thinking, theorised by the Portuguese sociologist Boaventura de Sousa Santos, among other authors concerned with the subject.

In a first moment, "abyssal thinking" will be presented as an important theoretical lens to read migration phenomena, particularly detention centres. Then, detention centres will be highlighted as important places in the context of one of the main paradoxes of our time: people movement restriction vs. good and services "free" circulation. The chapter ends by addressing some of the main questions focused by critical approaches on the issue: detention as a space "conducive" for violation of human rights and as "niche market" of a growing business.

[2] https://www.aclu.org/immigrants-rights/immigration-detention.

2 "Abyssal Thinking" and Other Critical Approaches

"Abyssal thinking" is a versatile theoretical instrument, a very interesting and useful lens to analyse various social contexts. That is, by its nature and its metaphorical plasticity it can be an excellent frame of reference for different realities.[3] In the context of migration, and particularly detention centres, abyssal thinking also acquires, in my view, an important analytical value, as I will demonstrate below.

To Santos, modern knowledge and modern law are the ultimate manifestations of abyssal thinking. The colonial territory embodies the notion of "the other side of the line". "Whatever could not be thought of as either true or false, legal or illegal was most distinctly occurring in the colonial zone (...) the colonial represents not the legal or illegal but rather the lawless (...) the colonial is the state of nature where civil society's institutions have no place" (Santos 2007, pp. 5–7).

> The other side of the abyssal line is the realm of beyond legality and illegality (lawlessness), of beyond true and falsehood (incomprehensible beliefs, idolatry, and magic). These forms of radical negation, together, resulted in a radical absence. The absence of humanity, modern sub-humanity. The exclusion is thus both radical and non-existent, as sub-humans are not conceivably candidates for social inclusion (...). The negation of one part of humanity is sacrificial, in that it is the condition of the affirmation of that other part of humanity it considers itself as universal. (Santos 2007, pp. 9–10)

Modern western thinking goes on operating through abyssal lines, which divide the human from the sub-human in such a way that human principles don't get compromised by inhuman practices (Santos 2007, p. 10). The author recognises three main continuities between colonial period and today: first, the creation and negation of the other side of the line are still the foundations of hegemonic principles and practices; second, the co-presence between the two sides remains impossible; third, the other side of the line is still seen as a place *par excellence* of incivility in contrast with civility legal and political force on this side of the line.

Guantánamo is mentioned in this seminal work, literally and metaphorically, as a paradigmatic example of the negation, invisibility and production of inexistence that occurs in "the other side of the line" and "one most grotesque manifestations of abyssal legal thinking". I suggest that detention centres can be seen as little Guantánamo in the sense that they represent locations where human rights, rule of law and democratic principles are dramatically violated. In general, immigrants belong to the "other side of the line". And this fact is further aggravated in the case of immigrants detained who are waiting for deportation.

In fact, the metaphorical character of abyssal lines increases their chances to be used as a good instrument of social analysis in various historical periods, i.e., they do not only divide macro spaces, such as the Old and New World, as they also separate spaces of smaller scale as countries, cities, neighbourhoods, homes, etc. (Santos 2007; Águas 2011). According to Santos, "the permanence of abyssal

[3] See, for example, an interesting application of the "abyssal thinking" to the Quilombos context (Águas 2011).

global lines throughout the modern period does not mean that they have remained fixed" (Santos 2007, p. 11). He highlights the two main "tectonic shake-ups" lines suffered in the last 60 years: one from the "other side of the line" originated by the anti-colonial struggles and processes of independence, and the other, which took place in "this side of the line", since 1970s and 1980s. "This second movement is made of a main movement—called return of the colonial and the return of the coloniser—and a subaltern counter-movement—called subaltern cosmopolitanism" (Santos 2007, p. 13). Colonial is once again used in its metaphoric meaning to refer to "those who perceive their live experiences as taking place on the other side of the line and rebel against it" (Santos 2007, p. 13). As so, the terrorist, the undocumented migrant worker and the refugee are the three main protagonists of the return of the colonial.[4]

Reflections of some other authors who also use strong and enlightening geographic metaphors, equally useful to grasp the realities of detention centres, must be highlighted. One of them is the Italian philosopher Giorgio Agamben, who compares detention centres to concentration camps, considered as "spaces of exception", as above mentioned:

> If this is true, if the essence of the camp consists in the materialization of the state of exception and in the subsequent creation of a space in which bare life and the juridical rule enter into a threshold of indistinction, then we must admit that we find ourselves virtually in the presence of a camp every time such a structure is created, independent of the kinds of crime that are committed there (Agamben 1998, p. 166).

This production of zones of exception makes possible the same type of "lawful lawlessness" that marked life in the colonies (Biswas and Nair 2010, p. 20). The comparison with the colonial period is reinforced when, for instance, some authors consider "ghettos, barrios, internment camps, and reservations as internal colonies" (Sharpe 2000, p. 105). But we can also compare detention centres with "Third World", following Duffield's analysis (2007), in the sense that we can view the detainees as "uninsured life", as people not "supported by regimes of social protection (...) and expected to be self-reliant" (Duffield 2008, p. 145).

Wacquant (1999, p. 73) calls detention centres "enclaves of non-right", where undocumented immigrants or immigrants waiting for deportation are arbitrarily detained. Some other authors identify the emergence of a "system of quasi-punitive immcarceration" (Kalhan 2010), in the broader framework of "crimmigration", a concept coined by Stumpf (2006), to refer to the global phenomenon that is characterised by an increasing association between immigrants and crime, and the consequent blurring of the distinction between criminal and immigration laws.

Hernández, in a paper on Detention and Latino Immigrants in the US, states that detention is an important instrument through which non-citizens are criminalised and doubly punished: "detention accentuates not simply the border separating who

[4] We can also identify expressions of what Santos terms as "return of the colonizer" and "indirect rules" in the privatisation of detention centres, a growing and profitable business which aggravate detainee's vulnerable situation, as we will see later.

remains in the US and who is deported, but the real weight of such processes is felt by the creation of a social class inside the US, but outside its legal protections" (Hernández 2008, p. 41).

Critical approaches on detention centres have been focusing on three interrelated aspects, which will be further analysed: first, the violation of immigrant (human) rights within these processes; second, the need for a broader approach, which considers these locations as part of a prison complex (in the United States, for instance, immigration detention centres should be included in the prison industrial complex); and, third, the existence of a business component, since detention facilities represent a very profitable sector.

3 Detention Centres and Movement's Paradoxes of Our Time

In the last decades, immigration unearthed two contradictions of globalisation era. First, if on the one hand goods and services circulate freely, on the other there are huge restrictions on the transnational circulation of the planet population. In other words, it seems to be that there is free pass for the flows of capital that is contrary to logic a growing number of barriers posed to people movement, to immigrants' flows. Second, the idea to integrate immigrants in hosting societies turns out to create an ethnic and racial division leading to discrimination and violence and to the emergence of "stigmatised minorities" (Fassin 2011, p. 217):

> The expulsion of immigrants – whether they are qualified as "illegal aliens" because of their lack of documents or as "criminal aliens" because of an offense they have committed, in both cases independent of the length of their stay in the receiving country – has become a powerful sign of contemporary politics (*apud* Fassin 2011, p. 220).

In this sense, migrants are condemned to "civil death" through "criminalization and exclusionary migration policy" and considered a category of people "who are not afforded the broadest range of rights and responsibilities afforded to the most privileged 'citizens'" (Loyd et al. 2009–2010, p. 86).

This paradox can also be expressed in other words: migrants are wanted and welcomed as labour power (preferably in irregular situation in order to be more vulnerable) on one hand, but on the other hand they are unwanted citizen (McDowell and Wonders 2009–2010, p. 55). Inspired by Karl Marx's and Max Weber's well-known reflections on "means of production" and "means of violence", respectively, Torpey (2000) states that our time is characterised by "state monopolization of the legitimate means of movement", in the sense that "modern states, and the international state system of which they are a part, have expropriated from individuals and private entities the legitimate "means of movement", particularly though by no means exclusively across international boundaries" (Torpey 2000, p. 4). It is in this context that the detention centres emerge as central locus where these paradoxes of our time acquire a relevant dimension.

As Gjergji states:

> immigrant detention centres are the emblem of this immigration policy, since they contribute to crime and stigmatize migration, without considering real individual behaviour. As a matter of fact, immigrants are detained in these centres only because of their immigrant status, not for having ever committed a crime. The detention of immigrant people is used to normalize the whole process of clandestine worker production, which is needed by western industry. (Gjergji 2006, p. 97)

The United Nations High Commissioner for Refugees defines detention as "Confinement within a narrowly bounded or restricted location, including prisons, closed camps, detention facilities or airport transit zones, where freedom of movement is substantially curtailed, and where the only opportunity to leave this limited area it to leave the territory" (ONHCR 1999, p. 3). So the network of detention structures is diversified. It includes distinct facilities scattered in the national territories.

The category of detainees is also very diverse:

> In general terms, detention is the practice of incarcerating noncitizens who are apprehended at ports of entry or within the nation's interior. Maintained in custody until they are released, bonded and paroled, or [deported from the United States], detainees consist of undocumented immigrants, lawful permanent residents and, at times, particular groups of citizens. To maintain the government's claim that detention is an "administrative process" – and not a punitive one – detention is theoretically utilized exclusively as a non-criminal procedure pursuant to deportation (Hernández 2008, p. 42).

States use diverse reasons to justify detention practices. The assumption of irregular migration as a criminal and security problem is one of the main reasons adduced by the states. Those against detention emphasise human rights violations (namely, arbitrary and lasting detentions), as well as the logic of securitisation due to the perceived dangers.

4 Detention Centres and Human Rights Violation

The political narrative presents detention (as well as deportation) as a simple administrative action, a "proper and natural response of the sovereign state to those who have violated its territorial sovereignty" (Cornelisse 2010, p. 101). The growing number of detention centres reflects the fact that detention is considered a natural and obvious answer to such a problem. Official discourse on detention also considers detention a civil response, but, as we have been examining, there are numerous criticism rebutting this argument, highlighting detention as a penal and punitive practice. The fact that inmates wear uniforms and the officer's criminal justice mentality are some of the most visible aspects of such detention's punitive nature.

In a context that makes hyper-visible the image of the immigrant "enemy", "outsider", "scapegoat", especially in periods of economic crisis, practices such as detention and deportation can easily become acceptable and supported. As Nair put it:

> In a global political economy where racialized, classed, sexualized and gendered representations of the immigrant "other" inform popular discourses and state practices, it has become acceptable to imprison migrants, to deny them basic legal rights and due process, and deport them whenever possible (Nair 2010, p. 101).

Thus, we can consider immigration detention as a form of state violence which is "(...) only possible because international human rights are incapable of fully addressing the human interests that are affected whenever the national state bases the exercise of power on territorial sovereignty" (Cornelisse 2010, p. 103).

The prevalence of the dominant notion of national sovereignty in face of human rights protection has as its main consequence the creation of "spaces near to rightlessness, such as the immigration prison" (Cornelisse 2010, p. 119), in Arendt's (2008) words, places where people are outside the legal normal order and where it is easier to deprive them of "the right to have rights", subjecting them to "total domination" (Arendt 2008).

Concerning migration issues, sovereignty is an unavoidable concept. In recent years and in an international context marked by securitarian giddiness, sovereignty as one of the main prerogatives of the modern nation (particularly in the aspect of controlling the entrance, residence and expulsion of foreigners) gained new expressions:

> Notions of sovereignty are thus being continually reworked and remapped by placement of insecure bodies in detention camps and wars zones, across heavily fortified and policed borders, in impoverished inner cities and unprotected sweatshops, and in variety of other transnational spaces, many of them increasingly regulated by out-sourced and unaccountable private outfits (Biswas and Nair 2010, p. 25).

So it is important to analyse the detention centres in a macro framework marked by the interception between violent colonial history and requirements of global capitalism. It is fundamental to be aware of the "broader constellation of detention-related practices, immigration laws "clothed with... many attributes of the criminal law", and a surrounding discourse that strongly associates immigration with criminality" (Kalhan 2010, p. 58), as previously mentioned.

The enforcement of immigration policies and practices, such as detention and deportation, is a way to prove that the government is in control and that it has a twofold purpose: one protective and other deterrent. It is also a way to transmit a double message: to the national citizens, showing them that they are protected from "external" enemies, those who endanger national security, and to asylum seekers and immigrants, dissuading their project to become part of "this side of the line", remembering them that they belong to the "other side of the line".

Universal Declaration of Human Rights, International Covenant on Civil and Political Rights, International Convention on the Protection of the Rights of All Migrant Workers and Members of their Families, Body of Principals for the

Protection of All Persons under Any Form of Detention or Imprisonment (A/RES 43/173), Vienna Convention on Consular Relations[5] constitute the wide corpus of law that safeguard the migrants' rights, particularly detained immigrants. So, there is a set of treaties and other regional and global juridical instruments that, in theory, protect immigrant's rights, although not satisfactorily applied in practice. This happens mainly due to the prevalence of sovereignty against human rights. States have the sovereign right to decide who may enter and remain in its territory; thus, it becomes essential to defend the non-negotiability of human rights. It should be stressed, however, that "human rights are not a matter of choice, but are legal obligations under international treaties which bind all governments that have accepted them" (Global Migration Group (GMC) 2010, p. 98). Protection of human rights cannot be dissociated from migration's management and control. In this sense, one of the main challenges continues to be to increase the number of countries that ratify, implement and enforce treaties in this field;

> Thus, the challenge is to protect the rights of migrants by strengthening the normative human rights framework relating to international migrants and by ensuring that its provisions are applied on a non-discriminatory basis at the national level (GMC 2010, p. 99).

It is therefore visible that international human rights discourse is impotent in what concerns "the imprisonment of thousands of people under exceptional conditions, not on account of what they have done but on account of what they are" (Cornelisse 2010, p. 102). However, starts to grow an international movement recognising the urgent need to find alternatives to the detention of immigrants and asylum seekers, particularly children detainees. United Nations Office of the High Commissioner for Human Rights (ONHCR) is, not surprisingly, one of the leading organisations of this process. Other international organisations have also been focusing more on migrant's rights recently, but there is still a long way to walk, particularly in what concerns coordination between the various entities that operate in this field (States, International Organizations, NGO, grassroots movements, etc.).

The International Detention Coalition states:

> (...) given the lack of one UN body with an overarching mandate on immigration detention, no international instrument on detention standards specifically for refugees, asylum seekers and migrants and the growing use of immigration detention worldwide, both the UN and civil society must remain vigilant, proactive and work collaboratively to ensure governments uphold international human rights standards for those in immigration detention (IDC 2011, p. 8).

[5] For a detailed list of legal instruments relevant to migration, see "Appendix B", Global Migration Group (GMC) 2008.

5 Detention Centres as Part of Prison Industrial Complex

There is certain unanimity in what concerns the main failures of the detention system, mainly in the United States. International human rights bodies, bipartisan groups and the U.S. government itself agree that detention centres are inadequate and excessively expensive (Human Rights First (HRF) 2011, p. ii).

If we analyse the detention system, particularly in the United States, with critical lens, there are some aspects that stand out. First, detention facilities mushroomed in the last years (there are more than the triple since 2001)—certainly due to the targets defined by ICE—and there are places where human rights are reported as systematically violated. Detention centres frequently do not have public scrutiny (civil society and media have restricted access to them, limiting the acquaintance of critical plights such as children in detention or other vulnerable groups), and in many cases not even lawyers have direct access to the detainees. In this sense, we can easily understand why the detention centres are spaces conducive to human rights violations and to physical, racial and sexual abuses. In this sense, "detention without accountability only increases mistreatment" (One America 2008, p. 9); it is an inappropriate and unnecessarily costly system (over $2 billion each year, according to HRF 2011) for asylum seekers and other immigration detainees, and it is a "patchwork system" comprising "ICE-run facilities, facilities operated by private prison contractors, and local jails and state prisons that also hold criminal inmates" (Human Rights First (HRF) 2011). So a detention facility can be a massive, privately run centre, such as Willacy Detention Center in Texas, or can have a few beds in a smaller country jail.

In 2009, a report by Dora Schriro, an official from the Department of Homeland Security (DHS), acknowledged those aspects and reinforced the need to change paradigm, moving from a penal and punitive system to a civil system and therefore adapting the detention centres to non-criminal detainees (Kalhan 2010).

Two years later, in 2011, Human Rights First (a non-profit, non-partisan international human rights organisation located in New York and Washington, D.C.) published a report focused essentially on demanding a "shift from a jail-oriented approach to immigration detention toward an approach that utilises conditions and environments more appropriate for civil immigration detainees" (Human Rights First (HRF) 2011, p. 3). Criticising the fact that some of the main aims outlined in Dora Schriro's report (Schriro 2009) towards a more appropriate approach to immigration detention (for instance, "asylum seekers and other immigrants still wear prison uniforms and are typically locked in one large room for up to 23 hours a day; they have limited or essentially no outdoor access, and visit with family only through Plexiglas barriers, and sometimes only via video, even when visitors are in the same building" (Human Rights First (HRF) 2011, p. i)) have not yet been attained,[6] the report concluded that "even with more appropriate detention conditions, however, detention can still be—and is—penal in nature when the detention

[6] Changes that ICE (Immigration and Customs Enforcement) proposed to carry out in 2–3 years.

itself runs afoul of other human rights protections—for example, when detention is not necessary, reasonable, or proportionate, or is unnecessarily prolonged" (Human Rights First (HRF) 2011, p. ii). In order to improve US detention policies and practices, Human Rights First recommended four main reforms, concerning the following:

1. Stop Using Prisons, Jails, and Jail-like Facilities, and When Detention Is Necessary Use Facilities with Conditions Appropriate for Civil Immigration Law Detainees;
2. Prevent Unnecessary Costs by Ensuring that Asylum Seekers and Other Immigrants Are Not Detained Unnecessarily;
3. Improve Access to Legal Assistance and Fair Procedures;
4. Take Other Steps to Address Deficiencies in Immigration Detention Conditions. (HRF 2011, pp. vi–vii)

Corroborating this perspective, Anil Kalhan states that

> to fully dismantle this quasi-punitive regime, it may not be sufficient to focus exclusively on improving conditions of confinement. Absent a more fundamental reconsideration of immigration control policies premised upon convergence with criminal enforcement, fully realizing "fairness and humanity" will remain an aspiration in tension with the "toughness" that has dominated immigration policy in recent years (Kalhan 2010, p. 58).

Therefore, such reforms cannot be, naturally, isolated from comprehensive immigration reform, so long in coming, and waiting to republican side support.

The exorbitant annual spending on detention is symptomatic of the "broken immigration system" (National Immigration Forum (NIF) 2012). The funding level for the current fiscal year (2013) "would amount to $5.4 million per day spent on immigration detention. The current cost to detain an immigrant is approximately $164 per day at a capacity of 32,800 daily detention beds" (National Immigration Forum (NIF) 2012, p. 1). Significant portions of this amount goes to the huge private prison corporations that feed U.S "prison industrial complex":

> It should not be surprising that the booming U.S. "prison industrial complex" would provide fertile ground for the growing industry of removals, which not only replicates the containment model but also models new methods of economic rationalization: flexibility, low-cost buildings, less organized labour, and increasing privatization. (Simon 1998). Indeed, the deportation process as a whole is perhaps best described as an industry (Walters 2002:266) that employs airlines, pilots, and private security companies in addition to DHS officials, deportation officers, and detention center staff (Peutz 2006, pp. 221–222).

Governments should choose more frequently less expensive community-based alternative to detention, but on the contrary, some countries are increasing detention and deportation practices. Alternatives to detention can reduce the risk of emotional and psychological damage and criminalisation and can represent significant cuts in costs borne by taxpayers:

> Given the predominantly non-criminal make-up of the immigration detention population and the expenses and concerns surrounding detention, more humane and cost-effective alternatives should be pursued. Many immigrants currently in ICE custody could be safely released and, if necessary, monitored with alternative methods, such as telephonic and in-person reporting, curfews, and home visits (NIF 2012, p. 7).

If ICE limited its use of detention to individuals who have committed violent crimes, the agency could save nearly $4.4 million a night, or $1.6 billion annually—an 82% reduction in costs (NIF 2012, p. 8).

In March 2012 was built a facility in Karnes, Texas, United States, conceived to be the "first civil detention center", housing low-risk adult male. One of the central questions that arise is whether these centres, even wanting to be "civil", will be the best alternative for "low-risk immigrants". Despite the increasing number of alternatives to detention programs, it remains residual compared to traditional detention.

In this sense, it is important to raise more research highlighting alternatives to detention's benefits and analysing what prevents governments from pursing or implementing them. Pro-immigrant rights organisations, anti-deportation activists, practitioners, advocates, etc. can also play a relevant role in this context (and in other aspects of detention and immigration phenomenon), acting as political actors and joining the migrants themselves as political actors.

These kinds of civil-society-led initiatives can be seen as an example of "subaltern cosmopolitanism movement", as an important contribution to avoid the "continuous reproduction of abyssal thinking" and to pursue a "post-abyssal thinking" in migration's field. It can be a way to bring detainees, in particular, and migrants, in general, to "this side of the line" (Santos 2007, p. 55).

6 The Portuguese Case: Some Brief Notes

In Portugal, like in many other countries, there are two different kinds of immigration detention facilities: transit zone sites—called Temporary Installation Centres (CITs) at the main airports—and one dedicated detention centre.

Act 23/2007 provides "the legal framework for entry, permanence, exit, and removal of foreigners into and out of national territory". Under Article 146, a person illegally entering or staying in Portugal who is detained by "a police authority"—including the Immigration and Borders Service (SEF), Guarda Nacional Republicana, Polícia de Segurança Pública, Polícia Judiciária, or Polícia Marítima—must be brought before a judge within 48 h. If a removal order is made, the person is to be detained "at a temporary lodging centre or a matching facility". Article 142 provides some alternative enforcement measures such as "a. Periodical presentations at SEF; b. The obligation of staying at home using electronic surveillance means according to law".[7]

The detention centre—Unidade Habitacional de Santo António (UHSA)—is located in Oporto and it serves the whole country. It can receive 30 adults (15 male and 15 female) and 6 children. The main purpose of UHSA is to accommodate irregular migrants awaiting deportation order[8] for a maximum length

[7] http://www.globaldetentionproject.org/countries/europe/portugal/introduction.html.

[8] In Portugal, an asylum seeker cannot be detained.

of 60 days. The majority of detainees come from South America and Balkans, and the average age of detainees is 30 years old (58 % male and 42 % female). Most of unaccompanied children (a particular vulnerable group) admitted in Portugal are Brazilian.

The centre is coordinated by the Portuguese Immigration and Borders Service in partnership with Jesuit Refugee Service, International Organization for Migration and Doctors of the World (Jesuit Refugee Service-Europe (JRS) 2010). The shared management between state institutions (SEF) and NGOs is the main reason why USHA is considered an example of good practice in what concerns immigrant detention. Since its foundation, UHSA has received about 1728 foreigners from countries such as Brazil, Ukraine, Morocco, China and Nigeria (SEF 2012, p. 55).

In the last years, UHSA has been evaluated by some universities and public institutions. In 2011, based on an evaluation held in 2009, the Portuguese Ombudsman's office concluded, as other prior assessments, that UHSA's environment is more humane than reclusive. Nevertheless, it made some important recommendations: to improve recreational programs and activities by creating better conditions to the practice of sports; to provide mandatory communication to Minors Protection Commission in case of unaccompanied minors; to increase the quantity of food; to do cost-benefit analysis in order to compare the spaces of detention at airports, for example, with other alternatives; to contact the embassies and consular services for the provision of literature in detainee's own languages (Provedor da Justiça 2011).

There is a long way to go on towards a less punitive and more human detention system in Portugal, as in other European countries. A regularly holistic assessment made by independent organisations is a key factor in this context (Jesuit Refugee Service-Europe (JRS) 2010).

7 Concluding Remarks

> It's hard to be away from people I love and lose my freedom. Everyone here is nice . . . but I feel like a criminal.[9]
>
> We were real prisoners. . . They put us in prison even though we didn't do anything. We didn't understand anything.[10]

These short testimonies highlight the role that detention can play in strengthening immigrant's criminalisation; they remember us that freedom of movement is not a prerogative of all humans in a globalised world. Thus, regardless of the specific conditions prevailing in different detention centres in the North or Global

[9] Testimony of a woman detained in UHSA (http://www.jrsportugal.pt).

[10] "Refugee from Democratic Republic of Congo who was detained in 2011 with her younger sister in a county jail in New York alongside criminal inmates" (Human Rights First (HRF) 2011, p. i).

South, the situation of suppression of freedom of foreigners, either as asylum seekers or as immigrants awaiting deportation, puts them on "the other side of the line" and creates or exacerbates several vulnerabilities inherent to their condition of the "other" or of "wasted lives".

"Bare", "uninsured", "insecure", "disposable", "spaces of exception", "spaces near to rightlessness", "enclaves of non-right", "system of quasi-punitive immcarceration" are some of the characteristics attributed to immigrants in the context of detention. They reveal the placement of the detainees "in the other side of the line", in a vulnerable and subaltern condition, which exposes them to violation of their most basic rights. At immigrations detention centres, what happens is a kind of voluntary interruption of human rights and negation of citizenship led by receiving countries' authorities, which also lead immigrants to the interruption of their project of life, their search for a better life.

This situation is powered by international institution's impotence to enforce legal instruments, compared to the almost omnipotence of national sovereignties. And it becomes easily acceptable and supported by receiving countries' public opinion due to a social and political context that makes hyper-visible the image of the immigrant as the "enemy", the "outsider", the "scapegoat", particularly during economic crisis.

Detention is being mostly used as a kind of "one size fits all" solution, in the sense that it is implemented in a plurality of situations, concerning irregular migrants, with regard to asylum seekers, from different ages and physical and psychological conditions, with or without special needs. As concluded in a recent European project, detention "is used in a mostly indiscriminate manner with little deference to personal choice and preferences" (Jesuit Refugee Service-Europe (JRS) 2010, p. 13). The DEVAS study also concluded that differences between Member States are notable, concerning length of time in detention, safeguards and living conditions (some offer psychosocial care, access to interpreters), detention facilities structures (some have prison-like architecture), etc.

Detention centres are part of a macro context marked by "the permanence of abyssal global lines", by continuities of a violent colonial history and of requirements of global capitalism. To bring detainees to "this side of the line" and to make them part of the social contract, it is urgent a "post-abyssal thinking". In order to accomplish that, it is essential that pro-immigrant rights organisations, anti-deportation activists, practitioners, advocates, researchers, etc., continue to report situations within the detention facilities and to demonstrate the advantages of alternatives to detention, in human and economic terms. Alternatives to detention that respect human dignity and fundamental rights must always take precedence. Detention period when inevitable should be proportional, suited to specific situations and transparent (in the sense that information should be provided to detainees on a regular basis and in a language they can understand) and should take place in the shortest period of time possible. Time is a crucial issue, given the fact that certain conditions become surely problematic in a long detention.

References

Agamben G (1998) O poder soberano e a vida nua. Homo Sacer (trans: Guerreiro A). Editorial Presença, Lisboa

Águas C (2011) Pensamento abissal e o contexto quilombola. O Cabo dos Trabalhos: Revista Electrónica dos Programas de Doutoramento do CES/FEUC/FLUC/III 5. http://cabodostrabalhos.ces.uc.pt/n5/ensaios.php. Accessed 5 Aug 2014

American Civil Liberties Union (ACLU) (nd) www.aclu.org/immigrants-rights/immigration-detention. Accessed 5 Aug 2014

Arendt H (2008) As origens do totalitarismo (trans: Raposo R; 3rd edn). Dom Quixote, Lisboa

Biswas S, Nair S (2010) Introduction: international relations and "states of exception". In: Biswas S, Nair S (eds) International relations and states of exception. Margins, peripheries, and excluded bodies. Routledge, London/New York, pp 1–30

Cornelisse G (2010) Immigration detention and the territoriality of universal rights. In: Genova ND, Peutz N (eds) The deportation regime. Sovereignty, space, and the freedom of movement. Duke University Press, Durham/London, pp 101–122

Duffield M (2007) Development, security and unending war. Governing the world of peoples. Polity Press, Cambridge

Duffield M (2008) Global civil war: the non-insured, international containment and post-interventionary society. J Refug Stud 21(2):145–165

Fassin D (2011) Policing borders, producing boundaries. The governmentality of immigration in dark times. Annu Rev Anthropol 40:213–226

Gjergji I (2006) Espulsione, trattenimento, disciplinamento Il ruolo dei CPT nella gestione della forza lavoro clandestina. DEP 5–6:97–119

Global Migration Group (GMC) (2010) International migration and human rights challenges and opportunities on the threshold of the 60th anniversary of the Universal Declaration of Human Rights. http://www.unfpa.org/public/home/publications/pid/5776. Accessed 5 Aug 2014

Hernández DM (2008) Pursuant to deportation: Latinos and immigrant detention. Latino Stud 6:35–63

Human Rights First (HRF) (2011) Jails and jumpsuits – transforming the U.S. immigration detention system—a two-year review. www.humanrightsfirst.org. Accessed 5 Aug 2014

International Detention Coalition (IDC) (2011) The issue of immigration detention at the UN level: Recent developments relevant to the work of the International Detention Coalition (IDC). http://idcoalition.org/wp-content/uploads/2011/01/idc-report_id-un-level-24jan2011-1.pdf. Accessed 5 Aug 2014

Jesuit Refugee Service-Europe (JRS) (2010) Becoming vulnerable in detention. Civil society report on the detention of vulnerable asylum seekers and irregular migrants in the European Union (The DEVAS Project). www.detention-in-europe.org. Accessed 5 Aug 2014

Kalhan A (2010) Rethinking immigration detention, 110 COLUM. L. REV SIDEBAR 24:42–58 http://columbialawreview.org/wp-content/uploads/2010/07/42_Anil_Kalhan.pdf. Accessed 5 Aug 2014

Loyd J, Burridge A, Mitchelson (2009–2010) Thinking (and moving) beyond walls and cages: bridging immigrant justice and anti-prison organizing in the United States. Soc Justice 36 (2):85–103

McDowell MG, Wonders NA (2009–2010) Keeping migrants in their place: technologies of control and racialized public space in Arizona. Soc Justice 36(2):54–72

Nair S (2010) Sovereignty, security, and migrants: making bare life. In: Biswas S, Nair S (eds) International relations and states of exception. Margins, peripheries, and excluded bodies. Routledge, London/New York, pp 95–115

National Immigration Forum (NIF) (2012) The math of immigration detention: runaway costs for immigration detention do not add up to sensible policies. http://www.immigrationforum.org/images/uploads/mathofimmigrationdetention.pdf. Accessed 5 Aug 2014

One America (2008) Voices from detention: a report on human rights violations at the Northwest Detention Center in Tacoma, Washington. Seattle University School of Law International Human Rights Clinic in collaboration with One America (formerly Hate Free Zone). http://www.weareoneamerica.org/sites/default/files/OneAmerica_Detention_Report.pdf. Accessed 5 Aug 2014
ONHCR (1999) Revised guidelines on applicable criteria and standards relating to the detention of asylum seekers. Geneva. http://www.unhcr.org.au/pdfs/detentionguidelines.pdf. Accessed 5 Aug 2014
Peutz N (2006) Embarking on anthropology of removal. Curr Anthropol 47(2):217–241
Portugal Detention Profile. http://www.globaldetentionproject.org/countries/europe/portugal/introduction.html. Accessed 5 Aug 2014
Provedor da Justiça (2011) A instalação temporária de cidadãos estrangeiros não admitidos em Portugal ou em processo de afastamento do território nacional. Relatório, Lisboa
Santos BS (2007) Para além do pensamento abissal: das linhas globais a uma ecologia de saberes. Revista Crítica de Ciências Sociais 78:3–46
Schriro DB (2009) Immigration detention overview and recommendations. US Department of Homeland Security, Immigration and Customs Enforcement
SEF (2012) Relatório de imigração, fronteiras e asilo. http://sefstat.sef.pt/Docs/Rifa_2011.pdf. Accessed 5 Aug 2014
Sharpe J (2000) Is the United States postcolonial? Transnationalism, immigration, and race. In: King RC (ed) Post-colonial America. University of Illinois Press, Urban and Chicago
Stumpf J (2006) The crimmigration crisis: immigrants, crime & sovereign power. Am Univ Law Rev 56:367–419
Torpey J (2000) The invention of the passport: surveillance, citizenship and the state. Cambridge University Press, Cambridge
Wacquant L (1999) As prisões da miséria (trans: Telles A). Jorge Zahar Editor, Rio de Janeiro

Statutes and Legislative Materials Cited

18 USC § 3142.
Anti-Drug Abuse Act of 1988, Pub. L. No. 100–690, § 7342, 102 Stat. 4469.
Anti-Drug Abuse Act of 1988, Pub. L. No. 100–690, § 7343, 102 Stat. 4181, 4470.
Antiterrorism and Effective Death Penalty Act (AEDPA), Pub. L. 104–132, 110 Stat. 1214.
Illegal Immigration Reform and Immigrant Responsibility Act (IIRIRA), Pub. L. 104–208, 110 Stat. 3009.
Immigration Act of 1990, P.L. 101–649, Nov. 29, 1990, 104 Stat. 4978.
Immigration and Nationality Act ("INA") § 212(d)(5); 8 USC. §1182(d)(5).
Immigration and Nationality Act ("INA") § 231 (b)(1)(B)(iii)(IV), (b)(2)(A); 8 USC. §1225(b)(1)(B)(iii)(IV), (b)(2)(A).
Immigration and Nationality Act ("INA") § 235 (b)(2)(c); 8 USC. §§1225(b)(2)(c)
Immigration and Nationality Act ("INA") § 236(c); 8 USC. § 1226(c).
Immigration and Nationality Act ("INA") § 236A; 8 USC. § 1226A.
Immigration and Nationality Act ("INA") § 241(a)(1)-(3); 8 USC.§ 1231(a)(1)-(3).
Immigration and Nationality Act ("INA") § 240a; 8 USC. § 1229a.
Hearing on H.R. 3333 before the Subcommittee on Immigration, Refugees, and International Law of the House Committee on the Judiciary, 101st Cong., 1st Sess., 54, 52 (1989)
George H.W. Bush, Statement on Signing the Immigration Act of 1990 (Nov. 29, 1990), P.L. No. 101–649, http://www.presidency.ucsb.edu/ws/index.php?pid=19117#axzz1OsUYZ1gw.
S. 744, "Border Security, Economic Opportunity, and Immigration Modernization Act." (2013) http://www.gpo.gov/fdsys/pkg/BILLS-113s744es/pdf/BILLS-113s744es.pdf.

Cases Cited

Moncrieffe v. Holder, No. 11–702 (Apr. 23, 2013)
Padilla v. Kentucky, 130 S. Ct. 1473, 1490 (2010)
Demore v. Kim, 538 U.S. 510 (2003)
Zadvydas v. United States, 533 U.S. 678 (2001)
Matter of Joseph, 22 I. & N. Dec. 799 (B.I.A. 1999)
Kansas v. Hendricks, 521 U.S. 346 (1997)
Reno v. Koray, 515 U.S. 50 (1995)

Mandatory Immigration Detention for U.S. Crimes: The Noncitizen Presumption of Dangerousness

Mark Noferi

Abstract Today in the United States, mandatory immigration detention imposes extraordinary deprivations of liberty following ordinary crimes—if the person convicted is not a U.S. citizen. Here, I explore that disparate treatment, in the first detailed examination of mandatory detention during deportation proceedings for U.S. crimes. I argue that mandatory immigration detention functionally operates on a 'noncitizen presumption' of dangerousness. Mandatory detention incarcerates noncitizens despite technological advances that nearly negate the risk of flight, with the risk posed by noncitizens increasingly seen as little different, at least those treated with dignity. Moreover, this 'noncitizen presumption' of danger contravenes empirical evidence and overdetains the nondangerous even more so than criminal pretrial detention practices, themselves under reform. Rather, the 'noncitizen presumption' rests on stereotypes of dangerous, recidivist 'criminal aliens'—which, because of a noncitizen's inherently speculative past, particularly bolster the tendency of preventive detention regimes to choose detention. I preliminarily offer two theories for the 'noncitizen presumption,' both reflecting expressive, symbolic characteristics of immigration detention law—government overcompensation for public 'blaming the gatekeeper' and, complementarily, a social construct of noncitizens as invitees, derived from property law.

1 Introduction

Today in the United States, if a noncitizen resident commits a crime, and later encounters immigration authorities, (s)he will likely never freely set foot on American soil again. (S)he will likely be 'mandatorily detained.' In other words, (s)he will be incarcerated for months or years, without even an individualized bail hearing, until deportation (unless (s)he defeats those proceedings while incarcerated without an appointed lawyer).

Mandatory detention applies, even for minor offenses committed long ago, no matter how long the noncitizen has lived in America or whether the noncitizen has a

M. Noferi (✉)
American Immigration Council, 2014-15, Washington, DC, USA
e-mail: marknoferi@gmail.com

M.J. Guia et al. (eds.), *Immigration Detention, Risk and Human Rights*,
DOI 10.1007/978-3-319-24690-1_13

lawful status (a.k.a. a 'green card'), family, property, or job or, indeed, whether any evidence of actual dangerousness exists. Mandatory detention applied, for example, to Melida Ruiz, a 52-year-old New Jersey grandmother who had lived in America for 30 years, supported her mother with Alzheimer's and her U.S. citizen children and grandchildren, and had one 9-year-old misdemeanor drug possession offense for which she never served jail time (Noferi and Koulish 2013). It applied to Bertha Mejia, a 53-year-old California grandmother who stole groceries (Mass 2013). It applied to Garfield Gayle, a 53-year-old Brooklyn carpenter and grandfather who was convicted of possessing marijuana in 1995, 17 years before U.S. Immigration and Customs Enforcement (ICE) authorities came to his house (Tan 2012). All were jailed for months or years during their deportation proceedings. I estimate the U.S. imposed 38,000 mandatory detentions in fiscal year 2011 (Noferi 2012, p. 67/n. 13).

In short, mandatory detention potentially imposes extraordinary deprivations of liberty following ordinary crimes—if the person convicted is not a U.S. citizen. This article examines this disparate treatment.

Here, I present the first detailed analysis of U.S. mandatory immigration detention on criminal grounds and its rationales and practices. My findings build on other scholars' questionings of immigration law's disproportionality while more specifically examining detention practices (and comparing them to pretrial criminal detention, which employs similar rationales of preventing flight risk or danger).[1]

Here, too, I isolate this particular context of prehearing mandatory immigration detention (i.e., during deportation proceedings), for postentry criminal activity (i.e., a U.S. crime). Doing so allows fuller examination of several heretofore-unexplored topics.[2] For one, I focus on detention for *criminal* grounds, rather than other forms of prehearing detention,[3] or mandatory detention.[4] Additionally, I explore the

[1] For example, Mary Fan argued that "criminal punishment and its costs should not turn just on the status of being an alien," but regarding U.S. laws criminalizing unlawful entry, rather than detention pending immigration proceedings (Fan 2014, p. 135). Jennifer Chacon, in analyzing deportation, noted "questions about why the criminal law is deemed to provide sufficient punishment for citizens, but not for non-citizens," without isolating detention (Chacón 2007, p. 1887).

[2] Geoffrey Heeren analyzed U.S. mandatory immigration detention generally. Here, I isolate prehearing, postentry mandatory detention on criminal grounds (Heeren 2010). Anil Kalhan primarily surveyed immigration detention conditions (calling them "quasi-punitive"), without focusing on particular detention laws or mandatory detention (Kalhan 2010).

[3] DHS also discretionarily detains noncitizens in deportation proceedings (8 U.S.C. § 1226(a)).

[4] Mandatory detention also exists postdeportation order, and for "arriving aliens" at the border (Heeren 2010, pp. 609–613; Noferi 2012, p. 83/n. 108). Postdeportation order detention seeks the same goals as preremoval order, but after adjudication of deportation, before execution of removal (Legomsky 1999, p. 534). An individual is mandatorily detained for ninety days after the removal order and, if not removed during those 90 days, may be released under supervision (INA § 241(a) (1)-(3), 8 USC.§ 1231(a)(1)–(3)). Additionally, 'arriving aliens'—noncitizens arriving to the United States, including returning LPRs and asylum seekers—are mandatorily detained if deemed inadmissible, without any immigration judge review (8 USC. §1225(b)(1)(B)(iii)(IV), (b)(2)(A)). They may be paroled into the United States, however (8 USC. §1182(d)(5)) (authorizing humanitarian parole). Also, such 'arriving aliens' from Mexico or Canada may be mandatorily detained

categorical nature of immigration mandatory detention, which does not consider noncitizens as individuals.[5] And notably, I explore constructions of migrants who enter and then commit a crime, distinct from scholars' constructions of the unlawfully entering migrants (the stereotypical 'illegal aliens') (Fan 2014, pp. 89–99; Schuck 1984, p. 6). Mandatory detention on criminal grounds applies to *all* noncitizens—lawful or not—which distinguishes the 'noncitizen presumption' I describe here from prior scholars' work.

First, I argue that prehearing mandatory detention on criminal grounds today functionally operates on a 'noncitizen presumption' of dangerousness. The U.S. effectively proceeds as if a noncitizen who has committed a crime remains especially dangerous beyond the period of conviction, even if supervised, compared to a U.S. citizen. Mandatory detention does not quite categorically incarcerate *all* noncitizens with criminal convictions during their deportation proceedings. But I argue that a 'noncitizen presumption' of dangerousness exists, based on the breadth of criminal activity encompassed, the absence of narrowing mechanisms for relief, and the empirical evidence I collect below.

I contrast this too with U.S. criminal pretrial detention practices. I argue that even though the U.S. criminal justice system overdetains relative to actual danger (despite recent reforms), mandatory immigration detention overdetains even more, because it categorically ensnares the less dangerous—the older, those with only one criminal charge, and those charged with fraud and public order criminal offenses (Baradaran and McIntyre 2012).

I arrive at the 'noncitizen presumption' of mandatory detention by examining prehearing detention's two rationales—flight risk and danger—and ruling out flight risk as legitimate. Little justification remains today for mandatory incarceration to prevent flight. Technological advances in alternatives to detention, such as GPS tracking bracelets, prevent flight nearly as well as detention. U.S. immigration and criminal authorities more routinely cooperate to identify and track noncitizens. More fundamentally, research preliminarily indicates that greater access to justice with supervision may encourage high compliance with proceedings—even, I argue, regarding noncitizens in immigration proceedings, traditionally presumed with higher incentives to "flee into the interior" (Noferi 2015; Tyler 2006; Tyler and Sunshine 2003).

Given this, the remaining rationale is danger. U.S. immigration officials cite danger, not flight risk, in their public statements and policies defending detention of "recidivist criminal aliens" (Morton 2013). Essentially, the U.S. does not trust noncitizens with convictions to remain at large, even if supervised and attending proceedings. This presumption ignores empirical evidence showing noncitizens as

during 'expedited removal,' a fast-track procedure that allows immigration officers to issue removal orders with no hearing or review (8 USC. §§1225(b)(2)(c), 1229a).

[5] César Cuauhtémoc García Hernández argues that immigration detention constitutes punishment in light of its legislative history, without isolating mandatory detention provisions (Hernández 2014).

less inclined to criminal activity and, even if so, less likely to recidivate. Thus, I argue, the 'noncitizen presumption' rather stems from well-familiar stereotypes of the dangerous 'criminal alien' than empirical evidence. Moreover, in a preventive detention context like prehearing immigration detention, the inherently speculative nature of noncitizens' lives *before* entering the U.S. bolsters the government's tendency to err towards detention.

Finally, although I mainly here establish the 'noncitizen presumption,' I also preliminarily explore its animating rationales.[6] I posit that the animating rationales are primarily expressive, not empirical—designed to send messages to the U.S. populace of active, competent government protection from dangerous criminal aliens. I explore two potentially complementary theories.

One I call 'blaming the gatekeeper.' I argue that the public perceives immigration officials to proximately cause noncitizen crime by failing their 'gatekeeping' function inherent to immigration law, more directly than the public blames criminal officials for citizen crime. The government then overcompensates to show protection via mandatory detention laws. Next, I argue that the U.S. socially constructs noncitizens as 'invitees,' per a property law analogy, which helps explain the categorical zero tolerance of mandatory detention even towards lawful immigrants' crimes. Both these theories help explain troubling disconnects between disproportionate immigration detention practices and individualized, rights-based norms. Indeed, mandatory detention does not speak to individual immigrants' circumstances because it is not speaking to them. The expressed message is categorical and designed for society at large, rather than individualized and designed for any particular noncitizen. I also largely reject two potential *sub rosa* rationales borrowed from criminal law, namely deterrence and punishment.

Most likely, given the expressive characteristics of mandatory detention laws, a change to mandatory detention will require a change to discourse regarding noncitizens with convictions. I preliminarily explore nascent seeds of this change last.

2 Overview: Mandatory Prehearing Immigration Detention of Noncitizens for U.S. Crimes

I examine here postentry, prehearing mandatory detention—*i.e.*, detention of one apprehended inside the U.S., pending a determination on his or her deportation.[7] In this section, I, first set out its facial rationales; second, provide an overview of the U.S. mandatory detention system; third, set out its historical development through

[6] I will explore these arguments further in future research.

[7] Immigration and Nationality Act (INA) § 236(c); 8 USC § 1226(c). My categorization of 'postentry' detention follows Daniel Kanstroom's categorization of "postentry social control" immigration laws, distinct from "extended border control" laws (Kanstroom 2000, pp. 1899–1914; Cox 2008, p. 350).

law; and, last, provide a parallel overview of criminal pretrial detention reforms, since passage of mandatory immigration detention laws.

2.1 *Rationales*

On its face, prehearing immigration detention is designed to prevent the putative deportee from committing either of two social ills during deportation proceedings. The first is flight from proceedings (a.k.a. abscondment). The second is crime (*Demore v. Kim* 2003, pp. 517–521; Legomsky 1999, p. 536). Mandatory detention seeks those same two goals via a categorical, rather than an individualized, determination (Legomsky 1999, p. 535). Here, the categorization is based on prior commission of a crime.[8]

Importantly, immigration detention, since it is legally civil, not criminal, is entirely preventive and should not be punishment (*Zadvydas v. Davis* 2001, p. 682). That said, immigration detention and *pretrial* criminal detention, before conviction, are both legally civil (Legomsky 1999, p. 536/n. 28). Indeed, both have the same two goals of preventing flight and crime.

Additionally, civil detention and criminal incarceration, whether pretrial or postconviction, both legitimately share the common mechanism of incapacitation, *i.e.*, separation from society.[9] Because of this overlap, with incapacitation in turn effecting complete deprivation of liberty, scholars have noted the functional resemblance between civil immigration detention and criminal incarceration (Stumpf 2006, p. 391/n. 130; Kanstroom 2000, p. 1895).[10]

2.2 *Current U.S. Prehearing Mandatory Detention Laws*

Since 1996, 8 USC § 1226(c) has governed U.S. mandatory detention of noncitizens in deportation proceedings. Under that statute, the U.S. government "shall take into custody" any noncitizen with prior criminal offense(s) that fit certain immigration law categories, all of which would also make the noncitizen deportable or

[8] The U.S. also can mandatorily detain one that the Attorney General certifies as a national security threat. INA § 236A; 8 USC § 1226A. This capability has never been exercised (Cooper Blum 2012, p. 691).

[9] "[W]hile incapacitation is a goal common to both the criminal and civil systems of confinement, retribution and general deterrence are reserved for the criminal system alone" (*Kansas v. Hendricks* 1997, Kennedy, J., concurring; Demleitner 2003, p. 1637).

[10] *But see* Hernández (2014) (arguing that immigration detention is punishment because legislative intent was punitive).

inadmissible[11] (Seipp and Feal 2010, pp. 5–6). If DHS determines a crime fits such a category, it detains the noncitizen without bail during proceedings, without any individualized hearing to assess flight risk or danger.

These immigration law categories encompass a broad range of criminal activity, much of it minor. One is mandatorily detained for a conviction of (a) an 'aggravated felony,' (b) two 'crimes involving moral turpitude' (CIMTs) at any time after U.S. admission, (c) one crime involving moral turpitude with a term of imprisonment of more than 1 year, (d) a controlled substance offense, or (e) a firearm offense.[12] Attempted possession of drugs, simple assault, subway turnstile jumping, petty theft or shoplifting, or disorderly person offenses have been held to qualify for mandatory immigration detention (Noferi 2012, pp. 89–94). Offenses may qualify even if no or little criminal jail time was served. Offenses may also qualify even if the criminal system absolved one of liability, via a dismissal, deferred adjudication, revoked sentence, expungement, nullification, pardon, or juvenile adjudication (Noferi 2012, pp. 94–95).

Offenses also qualify even if committed long ago. There are few statutes of limitations on detention and deportation for old convictions (Cox and Rodriguez 2009, p. 515). Indeed, U.S. immigration law changes were retroactive, turning pre-1996 convictions into new grounds for detention and deportation (Stumpf 2011, p. 1797). Detention and deportation for old convictions appears fairly common. For example, a 2013 study found that regarding ICE requests to local governments to hold noncitizens with convictions, about half involve convictions over 5 years old, almost a quarter involve convictions over 10 years old, and 4 % (about 4000 over 16 months) involve convictions over 20 years old[13] (TRAC Immigration, Syracuse University 2013b).

Regarding mandatory detainees specifically, along these lines, a significant portion are long-time U.S. residents, at least those who challenge deportation. For example, a 2013 expert report studied a sample of mandatory prehearing detainees who were detained 6 months or longer and found that 75 % had lived in the U.S. 5

[11] Federal immigration law primarily uses categories of crimes to trigger detention and deportation, rather than cross-referencing specific state or local criminal statutes (Das 2011, p. 1672).

[12] (8 USC. § 1226(c)(1)(A)–(D); Noferi 2012, p. 90).$6#The noncitizen has a high burden to challenge a DHS mandatory detention determination—essentially, to show DHS has no nonfrivolous argument supporting the determination. *Matter of Joseph*, 22 I. & N. Dec. 799 (B.I.A. 1999) (noncitizen must show that the government is 'substantially unlikely' to establish the mandatory detention charge(s) at the removal hearing). The analysis of whether a crime fits the mandatory detention categories is incredibly complicated and can include different modes of statutory analysis ("categorical" or "modified categorical" analysis), in different judicial circuits, as well as facts from the initial crime (Noferi 2012, pp. 89–96). Indeed, mandatory detention analysis spurred U.S. Supreme Court Justice Samuel Alito to say that "nothing is ever simple with immigration law" (*Padilla v. Kentucky* 2010, p. 1490).

[13] The study found some convictions over 40 years old (TRAC Immigration, Syracuse University 2013b).

years or longer, 55 % 10 years or longer, and 26 % 20 years or longer (Tan 2013, pp. 7–8).

Mandatory detention applies to all noncitizens—both those with lawful immigration status (such as a U.S. green card) and those without it (Grussendorf 2013, p. 6). About 20 % of those generally in immigration deportation proceedings appear to be lawful permanent residents,[14] who more likely have jobs and families.

Given all this, mandatory detention does not quite categorically encompass *all* noncitizens with criminal convictions pending their deportation proceedings. Some criminal convictions do not qualify one for mandatory detention. Data do not exist on the relative percentage of convictions that do qualify, among noncitizens.[15] But given the breadth of criminal activity covered, and the absence of avenues for relief, I argue that mandatory detention functionally creates a 'noncitizen presumption' of prehearing incarceration in deportation proceedings, where none exists in pretrial criminal proceedings.[16]

Existing data imply that mandatory detainees are a significant minority of the noncitizens placed into immigration proceedings. From 2005 to 2010, 9 % of New York ICE arrestees were mandatorily detained prehearing for crimes, which extrapolated nationwide would be over 38,000 mandatory detentions in fiscal year 2011 (of 429,000 the U.S. detained)[17] (NYU School of Law Immigrant Rights Clinic et al. 2012, p. 10; Noferi 2012, p. 67/n. 13). Or, from 2001 to 2011, 15.2 % of the nearly 2.3 million noncitizens placed into proceedings—over 346,000—were charged as deportable on criminal grounds (with some percentage of those mandatorily detained) (TRAC Immigration, Syracuse University 2011).[18]

Mandatory detainees also comprise a disproportionately high percentage of the long-term detention population. A 2009 government report stated that two-thirds of

---

[14] Human Rights Watch found that approximately 20 % of those deported on criminal grounds between 1997 and 2007 were lawful permanent residents (Human Rights Watch 2009, p. 4). Similarly, an NYU study of New York ICE arrestees from 2005 to 2010 found that 21.2 % were lawful permanent residents (NYU School of Law Immigrant Rights Clinic et al. 2012, p. 7).

[15] Human Rights Watch found that 72 % of those deported between 1997 and 2007 on criminal grounds were deported for nonviolent offenses, with the number rising to 78 % when considering lawful permanent residents (Human Rights Watch 2009, p. 4). It is unclear how many of these individuals were mandatorily detained.

[16] Cox and Rodriguez called "breathtaking" the scope of deportation statutes for criminal grounds (Cox and Rodriguez 2009, p. 516). For these reasons, several U.S. states and localities now refuse to hand over minor offender noncitizens to federal immigration authorities. These jurisdictions include California, Connecticut, New York City, Chicago, Los Angeles, Newark, New Orleans, and Washington, D.C. (New York Times 2013a).

[17] If 9 % does not seem high, consider that New York City criminal courts in 2010 denied bail to only 1 % of defendants in cases continuing past arraignment (Sect. 2.4).

[18] Recent data since 2011 is similar. For example, TRAC Immigration, a Syracuse University research project studying public immigration data, found that in fiscal year 2013 to date, approximately 14.3 % of those placed in proceedings were charged as deportable on criminal grounds, with slightly over 4 % charged with an 'aggravated felony' (which would automatically trigger mandatory detention) (TRAC Immigration, Syracuse University 2013a).

detainees then were 'mandatory,' although it is unclear what percentage were detained prehearing for U.S. crimes (Schriro 2009, p. 6; Kalhan 2010, p. 46). This high percentage may result from the length of mandatory detention for those who challenge deportation. A 2013 expert report found that of mandatory prehearing detainees who were detained 6 months or longer, the length of detention was about 14 months (Long 2013, p. B-1).[19]

More generally, mandatory detention has undeniably contributed to the U.S. immigration detention explosion, although it's exact contribution is unclear. In 1995, before the 1996 laws were passed, the U.S. detained 7500 on any 1 day (Schriro 2009, p. 2). Now, the U.S. Department of Homeland Security (DHS) detains 34,000 on any 1 day and 429,000 throughout the year, at a cost of $2 billion per year (U.S. DHS 2012, pp. 4–5; Nat'l Immigration Forum 2013, p. 1).

2.3 Historical Development of U.S. Mandatory Detention Laws

U.S. mandatory detention laws developed in three legislative enactments between 1988 and 1996. Initially, legislators focused on the danger posed by noncitizens with convictions and then shifted their focus to also encompass flight risk. I briefly summarize this history here.

Historically, prior to 1988, mandatory detention was not the norm. Although the U.S. possessed broad discretionary power to detain noncitizens pending their deportation on criminal or national security grounds, noncitizens (including 'criminal aliens') could be afforded 'liberal relief' from detention based on individual circumstances (Miller 2003, p. 622).[20] Detention appears to generally have been for short periods and not on the large scale implemented today (Kreimer 2012, p. 1486). In 1979 and 1980, however, the U.S. detained tens of thousands of Cubans arriving to the U.S. In 1982, U.S. President Ronald Reagan then by executive order mandatorily detained thousands of Haitians arriving by boat (Hernández 2014, pp. 1360–1361; Silverman 2010, p. 9; Cox and Rodriguez 2009, pp. 494–498).

In 1988, the U.S. first codified prehearing mandatory immigration detention in statute. Congress mandated detention pending deportation of noncitizens who had committed murder, illicit firearms trafficking, and drug trafficking, in the Anti-Drug Abuse Act, part of the U.S. then 'war on drugs'[21] (Hernández 2014,

[19] The expert report was filed in California federal litigation challenging the lack of individual bond hearings under mandatory prehearing detention laws. One-third of these detainees (33 %) won their cases, showing that challenging deportation was not a lost cause. Another 11 % had cases still pending at the time of the study (Long 2013, p. B-4).

[20] Allowable considerations included age, health, elapsed time of detention, and likelihood of resuming or engaging in deportable behavior.

[21] Anti-Drug Abuse Act of 1988, Pub. L. No. 100–690, § 7343, 102 Stat. 4181, 4470 (codified as amended at 8 USC. § 1252(a)(2) (2006)).

pp. 1366–1367). Congress did so by creating an immigration law category of crimes—i.e., 'aggravated felonies' (which included those three)—and mandating the then INS to take custody of any noncitizen convicted of these crimes after the criminal sentence.[22]

At this time, legislators' stated rationale was the dangerousness of those particular noncitizens. For example, New York Senator Alfonse D'Amato described aggravated felons as "a particularly dangerous class" and commended provisions that "put aggravated alien felons in detention" (Hernández 2014, p. 1367).

Subsequently, in 1990, the U.S. Congress expanded the 'aggravated felony' category to include more drug crimes, thus expanding mandatory detention.[23] The rationale remained danger. For example, in 1989, Congress heard evidence that criminal aliens committed more crimes before being deported.[24] Or then President George H.W. Bush stated after the 1990 Act that these noncitizens "jeopardize[d] the safety and well-being of every American resident" (Bush 1990).

Then, between 1990 and 1996, legislators developed evidence focusing on criminal aliens' flight from proceedings and recommended detention to prevent abscondment (and thus future crimes). For example, a 1995 U.S. Senate report stated, "[c]riminal aliens are a serious and growing threat to public safety," and "[p]roblems of undetained criminal aliens who fail to appear or who abscond... would be lessened if the INS detained more criminal aliens" (U.S. Senate Committee on Governmental Affairs 1995, p. 1). The report found that over 20 % of deportable "criminal aliens" failed to appear for removal hearings and called this a "high rate of no-shows" (U.S. Senate Committee on Governmental Affairs 1995, p. 32). This followed a 1994 Department of Justice report, which similarly found that 21 % of noncitizens failed to show for proceedings in 1992 (U.S. Department of Justice, Office of the Inspector General 1994, p. 5).

The 1995 Senate report did not estimate the numbers of crimes committed by noncitizens relative to citizens. Rather, it explicitly (if not empirically) connected unlawful immigration status to criminality. "[T]heir illegal situation conveys an 'outlaw' status, often leading them into the shadowy realms of criminal lifestyles" (U.S. Senate Committee on Governmental Affairs 1995, p. 5). Subsequently, Senator Orrin Hatch stated (without statistics), "Frankly, a lot of our criminality in this country today happens to be coming from criminal, illegal aliens who are ripping our country apart" (Chacón 2007, p. 1843).

The 1995 report also evinced a zero-tolerance attitude for criminality by noncitizens, whether lawful or unlawful. "[A] consensus seems to exist... there is just no place in America for non-U.S. citizens who commit criminal acts here. America

[22] Anti-Drug Abuse Act § 7342 (amending INA § 101(a)), § 7343) (amending INA § 242(a)).

[23] Immigration Act of 1990, P.L. 101–649, Nov. 29, 1990, 104 Stat. 4978; Hernández (2014), p. 1368.

[24] House Committee on the Judiciary 1989, p. 52 (after criminal aliens were identified as deportable, 77 % were arrested at least once more and 45 % were arrested multiple times before deportation proceedings began).

has enough criminals without importing more" (U.S. Senate Committee on Governmental Affairs 1995, p. 6).

In 1996, Congress then drastically expanded the categories of crimes qualifying for mandatory detention, whether by lawful or unlawful noncitizens, beyond crimes connected to the 'war on drugs'[25] (Miller 2003, p. 622). These categories are described above, and this law remains current today.

A note, however. Congress' language required mandatory "custody," not mandatory "detention" (i.e., incarceration) (8 U.S.C. § 1226(c)). Subsequently, though, U.S. immigration enforcement agencies administratively adopted the position that mandatory "custody" under INA § 236(c) requires incarceration rather than supervision[26] (American Immigration Lawyers Association (AILA) 2010). The U.S. government has declined to change this position without explanation[27] (Human Rights First (HRF) 2012, p. 8/n. 16).

2.4 Parallel Development of U.S. Pretrial Criminal Justice Reforms

The lack of change to mandatory immigration prehearing detention policies since 1996 contrasts with recent U.S. criminal pretrial detention practices. U.S. criminal authorities detain far less than immigration authorities, even though criminal pretrial detention shares the aims of preventing flight or danger. Moreover, U.S. criminal justice authorities are increasingly employing alternatives to incarceration, along with empirical tools to inform pretrial detention decisions, which reduce detention while still preventing flight and crime.

In practice, U.S. criminal authorities more readily employ a spectrum of supervision practices—from check-ins to community supervision and bond, to GPS tracking devices or house arrest, to jail[28] (Wiseman 2014, p. 1366). For example, while New York criminal judges denied bail to 1 % of defendants in cases that

---

[25] Antiterrorism and Effective Death Penalty Act (AEDPA), Pub. L. 104–132, 110 Stat. 1214 (codified as amended in scattered sections of 8, 18, 22, 28, 40, and 42 USC.); Illegal Immigration Reform and Immigrant Responsibility Act (IIRIRA), Pub. L. 104–208, 110 Stat. 3009 (codified as amended in scattered sections of 8 USC).

[26] In the U.S. criminal system, courts have reached the opposite conclusion (*Reno v. Koray* 1995 [defining "custody" to include those under prison system control]).

[27] 2013 U.S. Senate legislation would have changed this to explicitly define "custody" under INA § 236(c) to include electronic ankle devices ("Border Security, Economic Opportunity, and Immigration Modernization Act," § 3715(d)).

[28] Indeed, U.S. criminal laws rarely categorically impose detention without bail. The U.S. federal criminal code provides a rebuttable presumption that a defendant shall be denied bail on public safety grounds, if charged with certain serious crimes or crimes of violence, but the defendant is still provided a lawyer and a hearing to challenge that presumption (18 USC § 3142). U.S. mandatory immigration detention provides no similar hearing or appointed lawyer.

continued past arraignment, DHS mandatorily detained by law, without bail, 9 % of New York immigration arrestees[29] (NYU School of Law Immigrant Rights Clinic et al. 2012, p. 10).

Criminal authorities have also increasingly incorporated empirical evidence into pretrial justice practices. Nine states, multiple localities, and the federal system now use risk assessments, conducting an actuarial assessment of the likelihood of reoffense or flight that informs their detention decisions (Pretrial Justice Institute 2012a, p. 3; Pretrial Justice Institute 2012b, p. 14). Risk assessments can differentiate risk of flight or danger with high accuracy rates, according to studies (Pretrial Justice Institute 2012a, p. 4). For example, Kentucky has demonstrated a 90 % appearance rate and only 8 % re-arrest rate (Conference of State Court Administrators (COSCA) 2013, p. 6).

U.S. immigration authorities also recently introduced a risk assessment tool in March 2013 (Sampson and Mitchell 2013, p. 103). That said, for mandatory prehearing detainees, risk assessment offers no help. U.S. immigration authorities have not allowed alternatives to mandatory prehearing detention[30] (Koulish and Noferi 2013a).

Although the U.S. pretrial criminal system still overdetains, the immigration system overdetains even more. For example, a recent U.S. criminal empirical study found that up to 25 % of criminal pretrial detainees could be released without concomitantly increasing crime, generally in three categories—older defendants, defendants with previously clean records (i.e., one criminal charge at issue), and defendants charged with fraud and public order offenses (Baradaran and McIntyre 2012, p. 554).

Yet the immigration system overdetains these individuals even more, and categorically so. Mandatory immigration detention plausibly ensnares individuals in all three nondangerous categories. Immigration detainees are generally older, as the immigration system detains any time after a crime (unlike the criminal system, which detains immediately after a charge—crimes being more commonly committed by younger people)[31] (Schriro 2012; Stumpf 2011; Hirschi and Gottfredson 1983). Mandatory detention also holds individuals with only one criminal charge—

[29] Immigration authorities' tendency to detain more continues throughout their discretionary decisions. DHS denied bail discretionarily to another 71 % of New York ICE arrestees, and set bail for 20 % of immigration arrestees at markedly higher rates, while releasing less than 1 % on recognizance. Comparatively, New York criminal judges set bail for 20 % of defendants and released 68 % on recognizance (NYU School of Law Immigrant Rights Clinic et al. 2012, p. 10). I will address these vast discrepancies in future research.

[30] Other concerns exist regarding immigration risk assessments. The current lack of transparency, and concurrent possibility of overweighting towards detention, is one. More broadly, without transparency or process checks, risk assessment may facilitate a transition from mass incarceration to mass supervision, with its own attendant set of concerns (Koulish and Noferi 2013b). Robert Koulish and I have examined risk assessments in research, based on ICE immigration risk assessments received through FOIA (Noferi and Koulish 2014).

[31] As Dr. Dora Schriro notes, the immigration detention population thus has more stable individuals with families and jobs who are less dangerous (Schriro 2012). Even regarding immigration

for example, an 'aggravated felony,' which encompasses minor crimes like sharing a marijuana cigarette (*Moncrieffe v. Holder*, 2013). And mandatory detention holds individuals charged with fraud or public order offenses. Indeed, a 'crime involving moral turpitude' is typically one involving fraud, larceny, or intent to harm persons or property—for example, jumping a subway turnstile (as involving theft of services) or a disorderly person offense (as involving intent to harm property)[32] (Noferi 2012, p. 93).

In sum, while the U.S. criminal pretrial system begins to reform overdetention, mandatory immigration detention categorically inculcates overdetention into law. A noncitizen charged with a minor crime today will likely be released pretrial in the criminal system but, if convicted, will be quite likely mandatorily detained during deportation proceedings.

3 Mandatory Detention: The "Noncitizen Presumption" of Danger in Practice

Given this overview, I argue that U.S. mandatory immigration detention today functionally operates on a noncitizen presumption of dangerousness. More specifically, the presumption is that noncitizens who commit crimes are more dangerous than citizens, and remain so beyond the time period of punishment for their conviction, thus categorically warranting complete incapacitation through incarceration for their remaining time in the U.S.[33]

I reach this conclusion by examining the implementation of U.S. mandatory detention, in light of its two potential legitimate rationales—flight risk and danger—and ruling out flight risk as an explanation. Technological advances in alternatives to detention, such as GPS tracking bracelets, prevent flight nearly as well as detention. U.S. immigration and criminal authorities more routinely cooperate to identify and track noncitizens. More fundamentally, research preliminarily indicates that greater access to justice with supervision may encourage high compliance with proceedings—even, I argue, regarding noncitizens in immigration proceedings, traditionally presumed with higher incentives to 'flee into the interior.' Yet the U.S. refuses to employ alternatives for the mandatorily detained.

---

detainees with criminal histories, only 11 % had committed violent crimes (as of 2009) (Schriro 2009, p. 2).

[32] A separate 2009 study of immigration detention found that of the 42 % of detainees with a criminal record, 8 % were convicted of fraud, public order offenses, or forgery or counterfeiting. Thirty percent were convicted of drug crimes (Kerwin and Li 2009, pp. 20–21).

[33] Jennifer Chacon argued that U.S. policy incorporates a "misguided belief that non-citizens require extra incapacitation in the form of criminal removal" (Chacón 2007, p. 1887). Here, I argue that mandatory detention extends this "extra incapacitation" to the time period in removal proceedings, awaiting a determination.

This suggests that danger remains the primary concern. The discourse of immigration detention supports this, evidenced by U.S. immigration enforcement officials' statements that nearly exclusively focus on danger and policies that prioritize mandatory detainees as dangerous above all others. Essentially, the U.S. does not trust noncitizens with convictions to remain at large, even supervised by mechanisms that prevent flight like GPS tracking bracelets.

I argue that this danger rationale—which I call the 'noncitizen presumption'—is grounded in stereotype and bias towards immigrants, particularly 'criminal aliens,' rather than empirical evidence. This disconnect between immigrant criminality in discourse and fact is well established in law and social science literature, which I briefly reference below.

3.1 *Flight Risk*

Since 1996, when U.S. legislators last revisited mandatory immigration detention, lesser restrictive alternatives have emerged, such as electronic tracking, supervision, and case management that prevent flight nearly as well as complete incarceration at far less cost (Sampson and Mitchell 2013; Kreimer 2012, p. 1511; Legomsky 1999, p. 541; International Detention Coalition 2011). Advances have already been demonstrated in immigration proceedings. A 2000 study showed that 92 % of 'criminal aliens' released under supervisory conditions attended all of their hearings (Vera Institute of Justice 2000, p. 33/36).[34] Or Australia's individualized case management program achieved a compliance rate of 94 % between 2006 and 2009 (Nat'l Immigrant Justice Ctr. (NIJC) 2010, p. 6).

Some of these advances are technological. Electronic tracking bracelets, particularly, were not widely used in 1996, either in immigration or criminal proceedings (Kreimer 2012, p. 1511; Wiseman 2014, pp. 1364–1367). Today, U.S. immigration authorities do employ electronic monitoring, albeit not as widely as detention (Rutgers School of Law-Newark Immigrant Rights Clinic and American Friends Service Committee 2012; Koulish 2012) DHS' "Intensive Supervision Appearance Program," in FY 2014, supervised 22,000 individuals on a daily basis (albeit no prehearing mandatory detainees) (U.S. Department of Homeland Security 2014, p. 60; Lutheran Immigration and Refugee Service (LIRS) 2011, p. 31). This begins to parallel the greater use of electronic tracking in pretrial criminal justice (Wiseman 2014, p. 1365). Technological alternatives to detention also save significant money, costing $17/day or less versus $159/day for detention (Nat'l Immigration Forum 2013, p. 1).

[34] As the study found, "mandatory detention of virtually all criminal aliens is not necessary." Even 82 % of criminal aliens released on recognizance without supervision appeared, as did 77 % of those released on bond. The study did involve a selected group of detainees. On the other hand, the study also employed lesser restrictive alternatives such as supervision, in addition to electronic tracking bracelets.

Additionally, risk assessment tools now exist that allow officials to base detention decisions on empirical assessments of danger or flight (Koulish and Noferi 2013a). In 1996, immigration flight rates were high in part because DHS made release decisions arbitrarily, by bed space, without identifying those more likely to flee (*Demore v. Kim* 2003, pp. 563–564). Nor did DHS identify lawful permanent residents with families and jobs, with more incentive to stay in the U.S., as DHS can today (*Demore v. Kim* 2003, p. 563).

More generally, although some immigrants unquestionably fled proceedings then (and probably more than would today), more robust comparisons today to criminal pretrial practices illuminate the disproportionality of mandatory detention to remedy abscondment. For example, in U.S. criminal proceedings, studies show that a defendant's likelihood of failing to appear is "statistically unaffected by… immigration status." (Theophile 2009)

Also, comparisons of rates of appearance between immigration prehearing and criminal pretrial populations establish a baseline not present in the 1996 debate.[35] For example, 1990s U.S. immigration studies found that about 80 % of deportable 'criminal aliens' appeared for hearings, which a U.S. Senate Committee called a "high rate" of abscondment (U.S. Senate Committee on Governmental Affairs 1995, p. 1). Yet this rate was not much different than comparable criminal abscondment rates. Compliance figures for felony criminal defendants released under noncustodial measures before trial have historically ranged from 40 to 70%[36] (Field and Edwards 2006, para. 88), with higher rates recently as supervision techniques develop. For example, in 2009, 83 % of U.S. adult felony defendants released pretrial attended all court hearings (Reaves 2013, p. 21).

Put another way, immigration abscondment was never that high. Rather, the public tolerance for noncitizen crime following abscondment appears low (as Sect. 4 explores).

Additionally, greater coordination today between federal immigration and local criminal authorities has remedied prior failures to identify deportable noncitizens (as a precursor to thwarting absconders once identified) (Kreimer 2012, p. 1518). In the 1990s, the then INS was widely criticized for not identifying removable individuals after conviction (*Demore v. Kim*, p. 518). Recently, though, Secure Communities technology, which mandates local criminal authorities to share information with federal immigration authorities, makes it more possible to identify removable noncitizens.[37]

Most fundamentally, recent empirical immigration research may rebut the historical presumption that noncitizens are particularly likely to abscond immigration

[35] A 2003 U.S. Supreme Court decision upholding mandatory immigration detention discussed rates of immigration flight without comparing them to criminal rates (*Demore v. Kim* 2003).

[36] Thus, Field and Edwards' 2006 United Nations study assumed that an immigration compliance rate of over 80 % demonstrated effectiveness.

[37] Although ICE requires localities to share information, some states and cities now refuse to provide ICE noncitizen residents with criminal convictions (New York Times 2013b). This reflects public disagreement with ICE's policies, however, rather than technological capability.

proceedings and thus rebut a primary rationale for detention. Rather, recent research preliminarily indicates that providing dignity, via access to justice and less detention, fosters trust and subjective feelings of fairness, which Tyler and others correlate to compliance (Tyler 2006). I briefly describe potential implications here regarding mandatory immigration detainees.

Noncitizens have been presumed more likely to abscond immigration proceedings, since they seek additional time in the country and lose little by absconding (except eventual removal) (Legomsky 1999, p. 537; Schuck 1996, pp. 671–672). Along these lines, those with the least chance of success at a hearing have been thought least likely to attend it (Schuck 1996, p. 680). 'Criminal aliens' have in many cases no chance, since deportation is often mandatory (since 1996). Thus, so the argument goes, mandatory detention prevents flight by those most likely to flee (Heeren 2010, p. 631).

Yet recent research shows that supervising noncitizens, without detention but with dignity and fairness, significantly correlates with a predisposition to compliance—i.e., providing a proper and prompt hearing, by a consistent decision maker, and most importantly with access to early, reliable assistance and legal advice[38] (Costello and Kaytaz 2013; Sampson and Mitchell 2013, p. 110). For example, refugees acknowledged the necessity of a process to determine legitimate claims. But as Costello and Kaytaz found, refugees "expected not automatic protection, but a fair hearing" (Costello and Kaytaz 2013, p. 15).

For example, a 2013 UNHCR study examined Toronto asylum seekers released into shelters (not incarceration) pending immigration proceedings, with minimal reporting requirements but increased access to representation. As one asylum seeker said, "I do have trust in the system because I understand it." Toronto asylum seekers generally viewed the process as fair and remained cooperative with authorities (Costello and Kaytaz 2013, p. 18). This predisposition to comply extended to adverse orders (Costello and Kaytaz 2013, p. 24). Conversely, asylum seekers in Geneva, detained in worse conditions, with delayed hearings, and without ready access to legal advice, viewed the process as deeply unfair, evincing a predisposition not to comply with orders (Costello and Kaytaz 2013).

Tyler identified these subjective views of fairness, produced by procedural justice, as correlative with perceived legitimacy and thus compliance (Tyler 2006). This research has potential significance for immigration proceedings, although more research should be done—particularly regarding compliance by noncitizens with varying membership claims and little relief.[39] Notably, however, alternatives to detention are proving to be successful even for 'criminal aliens' without relief. Canada's Toronto Bail Program, for example, supervises many

[38] A 2011 survey of European detention similarly stressed early access to reliable assistance and legal advice (Amaral 2013).

[39] For example, Tyler's conception of legitimacy presumes membership and shared purposes, while noncitizens have varying membership claims (Tyler and Jackson 2014, p. 80 (studying U.S. citizens); *compare* Walzer 1996).

criminal aliens with 90 % compliance rates (although it screens clients for amenability to supervision) (Field and Edwards 2006, pp. 85–89). And through caseworker management, Sweden showed high rates of voluntary compliance with adverse removal orders, with 82 % of refused migrants arranging their own return (Phelps 2013, p. 46).

Still, the U.S. refuses to employ alternatives for those subject to mandatory detention. Even assuming theoretically that criminal aliens in removal proceedings pose greater flight risk—an assumption research increasingly rebuts—no evidence supports that flight risk is so much greater than ordinary criminal pretrial risk to categorically warrant total incarceration. Indeed, U.S. government officials do not argue this but rather defend mandatory detention on danger grounds. I examine these arguments next.

3.2 Public Danger

U.S. immigration enforcement officials since 1996 have essentially presumed mandatory detainees too dangerous to release, even with supervision. As such, prehearing mandatory detention has become a particularly excessive, blunt, and empirically unsound tool for "domestic crime control" (Kreimer 2012, p. 1514; Heeren 2010, p. 633). Here, I contrast public statements and policies with empirical evidence.

U.S. executive branch and immigration enforcement officials have continually characterized their enforcement efforts as promoting "security" and ensuring "public safety" by deporting "criminal aliens"[40] (McLeod 2012, p. 164). Indeed, the Obama Administration dubbed its information-sharing requirements for local police 'Secure Communities.' More specifically, in 2011 ICE Director John Morton issued a 'prosecutorial discretion' memorandum setting ICE's priorities as "serious felons, repeat offenders, or individuals with a lengthy criminal record" (Morton 2011a). Moreover, immigration officials cast criminal aliens as natural recidivists. For example, in 2011 Morton stated Secure Communities was "removing those aliens whose criminal history demonstrates a willingness to violate our laws…" (Morton 2011b).

Detention, concomitantly, is promoted as protecting the public from future crimes. For example, ICE characterizes its detention efforts as ensuring "security," by focusing resources on "the most serious criminal offenders…in a way that maximizes public safety" (U.S. Immigration and Customs Enforcement 2012; McLeod 2012, p. 127). Or a 2009 government report characterized ICE detention

[40] *See* U.S. Immigration and Customs Enforcement, *Secure Communities*, available at http://www.ice.gov/secure_communities/ ("The highest priority of any law enforcement agency is to protect the communities it serves," and thus "ICE prioritizes the removal of criminal aliens").

as focusing on "dangerous and repetitive" criminal aliens (Schriro 2009, p. 11; Kreimer 2012, p. 1513).

Perhaps most specifically, in 2013, Morton characterized detention as protecting "local communities [from] risks from suspected and convicted sex offenders, weapons violators, drunk drivers, and other violent criminals" (Morton 2013). He continued, "These are not hypothetical risks.... additional crimes being committed by these recidivist criminal aliens... include the possession of a controlled substance, money laundering, burglary, spousal battery, aggravated driving under the influence, and even attempted murder" (Morton 2013).

Mandatory detention, in turn, is characterized as protecting public safety—perhaps unsurprising, since mandatory detention by law detains noncitizens who have committed at least one crime. Yet ICE's prioritization of mandatory detainees is surprisingly high, even higher than those it individually identifies as dangerous. For example, a 2004 ICE policy memo, still in effect, places mandatory detainees first among detention priorities, above "national security interest aliens"; "aliens who exhibit specific, articulable intelligence-based risk factors for terrorism"; "aliens who present an articulable danger to the community"; or "suspected alien and narcotics smugglers" (Hutchinson 2004, p. 2). The memo provides no distinction between the various classes of mandatory detainees—e.g., terrorism grounds, criminal grounds, or asylum seekers at the border. Moreover, "[i]n the case of mandatory detention," guidelines must be heeded "strictly," with ICE managers given no discretion to deviate (unlike other categories) (Hutchinson 2004, p. 2).

ICE's 2011 'prosecutorial discretion' memo does not change these detention priorities. Indeed, it reaffirms allocation of detention resources either to support its public safety priorities or for "aliens subject to mandatory detention by law" (Morton 2011a, p. 3). Moreover, it excepts mandatory detainees from its relaxation of detention for certain categories, such as "primary caretakers," the seriously physically or mentally ill, or the disabled, elderly, pregnant, or nursing (Morton 2011a, p. 3). ICE could have allowed tracking bracelets for mandatory detainees, as alternative forms of 'custody,' but has not.

In essence, ICE sets its mandatory detention policy by relying on Congress' legislative, categorical determination of danger over its own agents' identifications of individualized danger. One might counterargue that Congress' legislative determination left ICE with little choice, except ICE has declined at least one choice it has—interpreting "custody" to include supervision.[41] One explanation may be the Congressional criticism ICE has faced for releasing detainees. For example, when ICE recently released detainees due to budget cuts, several elected officials assailed the releases as "needlessly endangering American lives" (Washington Post 2013),

[41] Contrastingly, the Obama Administration chose to implement a "deferred action" policy for undocumented youth, despite Congress' failure to pass legislation.

an "abrogation of [ICE's] mission to ensure the safety and security of Americans" (Grassley 2013), and a "federally sponsored jailbreak"[42] (Perry 2013).

Notably, these immigration officials' statements and policies regarding mandatory detainees do not cite flight risk. Indeed, ICE can now more readily find noncitizens with convictions and supervise them at modest cost. Rather, the apparent rationale is that noncitizens with convictions would commit more crimes if on the streets during proceedings, even supervised—enough to categorically, drastically reverse the normal presumptions towards release in the criminal system (Legomsky 1999, p. 541).

Concomitantly, noncitizens are presumed vastly more likely to reoffend (and violently) than citizens who committed similar crimes. This appears empirically untrue. A 2012 Congressional Research Service study found that criminal recidivism by ICE arrestees was significantly lower than recidivism by the general prison population[43] (Congressional Research Service (CRS) 2012). If anything, mandatory immigration detention results in greater overdetention relative to actual danger of recidivism than in the criminal system, as noted above. Yet mandatory detention persists.

3.3 Stereotype and Bias Supporting the Noncitizen Presumption

Given this, I argue that U.S. mandatory immigration detention today operates on a 'noncitizen presumption' of dangerousness, which relies primarily on historical stereotypes of foreigners as 'dangerous others,' rather than any empirical evidence of greater noncitizen criminality. Moreover, this stereotype particularly bolsters the detention rationale, since the inherently speculative nature of noncitizens' lives before entering the U.S. amplifies the inherently speculative nature of preventive detention decision making.

There is no evidence that noncitizens are more disposed towards criminality than citizens. Indeed, empirically, immigrants are generally more law abiding than natural-born citizens (Chavez and Provine 2009, p. 83; Alba et al. 2005, pp. 901–919; Reid et al. 2005, pp. 757–780). Migration, if anything, contributes to a decrease in violent crime rates (Guia 2012, pp. 27–29; Rumbaut and Ewing 2007; Stowell et al. 2009; Wadsworth 2010). Moreover, there is no evidence that a noncitizen poses greater danger after a criminal sentence (Legomsky 1999, p. 539).

[42] Not all elected officials posed this criticism. For example, Rep. Spencer Bachus (R-AL) asked, "Are you overusing detention? Are some of these mandatory detainees where we [Congress] could recommend they not be?" (Koulish and Noferi 2013b).

[43] Sixteen percent of ICE arrestees were rearrested for criminal activity within 3 years, compared to 43 % of U.S. criminal prisoners released in 2004 that were convicted and returned to prison within 3 years (Bennett 2012; Waslin 2012).

If anything, noncitizen recidivism rates appear lower than the general population, as noted. In any case, a criminal conviction is not necessarily a 'reliable indicator' of dangerousness—particularly minor convictions, many of which trigger mandatory immigration detention[44] (McLeod 2012, p. 149).

Yet the public perception of immigrants as 'dangerous others' persists (Guia 2012, pp. 27–29; Chacón 2007, p. 1887; Demleitner 1997; Garland 1996). Immigrants, lawful or not, are regularly conflated with criminals. As McLeod argues, a "stock crime-narrative framework" dominates immigration discourse and thus criminal aliens ostensibly "threaten the security and well-being of U.S. society" (McLeod 2012, p. 164). Indeed, the use of detention—similar to criminal jail—reinforces the conflation of immigration with crime (McLeod 2012, p. 154). Or immigrants are conflated with other 'dangerous others'—i.e., security threats, particularly terrorists after 9/11 (Massey 2013, pp. 7–9; Baili 2006, p. 54). The legal characterization of noncitizens as "aliens" contributes to immigrants being viewed as an invading flood (Cunningham-Parmeter 2011, p. 1559). Racial or ethnic prejudice is historically part of the equation as well (Chavez and Provine 2009, p. 80). Thus, U.S. mandatory detention law functionally assumes that detention is necessary for a noncitizen's remaining time in the U.S.

Additionally, the 'dangerous other' trope particularly infects detention policy because immigration detention is inherently predictive—informed by past acts, but ultimately preventive and speculative. As David Cole argued, "no one can predict the future," and thus detention "decision makers all too often fall back on stereotypes and prejudices as proxies for dangerousness" (Cole 2009, p. 696; Noferi 2012, p. 120; Robinson 2001, p. 1432). Moreover, a noncitizen's life before entering the U.S. is inherently speculative, and unknowable to immigration officials (Koulish 2012, pp. 63–64/71). As Peter Schuck argued, "aliens who appear to be first-time offenders may well have been convicted of other crimes in their home countries... of which the INS simply has no record" (Schuck 1997, p. 677). Or, as U.S. Supreme Court Justice Anthony Kennedy stated, a "significant risk may still exist" from "aliens who have completed prison terms," since "[u]nderworld and terrorist links are subtle and may be overseas," not reflected in U.S. criminal records (*Zadvydas v. Davis* 2001, p. 714).

Regarding immigration detention, I argue, the noncitizen's inherently speculative, potentially dangerous past amplifies the already-speculative nature of preventive detention to a greater degree than a criminal conviction based on tested evidence (Robinson 2001). Thus, it accentuates a government's tendency to err towards preventive detention (Cole 2009, p. 696). Errors of detention are unknowable, but errors of release are criticized.[45] When any noncitizen could be a recidivist

---

[44] Nor is a conviction a reliable indicator of undesirability (Cox and Posner 2007, p. 846). As McLeod points out, a noncitizen may have "possessed narcotics, trespassed, shoved someone during a verbal altercation or pulled their hair, jaywalked, jumped a subway turnstile," and on and "still be a valued contributor" to the U.S., let alone not dangerous (McLeod 2012, p. 149).

[45] "How can one prove what someone would or would not have done had he been free?" (Cole 2009, p. 696).

criminal, the safer course is to detain, even after lengthy U.S. residency without criminal activity. I return to these arguments in Sect. 4.2.1.

4 Examining Mandatory Detention's Animating Rationales

Here, I preliminarily analyze the animating rationales behind the 'noncitizen presumption' of danger, and mandatory detention generally. First, I largely reject *sub rosa* criminal law rationales, and second, I explore expressive rationales.

4.1 Rejecting Sub Rosa *Criminal Rationales*

Deterrence or punishment, rationales customary to criminal law, likely does not play an improper *sub rosa* role in prehearing mandatory immigration detention for U.S. crimes. Deterrence plays little, if any, role in the detention of residents committing crimes after entry. As to punishment, I argue that mandatory detention more likely (but not mutually exclusively) is animated by preventing future crimes, not punishing past crimes. Moreover, to the extent mandatory detention sends a message, it primarily expresses protection of the populace rather than the individual condemnation emblematic of criminal punishment, which I explore further in Sect. 4.[46]

4.1.1 Deterrence

Firstly, deterrence plays little, if any, animating role in prehearing, postentry mandatory detention of noncitizens.

Deterrence certainly animated policies to deter arriving noncitizens, particularly asylum seekers. For example, when the U.S. mandatorily detained arriving Haitians by executive order in the 1980s, the deterrence rationale was explicit (Taylor 1997, pp. 154–155; Pistone 1999, pp. 25–228). As then Attorney General William French

[46] Briefly, I note too that the rehabilitation rationale, present in criminal incarceration, likely plays little role in prehearing immigration detention. For one, immigration detention's baseline assumption has historically been deportation of detainees, rather than their return, and as a corollary rehabilitation has been presumed unnecessary from society's standpoint (Stumpf 2011, p. 1709). (That said, as more detainees receive procedural rights like appointed counsel and win deportation cases, this might change) (Noferi 2012, pp. 127–128). For another, rehabilitation presumes remorse by the individual, which is less likely present (nor legally required) regarding civil immigration law violations (Hernández 2014, p. 1401).

Smith stated, "[d]etention of aliens seeking asylum was necessary to discourage people like the Haitians from setting sail"[47] (Silverman 2010, pp. 18–20).

That said, the deterrence rationale has much less salience to postentry detention of residents already here. Theoretically, mandatory immigration detention on criminal grounds could serve a deterrent effect on criminal activity by residing noncitizens. But I agree with Stephen Legomsky that detention pending a deportation proceeding likely serves no meaningful deterrent effect, over and above the applicable criminal punishment and deportation[48] (Legomsky 1999, p. 541; Hernández 2014, pp. 1400–1401). Moreover, recent U.S. government statements regarding detention emphasize its incapacitative nature—i.e., protecting the public from dangerous criminals—rather than its deterrent impact—i.e., sending a particular message to noncitizens that immigration detention will be imposed for crime.

4.1.2 Punishment

Secondly, I acknowledge that detention may plausibly reflect extra punishment for noncitizens committing crimes, beyond the criminal sentence.[49] But I argue that detention more likely (but not mutually exclusively) reflects a perceived need for prevention, based on noncitizen dangerousness, rather than punishment.[50]

César Cuauhtémoc García Hernández argues persuasively that immigration detention is legally punitive under U.S. Constitutional Law, as constitutional tests define 'punishment' by focusing on legislative intent (Hernández 2014). Hernández calls attention to legislators' inclusion of immigration detention laws (including mandatory detention laws) in anti-crime legislation to fight the 'war on drugs' and argues that immigration detention was intended to sanction and stigmatize criminal behavior (Hernández 2014, p. 1350). In support, Hernández notes some statements above, such as Senator D'Amato's calling aggravated felons "a particularly dangerous class" or President Bush's terming of criminal aliens as jeopardizing "the safety and well-being of every American resident" (Hernández 2014, p. 1368).

Although legally Hernández' argument has merit, expressively I argue that the particular mandatory detention provisions evince a prevention rationale more than punishment. These statements, and subsequent executive branch statements, focus

[47] Similarly, Australia passed its mandatory detention law to discourage so-called boat people from arriving (Nat'l Immigrant Justice Ctr. (NIJC) 2010, p. 2).

[48] In any case, when the U.S. retroactively passed these mandatory detention laws, many individuals had *already* committed crimes which could not possibly be deterred.

[49] Such punishment would of course be illegitimate, as immigration detention is legally civil and preventive, not punitive. As Legomsky notes, no scholar has "sought to justify [pre-hearing immigration] detention on punishment grounds" (Legomsky 1999, p. 540; Schuck 1996, p. 670).

[50] Here, I consider whether mandatory immigration detention is extra punishment for the crime, not the immigration violation, because the crime triggers the immigration detention, not immigration status. Indeed, lawful permanent residents may have no immigration violation, save the impact of the criminal conviction.

more on immigration detention as protecting the American public from danger, rather than a tool for moral condemnation of noncitizen crimes.[51]

Even assuming a punishment or quasi-punishment rationale exists in immigration detention, mandatory detention appears more designed to expressively send a message to society at large, rather than the individual detainee (Kahan 1996). Indeed, mandatory detention law is by nature categorical, without reference to individual characteristics, and thus lacks one aspect of the expressive condemnation associated with criminal punishment.[52] Even statements like the 1995 Senate report, which state that "America has enough criminals without importing more," appear to reflect society's tolerance level for noncitizen criminality and conception of desirable migration, rather than direct individual condemnation.

It is possible that immigration detention is designed both to punish past crimes and prevent future crimes; indeed, criminal incarceration can serve both those functions. Yet any expressive condemnation appears eclipsed in practice by government expressions of robust enforcement and protection. I further consider these expressions next.

4.2 Expressive Characteristics of Mandatory Detention

Finally, I offer preliminary thoughts regarding the expressive characteristics of U.S. immigration detention and explore two theories for the animating rationales behind prehearing mandatory detention for U.S. crimes.[53] In my view, these expressive characteristics explain much of the above-described disconnect between the noncitizen presumption of danger and empirical reality.

Law has expressive, symbolic value, as many have set out (Stuntz 2001, p. 533; Anderson and Pildes 2000; Sunstein 1996; Lessig 1995; Edelman 1964). Yet immigration law is uniquely, especially expressive, since it embodies decisions by the polity through their government to pick new members and exclude others[54] (Cox and Rodriguez 2009, p. 462/540; Stumpf 2006, p. 377; Walzer 1996, pp. 82–95). The spatial and physical structures created by immigration law also possess expressive content. For example, several scholars have explored the border

[51] That said, the criminal provisions regarding those drug crimes, which increased criminal sentences and imposed mandatory minimums, certainly conveyed a sense of moral condemnation to the individuals involved (Hernández 2014, pp. 1372–1375).

[52] Dan Markel has distinguished the two forms of communication of the social meaning of criminal punishment—communication to society and communication to the individual offender (Markel 2001, pp. 2206–2207).

[53] I plan to further explore these ideas in future research.

[54] For example, Cox and Rodriguez alluded to the fact that "lawmakers and the public regard immigration law as different from other regulatory arenas in fundamental ways," one being the importance of the "illusion of democratic control over membership decisions" (Cox and Rodriguez 2009, p. 540).

and the physical fence along it (Bosniak 2007, p. 276; Fan 2008, p. 711; Gulasekaram 2012, pp. 161–162/169–170).

Here, I preliminarily explore the expressive dimensions of immigration detention, the physical embodiment of enforcement inside the border. By increasing the public severity of immigration enforcement, I argue that mandatory detention for U.S. crimes amplifies the expressive messages already inherent to citizenship and membership delineations[55] (Stumpf 2006, p. 396; Demleitner 1999, p. 158; Bosniak 1994, p. 1055).

I proffer that mandatory detention is primarily motivated by expressive qualities—to 'send a message' to the U.S. populace, in common parlance. The message is twofold—of active, competent protection of the populace from the dangerous 'criminal alien' and of zero tolerance for criminality by noncitizens. Nothing expresses protection of the public in a preventive detention regime or revocation of a noncitizen's presumptive ability to remain, like total incarceration without possibility of release for the remaining time in the U.S.

Here, I analogize Dan Kahan's articulations of expressive functions of criminal incarceration but distinguish arguments for the immigration context. Kahan and other criminal theorists posit that nothing expresses condemnation in our modern liberal society like incarceration's complete deprivation of liberty (Kahan 1996; Markel 2001). With immigration detention, designed to effect incapacitation, not condemnation, I posit that the physical structures and categorical severity of mandatory detention effectively send an analogous message of protection. Moreover, the larger the scale of detention is, the more visible is the message to the public (Taylor 1997, p. 157). And as ICE's director once said, ICE detains on a "grand scale" (Kalhan 2010, p. 44).

Viewing prehearing, postentry mandatory detention as expressive helps explain several disconnects that commonly trouble immigration law scholars. For one, it helps explain the 'noncitizen presumption's' vitality in the face of parallel, empirically based advances in criminal law. More broadly, expressive analysis helps explain the disconnect between severe, incapacitative detention practices and individualized, rights-based norms that recognize U.S. lives, family, and employment ties (McLeod 2012, pp. 132–142). Importantly, the expressed message is categorical and designed for society at large, rather than individualized to any case and designed for that immigrant. Mandatory detention does not speak concerning individual immigrants' circumstances, because it is not speaking to them (Miller 2003, pp. 653–654; Pistone 1999, p. 225).[56]

I theorize two, potentially complementary, theories for the animating rationales behind these messages. The first I term 'blaming the gatekeeper,' by which the

[55] I build upon Margaret Taylor's helpful analysis of detention's deterrent messages towards potential arrivals from outside the country (Taylor 1997).

[56] As Teresa Miller stated, "A discourse that focuses on categories and sub-populations rather than individuals... serves different objectives than one based on moral or clinical judgments about individuals" (Miller 2003, pp. 653–654). While "safety and absconding rationales are capable of being directly applied to individual cases," symbolic detention is not (Pistone 1999, p. 225).

public assigns blame to the government for its failure to exclude or deport a noncitizen who later commits a crime, and the government responds by overcompensating to show protection via mandatory detention laws. The second is a property-law-derived theory of noncitizens as 'invitees,' with mandatory detention revoking the invitation upon commission of a crime and returning the noncitizen to the fiction of *status quo ante* when seeking admission at the border (or, at least, as close as physically possible inside it).

In setting out these theories, I aim to integrate institutional design analysis of immigration law, by Adam Cox and other scholars, with the social and political analysis more traditional to immigration scholarship (Cox and Rodriguez 2009; Cox and Posner 2007; Cox 2008). I offer a short preview here of these arguments, with future research to follow.

4.2.1 Blaming the Gatekeeper

The title 'blaming the gatekeeper' stems from an essential function of government under immigration law to admit desired types and exclude others[57] (Cox and Posner 2007, p. 846; McLeod 2012, p. 164; Eagly 2010, p. 1296). It also stems from the U.S. government's own self-conception, expressed in 1990s initiatives like "Operation Gatekeeper" that allocated additional funding, fencing, and agents to the U. S.–Mexico border (Hing 2001; Massey 2013, p. 11).

Because of this gatekeeping function, I argue, the public uniquely assigns blame to the government for noncitizens who commit crimes. The government's perceived failure is generally insufficient *ex ante* exclusion—either insufficient enforcement, for those who unlawfully enter, or erroneous prediction, for those who lawfully enter but later commit a crime[58] (Cox and Posner 2007). For those who enter and commit one crime, the failure to prevent a second crime becomes one of perceived insufficient *ex post* enforcement (with the first crime putting the government on notice that removal is possible).

In each case, the government's gatekeeping role creates the perception that it proximately causes any subsequent noncitizen crime, to employ a tort law analogy—that the crime "never would have happened" absent government failure (Prosser and Keeton 1984, p. 284). Put simply, the public holds the government more accountable for noncitizen crime than citizen crime. While a citizen is 'here,' for a noncitizen, the possibility always exists to be somewhere else besides 'here.' Immigration officials thus face uniquely targeted criticism for crimes by those who 'shouldn't be here.'

---

[57] For example, Ayelet Shachar termed the "crucial realm of responsibility" of immigration regulators to "determine who to permit to enter, who to remove, and who to keep at bay" (Shachar 2009, p. 811).

[58] To illustrate the second scenario, some U.S. legislators criticized DHS for admitting the Boston Marathon bombers as asylees when they were children (Weigel 2013).

This societal construction of government proximate cause repeats throughout discourse on noncitizen crime. For example, consider the case of Carlos Martinelly-Montano, a Bolivian unauthorized immigrant (and then potential DREAMer) who, in 2010, killed one nun and injured two others while driving drunk in Virginia (Boorstein 2010). Martinelly-Montano had two prior convictions for drunk driving, neither of which ICE determined triggered mandatory detention. Upon the second conviction, ICE released Martinelly-Montano with a GPS tracking device, and Martinelly-Montano complied with supervision conditions (Vendantam 2011). Local police subsequently stopped Martinelly-Montano for two other driving violations, but he was not convicted. After multiple immigration court continuances, Martinelly-Montano crashed into the nuns 18 days before his rescheduled deportation hearing while still under ICE supervision (Vendantam 2011).

The incident sparked criticism that cast ICE as proximately causing the crime because it failed to expeditiously detain and deport Martinelly-Montano. For example, U.S. Rep. Harold Rogers criticized ICE's prioritizing of those with only "serious" criminal records and said "A life could have been saved had ICE just simply done their job to begin with" (Boorstein 2010). Similarly, the local county supervisor blamed federal immigration authorities, stating, "This crime *need not have happened*... if federal authorities, who now have blood on their hands, had done their job in the first place and had this sleazebag deported" (Boorstein 2010).

Or when a New York unauthorized immigrant killed a mother and daughter in a drunk driving accident, a group representing families of 9/11 victims criticized the federal government's immigration policies. "While crime is crime and the victims suffer equally whether the perpetrator is a citizen or illegal alien, what makes illegal alien crime so different is that the crime *would have never happened* if our government was doing its constitutionally mandated duty and enforcing immigration laws..." (Rae 2009).

The fear of subsequent crime is inherent to preventive detention determinations, such as criminal bail. Indeed, as David Cole noted, false positives are unknowable while false negatives are "emblazoned across the front pages" (Cole 2009, p. 696). But this perception of proximate cause for noncitizen crime amplifies that fear and helps explain why, as Legomsky put it, "false negatives [are] tolerated in the criminal context but not in the [immigration deportation] context" (Legomsky 1999, p. 546).

Yet although the specter of proximate cause might explain why DHS or an individual immigration judge might choose detention—and indeed, DHS invariably does in individual cases[59]—it does not quite explain categorical detention even for minor crimes. Here, I preliminarily argue that mandatory detention represents an overcompensation by Congress and ICE to public 'blaming the gatekeeper,' to send a message to the U.S. populace of active, competent protection from dangerous

[59] As noted, DHS denied bail to 71 % of ICE arrestees on discretionary, not mandatory, grounds (NYU School of Law Immigrant Rights Clinic et al. 2012, p. 10).

'criminal aliens.'[60] Because individualized decisions lack the symbolic value of law, individualized detention by judges would not send a message so effectively (Stuntz 2001, p. 533).

Mandatory detention law, implemented through physical detention facilities, provides symbolic order, analogous to the border fence's symbolic sense of order for those who seek "the omniscient power of the government and the law to fix things" (Fan 2008, p. 704; Taylor 1997, p. 154; Motomura 2007). Indeed, mandatory detention establishes a kind of border within borders, in placing a wall (or, literally, four walls) between noncitizens who have committed crimes and the U.S. public (Shachar 2009, p. 811).

4.2.2 A Property Law Analogy: Detention of Noncitizens as Invitees

Although 'blaming the gatekeeper' may explain the symbolic value of mandatory detention legislation, it does not quite explain its categorical severity towards lawful noncitizen residents. Indeed, minor noncitizen crimes should theoretically create minor blame and resultant minor government response—not the drastic remedy of detention without bail until deportation.[61]

Thus, I explore here a complementary theory—that noncitizens who commit crimes are viewed as 'invitees,' per property law analogies, whom upon committing a crime presumably violate the scope of permission granted by the landowner (i.e., the U.S. public). This better explains the categorical, nearly zero-tolerance attitude towards *ex post* crime expressed by mandatory detention law.

Property-law-derived constructs of immigration law—related but distinct from contract law constructs, as Hiroshi Motomura described (Motomura 2006, pp. 15–16)—have a special salience because of migration's inherently geographic component. Moreover, as Pratheepan Gulasekaram argues, property law analogies gain societal acceptance because they transplant "innately recognizable neighborly norms into the complicated arena of immigration law"[62] (Gulasekaram 2012, p. 176). Several scholars, notably Peter Schuck, have explored the analogy of

---

[60] Here, Congress has passed the law, and ICE subsequently interpreted it as strictly as possible by requiring detention rather than 'custody.'

In future research, I plan to more fully delineate the public blame ascribed to each political branch actor, building on Cox's and Rodriguez's description of each's enforcement functions (Cox and Rodriguez 2009, pp. 519–528). It is highly plausible, though, that Congress passed mandatory detention laws in order to shift the blame to the Executive for purportedly 'causing' crime. As Rodriguez said, "Congress never faces direct or exclusive blame for the rise of illegal immigration. Instead, it can easily deflect that blame to the president and the failure of his dysfunctional agencies to enforce the law…" (Rodriguez 2010, p. 1841).

[61] For example, one could envision legislation imposing mandatory immigration detention for drunk driving that results in death, rather than subway turnstile jumping.

[62] Gulasekaram argued that U.S. border fence initiatives reflect and reinforce the societal trespass analogy (Gulasekaram 2012, p. 176).

unlawful immigrants as "trespassers"[63] (Schuck 1984, p. 7; McLeod 2012, pp. 128–133; Fan 2008, pp. 727–728; Boland 2006). For example, Schuck argued that "Americans believe that illegal aliens. . . are like trespassers; they have no right to enter or remain. Control of illegal migration, then, is not merely a pragmatic policy goal; it assumes the character of a legal duty and a moral crusade. . . [and] Americans' conceptions of citizenship reflect these imperatives" (Schuck 1997, pp. 7–8).

I posit here that mandatory detention laws reflect an 'invitee' construction, more applicable to postentry conduct and not necessarily dependent on unlawful entry. Under this theory, although the landowner (here, the U.S.) owes duties to invitees, violating the terms of the granted permission forfeits the right to be present (Restatement Second of Torts 1965, § 332). Mandatory detention law thus expresses government withdrawal of permission to be present, as much as (or more than) the actual dangerousness implied by a noncitizen's crime[64] (Chacón 2007, p. 1890). As the 1995 Senate report stated, "there is just no place in America for non-U.S. citizens who commit criminal acts here. America has enough criminals without importing more" (U.S. Senate Committee on Governmental Affairs 1995, p. 6).

In doing so, mandatory detention approximates the fiction of the liminal 'arriving alien' state, outside society pending the government's decision to admit—or as close as practically possible, by presuming detention unless deportation is defeated[65] (Chavez and Provine 2009, p. 80; Menjivar 2006). This is true even for lawful permanent residents, for whom the governing presumption is changed from citizenship in waiting to "liminal legality" (Valverde 2010, pp. 224–229; Motomura 2006). The expressive presumption is banishment. Detention serves as a physical way station on that conceptual path, unless and until someone defeats deportation in immigration proceedings[66] (Sweeney 2010, p. 84).

An 'invitee' construct may help resolve several troubling disconnects. For one, the 'invitee' theory may help explain why mandatory detention applies equally to lawful entrants (or residents) and to unlawful, and thus the disconnect between the categorical harshness of detention and rights-based norms for long-term residents with jobs and families. Trespass theory cannot account for those lawfully admitted, since there is no "entry without invitation" (McLeod 2012, p. 131). But under the 'invitee' theory, no trespass need exist for the 'criminal alien' to violate social

[63] Villazor and Shachar also explore the connections between property law and immigration (Villazor 2010; Shachar 2011).

[64] As Chacon surmised, "[t]he crime is not the underlying offense so much as it is the act of committing any transgression, whether great or small, while being present in the United States as a non-citizen" (Chacón 2007, p. 1890). I depart from Chacon in specifically analyzing detention pursuant to removal and by raising a different analogy than one to criminal law.

[65] Valverde noted that "practices of detention" play a role in creating "liminal citizenship" status (Valverde 2010, pp. 224–229).

[66] Indeed, prehearing mandatory detainees are treated worse than actual 'arriving aliens' in one respect—that prehearing mandatory detainees are ineligible for parole.

norms. Indeed, criminal activity would violate U.S. terms of permission under any status short of citizenship.

Moreover, an 'invitee' construct may help explain the nearly zero-tolerance presumption for noncitizen crime that mandatory detention effects.[67] Under an 'invitee' theory, the expressed message is not only protection from the dangerous but also *post hoc exclusion* of noncitizens committing crimes, even minimally dangerous crimes. This may explain the departure from criminal pretrial practices, which do not categorically impose a 100 % incapacitation rate upon categories of prior offenders (although some released pretrial invariably reoffend). That said, this social 'invitee' construct is imperfect, and I plan to further explore it in future research.[68]

5 Conclusion

As a conclusion, I offer final thoughts as to the realistic chance that U.S. mandatory detention will change.

If mandatory detention is primarily expressive and designed to send a message, then changes to mandatory detention are unlikely absent change in the underlying discourse characterizing immigrants as dangerous 'criminal aliens[69] (McLeod 2012, p. 173; Harvard Law Review 2012, pp. 1482–1484/1486; Dolovich 2011, pp. 266–267). There is potential for that change in discourse, however.

For one, the sheer numbers in the deportation system, as the numbers of undocumented has risen to "unprecedented heights" and the U.S. has ramped up enforcement (Massey 2013, p. 11),[70] may result in greater recognition of the humanity of even 'criminal aliens.' President Obama alone has deported nearly two million from the U.S. (Gonzalez 2013), which means two million sets of families, friends, and colleagues affected by deportation.

Concurrently, immigrants' rights advocates have increasingly challenged the dichotomous discourse of good and bad immigrants (with "criminal aliens" of course "bad") (Nat'l Immigrant Justice Ctr. (NIJC) 2013). Indeed, a current rallying cry against deportation is 'not one more'—which omits a good/bad dichotomy.

Moreover, as more noncitizens are placed in proceedings, more are defeating deportation and thus rebutting the presumption that one in immigration detention

[67] Schuck, for example, justified prehearing detention of criminal aliens on the ground that it might prevent "twelve crimes a year" (Schuck 1996, p. 668).

[68] Indeed, although the rules set the norms, property law rules admit of exceptions—"attractive nuisance," for example (Schuck 1984, p. 7), or "adverse possession" for the long-term unauthorized (Gomez 2007).

[69] As Sharon Dolovich noted, "a political strategy emphasizing the financial costs of incarceration is bound to fail unless it also generates an ideological reorientation towards recognizing the people the state incarcerates as fellow human beings and fellow citizens" (Dolovich 2011, pp. 266–267).

[70] Massey points out the circular causality of these two trends (Massey 2013, p. 11).

will not return to his or her American life. This trend may increase as immigrants in proceedings are provided greater access to procedural rights such as appointed counsel.[71] These developments may cause greater public recognition of the disproportionality of mandatory detention and the deprivations that follow from long-term residency.

Acknowledgements I thank for feedback, guidance, and support Farrin Anello; Kristina Campbell; Stacy Caplow; Stewart Chang; Alina Das; Maryellen Fullerton; Maria João Guia; César Cuauhtémoc García Hernández; Geoffrey Heeren; Robert Koulish; Frances Kreimer; Juliet Stumpf; Yolanda Vasquez; the participants in the 2012 First Crimmigration Control Conference at the Universidade de Coimbra, Portugal; and the participants in the 2013 *Emerging Immigration* Law *Scholars* Conference at UC-Irvine, California. I also thank Setenay Akdag, Elizabeth Komar, and Rebecca McBride for excellent research assistance.

References

Alba R, Rumbaut RG, Marotz K (2005) A distorted nation: perceptions of racial/ethnic group sizes and attitudes toward immigrants and other minorities. Soc Forces 95:901–919

Amaral P (2013) Immigration detention: looking at the alternatives. Forced Migr Rev 44:40–42. http://www.fmreview.org/detention/amaral#sthash.Rhsew2YC.dpuf. Accessed 5 Aug 2014

American Immigration Lawyers Association (AILA) (2010) Memorandum to David Martin, Office of General Counsel, U.S. Department of Homeland Security: the use of electronic monitoring and other alternatives to institutional detention on individuals classified under INA § 236(c). www.nilc.org/document.html?id=94. Accessed 5 Aug 2014

Anderson E, Pildes R (2000) Expressive theories of law: a general restatement. Pa Law Rev 148:1503–1575

Baili A (2006) Scapegoating the vulnerable: preventative detention of immigrants in America's war on terror. Stud Law Polit Soc 38:25–69

Baradaran S, McIntyre F (2012) Predicting violence. Tex Law Rev 90:497–554

Bennett B (2012) Illegal immigrant rearrest rate is 16%, study says. Los Angeles Times, August 1. http://articles.latimes.com/2012/aug/01/nation/la-na-illegal-immigrants-20120801. Accessed 5 Aug 2014

Boland M (2006) Comment: no trespassing: the states, the Supremacy Clause, and the use of criminal trespass laws to fight illegal immigration. Pa State Law Rev 111:481–503

Boorstein M (2010) Nuns decry focus on immigration status of driver in fatal Va. crash. Washington Post: August 3. http://www.washingtonpost.com/wp-dyn/content/article/2010/08/03/AR2010080302519.html?hpid=topnews. Accessed 5 Aug 2014

Bosniak L (1994) Membership, equality, & the difference that alienage makes. N Y Univ Law Rev 69:1047–1149

Bosniak L (2007) Between the domestic and the foreign: centering the nation's edges. Const Comment 24:271–284

[71] For example, a New York study found that 74 % of those not detained but have a lawyer won their immigration removal proceedings, while even 18 % of those detained with lawyers won (New York Immigrant Representation Study 2011, pp. 363–364). New York City subsequently funded a pilot project to provide lawyers to the detained in immigration proceedings, and other cities are exploring similar efforts (Noferi 2012).

Bush G (1990) Statement on signing the immigration act of 1990. http://www.presidency.ucsb.edu/ws/?pid=19117. Accessed 23 Jan 2016
Chacón J (2007) Unsecured borders: immigration restrictions, crime control and national security. Conn Law Rev 39:1827–1891
Chavez JM, Provine DM (2009) Race and the response of state legislatures to unauthorized immigrants. Ann Am Acad Pol Soc Sci 623:78–83
Cole D (2009) Out of the shadows: preventive detention, suspected terrorists, and war. Calif Law Rev 97:693–750
Conference of State Court Administrators (COSCA) (2013) 2012–2013 Policy paper: evidence-based pretrial release, final paper. http://www.colorado.gov/ccjjdir/Resources/Resources/Ref/EBPre-TrialRelease_2012.pdf. Accessed 5 Aug 2014
Congressional Research Service (CRS) (2012) Analysis of data regarding certain individuals identified through secure communities: updating the previous analysis with citizenship data. July 27, 2012. http://judiciary.house.gov/news/pdfs/Criminal%20Aliens%20Report.pdf. Accessed 5 Aug 2014
Cooper Blum S (2012) "Use It and Lose It": an exploration of unused counterterrorism laws and implications for future counterterrorism policies. Lewis Clark Law Rev 16:677–739
Costello C, Kaytaz E (2013) Building empirical evidence into alternatives to detention: perceptions of asylum-seekers and refugees in Toronto and Geneva. UNHCR, Geneva. http://www.refworld.org/pdfid/51a6fec84.pdf. Accessed 5 Aug 2014
Cox A (2008) Immigration law's organizing principles. Pa Law Rev 157:341–393
Cox A, Posner E (2007) The second-order structure of immigration law. Stanford Law Rev 59:809–856
Cox A, Rodriguez C (2009) The president and immigration law. Yale Law J 119:458–547
Cunningham-Parmeter K (2011) Alien language: immigration metaphors and the jurisprudence of otherness. Fordham Law Rev 79:1545–1598
Das A (2011) The immigration penalties of criminal convictions: resurrecting categorical analysis in immigration law. N Y Univ Law Rev 86:1669–1760
Demleitner N (1997) The fallacy of social "citizenship," or the threat of exclusion. Georget Immgr Law J 12:35–64
Demleitner N (1999) Preventing internal exile: the need for restrictions on collateral sentencing consequences. Stanford Law Policy Rev 11:153–163
Demleitner N (2003) Abusing state power or controlling risk? Sex offender commitment and sicherungverwahrung. Fordham Urban Law J 30:1621–1669
Demore v. Kim (2003) 538 U.S. 510
Dolovich S (2011) Exclusion and control in the carceral state. Berkeley J Crim Law 16:259–335
Eagly I (2010) Prosecuting immigration. Northwest Law Rev 104:1281–1360
Garland D (1996) The limits of the sovereign state: strategies of crime control in contemporary society. Br J Criminol 36:445–471
Edelman M (1964) The symbolic uses of politics. University of Illinois Press, Urbana
Fan M (2008) When deterrence and death mitigation fall short: fantasy and fetishes as gap-fillers in border regulation. Law Soc Rev 42:701–729
Fan M (2014) The case for crimmigration reform. North Carol Law Rev 92:75–146. http://nclawreview.org/documents/92/1/Fan.pdf
Field O, Edwards A (2006) United Nations High Commissioner for Refugees, Alternatives to detention of asylum seekers and refugees. http://www.refworld.org/cgi-bin/texis/vtx/rwmain?page=search&docid=4472e8b84&skip=0&query=alternatives%20to%20detention%20of%20asylum%20seekers%20and%20refugees. Accessed 5 Aug 2014
Gomez M (2007) Note, immigration by adverse possession: common law amnesty for long-residing illegal immigrants in the United States. Georget Immgr Law J 22:105–125
Gonzalez J (2013) President Obama heads toward deportation milestone as immigration reform flounders. N.Y. Daily News. October 4. http://www.nydailynews.com/news/politics/obama-heads-deportation-milestone-article-1.1476073#ixzz2l2ze8zAW. Accessed 5 Aug 2014

Grassley C (2013) Grassley, Goodlatte Press Napolitano for answers on release of illegal immigrants from detention facilities. February 28. http://www.grassley.senate.gov/news/news-releases/grassley-goodlatte-press-napolitano-answers-release-illegal-immigrants-detention. Accessed 5 Aug 2014

Grussendorf P (2013) Building an immigration system worthy of American values: testimony before the U.S. Senate Committee on the Judiciary. Wednesday, March 20 2013. http://www.judiciary.senate.gov/imo/media/doc/CHRG-113shrg81774.pdf. Accessed 5 Aug 2014

Guia MJ (2012) Crimmigration, securitisation and the criminal law of the crimmigrant. In: Guia M, Van der Woude M, Van der Leun J (eds) Social control and justice: crimmigration in the age of fear. Eleven, London, pp 17–39

Gulasekaram P (2012) Why a wall? UC Irvine Law Rev 2:147–191

Harvard Law Review (2012) Note, improving the carceral conditions of federal immigrant detainees. Harv Law Rev 125:1476–1497

Heeren G (2010) Pulling teeth: the state of mandatory immigration detention. Harv Civ Rights Civil Lib Law Rev 45:601–634

Hernández C (2014) Immigration detention as punishment. UCLA Law Rev 61:1346–1414

Hing B (2001) The dark side of operation gatekeeper. UC Davis J Int Law Policy 7:121–165

Hirschi T, Gottfredson M (1983) Age and the explanation of crime. Am J Sociol 89:552–584

Human Rights First (HRF) (2012) How to repair the U.S. immigration detention system: blueprint for the next administration. http://www.humanrightsfirst.org/wp-content/uploads/pdf/immigration_detention_blueprint.pdf. Accessed 5 Aug 2014

Human Rights Watch (2009) Forced apart (by the numbers): non-citizens deported mostly for nonviolent offenses. http://www.hrw.org/reports/2009/04/15/forced-apart-numbers-0. Accessed 5 Aug 2014

Hutchinson A (2004) Memorandum from Asa Hutchinson, Undersec'y for Border and TransSec., to Robert C. Bonner, Comm'r, U.S. Customs & Border Prot. 1–2 (October 18, 2004). http://www.ice.gov/doclib/foia/dro_policy_memos/detention_prioritization_and_notice_to_appear_documentary_requirements-oct2004.pdf. Accessed 5 Aug 2014

International Detention Coalition (2011) There are alternatives. http://idcoalition.org/cap/. Accessed 5 Aug 2014

Kahan D (1996) What do alternative sanctions mean. Univ f Chic Law Rev 63:591–653

Kalhan A (2010) Rethinking immigration detention. Columbia Law Rev Sidebar 110:42–58

Kansas v. Hendricks (1997) 521 U.S. 346

Kanstroom D (2000) Deportation, social control, and punishment: some thoughts about why hard laws make bad cases. Harv Law Rev 113:1890–1935

Kerwin D, Li S (2009) Migration Policy Institute, immigration detention: can ICE meet its legal imperatives and case management responsibilities? http://www.migrationpolicy.org/pubs/detentionreportSept1009.pdf. Accessed 5 Aug 2014

Koulish R (2012) Entering the risk society: a contested terrain for immigration enforcement. In: Guia M, Van der Woude M, Van der Leun J (eds) Social control and justice: crimmigration in the age of fear. Eleven, London, pp 61–86

Koulish R, Noferi M (2013a) Unlocking immigration detention reform. The Baltimore Sun, 20 February. http://www.baltimoresun.com/news/opinion/oped/bs-ed-immigrant-detention-20130220,0,5653483.story. Accessed 5 Aug 2014

Koulish R, Noferi M (2013b) ICE risk assessments: from mass detention to mass supervision? Crimmigration.com, May 16. http://crimmigration.com/2013/05/16/ice-risk-assessments-from-mass-detention-to-mass-supervision.aspx. Accessed 5 Aug 2014

Kreimer F (2012) Dangerousness on the loose: constitutional limits to immigration detention as domestic crime control. N Y Univ Law Rev 87:1485–1522

Legomsky S (1999) The detention of aliens: theories, rules, and discretion. Miami Inter Am Law Rev 30:531–549

Lessig L (1995) The regulation of social meaning. Univ Chic Law Rev 62:943–1045

Long S (2013) Exhibit A, Expert report of Professor Susan B. Long, Rodriguez v. Hayes, No. 07–3239. August 6. U.S. District Court for the Central District of California

Lutheran Immigration and Refugee Service (LIRS) (2011) Unlocking liberty: a way forward for U.S. immigration detention policy. http://www.lirs.org/wp-content/uploads/2012/05/RPTUNLOCKINGLIBERTY.pdf. Accessed 5 Aug 2014

Markel D (2001) Are shaming punishments beautifully retributive? Retributivism and the implications for the alternative sanctions debate. Vanderbilt Law Rev 54:2157–2242

Mass J (2013) The problem of prolonged incarceration of immigrants. February 7. http://www.aclu.org/blog/immigrants-rights/problem-prolonged-incarceration-immigrants. Accessed 5 Aug 2014

Massey DS (2013) America's immigration policy fiasco: learning from past mistakes. Daedalus 142:5–15

McLeod A (2012) The U.S. criminal-immigration convergence and its possible undoing. Am Crim Law Rev 49:105–178

Menjivar C (2006) Liminal legality: Salvadoran and Guatemalan immigrants' lives in the United States. Am J Sociol 111:999–1037

Miller T (2003) Citizenship & severity: recent immigration reforms and the new penology. Georget Immgr Law J 17:611–666

Moncrieffe v. Holder (2013) 133 S. Ct. 1678

Morton J (2011a) Memorandum from John Morton, Director, U.S. Immigration and Customs Enforcement, to all Field Office Directors, all special agents in charge, all Chief Counsel. June 17. http://www.ice.gov/doclib/secure-communities/pdf/prosecutorial-discretion-memo.pdf. Accessed 5 Aug 2014

Morton J (2011b) Letter from John Morton, Assistant Secretary of Department of Homeland Security to Rep. Zoe Lofgren. April 28. http://ndlon.org/pdf/2011-05cadman.pdf. Accessed 23 Jan 2016

Morton J (2013) Letter from John Morton to Julie Kirchner, Executive Director, Federation for American Immigration Reform. August 23, 2013. http://www.ndlon.org/en/pressroom/press-releases/item/553-morton-fair-letter. Accessed 5 Aug 2014

Motomura H (2006) Americans in waiting: the lost story of immigration and citizenship in the United States. Oxford University Press, New York

Motomura H (2007) Comment – Choosing immigrants, making citizens. Stanford Law Rev 59:857–870

Nat'l Immigrant Justice Ctr. (NIJC) (2010) Creating 'truly civil' immigration detention in the United States: Lessons from Australia. http://www.immigrantjustice.org/sites/immigrantjustice.org/files/Australia%20Civil%20Detention%20Report%202010.pdf. Accessed 5 Aug 2014

Nat'l Immigrant Justice Ctr. (NIJC) (2013) Rethink immigration: minor crimes should not lead to immigration exile. April 10. http://www.immigrantjustice.org/staff/blog/rethink-immigration-minor-crimes-should-not-lead-immigration-exile#.UoqywXAqhng. Accessed 5 Aug 2014

Nat'l Immigration Forum (2013) The math of immigration detention. http://www.immigrationforum.org/images/uploads/mathofimmigrationdetention.pdf. Accessed 5 Aug 2014

New York Immigrant Representation Study (2011) Accessing justice: the availability and adequacy of counsel in immigration proceedings. Cardozo Law Rev 33:357–416

New York Times (2013a) A brighter line on immigration policing. August 17. http://www.nytimes.com/2013/08/18/opinion/sunday/a-brighter-line-on-immigration-policing.html. Accessed 5 Aug 2014

New York Times (2013b) Fixing immigration from the Ground Up. October 6. http://www.nytimes.com/2013/10/07/opinion/fixing-immigration-from-the-ground-up.html?_r=0. Accessed 5 Aug 2014

Noferi M (2012) Cascading constitutional deprivation: the right to appointed counsel for mandatorily detained immigrants pending removal proceedings. Mich J Race Law 18:63–129

Noferi M (2015) A humane approach can work: the effectiveness of alternatives to detention for asylum seekers. American Immigration Council and Center for Migration Studies, Washington

and New York. http://www.immigrationpolicy.org/special-reports/humane-approach-can-work-effectiveness-alternatives-detention-asylum-seekers. Accessed 23 Jan 2016
Noferi M, Koulish R (2013) Boost protections for detained immigrants. Newark Star-Ledger. May 1. http://blog.nj.com/njv_guest_blog/2013/05/boost_protections_for_detained.html. Accessed 5 Aug 2014
Noferi M, Koulish R (2014) The immigration detention risk assessment. Georgetown Immigr Law J 29:45–94
NYU School of Law Immigrant Rights Clinic et al (2012) Insecure communities, devastated families: new data on immigrant detention and deportation practices in New York City. http://immigrantdefenseproject.org/wp-content/uploads/2012/07/NYC-FOIA-Report-2012-FINAL.pdf. Accessed 5 Aug 2014
Padilla v. Kentucky (2010) 559 U.S. 356
Perry R (2013) Release of criminal aliens into our communities is unconscionable. March 4. http://governor.state.tx.us/news/press-release/18220/. Accessed 5 Aug 2014
Phelps J (2013) Alternatives to detention in the UK: from enforcement to engagement? Forced Migr Rev 44:45–48. http://www.fmreview.org/detention/phelps#sthash.QjAfSeNG.dpuf. Accessed 5 Aug 2014
Pistone M (1999) Justice delayed is justice denied: a proposal for ending the unnecessary detention of asylum seekers. Harv Hum Rights J 12:197–265
Pretrial Justice Institute (2012a) Pretrial Risk Assessment 101: science provides guidance on managing defendants. http://www.pretrial.org/download/advocacy/PJI%20Risk%20Assessment%20101%20%282012%29.pdf. Accessed 5 Aug 2014
Pretrial Justice Institute (2012b) Using technology to enhance pretrial services: current applications and future possibilities. http://www.pretrial.org/download/pji-reports/PJI%20USING%20TECHNOLOGY%20TO%20ENHANCE%20PRETRIAL%20SERVICES.pdf. Accessed 5 Aug 2014
Prosser W, Keeton W (1984) The law of torts, 5th edn. St. Paul, West
Rae L (2009) Fact-check: illegal immigrants and crime. LoHud.com: June 24. http://immigration.lohudblogs.com/2009/06/24/fact-check-illegal-immigrants-and-crime/. Accessed 5 Aug 2014
Reaves B (2013) Felony defendants in large urban counties, 2009 - statistical tables. U.S. Department of Justice, Office of Justice Programs, Bureau of Justice Statistics, Washington. http://www.bjs.gov/content/pub/pdf/fdluc09.pdf. Accessed 23 Jan 2016
Reid LW, Weiss H, Adelman R, Jaret C (2005) The immigration-crime relationship: evidence across U.S. metro areas. Soc Sci Res 34:757–780
Restatement (Second) of Torts (1965) American Law Institute, Philadelphia
Robinson P (2001) Punishing dangerousness: cloaking preventive detention as criminal justice. Harv Law Rev 114:1429–1456
Rodriguez C (2010) Constraint through delegation: the case of executive control over immigration policy. Duke Law J 59:1787–1846
Rumbaut R, Ewing W (2007) The myth of immigrant criminality and the paradox of assimilation. American Immigration Law Foundation, Washington DC
Rutgers School of Law-Newark Immigrant Rights Clinic and American Friends Service Committee (2012) Freed but not free. http://www.law.newark.rutgers.edu/files/FreedbutnotFree.pdf. Accessed 5 Aug 2014
Sampson R, Mitchell G (2013) Global trends in immigration detention and alternatives to detention: practical, political and symbolic rationales. J Migr Hum Secur 1:97–121
Schriro D (2009) U.S. Department of Homeland Security, Immigration and Customs Enforcement. Immigration detention overview and recommendations. http://www.ice.gov/doclib/about/offices/odpp/pdf/ice-detention-rpt.pdf. Accessed 5 Aug 2014
Schriro D (2012) Dialogues on detention: what is "civil" detention? (transcript of public comments on file with author). http://www.youtube.com/watch?v=QM7zZe7I1OM&list=SPpgRk1PtLwuqaglY0IzUyLQMLuPTjNcam&index=3. Accessed 5 Aug 2014
Schuck PH (1984) The transformation of immigration law. Columbia Law Rev 84:1–90

Schuck PH (1996) INS detention and removal: a white paper. Georget Immgr Law J 11:667–708
Schuck PH (1997) The re-evaluation of American citizenship. Georget Immgr Law J 12:1–34
Seipp G, Feal S (2010) The mandatory detention dilemma: the role of the federal courts in tempering the scope of INA §236(c). Immigration Briefings 10-07:1
Shachar A (2009) Immigration beyond territory: the shifting border of immigration regulation. Mich J Int Law 30:809–839
Shachar A (2011) Earned citizenship: property lessons for immigration reform. Yale J Law Humanit 23:110–158
Silverman S (2010) Immigration detention in America: a history of its expansion and a study of its significance, University of Oxford Working Paper No. 80. http://ssrn.com/abstract=1867366. Accessed 5 Aug 2014
Stowell J, Messner S, McGeever K, Raffalovich L (2009) Immigration and the recent violent crime drop in the U.S.: a pooled, cross-sectional time-series analysis of metropolitan areas. Criminology 47:889–928
Stumpf J (2006) The crimmigration crisis: immigrants, crime, and sovereign power. Am Univ Law Rev 56:367–419
Stumpf J (2011) Doing time: crimmigration law and the perils of haste. UCLA Law Rev 58:1705–1748
Stuntz W (2001) The pathological politics of criminal law. Mich Law Rev 100:505–600
Sunstein C (1996) On the expressive function of law. Pa Law Rev 144:2021–2053
Sweeney M (2010) Fact or fiction: the legal construction of immigration removal for crimes. Yale J Regul 27:47–89
Tan M (2012) ACLU files class action lawsuit challenging mandatory immigration lock-up. November 15. http://www.aclu.org/blog/immigrants-rights/aclu-files-class-action-lawsuit-challenging-mandatory-immigration-lock. Accessed 5 Aug 2014
Tan M (2013) Declaration of Michael Tan of February 8, 2013, *Rodriguez v. Hayes*, No. 07-3239 (C.D. Cal.)
Taylor M (1997) Symbolic detention. In Defense of the Alien 20:153–159
Theophile A (2009) Pretrial risk assessment and immigration status: a precarious intersection. Fed Probat 73:2
TRAC Immigration, Syracuse University (2011) Immigration enforcement since 9/11: a reality check. http://trac.syr.edu/immigration/reports/260/. Accessed 5 Aug 2014
TRAC Immigration, Syracuse University (2013a) Nature of charge in new filings seeking removal orders through September 2013. http://trac.syr.edu/phptools/immigration/charges/apprep_newfiling_charge.php. Accessed 5 Aug 2013
TRAC Immigration, Syracuse University (2013b) Few ICE detainers target serious criminals. http://trac.syr.edu/immigration/reports/330. Accessed 5 Aug 2013
Tyler TR (2006) Why people obey the law. Princeton University Press, Princeton
Tyler TR, Jackson J (2014) Popular legitimacy and the exercise of legal authority: motivating compliance, cooperation and engagement. Psychol Public Policy Law 20:78–95. http://papers.ssrn.com/sol3/papers.cfm?abstract_id=2292517. Accessed 5 Aug 2014
Tyler TR, Sunshine J (2003) Moral solidarity, identification with the community, and the importance of procedural justice. Soc Psychol Q 66(2):153–165
U.S. Department of Homeland Security (2012) Office of Immigration Statistics, immigration enforcement actions: 2011. http://www.dhs.gov/sites/default/files/publications/immigration-statistics/enforcement_ar_2011.pdf. Accessed 5 Aug 2014
U.S. Department of Homeland Security (2014) Immigration & Customs Enforcement: Salaries and expenses, fiscal year 2015 congressional budget justification. http://www.dhs.gov/sites/default/files/publications/DHS-Congressional-Budget-Justification-FY2015.pdf. Accessed 5 Aug 2014
U.S. Department of Justice, Office of the Inspector General (1994) Case hearing process in the Executive Office for Immigration Review. ReNo. I-93-03

U.S. Immigration and Customs Enforcement (2012) FY 2012: ICE announces year-end removal numbers, highlights focus on key priorities and issues new national detainer guidance to further focus resources. December 21. http://www.ice.gov/news/releases/1212/121221washingtondc2.htm. Accessed 5 Aug 2014

U.S. Senate Committee on Governmental Affairs (1995) Criminal aliens in the United States. S. ReNo:104–48

Valverde M (2010) Practices of citizenship and scales of governance. New Crim Law Rev 13:216–240

Vendantam S (2011) Undocumented immigrant charged in crash that killed nun was not flight risk, report says. Washington Post, March 5. http://www.washingtonpost.com/wp-dyn/content/article/2011/03/04/AR2011030406636.html. Accessed 5 Aug 2014

Vera Institute of Justice (2000) Testing community supervision for the INS: an evaluation of the appearance assistance program

Villazor RC (2010) Rediscovering Oyama v. California: at the intersection of property, race, and citizenship. Wash Univ Law Rev 87:979–1042

Wadsworth T (2010) Is immigration responsible for the crime drop? An assessment of the influence of immigration on changes in violent crime between 1990 and 2000. Soc Sci Q 91 (2):531

Walzer M (1996) What it means to be an American. Marsilio Publishers, Venice

Washington Post (2013) DHS releases hundreds of illegal immigrants from immigration jails ahead of sequester. February 26

Waslin M (2012) Restrictionists misrepresent data on immigration enforcement. Immigration Impact, August 1. http://immigrationimpact.com/2012/08/01/restrictionists-misrepresent-data-on-immigration-enforcement/. Accessed 5 Aug 2014

Weigel D (2013) Lost in translation. Slate: April 19. http://www.slate.com/articles/news_and_politics/politics/2013/04/tamerlan_and_dzhokhar_tsarnaev_suspects_the_origins_of_the_boston_marathon.html. Accessed 5 Aug 2014

Wiseman S (2014) Pretrial detention and the right to be monitored. Yale Law J 123:1344–1404. http://yalelawjournal.org/article/pretrial-detention-and-the-right-to-be-monitored. Accessed 25 Aug 2014

Zadvydas v. Davis (2001) 533 U.S. 678

Let Us In: An Argument for the Right to Visitation in U.S. Immigration Detention

Christina M. Fialho

Abstract Since the creation of U.S. Immigration & Customs Enforcement (ICE) in 2003, approximately 2.5 million individuals have passed through ICE detention facilities in a network of over 250 jails and private prisons. Men, women, and children can spend weeks, months, and sometimes years inside of these facilities with little connection to the outside world and limited access to legal, medical, or social resources. To combat the isolating experience of immigration detention and promote government accountability, communities throughout the United States are establishing volunteer-based visitation programs.

However, establishing a community visitation program (CVP) at a U.S. immigration detention facility often takes longer than a year. The problem is that no U.S. law mandates these programs or even acknowledges a right to receive visits while in immigration detention. Additionally, whether any one program remains in operation is nearly entirely within the discretion of the individual detention facility. While the right to receive visits is an emerging international norm and member states of the European Union are beginning to protect a person's right to receive visits in immigration detention, the U.S. government has been slow to recognize the benefits of visitation.

This article sets forth the first comprehensive look at the challenges associated with starting and maintaining a CVP in the U.S. immigration detention system and the domestic and international laws that affect immigration detention visitation.

1 Introduction

> How difficult would it be for the government to accept a group of people to come and give somebody else moral support and a little breath of fresh air? Why would that be a bad thing? (Carlos Hidalgo)[1]

[1] A member of Community Initiatives for Visiting Immigrants in Confinement (CIVIC) who was in immigration detention at the Adelanto Detention Center for 8 months in 2013 and redetained in February 2015.

C.M. Fialho (✉)
Attorney & Co-Founder/Executive Director, Community Initiatives for Visiting Immigrants in Confinement (CIVIC), San Francisco, CA, USA
e-mail: CFialho@endisolation.org

M.J. Guia et al. (eds.), *Immigration Detention, Risk and Human Rights*,
DOI 10.1007/978-3-319-24690-1_14

The United States of America imprisons over 400,000 people in 250 jails and private prisons each year as part of the country's civil immigration detention system (DHS 2013).[2] Men, women, and children can spend weeks, months, and sometimes years inside of these facilities with little connection to the outside world and limited access to legal, medical, or social resources (Amnesty International 2009). Additionally, no independent oversight system exists in immigration detention. Only U.S. Immigration and Customs Enforcement (ICE) and its umbrella agency, the Department of Homeland Security (DHS), conduct audits of immigration detention facilities. As there is no independent oversight, there are untold and unrecorded abuses. Immigrants who have been abused by detention guards are made invisible by a code of silence, the threat of retaliation, and a culture that stigmatizes incarcerated people.

To promote government accountability and combat the isolating experience of immigration detention, communities throughout the United States are establishing volunteer-based visitation programs offering a connection to the outside world and the only consistent community presence inside these detention facilities. Each community visitation program (CVP) is unique, but all of them connect people in immigration detention to community members on the outside for weekly or monthly visits. Visitor volunteers include retired teachers, formerly detained individuals, students, leaders from nearly all faith traditions, and many more. Some visitation programs operate behind Plexiglas during regular visiting hours, and others operate in a classroom-style setting outside the regular visiting hours.

Some visitation programs also operate monthly inspection tours of the facility. Others run a hotline, which provides people in immigration detention with the ability to call community volunteers for free. Other programs ensure that persons in immigration detention can maintain family and community ties by transporting family members to the detention facility for visits.

Despite these benefits, establishing a CVP at a U.S. immigration detention facility often takes longer than a year (see *infra* Sect. 3). The problem is that no U.S. law mandates these programs, and ICE's Performance-Based National Detention Standards (PBNDS) do not protect a right to receive visits while in immigration detention (see *infra* Sect. 4). Therefore, whether any one program remains in operation is almost entirely within the discretion of the individual detention facility. While the right to receive visits is an emerging international norm (see *infra* Sect. 5) and some European Union member states are beginning to protect a person's right to receive visits in immigration detention (see *infra* Sect. 5.2), the U.S. government has been slow to recognize the advantages of CVPs and the rights of volunteer visitors.

Thus, the purpose of this article is to present an overview of the law as it pertains to the right to visitation in immigration detention, as well as highlight the

[2] See section on "immigration enforcement actions" and subsection on "detentions" showing that ICE detained 477,523 people in immigration detention during 2012 and a total of 2,166,095 persons between 2004 and 2010.

restrictions and roadblocks people in detention and their visitors have encountered when trying to simply connect with one another.

Before introducing the structure of this article, it is important to carefully define immigration detention and CVPs. This article defines immigration detention as the deprivation of liberty of *persons* due to their immigration status. In the international arena, immigration detention often is described as a deprivation of liberty of *non-citizens* (Flynn 2011).[3] In the United States, immigrant rights' advocacy groups refer to persons in detention as "immigrants," choosing sometimes not to distinguish between immigrants with lawful status and immigrants who are undocumented. Conversely, U.S. statutes authorizing immigration detention refer to persons subject to immigration detention as "aliens."[4] While the all-encompassing term "persons" departs from traditional distinctions between noncitizen groups that U.S. courts have recognized (*Mathews v. Diaz*, 426 U.S. 67 1976),[5] the term "persons" underscores the humanity of each individual in detention. Furthermore, this all-encompassing classification recognizes the reality that ICE has wrongfully detained U.S. citizens on several occasions (Preston 2011; Hendricks 2009). Thus, this article intentionally places asylum seekers, undocumented immigrants, lawful permanent residents, and U.S. citizens into a single category—persons.

This article defines CVPs[6] as primarily volunteer-run groups that provide persons in immigration detention with a connection to the outside world through a volunteer visitor. University student groups and faith communities establish and manage most CVPs. While some CVPs operate with approval and minimal support from ICE and the detention facility itself, other CVPs function without these relationships. A typical CVP coordinator will connect volunteer visitors to persons in detention on a weekly basis. While some visitor volunteers act as de facto case managers who connect persons in detention to resources on the outside and monitor abuse, all visitors are invited to serve as friends to persons in immigration detention and no visitor is tasked with providing legal, psychological, or pastoral services. While each CVP is independently run and has its own unique mission, all current U.S. immigration detention visitation programs are affiliated with the national visitation network, Community Initiatives for Visiting Immigrants in Confinement (CIVIC). CIVIC's mission is to end the isolation and abuse of individuals in U.S. immigration detention through visitation, independent monitoring, storytelling, and advocacy with the ultimate goal of defunding detention.

[3] Defining "migration-related detention" as "the deprivation of liberty of noncitizens because of their status."

[4] 8 U.S.C. § 1225(b) (2000); 8 U.S.C. § 1226 (2000); 8 U.S.C. § 1231 (2000).

[5] Explaining that courts do not place all persons in a single homogeneous legal classification for due process consideration.

[6] CVPs refer to themselves as "visitation programs" or "visitation groups," and therefore this article uses the two phrases interchangeably.

This article proceeds as follows: Sect. 2 uses responses gathered from an online assessment tool, phone interviews, emails, and my own experience coestablishing a CVP in Northern California to summarize the positive effects of CVPs on persons in immigration detention, the greater community, and the government. Section 3 uses the same responses and personal experience to provide an overview of how federal and local governments hinder the creation and expansion of CVPs. Section 4 explains that notwithstanding First Amendment limits on government action, U.S. law fails to establish a person's right to receive visits while in civil immigration detention. Section 5 provides a synopsis of the international law instruments pertaining to the right to receive visitors and how the European Union and some member states encourage community visitation within the immigration detention context. The article concludes by offering three proposals in Sect. 6 for expanding community visitation in the U.S. immigration detention system.

2 CVPs Benefit People in Immigration Detention and the U.S. Government

CIVIC—and its predecessor, the National Detention Visitation Network—was originally formed in November 2009 by four existing immigration detention visitation programs. CIVIC's purpose was to address the expanding U.S. immigration detention system—only one part of the prison industrial complex—that has privileged mass incarceration over the sanctity of human life, rights, and justice. The group's mission was simply to end isolation and human rights abuses. Over the next two and a half years, these programs grew to become an alliance of 16 community-initiated visitation programs. In 2012, the group filed for 501(c)(3) nonprofit status and brought on its first two paid coordinators through the support of an Echoing Green Fellowship. In the first year and half, the visitation coalition doubled in size to a total of 32 visitation programs in 16 states. At the time of publication, visitation programs were operating at over 40 immigration detention facilities in the United States.

This section uses responses gathered from a 2012 online assessment, phone interviews, emails, and my own experience in coestablishing a CVP called Detention Dialogues and in running CIVIC to highlight the benefits of CVPs.[7] While this section focuses on the benefits of volunteer-led visitation, the volunteer model does present some noteworthy limitations. For instance, CVPs often operate on budgets less than $5000 per year and volunteers themselves have limited hours of availability. Despite these limitations, CVPs are doing remarkable work.

---

[7] Online assessment tool created primarily by Christina Mansfield, Cultural Anthropologist and cofounder/executive director of CIVIC with input from David Fraccaro, Executive Director, FaithAction International House, and Christina Fialho in 2012. *Available at* https://docs.google.com/spreadsheet/viewform?formkey=dEEyTU9JTUl3c256Tlp5cGFqUUExelE6MQ (data on file with author).

2.1 CVPs Hold the Government Accountable, Ensure the Maintenance of Family and Community Ties, and Facilitate Entry or Reentry Post Release

Community visitation accomplishes three important tasks. First, ICE has recognized that "accountability" is a "keystone to detention reform" (Schriro 2009). Visitors help ICE remain accountable to human rights standards and basic decency principles by advocating for everything from fundamental necessities—such as pillows—to sufficient medical care (Bernstein 2010). Many visitation groups also monitor compliance with ICE's PBNDS, using various means to track compliance. In fact, visitors often refer to themselves as the "eyes and ears of detention facilities." Second, preserving contact with family and the community is important for the psychological well-being of the person in detention (Loyo and Corrado 2010). Visitors facilitate contact with the outside world by making phone calls on behalf of persons in detention, receiving mail for persons in detention, compiling important personal documents, and contacting pro bono attorneys.

Third, ICE has noted, "reentry planning should be completed by caseworkers and carried out in cooperation with nearby NGOs" (Schriro 2009, p. 22). Many visitors act as de facto case managers who have the ability to ease the transition into life after detention. By assisting persons in immigration detention with maintaining communication with their families and communities, CVPs act as a vehicle for sustaining a "safety net" that will be valuable and available upon release. Furthermore, upon release, visitors can help connect those persons formerly detained to employment agencies or to refugee resettlement agencies if granted asylum in the United States (Loyo and Corrado 2010, p. 8). For those individuals who are deported, visitors can help them establish contact with family or friends in the country of origin and help tie up affairs in the United States (Loyo and Corrado 2010, p. 4).

2.2 As CVPs Operate Independently of the Government, CVPs Do Not Burden Taxpayers but Rather Expand Services to Persons in Immigration Detention

ICE has recognized the need to expand services, particularly visitation services, to immigrants in detention (Schriro 2009, p. 24). In fact, Dr. Dora Schriro—a former appointed Special Adviser to ICE—called on ICE to expand access to visitation (Schriro 2009, p. 3) and to "reengage" nongovernmental stakeholders in developing standards on visitation (Schriro 2009, pp. 18–19). Specifically, Dr. Schriro recommended that family visitation be improved with expanded hours, appropriate space, affordable phone calls, and accessible mail service (Schriro 2009, p. 24).

CVPs can fulfill some of these recommendations without costing ICE or each individual detention facility a dime. As volunteers run CVPs, ICE and local detention facilities have relatively no overhead cost for providing such a service to persons in immigration detention. CVPs recruit volunteers, collect the appropriate information for any necessary background checks, and train the volunteers on the applicable rules and procedures of the detention facility at which they will visit.

CVPs also help detention facilities create a more open dialogue with the communities in which they operate. In fact, CVPs offer visitors and other immigrant rights advocates, detention facilities, and ICE employees a platform for discussion. Often, to start a visitation program, CIVIC helps communities schedule meetings with ICE and detention facility staff. In these meetings, volunteers are encouraged to ask questions and learn more about the policies of the facility and the individuals administering those policies. Despite widely different beliefs about the viability of immigration detention, this opportunity gives community members a better understanding of the mindset of detention facility administrators, which can provide a foundation of respect from which communities and detention facilities can resolve future issues collaboratively.

3 The United States Government Creates Unnecessary Roadblocks for CVPs

As immigration detention has expanded, people in immigration detention have had an increasingly difficult time maintaining social support networks. Mailed letters are slow, and phone calls are prohibitively expensive. Visits from family and friends may be the best option for maintaining social support networks, but visitation is often limited.

Families, friends, and communities have a difficult time visiting people in immigration detention for three main reasons. First, most immigration detention facilities are located in rural areas far from a city center. Take Adelanto, California, or Lumpkin, Georgia, as examples. Second, few immigration detention visitation policies are designed to encourage visits. For example, at the Ramsey County Jail in Minnesota, families are allowed only 20-min visits that they must book in advance through a system that only allows them to visit their loved ones through video conferencing. Third, the government sets up roadblocks at nearly every step of the visitation process.

The purpose of this section is to illustrate the roadblocks to establishing a CVP and the ways communities have worked together to overcome them. This section uses responses gathered from an online assessment tool, phone interviews, emails, and my own experience in coestablishing a CVP in Northern California and running CIVIC. In particular, this section proceeds as follows: Sect. 3.1 discusses the difficulties CVPs have in locating detention facilities, Sect. 3.2 looks at general barriers to visiting persons detained at these facilities, Sect. 3.3 focuses on the reasons why detention facilities often refuse to support the establishment of ICE-approved CVPs, Sect. 3.4 provides an overview of how ICE and detention facilities have tried to suspend visitation programs after volunteers exercise their First Amendment rights.

3.1 Determining the Location of Immigration Detention Facilities Is Difficult Because the Government Provides Incomplete Information

Establishing a CVP requires locating an immigration detention facility. Prior to July 2010, ICE did not publically disclose the locations of its contracted detention facilities. Therefore, communities had to file Freedom of Information Act (FOIA) requests or public record requests to determine the location of current immigration detention facilities. For example, when my colleague Christina Mansfield and I were first trying to establish Detention Dialogues in California, our research began by poring over results of FOIA requests and talking with immigration attorneys to determine where immigrants were being detained in Northern California.

We first reviewed records obtained through a FOIA request by the Switzerland-based Global Detention Project (ICE 2007). The records were overinclusive in that they showed that dozens of jails and prisons in California had the potential to house immigrants in detention, but the records also were underinclusive because they only provided a glimpse of detention during 1 month. In particular, the records indicated that 35 cities in California in September 2007 had the ability to hold "ICE detainees" in jails, state prisons, or private prisons located within their city (ICE 2007).[8] However, not all of these cities actually housed persons in immigration detention during the month of September 2007. For example, while the Santa Clara County Main Jail in San Jose housed 218 persons in immigration detention in September 2007, the Corcoran State Prison housed zero (ICE 2007). Simply knowing that a facility had an agreement with ICE did not tell us anything about how often ICE used the facility to hold immigrants in custody. Thus, in order to determine where immigrants were being detained in 2010, we had to contact individual counties.

However, counties that were holding immigrants in detention through intergovernmental service agreements were not forthcoming about these agreements. For example, Santa Clara County's public information officer provided Detention Dialogues with misinformation about its agreement with ICE. I first contacted the

[8] Lancaster, San Diego, San Pedro, El Centro, San Jose, Westminister, Bakersville, Marysville, Santa Ana, San Bernadino, El Cajon, Sacramento, Camarrillo, San Rafael, San Mateo, French Camp, Woodland, Fresno, Corcoran (California State Prison), Castro Valley, Redwood City, Milpitas, Calipatria (State Prison), Salinas, Vacaville, Merced, Santa Cruz, Oakland, Ventura, Willows, Los Angeles, Red Bluff, Atwater, Lompoc, and Riverside.

Santa Clara County Public Record Officer, Sergeant Rick Sung, in late 2010. In a phone call and in a follow-up email on November 22, 2010, Sergeant Sung said, "Please be advised that the Santa Clara County Department of Correction never had an MOU [Memorandum of Understanding] or interagency service agreement with ICE."[9] In order to obtain accurate information, I had to file a California Public Records Request, and the results revealed that Santa Clara County in fact had been detaining immigrants for the federal government since 1984 when it began contracting with the U.S. Marshals Services (before ICE's creation in 2003) and had recently ended its contract with ICE in 2010.[10]

Today, ICE does maintain a Facility Locator program on its website,[11] which allows the public to search for detention facilities by state, region, or name. However, this list is not comprehensive. For example, while it lists nine facilities in California, it fails to list all of the facilities holding immigrants in California, such as the James A. Musick Facility and Theo Lacy in Southern California.[12]

3.2 *After Determining Where Persons Are Held in Immigration Custody, the Next Obstacle Is Establishing a Way to Visit Persons Detained at These Facilities*

The visitation policy of a detention facility can affect whether or not a community group must obtain prior approval from the facility and from ICE to start an immigration detention CVP. For example, Detention Dialogues operates an ICE-approved program at the West County Detention Facility (WCDF) in

[9] Email from Rick Sung, Public Information Officer, Santa Clara County Sheriff's Office, to Christina Fialho (Nov. 22, 2010, 7:43 PST).

[10] California Public Records Act (Govt. Code §§ 6250-6276.48), to Christina Fialho (Dec. 17, 2010) (on file with author) ("The USM has contracted with the County to house federal prisoners since 1984. The initial agreement, followed by five subsequent amendments, was valid until January, 1998. In February, 1998 the DOC negotiated a new Agreement with the USM for an indefinite time period. The Agreement can be terminated when either party informs the other in writing 30 days in advance of the effective date of termination or a new Agreement is put into place. Two amendments to the Agreement were completed in July 1998, and February 2000. On August 19, 2003, the Board of Supervisors delegated authority to the Chief of Correction to approve two additional addendums to the Agreement: one to include transportation services for federal prisoners, and the other to include ICE as a user agency in the Agreement with the U.S. Marshall's Service.")

[11] U.S. Immigration and Customs Enforcement, Detention Facility Locator. http://www.ice.gov/detention-facilities/. Accessed 29 Jan 2014.

[12] U.S. Immigration and Customs Enforcement, Detention Facility Locator. http://www.ice.gov/detention-facilities/. Accessed 29 Jan 2014.

California, while Georgia Detention Watch operates an informal program at the Stewart Detention Center.[13]

The California-based facility requires visitors to have a prior approved visitation appointment, scheduled by the person in immigration detention. This policy requires persons in detention to request a visit with their on-duty lieutenant, fill out a paper visitation request slip in English, and then call their loved one and let them know the date and time when they can visit. This means that immigrants in detention must have enough money to make a call. This also means that visitors cannot simply obtain a person's Alien Registration Number, or A-number, from an attorney or family member and begin visits. For Detention Dialogues, this policy meant that we needed to obtain prior approval from WCDF and from ICE in order for us to start a CVP at the facility. We now are allowed to visit every Friday morning, outside of the facility's regular visitation hours.

At Stewart, community members and family members can visit a person in immigration detention without any reservation. For example, the Stewart Detention Center allows community members to visit with persons in detention after providing the detention center with the person's A-number. While this visitation policy allows for more liberal visitation in theory, the visitation program still encounters numerous roadblocks. For example, there are only a few visitation booths available for use and limited visitation hours. Each person at Stewart is allowed only one visit per week, and visits are noncontact and occur behind glass and through a telephone. As there are only five visitation booths in total at Stewart, the visitation group only visits with approximately five to ten individuals per week. Additionally, due to the lack of visitation space in a facility that detains up to 1924 people each day,[14] family members and visitor volunteers sometimes are denied visits after traveling hours to get to the rural facility in Lumpkin. This reality spurred the visitation group's creation of El Refugio, which provides hospitality to families outside the gates of Stewart Detention Center.

3.3 Detention Facilities and ICE Often Refuse to Support the Establishment of Immigration Detention CVPs

Since the creation of the first two U.S. immigration detention CVPs in the late 1990s, 42 additional CVPs have been formed across the country, as of November 2015. Most CVPs have had to overcome significant resistance from ICE and the

[13] Stewart is owned by the private prison corporation, Corrections Corporation of America.

[14] Email from Melissa Jaramillo, Chief of Staff to the Public Advocate, U.S. Immigration and Customs Enforcement, to Christina Fialho (October 24, 2012) (email contained Excel document with the top 25 authorized facilities by maximum capacity, obtained on October 15, 2012, from IIDS, which ICE defines as a data warehouse that contains dynamic data extracts from the Enforcement Integrated Database (EID). Stewart is the largest immigration detention facility by capacity).

detention facility in order to be approved. For example, it took over a year for CVPs to begin at the Middlesex County Adult Correction Center (MCACC) in New Jersey, the Ramsey County Detention Center in Minnesota, WCDF in California, and the McHenry County Jail in Illinois.

After the death of an elderly person in immigration detention at MCACC in March 2008, Middlesex County First Friends began a series of failed negotiations with county officials and the ICE Field Office in Newark to start a CVP. Eventually, the county and ICE approved a CVP over a year later in May 2009, allowing a group of visitor volunteers to meet twice a week for 2 h in a classroom space with persons in immigration detention. However, 5 months after gaining access, the program ended when the county terminated its contract with ICE in October 2009. Middlesex County First Friends received no advance notice of the contract termination and only learned about it from persons in immigration detention.

"I can't say whether our program influenced the termination," said Karina Wilkinson, program coordinator of the CVP, "If you think of it as a 'success,' 'success' has many parents." Wilkinson explains that ICE transferred persons who had been detained at MCACC to three other jails in a "very chaotic way" after the contract termination. Neither MCACC nor ICE notified attorneys or families of these transfers, and many of these individuals were transferred multiple times within a few month period due to the termination of MCACC's contract. Most of the individuals with whom Wilkinson's program visited were eventually transferred to the Essex County Correctional Facility.

Despite Wilkinson's success in establishing a CVP at MCACC, ICE and two nearby counties contracting with ICE prevented Wilkinson from replicating her CVP at other detention facilities. "We first met with Newark ICE in early 2010 to ask for a program or at least access to our former Middlesex detainees now in Essex County, and we were told we should visit during regular visiting hours," said Wilkinson. In early 2010, visitation during regular visiting hours was "a joke" at the Essex Correctional Facility, according to Wilkinson. Visitors waited usually one and a half hours before being permitted to visit with a person in immigration detention for no more than 30 min.

Therefore, Wilkinson tried to secure a CVP in Monmouth County. Approximately an hour and half away from New York City, Monmouth County is difficult to access via public transportation. "It is very difficult for any church groups and even lawyers to get to the facility on a regular basis," explains Wilkinson. Therefore, a CVP could fill an important gap in services to persons detained by ICE in this isolated county. For example, a CVP could help transport family members to the detention facility. However, Monmouth County and ICE's New York Field Office refused to work with Wilkinson. Eventually, the detention facility in Monmouth County closed, too (Lee 2013).

Like Wilkinson's former program at MCACC, Conversations with Friends obtained an in-person CVP at the Ramsey County Detention Center in Minnesota after a year of discussions with county officials. Conversations with Friends is led by Rev. John Guttermann. Rev. Guttermann explains, "We assumed that a credential as a member of the clergy gave us the right to have in-person visits with immigrants in detention." The group soon learned that was not the case in Ramsey County. Conversations with Friends launched a public information campaign, which included coordinated vigils and the collection of support letters from groups such as the Immigrant Law Center of Minnesota and Advocates for Human Rights.

Rev. Guttermann attended countless meetings with the detention center staff, who eventually told him that a program could not be approved without the support of ICE. Therefore, Rev. Guttermann sent a letter to ICE's Field Office and obtained verbal approval from ICE. However, jail administrators remained uncomfortable about the idea of contact visits and about starting a new program just prior to the swearing in of a new Sherriff. After many more months of persistent negotiation, the group conducted its first contact visit at the Ramsey County Detention Center in March 2011.

Detention Dialogues also met resistance in establishing its approved CVP at the West County Detention Facility (WCDF) in Contra Costa County, California. Our first contact with the jail was in December 2010; we began by establishing a rapport with the county jail's program department by attending Know Your Rights (KYR) presentations at WCDF, conducted by U.C. Davis Law School and Centro Legal de la Raza. This relationship with program administrators led to an email introduction to the Director of Support Services for WCDF. Unfortunately, she could not accommodate our request: "adding a new program, at this time, would increase the daily demand on our already-strained custody staffing levels."[15] We responded with an email that explained the nature of our visitation services. A few days later, we received an email from WCDF's Federal Program Manager, which suggested that we contact ICE as WCDF could not approve our program without ICE's approval: "The very nature of your unique proposal precludes me or any one from the Contra Costa County of the Sheriff to authorize visits, of the kind you suggest to ICE detainees in our custody."[16]

Although WCDF and ICE both believed a CVP was a good idea, each group punted our request to start the program back and forth between each other. In the absence of an enforceable regulation or policy, our only recourse was polite persistence. After a month of calls, voicemails, and a mailed letter to ICE's Field Office Director, we received a voicemail from ICE's Deputy Field Office Director in May 2011. The Deputy Director thought a CVP was a great idea, but he could not approve it without the support of WCDF. When we relayed this news to WCDF, the lieutenant with whom we had previously communicated told us that we could not start the program for security purposes. However, follow-up negotiations secured us a meeting in July 2011, which resulted in approval from both ICE and WCDF to start a CVP for persons in immigration detention. Visits began in November 2011.

---

[15] Email from Mary Jane Robb, Director of Support Services, Office of the Sheriff, Contra Costa County, to Christina Fialho (Apr. 18, 2011, 12:32 PST).

[16] Email from Jeff Hebel, Federal Program Manager, Emergency Services Division, Contra Costa County, to Christina Fialho (Apr. 26, 2011, 13:49 PST).

Another example of the trials and tribulations of starting an immigration detention CVP arose out of the experience of two Catholic nuns in Chicago, Illinois. In an effort to establish a recognized CVP and in the hopes of creating more opportunities for persons in immigration detention to connect to the outside world, the Sisters of Mercy in Chicago, Illinois, embarked on a 3-year journey. In September 2007, Sr. Pat Murphy and Sr. JoAnn Persch approached the staff at the Broadview Staging Center, asking for the permission to visit with persons being detained and deported. The Staff referred the Sisters to ICE, and ICE's Field Office Deputy Director suggested that the Sisters try to conduct visits at McHenry County Jail. After close to a year of emails and phone calls to McHenry County Jail, the Sisters obtained a meeting in May 2008 with ICE and McHenry County Jail. Unfortunately for the Sisters, McHenry County Jail staff believed they had all they needed in terms of services for those persons held in immigration detention at their facility.

Refusing to take "no" for an answer, the Sisters worked with Fred Tsao of the Illinois Coalition for Immigrant and Refugee Rights (ICIRR) to write and lobby for a new state law to allow them to start a CVP. On November 20, 2008, H.B. 4613 passed unanimously in the Illinois House and Senate. The bill, which provided that religious workers shall be granted access to ICE-contracted facilities in Illinois, was signed into law by the Governor in December 2008 and became law in June 2009. The law created the Access to Religious Ministry Act of 2008, which amended the Illinois County Jail Act. The new law provides "that any county jail in the State of Illinois for which an intergovernmental agreement has been entered into with United States Immigration and Customs Enforcement (ICE) for detention of immigration related detainees shall be required to provide to religious workers reasonable access to such jail." The new law also provides "that the sheriff or his or her designee shall have the right to screen and approve individuals seeking access to immigration detainees at the facility under the Act."

Despite the passage of this new law, the Broadview Staging Center and McHenry County Jail continued to refuse to allow the Sisters to conduct visits. The Sisters, along with other religious leaders, threatened to lie down in front of ICE's buses as they left the Staging Center to go to the airport for deportation. "ICE did not want us to lie in front of the buses, and so, ICE negotiated with us about praying on the buses," said Sister JoAnn. The Sisters also had to request Representative Dan Burke and Representative Jack Franks, who had sponsored H.B. 4613 in the House, to meet with Sheriff Keith Nygren and the McHenry County Jail. After another 6 months, Sheriff Nygren agreed to allow the Sisters to begin a CVP at McHenry County Jail. The Sisters' first visit occurred in January 2010, almost two and a half years after their first attempt to enter a detention facility as visitors.

3.4 ICE Suspends Visitation Programs

Once a visitation program is established, ICE and the detention facilities can still terminate the visitation program without any advance notice. Between 2013 and 2015, ICE and its contractors suspended 6 CIVIC-affiliated visitation programs after volunteers publically criticized the immigration detention system. In July 2013, ICE suspended three immigration detention visitation programs and blacklisted certain volunteers from any type of visit with people in detention, in clear violation of the ICE PBNDS (ICE 2011).[17] At the time of the suspensions, there existed 28 CIVIC-affiliated CVPs across the country, including two in Southern California: Friends of Orange County Detainees, which had been conducting visits at the Santa Ana City Jail and James A. Musick Facility since 2012, and the Friends of Adelanto Detainees, which had been recently approved by ICE and had begun visits at the Adelanto Detention Center. Together, the two groups had more than 130 volunteers.

These programs were abruptly suspended on July 24, 2013 (Linthicum 2013). The suspension occurred less than 48 h after I published a blog post on the Huffington Post in which I criticized ICE's treatment of LGBT immigrants in detention at the Santa Ana City Jail and called for certain reforms. In subsequent conversations with ICE's national office, ICE made clear that it suspended the programs because of my blog post and because of certain Facebook posts by visitor volunteers who were critical of conditions at detention centers. ICE requested that CIVIC and its volunteers remove the Facebook posts and cease public criticism of ICE.

CIVIC and the American Civil Liberties Union (ACLU) of Southern California, along with other legal service providers and advocates, sent two letters to ICE requesting that ICE reinstate the community visitation programs immediately and issue a public statement explaining its actions (ACLU 2013). The ACLU explained that the suspensions raised grave First Amendment concerns and gave the clear appearance that ICE was trying to silence its critics and shield the public's awareness of detention conditions (ACLU 2013).

After a vigil outside of the Adelanto Detention Center and media attention from the Los Angeles Times, the Associated Press, and other news media, ICE resumed visitation (Visitations resume in California immigration detention 2013; Fowler 2013).

A few months later, the visitation program at the Otay Detention Center in San Diego, California, experienced a similar suspension. This time, the SOLACE visitation program had raised the following three issues with ICE's San Diego Field Office: (1) SOLACE had received a complaint from a woman detained at Otay that a female guard had sexually assaulted her and that the guard still remained on active duty in her pod; (2) there was a severe bacterial infection in the legs of people in detention causing their legs to swell and weep fluid, and despite the spreading of this infection, it had not been addressed in the women's pod; and (3) there were concerns that transgender immigrants were not being housed according to their gender identification and were subject to harassment and abuse by other people in detention. ICE responded by providing SOLACE with a form to sign, which required volunteers to waive their First Amendment rights. As visitors

[17] Providing that visits "shall be permitted" by "non-relatives and friends."

refused to give up their Constitutional rights, the visitors were blacklisted from visiting Otay (Eichelberger 2014; CIVIC 2014). After CIVIC and SOLACE met with ICE's San Diego Field Office, sent a formal complaint to the Office of Civil Rights and Civil Liberties, and secured an exclusive article in Mother Jones, ICE resumed visitation.

In October 2014, ICE's contractor GEO Group also shut down the Friends of Broward County Detainees, a visitation program at the Broward Transitional Center in Florida. The program's leaders had presented testimony criticizing the detention system at a congressional hearing in Broward County hosted by Florida U.S. Reps. Joe Garcia and Ted Deutch. After CIVIC sent an email to the Field Office, the program was immediately restored.

A year later in August 2015, the visitation program at the Etowah County Detention Center in Alabama was terminated, after CIVIC filed a civil rights complaint on behalf of 20 currently and formerly detained men at the facility. The complaint described physical abuse, including beatings to coerce men in detention into signing deportation documents, as well as race-based harrassment, and inadequate medical care. After CIVIC and and the Southern Povery Law Center sent a formal complaint to ICE and the Etowah County Sherrif's Department and secured widespread media coverage, the County resumed the visitation program.

4 U.S. Law Does Not Protect a Person's Right to Receive Visits While in Immigration Detention

The difficulty of starting and maintaining a visitation program begs the question, is there a legally protected right to visitation? This section provides an overview of U.S. case law on the right to visitation in immigration detention.

4.1 The U.S. Constitution Does Not Establish a Legally Protected Right to Visitation

While no published case in any U.S. jurisdiction has addressed whether a person in immigration detention has a constitutional right to visitation, the right to visitation is not protected for prisoners or pretrial detainees in the U.S. criminal justice system. Although prison walls do not form a barrier separating prison inmates from the protection of the United States Constitution (*Hudson v. Palmer*, 468 U.S. 517 1984),[18] lawful incarceration brings about the withdrawal or

[18] Holding that a prisoner has no reasonable expectation of privacy in his prison cell under the Fourth Amendment and that an unauthorized intentional deprivation and destruction of a prisoner's property by a state prison guard did not constitute a violation of the due process clause of the Fourteenth Amendment.

limitation of many privileges and rights (*Sandin v. Conner*, 515 U.S. 472 1995). Traditionally, prison officials have strictly limited visitation for persons incarcerated in the criminal justice system (Palmer 2010, para. 3.1).[19] Cases concerning inmates' rights to visitation "generally hold that controlling this activity is within the prison officials' discretion and that such control is not subject to judicial reversal unless a clear abuse of discretion is shown" (Palmer 2010, p. 51). This deference to prison officials stems from the fact that courts have not found any inherent, absolute constitutional right to visits for prisoners.[20] As long as limitations on visitation are reasonably related to legitimate penological interests, an inmate's constitutional rights have not been violated (*Turner v. Safley*, 482 U.S. 78 1987). For example, in 2003, the U.S. Supreme Court held in *Overton v. Bazzetta* that it is not unconstitutional to deprive inmates, who have engaged in drug offenses while incarcerated, of all forms of family and personal visits for up to 2 years (*Overton v. Bazzetta*, 539 U.S. 126 2003). Lower courts have held similarly.[21] Moreover, it is irrelevant whether these limitations on visitation affect persons outside of prison.[22]

In addition, the U.S. Supreme Court has refused to find that the right to visitation exists for pretrial detainees in the criminal justice system. Pretrial detainees constitute a special category of inmates (Palmer 2010, para. 3.2). In *Bell v. Wolfish* (441 U.S. 520 1979), the U.S. Supreme Court held that the fact that a pretrial detainee is subject to some of the same restrictions as convicted persons does not in itself create an injury of constitutional dimension, as long as the restrictions do not amount to punishment (*Bell v. Wolfish* 1979, pp. 536–537). It is unclear whether a blanket prohibition on visitation for persons in pretrial detention would amount to punishment. However, as Justice Marshall explained in his dissent in *Bell*, in determining whether a restriction is punitive, the Court makes the "detention officials' intent the critical factor" and requires the detainee challenging these policies to bear the substantial burden (*Bell v. Wolfish* 1979, pp. 564).[23] The Court accords "virtually unlimited deference to detention officials' justifications for particular impositions" and overlooks "the most relevant factor, the impact that restrictions may have on [detainees]" (*Bell v. Wolfish* 1979, pp. 563). Thus, the

---

[19] Citing *Walker v. Pate*, 356 F.2d 502 (7th Cir. 1966), cert. denied, 384 U.S. 966 (1966).

[20] *See Bellamy v. Bradley*, 729 F.2d 416, 420 (6th Cir.) ("Prison inmates have no absolute constitutional right to visitation."), *cert. denied*, 469 U.S. 845 (1984).

[21] *Dunn v. Castro*, 621 F.3d 1196 (9th Cir. 2010) (holding that prisoners do not have a right to receive visits from their children); *Samford v. Dretke*, 562 F.3d 674, 682 (5th Cir. 2009) (per curiam) (holding the removal of prisoner's sons from the approved visitors list did not violate his constitutional rights); *Wirsching v. Colorado*, 360 F.3d 1191, 1198–1201 (10th Cir. 2004) (upholding prison regulation that prohibited a prisoner from receiving any visits from his children so long as he refused to participate in a treatment program).

[22] *Thornburgh v. Abbott*, 490 U.S. 401, 410 n.9 (1989) (explaining that the three cases on which the U.S. Supreme Court expressly relied in *Turner v. Safley* when it announced the reasonableness standard for inmates' constitutional rights cases all involved regulations that affected rights of prisoners *and* outsiders).

[23] Marshall, J. dissenting.

detainee's "burden will usually prove insurmountable" as most detention officials believe, erroneously but in good faith, that a specific restriction is necessary for institutional security (*Bell v. Wolfish* 1979, pp. 566).[24]

The Supreme Court's subsequent decision in *Block v. Rutherford* (468 U.S. 576 1984) advances this seemingly unlimited deference to detention officials. The Court explained that a complete prohibition on *contact* visits for any pretrial detainee is not considered punishment as long as the prohibition is a reasonable, nonpunitive response to legitimate security concerns (*Block v. Rutherford* 1984, p. 584). It is not clear from the Supreme Court's holding in *Block* whether a complete ban on all forms of visitation would be constitutional, as the Court referred specifically to "contact visits," which are visits free from any physical barrier between the inmate and the visitor. At least one lower court prior to *Block* found that pretrial detainees must be allowed reasonable visitation privileges,[25] but it is not clear this lower court case would have been decided the same way post-*Block*. In fact, post-*Block* cases have held that pretrial detainees cannot bring cognizable claims for deprivation of visitation privileges because no constitutional right to visitation exists under *Block*.[26] As the right to visitation is not protected for U.S. citizens in the criminal justice system, it is unlikely that a court would find that noncitizens have a constitutional right to visitation absent a congressional statute or state law.

4.2 No Federal Statute Provides for a Legally Protected Right to Visitation, and ICE's Standards Do Little to Support Visitation

No federal statutory right to visitation exists for persons in immigration detention. While some states, such as Texas, have passed laws requiring county jails and or state prisons to provide a certain number of visitation opportunities per week, these local laws do not guarantee an affirmative individual right to visitation. In the absence of a federal statutory right to visitation, ICE has established Performance-

[24] Marshall, J. dissenting.

[25] *E.g., Nicholson v. Choctaw County, Ala.,* 498 F. Supp. 295 (S.D. Ala. 1980).

[26] The author was unable to find any cases holding that a deprivation of visitation privileges resulted in a constitutional violation post-*Block*. *See, e.g., Dies v. Fries*, 2011 WL 3155038 (holding that a pretrial detainee denied all visitation and phone privileges did not state a claim as pretrial detainees do not have a constitutional right to visitation); *Hazel v. McElvogue*, 2011 WL 1559231 (2011) (holding that a pretrial detainee denied visits for 2 weeks did not allege any injury from the denial of his visitation privilege, and thus there was no constitutional violation); *Jones v. California Dep't of Corrections*, 2011 WL 902480 (2011) (holding that a pretrial detainee denied visitation with his wife on one occasion did not identify a liberty interest and therefore had failed to state a cognizable claim for a constitutional violation); *Hastings v. May*, 2010 WL 6560269 (2011) (holding that a pretrial detainee denied visitation with his family on one occasion did not state a cognizable claim for a constitutional violation).

Based National Detention Standards (PBNDS) for ICE and ICE-contracted facilities. Different versions of the three sets of PBNDS currently apply to ICE's various detention facilities. Standard 5.7 of the 2011 PBNDS, Standard 32 of the 2008 PBNDS, and the Standard on Visitation of the 2000 PBNDS all encourage community visitation. ICE's most recent standard on visitation, Standard 5.7 of the 2011 PBNDS, ensures that persons in detention will be able to maintain morale and ties through visitation with their families, the community, legal representatives, and consular officials, within the constraints of safety, security, and good order (ICE 2011, para. 5.7). ICE's PBNDS specifically prohibit detention facilities from blocking family and friends from visiting pursuant to the detention facilities' regular visitation policies (ICE 2011, para. 5.7.I.2.c).[27] ICE has begun implementing the 2011 PBNDS across its detention facilities, with priority given to facilities housing the largest populations of persons in immigration detention (ICE 2012).

For three reasons, ICE's PBNDS on visitation do little to incentivize detention facilities to welcome CVPs. First, these standards are neither statutory nor incorporated into regulation (Stannow 2012;[28] see also Women's Refugee Commission 2000). Therefore, they are not legally enforceable and lack disciplinary and financial consequences for facilities that fail to comply (Midwest Coalition for Human Rights & Heartland Alliance 2011, p. 5). In the absence of an enforceable regulation or policy, CVPs report that grave inconsistencies among detention facilities exist. Moreover, due to the lack of uniform application of binding detention standards, community groups hoping to establish a CVP cannot rely on the standards to help them achieve this goal. Second, Standard 5.7 of the 2011 PBNDS gives detention facilities broad discretion with regard to visitation, as visitation may be restricted for "safety, security, and good order" (ICE 2011, para. 5.7). The 2008 and 2000 PBNDS on visitation contain comparable language. Thus, without violating Standard 5.7, detention facilities can refuse to work with groups advocating for increased visitation services by simply saying that an increase in visitors might negatively impact safety or security.

Third, the phrase "constraints of safety, security, and good order" (ICE 2011, para. 5.7) sounds eerily similar to the requirement announced in *Bell v. Wolfish* and *Block v. Rutherford*. In *Bell* and *Block*, the Supreme Court was assessing restrictions within the criminal context, explaining that restrictions in that context must be reasonable, nonpunitive responses to legitimate security concerns (*Block v. Rutherford* 1984, p. 584). It is no coincidence that Standard 5.7 reflects language from cases arising out of the criminal justice setting because the PBNDS are largely derived from American Correctional Association standards (ICE 2011, para. 5.7).[29]

[27] Providing that visits "shall be permitted" by "non-relatives and friends."

[28] Explaining that the 2011 PBNDS are internal agency policies and not enforceable regulations or legally binding because they were drafted without public review or comment.

[29] See section IV, referencing American Correctional Association, *Performance-Based Standards for Adult Local Detention Facilities*, 4th Edition: 4-ALDF: 5B-01, 5B-02, 5B-03, 5B-04, 2A-21.

However, immigration detention is an entirely different context involving persons held in civil custody who are not being charged with a crime. ICE even admitted in 2009 that it's PBNDS as a whole "impose more restrictions and carry more costs than are necessary to effectively manage the majority of the detained population" (Schriro 2009, pp. 2–3).[30] Yet, when ICE revised its PBNDS in 2011, it left the standard on visitation functionally untouched.

4.3 Although No Freestanding Right to Visitation Exists, the First Amendment Places Limits on Government Action to Eliminate CVPs

While there is no freestanding right to visitation, there are limits on the government's ability to eliminate a person's ability to visit someone in immigration detention. Most notably, the U.S. Supreme Court has long held that the government cannot terminate volunteer positions or obstruct volunteer access to inmates in correctional facilities simply because the volunteer exercised his or her First Amendment rights. The very act of denying or depriving a person of a governmental benefit or privilege in retaliation against that person for his/her exercise of his/her First Amendment rights is unconstitutional and violates that person's civil rights (*Perry v. Sindermann,* 408 U.S. 593, 597 1972). There is no need to further inquire if the retaliatory denial or deprivation of governmental benefits or privileges would "chill" a person of ordinary firmness from exercising his/her First Amendment rights. The courts have long held that the retaliatory denying or depriving of someone of governmental benefits or privileges would always chill a person of ordinary firmness from exercising his/her First Amendment rights.[31] Essentially, this means that the government cannot suspend or terminate a CVP or an individual visitor volunteer in retaliation for speaking publically against the detention system, attending a vigil in protest of a detention facility, or engaging in any other activity or speech protected by the First Amendment.

---

[30] Discussing ICE's 2008 Performance-Based National Detention Standards.

[31] See *Perry v. Sindermann,* 408 US 593,597 (1972); *Hyland v. Wonder,* 972 F.2d 1129, 1134 (9th Cir. 1992); *Andersen v. McCotter,* 100 F.3d 723, 727 (10th Cir. 1996). Other courts have held similarly. *McCollum v. California*, No. C 0403339 CRB, 2006 U.S. Dist. LEXIS 58026, at *22-*23 (N.D.Cal. Aug. 8, 2006) (holding plaintiff had stated First Amendment retaliation claim by alleging that correctional facility had punished his speech by hindering his ability to visit inmates as volunteer chaplain). See also *Mosely v. Bd. of Educ.*, 434 F.3d 527, 535 (7th Cir. 2006) (holding that retaliatory acts against volunteer were actionable because "she cannot be muzzled or denied the benefit of participating in public school governance because she engaged in constitutionally protected activity").

5 The Right to Receive Visitors in Immigration Detention Is an Emerging International Norm

Despite both the expansion of U.S. immigration detention and the restrictions on a person's ability to connect to the outside world while in detention, international law defends the right to visitation during immigration detention. This section will analyze international law, underscoring how international conventions and guidelines provide a basis for individuals to claim a right to unimpeded community visitation while in immigration detention. This section is not concerned with the enforceability of international legal standards in the United States. Instead, this section demonstrates that the right to community visitation is an emerging norm (Finnemore and Sikkink 1998)[32] in international law and that the European Union is leading the way toward a recognized right to receive visits in immigration detention.

5.1 The Right to Receive Visits While in Immigration Detention Is an Emerging International Norm

The foundational document of international human rights law, the Universal Declaration of Human Rights (United Nations General Assembly 1948),[33] established that the "human rights of people, regardless of citizenship, was to be the primary subject of international law" (Steinhardt et al. 2009, p. 264). Specifically, the Universal Declaration encouraged freedom of movement (The United Nations General Assembly 1948, art. 13) and protected against cruel, inhumane, and degrading treatment (United Nations General Assembly 1948, art. 5), as well as arbitrary detention (United Nations General Assembly 1948, art. 9). This instrument set forth the first global statement of what many countries now take for granted—the inherent dignity and equality of all human beings. In other words, the Universal Declaration took what was at the time an emerging norm and, over decades, assisted in the fight to solidify human dignity as a recognized international and domestic norm.

Today, the right to receive visits while in any form of government-imposed confinement is an emerging norm enshrined in various international law instruments. According to the Standard Minimum Rules for the Treatment of All

[32] Norm creation is a three-step process requiring the promotion of the new norm often through organized civil disobedience, adoption of the norm by a critical mass—usually one-third—of state actors, and societal internalization of the norm.

[33] The Universal Declaration was passed by the United Nations General Assembly by 48 votes in favor, none opposed, and 8 abstentions. The United States voted in favor. The Universal Declaration "established an aspirational – and gradually a legal – framework for denying the premise that human rights were strictly domestic in the first place" (Steinhardt et al. 2009, p. 264).

Prisoners (United Nations General Assembly 1955),[34] "Prisoners shall be allowed under necessary supervision to communicate with their family and reputable friends at regular intervals, both by correspondence and by receiving visits" (United Nations General Assembly 1955, art. 37; see also arts. 38–39). While this standard applies specifically to "prisoners," the United Nations Body of Principles for the Protection of All Persons under Any Form of Detention or Imprisonment (United Nations General Assembly 1988) promotes a comparable principle for persons in detention: "communication of the detained or imprisoned person with the outside world, and in particular his family or counsel, shall not be denied for more than a matter of days" (United Nations General Assembly 1988, princ. 15). If a person is detained or transferred from one detention facility to another, that person also "shall be entitled to notify or to require the competent authority to notify members of his family or other appropriate persons of his choice" (United Nations General Assembly 1988, princ. 16(1)). Additionally, according to Principle 19, persons deprived of their liberty have the right to receive visits and correspond with the outside world (United Nations General Assembly 1988, princ. 19).

Other international law instruments unambiguously apply to migrants and asylum seekers in detention. The International Convention on the Protection of the Rights of All Migrant Workers and Members of Their Families (United Nations General Assembly 1990) explains that "migrant workers and members of their families shall enjoy the same rights as nationals to visits by members of their families" while under any form of detention (United Nations General Assembly 1990, art. 17(5)). Guideline 10(iv) of the United Nations High Commissioner for Refugees (UNHCR)'s Revised Guidelines on Applicable Criteria and Standards relating to the Detention of Asylum-Seekers (UNHCR 1999) emphasizes that asylum seekers in detention should have "the opportunity to make regular contact and receive visits from friends, relatives, religious, social and legal counsel" (UNHCR 1999, art. 10(iv)). Moreover, facilities should be constructed in a way to enable such visits and when "possible such visits should take place in private unless there are compelling reasons to warrant the contrary" (UNHCR 1999, art. 10 (iv)).

5.2 Visitation Rights in the European Union Provide the United States with a Lesson for Reforming Visitation Policies

The European Union and member states have begun to protect the right of persons in immigration detention to receive visits. European Union member states currently

[34] These Rules were adopted by the First United Nations Congress on the Prevention of Crime and the Treatment of Offenders, held at Geneva in 1955, and approved by the Economic and Social Council by its resolutions 663 C (XXIV) of July 31, 1957, and 2076 (LXII) of May 13, 1977.

place persons in over 220 immigration detention centers with capacity for over 30,000 persons (United States Committee for Refugees and Immigrants 2009). In a study released in September 2013, researchers found that parliamentarians across Europe have a right to visit immigration detention facilities as part of their mandate as national parliamentarians (Committee on Migration, Refugees and Displaced Persons of the Parliamentary Assembly 2013, p. 12). More specifically, in 10 of the 36 Council of Europe member states studied, this right is "either expressed (Belgium, Italy, France, Lithuania, and Poland) or implicit in law or regulations (such as Austria and Norway) or a right that simply derives from the general status of members of parliament (Hungry, Moldova, and Portugal)" (Committee on Migration, Refugees and Displaced Persons of the Parliamentary Assembly 2013, p. 20). Despite this right for government officials, approximately 80 % of asylum seekers in the European Union's immigration detention facilities do not receive any visits from family and friends, and over half do not have any family or friends in the host country (Jesuit Refugee Service-Europe 2010, p. 4).

Therefore, the European Union has taken steps to create a framework for persons in immigration detention to receive visits from nongovernmental organizations. In 2008, the European Parliament and the Council of the European Union established the Return Directive, which is the first binding (Treaty on the Functioning of the European Union)[35] supranational document providing for a maximum length for preremoval detention in European Union member states (Return Directive 2008). It also dictates, "Relevant and competent national, international and nongovernmental organizations and bodies shall have the possibility to visit detention facilities" (Return Directive 2008, article 16 paragraph 4). The purpose of these visits is not explicit in the Return Directive, but as the Council of Europe's Committee for the Protection of Torture explains, "immigration detainees should be entitled to maintain contact with the outside world during their detention, and in particular to have access to a telephone and to receive visits from relatives and representatives of relevant organizations" (The Council of Europe 2002, p. 55).

Within this framework, some European Union member states, such as Finland and Cyprus, have passed specific laws to create a system of access to detention facilities for nongovernmental organizations, families, and friends (European Commission 2013). Other member states are still trying to conform their domestic laws to the Return Directive; for example, although Italy and Estonia provide nongovernmental organizations in theory with the possibility of visiting detention facilities, these countries—like the United States—still require the organizations to request admittance to visit detention facilities from the local authorities (European Commission 2013).

In the United Kingdom, while there is no statutory right to receive visits from nongovernmental organizations and the community, the government does offer additional incentives to detention facilities to provide persons in these facilities

[35] Article 288 states that a directive is binding upon those to whom it is addressed. It is binding in its entirety and so may not be applied incompletely, selectively, or partially.

with family and community visitation. Within the United Kingdom, a national community-based immigration detention visitation network, Association of Visitors to Immigration Detainees (AVID), has emerged over the last two decades. AVID has served as an organizational platform from and through which immigrant rights advocates have promoted visitation and have used their expertise in this area to change the behavior of detention facilities (Finnemore and Sikkink 1998, p. 899).[36] For example, AVID worked with the U.K.'s Detention Services to include a clause in the Detention Services' Operating Standards Manual for Immigration Service Removal Centres stipulating, "The Centre must maintain up-to-date lists of local befriending groups and contact details of the Association of Visitors to Immigration Detainees (AVID) and ensure that detainees are aware of their services" (United Kingdom Detention Services 2005, p. 21). While the Operating Standards, like ICE's PBNDS, are not legally enforceable, they have provided AVID with a means to advocate expanded visitation.

In fact, communities in the United Kingdom have not been prevented from starting CVPs at U.K. detention facilities since the creation of an Operation Standard that specifically addresses AVID members.[37] The standard, combined with AVID's growth as a national organization, helped CVPs expand throughout the United Kingdom. Today, an AVID-affiliated visitation group exists in every U.K. long-term detention facility, and the U.K.'s prison inspectorate (HMIP) often commends the visitor groups for their welfare and befriending support. "So for a centre to deny access to an AVID-affiliated group," says AVID's Director Ali McGinley, "would certainly reflect poorly on their inspection reports." For example, McGinley explains that when AVID was helping to develop a CVP at one of the U.K.'s newer detention centers in Lincolnshire, "the staff there were very keen to meet AVID and to ensure a voluntary group was set up, as they knew that all other centers have these groups and that they are beneficial to detainees."

However, this does not mean that visitation groups operate seamlessly in U.K. detention facilities. "I wouldn't say there is a blanket acceptance," says McGinley, "but not resistance either. Perhaps they view us as a critical friend." Some U.K. facilities place restrictions on visitation groups, while other groups encounter difficulties with providing different services at a particular facility. In these cases, AVID intervenes on behalf of the local visitation group and provides a "national voice"[38] to compare and contrast the situation in a particular facility with

---

[36] Explaining that all "norm entrepreneurs" at this stage need some form of organizational platform from and through which they may promote their norms.

[37] Email from Ali McGinley, Director, Association of Visitors to Immigration Detainees (AVID), to Christina Fialho (Mar. 22, 2012, 10:32 PST) (all information contained in this article regarding AVID was provided through this email).

[38] By "national voice," McGinley does not necessarily mean publicity and press but, instead, a unified voice advocating for those persons in detention who have no political voice. It is noteworthy that AVID does engage in speech against the detention system and even submitted written evidence for the first-ever Parliamentary Inquiry into the use of Immigration Detention in the U.K., advocating for a moratorium on detention expansion, increased transparency, expanded internet access, statutory detention center rules, and other recommendations.

the circumstances at other facilities. AVID's ability to provide a "national voice," says McGinley, "is immensely helpful for individual groups in those circumstances." McGinley continues, "I think there is an understanding that AVID encourages good practice, that all volunteers are properly trained, and that we've been around for so long and have such a long history of supporting detainees, that it would be *very* difficult to come up with a good solid reason to resist a new group completely."

Although the right to receive community visits while in immigration detention is not a norm that the general public has internalized (Finnemore and Sikkink 1998, p. 895)[39] and accepts without hesitation in the United Kingdom, AVID believes that the right to visitation is an emerging norm, especially given the fact that some European Union members states have already codified the right to visitation.

6 A Role for Everyone: Proposals for Expanding Community Visitation in U.S. Immigration Detention

6.1 Congress Should Pass a New Federal Statute That Provides Families and Community Groups with Reasonable Access to Visiting Persons in Immigration Detention

In 2008, the Illinois House and Senate unanimously passed a forward-thinking bill, H.B. 4613. The law created the Access to Religious Ministry Act of 2008 and provides "that any county jail in the State of Illinois for which an intergovernmental agreement has been entered into with United States Immigration and Customs Enforcement (ICE) for detention of immigration related detainees shall be required to provide to religious workers reasonable access to such jail." While this law assisted the Catholic Sisters of Mercy to establish a CVP at McHenry County Jail in Illinois, the law would not have been as useful to a nonreligious group. Additionally, this law does not apply to detention facilities run by private corporations, such as Corrections Corporation of America or GEO Group. Moreover, this law only expands community visitation access within one state, even though immigration detention is based on federal statutes.[40] To ensure that persons detained by ICE in one state are treated equally to persons detained in another state, Congress should enact a law similar to the Illinois state law.

---

[39] Explaining that the third stage of norm creation requires internalization, where "norms acquire a taken-for-granted quality and are no longer a matter of broad public debate."

[40] *See* 8 U.S.C. § 1225(b) (authorizing detention of aliens seeking admission), 8 U.S.C. § 1226 (authorizing detention of aliens pending a determination of removability), and 8 U.S.C. § 1231 (authorizing detention of aliens with final orders of removal).

In particular, Congress should pass a law that requires all government or private correctional facilities in the United States for which an intergovernmental service agreement or contract has been entered into with U.S. Immigration and Customs Enforcement (ICE) or other relevant government agency for detention of immigration-related detainees shall be required to provide to family and community groups reasonable access to weekly in-person visitation. Reasonable access should be clearly defined with input from relevant stakeholders.

This congressional law would ensure that persons detained in one state would be afforded reasonably similar access to the outside world—especially to their family and their community—as any other person detained in another state by ICE. Additionally, this law would encourage volunteers from communities across the country to establish CVPs without the burden of having to advocate for years for access to their local detention facility. This law also would take a cue from international human rights law, which recognizes the right to receive visits while in immigration detention (see *supra* Sect. 5.1). Furthermore, this law would assist ICE in ensuring that its Standard 5.7 on visitation is upheld at all of its contracted facilities while providing detention facilities with an incentive to capitalize on the goodwill of community volunteers to expand services to persons in immigration detention.

6.2 ICE Should Update Standard 5.7 to Ensure That Persons in Immigration Detention Are Aware of CVPs

Short of congressional action, ICE should amend its Standard 5.7 on visitation to include the following language: "Facilities are encouraged to maintain up-to-date contact lists of local community-based visitation groups and contact details of Community Initiatives for Visiting Immigrants in Confinement (CIVIC), grant reasonable access to the facilities to these groups, and ensure that detainees are aware of their services." This addition to Standard 5.7 would begin to remedy some of the problems inherent in the current provision of Standard 5.7 (see *supra* Sect. 4.2). First, while it would remain true that holding a detention facility accountable to Standard 5.7 would be almost impossible as it is not legally enforceable, visitation groups would be able to exert other pressures on the facilities to comply. For example, similar to AVID's approach, U.S.-based CVPs would be able to help ICE push for compliance with Standard 5.7 by encouraging facilities to "emulate" the facilities that have CVPs "praise" the ones that conform their behavior to the Standard and "ridicule" others for their nonconformist behavior (Finnemore and Sikkink 1998, p. 902).[41] Second, this language in the Standard would guide detention facilities and ICE Field Offices in approving CVPs.

[41] The cycle for norm creation is a three-step process requiring the promotion of the new norm, adoption of the norm by a critical mass—usually one-third—of state actors, and societal internalization of the norm.

As a practical matter, in order for this addition to Standard 5.7 to have any real effect within detention facilities, ICE should provide CIVIC and its affiliated CVPs with an ICE pro bono telephone extension at all 250 immigration detention facilities. As telephone costs are expensive in immigration detention (Bernstein 2010), those persons in detention who receive the list of local community-based visitation groups may not be able to afford to call the visitation groups. A few of ICE's Field Offices across the country already have provided pro bono extensions to CIVIC-affiliated CVPs. The advantage to ICE is twofold: first, as the extension will be run by CIVIC, the operation of the telephone line will not cost ICE a dime to operate; second, persons in immigration detention will likely use it as it is operated by a nongovernmental group.

CVPs recognize that amending the Standards may not be possible in the foreseeable future as they were recently updated in 2011. Therefore, in the meantime, ICE's intergovernmental service agreements or contracts should require the facility holding ICE detainees to maintain up-to-date contact lists of local community-based visitation groups, grant reasonable access to the facilities to these groups, and ensure that detainees are aware of their services.

6.3 ICE Should Release a Memo Explaining the Benefits of CVPs

While Congress should codify a federal statute as outlined above and ICE should amend Standard 5.7 as outlined above, CVPs recognize that there are many competing political forces that might prevent these results in the short term. Thus, ICE should release a memo explaining the benefits of CVPs. While an ICE memo will not create any right to visitation enforceable at law by any party, a memo on point will provide detention facilities and ICE Field Offices with guidance on ICE's national stance on CVPs. The memo, therefore, will create an avenue through which community groups may advocate the creation of a CVP at their local detention facility.

7 Conclusion

If the U.S. government, particularly ICE, is serious about promoting accountability and improving a deeply flawed immigration detention system, it should make improving access to family and the community a top priority. It is time for the United States to recognize visitation as a right for all people locked up. It is time to let us in.

Acknowledgements Christina Mansfield and David Fraccaro provided essential guidance during the research process, and I am indebted to Karina Wilkinson, Rev. John Guttermann, Sr. Joann

Persch, Sr. Pat Murphy, Katie Beno-Valencia, Sally Pillay, Ali McGinley, and Michael Kaufman for their time, enthusiasm, and ideas. Special thanks to W. David Ball, Professor at Santa Clara University School of Law and Co-Chair of the Corrections Committee of the American Bar Association's Criminal Justice Section, who reviewed earlier drafts of this paper. Any errors are mine alone.

References

ACLU (2013) Press release: groups call on ICE to reinstate community-based visitation programs. American Civil Liberties Union of Southern California. http://www.aclusocal.org/press-release-groups-call-on-ice-to-reinstate-community-based-visitation-programs/. Accessed 29 Jan 2014

Amnesty International (2009) Jailed without justice. http://www.amnestyusa.org/pdfs/JailedWithoutJustice.pdf. Accessed 8 Aug 2014

Bell v. Wolfish, 441 U.S. 520 (1979)

Bernstein N (2010) Volunteers report on treatment of immigrant detainees. N.Y. Times, 29 Apr 2010, at A26

Block v. Rutherford, 468 U.S. 576 (1984)

CIVIC (2014) Wednesday, August 13, 2014 – Congressional Testimony. http://blog.endisolation.org/wp-content/uploads/2014/08/CIVIC_Congressional_Testimony_Final_reduced2.pdf. Accessed 2 Sept 2014

Committee on Migration, Refugees and Displaced Persons of the Parliamentary Assembly (2013) Visiting immigration detention facilities: a guide for parliamentarians. http://www.apt.ch/content/files_res/guide-for-parliamentarians-visiting-detention-centres-en.pdf. Accessed 6 Feb 2014

Council of Europe (2002) The CPT Standards – 'Substantive' sections of the CPT's General Reports [CPT/Inf/E (2002) 1, Rev. 2010]

Detention Watch Network, Visiting Immigrants in U.S. Detention Facilities, Available at http://fcnl.org/assets/detention_visitation_manual.pdf. Accessed 2 Sept 2014

DHS (2013) Annual Report, Immigration Enforcement Actions: 2012. Department of Homeland Security. http://www.dhs.gov/sites/default/files/publications/ois_enforcement_ar_2012_1.pdf. Accessed 8 Aug 2014

Eichelberger E (2014) Watchdog: feds are muzzling us for reporting alleged immigrant detainee sex abuse. Mother Jones, 19 March 2014. http://www.motherjones.com/politics/2014/03/ice-sexual-abuse-immigrant-detention-oversight. Accessed 2 Sept 2014

European Commission (2013) Ad hoc query on access to detention centres. http://ec.europa.eu/dgs/home-affairs/what-we-do/networks/european_migration_network/reports/docs/ad-hoc-queries/protection/483_emn_ad-hoc_query_on_detention_of_asylum_seekerswider_dissemination_en.pdf. Accessed 6 Feb 2014

Finnemore M, Sikkink K (1998) International norm dynamics and political change. In the special issue international organization at fifty: exploration and contestation in the study of world politics. Int Organ 52(4):887–917

Flynn M (2011) Immigration Detention and Proportionality 7. Global Detention Project, Working Paper No. 4

Fowler L (2013) ICE visitation ban lifted at detention centers. San Bernardino Sun, 11 September 2013. http://www.endisolation.org/wp-content/uploads/2013/03/ICE_visitation_ban_lifted_at_detention_centers.pdf. Accessed 29 Jan 2014

Hendricks T (2009) U.S. citizens wrongly detained, deported by ICE. San Francisco Chronicle, July 27, 2009, at A-1

ICE (2007) Letter to Michael Flynn under the Freedom of Information Act (FOIA) (7 Nov 7, 2007). U.S. Immigration and Customs Enforcement. http://www.globaldetentionproject.

org/fileadmin/docs/US_Department_of_Homeland_Security_2007_1_.pdf. Accessed 29 Jan 2014
ICE (2011) Performance-Based National Detention Standards. U.S. Immigration and Customs Enforcement. http://www.ice.gov/detention-standards/2011/. Accessed 29 Jan 2014
ICE (2012) Fact Sheet: ICE Detention Standards. U.S. Immigration and Customs Enforcement. http://www.ice.gov/news/library/factsheets/facilities-pbnds.htm. Accessed 29 Jan 2014
Jesuit Refugee Service-Europe (2010) Becoming vulnerable in detention. http://www.jrseurope.org/publications/JRS-Europe_Becoming%20Vulnerable%20In%20Detention_June%202010_PUBLIC_updated%20on%2012July10.pdf. Accessed 6 Feb 2014
Lee E (2013) Immigrant detention operation shuts down at Monmouth County Jail. The Star-Ledger, 29 April 2013. http://www.nj.com/monmouth/index.ssf/2013/04/monmouth_county_jail_shuts_down_immigrant_dention_operations.html. Accessed 29 Jan 2014
Linthicum K (2013) U.S. suspends visitation programs at 3 immigrant facilities in the Southland. Los Angeles Times, 20 Aug 2013. http://articles.latimes.com/2013/aug/20/local/la-me-immigrant-detention-20130820. Accessed 29 Jan 2014
Loyo R, Corrado C (2010) Locked up but not forgotten 7–8. New York University School of Law Immigrant Rights Clinic. https://afsc.org/resource/locked-not-forgotten. Accessed 29 Jan 2014
Midwest Coalition for Human Rights & Heartland Alliance (2011) Not too late for reform. http://www.immigrantjustice.org/publications/report-not-too-late-reform. Accessed 29 2014
Palmer J (2010) Constitutional rights of prisoners. Elsevier. https://www.elsevier.com/books/constitutional-rights-of-prisoners/palmer/978-1-59345-503-3
Preston J (2011) Immigration crackdown also snares Americans, N.Y. Times, 14 Dec 2011, at A-20
Schriro D (2009) Immigration detention overview and recommendations. U.S. Immigration and Customs Enforcement, United States. http://www.ice.gov/doclib/about/offices/odpp/pdf/ice-detention-rpt.pdf. Accessed 29 Jan 2014
Stannow L (2012), When good isn't enough. Huffington Post, 6 March 2012
Steinhardt RG et al (2009) International human rights Lawyering: cases and materials. West Academic Publishing. http://www.amazon.com/International-Human-Rights-Lawyering-Materials/dp/031426020X
United Kingdom Detention Services (2005) Detention Services Operating Standards Manual for Immigration Service Removal Centres, Communications Standard #22. http://www.ukba.homeoffice.gov.uk/sitecontent/documents/managingourborders/immigrationremovalcentres/operatingstandards/operatingstandards_manual.pdf?view=Binary. Accessed 6 Feb 2014
UNHCR (1999) Revised guidelines on applicable criteria and standards relating to the Detention of Asylum-Seekers. United Nations High Commissioner for Refugees. http://www.unhcr.org/refworld/docid/3c2b3f844.html. Accessed 21 Jan 2012
United Nations General Assembly (1948) Universal Declaration of Human Rights. G.A. Res. 217 (III) A, U.N. Doc. A/RES/217(III) (10 Dec 1948)
United Nations General Assembly (1955) United Nations, Standard Minimum Rules for the Treatment of Prisoners. http://www.unhcr.org/refworld/docid/3ae6b36e8.html. Accessed 21 Jan 2012
United Nations General Assembly (1988) Body of Principles for the Protection of All Persons under Any Form of Detention or Imprisonment. G.A. Res. 43/173 A. U.N. Doc A/RES/23/173 (9 Dec 1988)
United Nations General Assembly (1990) International Convention on the Protection of the Rights of All Migrant Workers and Members of Their Families. G.A. Res. 45/158 A. U.N. Doc A/RES/45/158 (18 Dec 1990)
United States Committee for Refugees and Immigrants (2009) World Refugee Survey 2009 – Europe 17 Jun 2009. http://www.unhcr.org/refworld/country,,USCRI,,CYP,,4a40d2a6c,0.html. Accessed 5 Feb 2014

Visitations resume in California immigration detention (2013) Associated Press, 11 Sep 2013. http://www.endisolation.org/wp-content/uploads/2013/03/Visitation_Resumed_APArticle.pdf. Accessed 29 Jan 2014

Women's Refugee Commission (2000) Behind locked doors. Abuse of refugee women at the Krome Detention Center. Women's Refugee Commission, New York

Who Wants to Go to Arizona? A Brief Survey of Criminalization of Immigration Law in the U.S. Context

Gabriel Haddad Teixeira

Abstract The state of Arizona, dissatisfied with circumstances arising from U.S. immigration policy, sought to promote adjustments in U.S. immigration law through the issue of local regulations: Arizona Senate Bill 1070, House Bill 2162. These statutes pursue to combat illegal immigration and harden the criminalization of immigration law by criminalizing the immigrants and conducts related to illegal immigration as labor issues. In this scenario, the purpose of this article is to promote a brief debate about the legal adequacy of Arizona's acts, as well as the validity of the factual arguments that fostered the editing of such acts. The relationship between immigration and crime also may be questioned. Thus, this article promotes a brief analysis of the relationship between immigration and crime within the context of the paradigm shift of criminology—the passage of the etiological paradigm to the paradigm of critical criminology—and the effects of risk society and actuarial methodology on the way of thinking the issues pertaining to immigration and its relationship to crime. Finally, it questions the validity of Arizona's acts based on empirical results about crime collected in recent surveys.

1 Introduction

The people of a state are defined by Kelsen as "personnel sphere of validity of the National Legal Order," in other words, as the unity of those subjected to state regulation (Kelsen 2000, p. 334). Thereby, it is necessary to define the criteria, according to which the personal sphere would be settled, implying distinctions between pernationals and nonnationals. Likewise, it is necessary to regulate the movement of people through immigration law.

Indeed, the power to establish the criteria of nationality and the immigration law stems from the exercise of sovereignty. The immigration law, as a rule, is established considering a wide range of elements as state's interests and its commitments undertaken either in national law or international law. Therefore, the national immigration law is volatile and can vary throughout history.

G.H. Teixeira, LLM (✉)
Law Department, Centro Universitário de Brasília (UniCEUB), Brasília, Brazil
e-mail: gabrielht@me.com; gabriel.teixeira@uniceub.br

M.J. Guia et al. (eds.), *Immigration Detention, Risk and Human Rights*,
DOI 10.1007/978-3-319-24690-1_15

In the United States, it is no different. The U.S. immigration law has changed to fit to the new realities that arise. There is an oscillation between permissive periods—in which there was a demand for labor—and restrictive periods—when it was necessary to control the entry of new immigrants due to the scarcity of resources or on behalf of greater national security. These oscillations can be caused by many different factors, whether internal or external order.

The state of Arizona, dissatisfied with circumstances arising from U.S. immigration policy, sought to promote adjustments in U.S. immigration law through the issue of local regulations: Arizona Senate Bill 1070, House Bill 2162.[1] These statutes pursue to combat irregular immigration and harden the criminalization of immigration law by criminalizing the immigrants and conducts related to irregular immigration as labor issues.

Arizona's discourse presents irregular immigration as a generating element of disorder and reason of the massive increase in crime rates in the region. It is inferred from public shared opinion that immigration—especially irregular immigration—and immigrants come to be considered as elements of risk in that social context.

In this scenario, the purpose of this article is to promote a brief debate about the legal adequacy of Arizona's acts. The assumption is that the factual arguments that fostered the editing of such acts are misleading.

First, in order to facilitate the study, a brief summary of the case of Arizona—highlighting relevant points of the constitution of normative acts and emphasizing some of the most controversial points—will be presented.

Afterward, it is necessary to question the legitimacy (competence) of a state to regulate issues related to immigration, in the context of federalism. Without further claims, it is a simple check of legal adequacy of Arizona's acts based on arguments raised by the Federal Government and by Arizona's Government in legal challenges that followed the publication of the acts.

The circumstances of the creation of Arizona's acts and some of the arguments presented in favor of the issue indicate that, by this endeavor, Arizona aims to combat crime that stems from immigration, especially irregular immigrants.

However, the relationship between immigration and crime must be questioned. Thus, this article promotes a brief analysis of the relationship between immigration and crime within the context of the paradigm shift of criminology—the passage of the etiological paradigm to the paradigm of critical criminology—and the effects of risk society and actuarial methodology on the way of thinking the issues pertaining to immigration and its relationship to crime. Finally, it questions the validity of Arizona's acts based on empirical results about crime collected in recent surveys.

[1] In the 1850s, A Tennessee's Senator proposed a project whereby the regulation of immigration would be the burden of the states; however, it was decided at the time for another project which provided for a stronger federal jurisdiction on the matter (Edwards 2001, p. 501).

2 Arizona's Case

On 23 April 2010, the state of Arizona enacted a law named Support Our Law Enforcement and Safe Neighborhoods Act, known as Arizona Senate Bill 1070 (SB 1070). The law was reformed just after its publication by the House Bill 2162 (HB 2162). This set of laws introduces a new context regarding the enforcement of immigration laws in Arizona. This new scenario has been the target of numerous protests and of some legal action even before its entry into force, which took place on July 29 of that year.

SB 1070 was enacted with the intent to discourage and to deter the entry, presence, and economic activity of irregular immigrants in Arizona's territory. It is believed that with the enactment of those acts, the enforcement of immigration law by the state and local agencies will be facilitated. Hence, Arizona sought to legitimize the act grounded on the discourse of need of cooperation between the federal and state levels to combat irregular immigration in Arizona.[2]

Arizona is one of the U.S. states known as destinations for immigrants;[3] it appears that part of the population shows itself sensitive to an increase in irregular immigration.[4] This restlessness probably arises from the notion very reproduced in the common sense whereby the irregular immigration is an aggravating factor, or even reason of certain social problems. In this context, immigration—especially irregular immigration—is often associated with crime rate increase, as it is possible to infer from the discourse of the national organization Stand With Arizona Against Irregular Immigration:

> ARIZONA IS BESIEGED by illegal immigration--more people and drugs cross illegally into the United States through Arizona than any other state. And Arizonans suffer the massive levels of crime that go with it. Drug and human smuggling, extortion, kidnapping

[2] The provisions of this act are intended to work together to discourage and deter the unlawful entry and presence of aliens and economic activity by persons unlawfully present in the United States (Arizona 2010b, section 1).

[3] The Hispanic or Latino origin population represents 29.6 % of the inhabitants of the state—a rate considered median if compared with the other states which border Mexico. Still according to the official data from the census, between 2000 and 2010 there was an increase of 24.6 % in the total population of Arizona—46.3 % of increase considering only the Hispanic or Latino origin population in the territory. The state with the largest Hispanic population among the states that border Mexico is the New Mexico, with 46.3 % of the population consisting of Hispanics and Latinos, and the smallest is the state of Mississippi with only 2.7 % of the population (U.S. Census 2010).

[4] Arizona had already edited prior law aimed at combating irregular immigration. In the 1980s struggled a proposed amendment to state's constitution considering the English Only politics, in order to set English as the official language of work in the state administration. This measure was challenged by the American Civil Liberties Union (ACLU) for violating freedom of speech protection provided in the First Amendment. Another episode occurred in 2007 with the enactment of state laws designed to inhibit the hiring of irregular immigrants by punishing the employers (Zeman 2001, p. 486; National Conference of State Legislatures 2012).

and murders. And the Federal government has done NOTHING to stop it. (Stand With Arizona 2012)

It was in this scenario that SB 1070 was enacted, resulting in a controversial text, in which three provisions were elected for analysis in the current article: (1) provisions concerning procedures for verification of immigration status, (2) the primary criminalization of willful failure to complete or carry an alien registration document as established on the local act, and (3) the possibility of immigrant detention in certain cases.

The procedures for verification of immigration status are one of the most controversial points of the act. According to SB 1070, local actors should try to determine the immigration status whenever facing any reasonable suspicion of unlawful presence in U.S territory. The suspicion can arise from any lawful contact, as a legal stop or detention.[5]

Note that the use of the expression "reasonable suspicion"—in the immigration context[6]—makes possible the application of the law based on discrimination of race, color, and gender, which is expressly interdicted by federal order and also repudiated in international context.[7] Therefore, the amendment carried out by HB 2162 added that, in applying the provisions under discussion, no local actors may take into consideration race, color, or national origin, subject to constitutional exceptions. The reform also creates a presumption of legality for immigrants who present one of the listed documents.[8]

[5] For any lawful contact made by a law enforcement official or agency of this State or a Country, City, Town or other political subdivision of this State where reasonable suspicion exists that the person is an alien who is unlawfully present in the United States, a reasonable attempt shall be made, when practicable, to determine the immigration status of the person. The person's immigration status shall be verified with the Federal Government pursuant to 8 United States Code Section 1373(c) (Arizona 2010b, Article 8(b)).

[6] Although "reasonable suspicion" is a legal term often used in the amendment case law, and there is consensus that the term does not allow discrimination. However, thinking about immigration it should be revalued.

[7] The International Covenant on Civil and Political Rights—specifically in Article 2, § 1, and Article 26—rejected any kind of discrimination such as of race, color, sex, language, religion, political opinion, or any other opinion, national origin or social origin, property, birth, or other status. The Covenant was signed by the United States on October 5, 1977, and ratified on June 8, 1992. It was presented a statement of interpretation by which the U.S. declares, "that the Constitution and laws of the United States guarantee all persons equal protection of the law and provide extensive protections against discrimination. The United States understands distinctions based upon race, colour, sex, language, religion, political or other opinion, national or social origin, property, birth or any other status - as those terms are used in article 2, paragraph 1 and article 26 - to be permitted when such distinctions are, at minimum, rationally related to a legitimate governmental objective [. . .]" (Recueil des Traités des Nations Unies 1966).

[8] [. . .] A law enforcement official or agency of this state or a country, city, town or other political subdivision of this state may not consider race, color or national origin in implementing the requirements of this subsection except to the extent permitted by the United States or Arizona Constitution. A person is presumed to not be an alien who is unlawfully present in the United

The second provision establishes as state class 1 misdemeanor the "willful failure to complete or carry an alien registration document" inasmuch as the USC-8 establishes that the immigrants must always remain with its documents. The question is not the criminalization but the punishments set by SB 1070—since the same acts are considered federal misdemeanor under the USC-8–1304 (e), 1306 (a). However, SB 1070 fixed punishments far more severe than those specified in the federal legislation, which were subsequently attenuated.

These facts—federal primary criminalization and local establishment of harsher punishments—highlight the intolerance of the local population with irregular immigration and other correlated issues, and also their unwillingness to deal with the dangers arising from Federal Government's decisions on immigration law.

The population's unwillingness to manage the immigration issues is also evidenced in several other provisions besides those already mentioned, such as the power to arrest a person, without a warrant, whenever there is enough evidence that leads to believe that the person has committed a crime that makes the person removable from U.S. territory.[9] There are also a number of other provisions about labor issues correlated to immigrants or transport of immigrants, all in order to make irregular immigration harder or to inhibit it.

Arizona's efforts corroborate the society's fear according to which the increase in crime rates in the state is linked to the irregular immigration issue. This fear is of such intensity that authorizes civil rights violations, as those cited. However, the rush may lead to measures taken without a legal adequacy or factual evidence about the impacts of irregular immigration on crime rates. The legal system—based on the legality criteria—will take care of the first analysis (legal adequacy), while criminology is engaged on the second analysis (irregular immigration effects on the process of defining the deviation/crime).

3 Legal Adequacy

SB 1070 has raised a lot of controversy, and its constitutionality has been challenged by U.S. Government,[10] which requests a declaratory judgment stating that "Sections 1–6 of SB 1070 are invalid, null, and void." Therefore, so as to reduce the impacts SB 1070 enacted, Arizona's Government issued, on the same day, an order to properly train the agents state law enforcement. However, this measure was

States if the person provides to the law enforcement officer or agency any to the following: [...] (Arizona 2010a, Section 5.D).

[9] Article 8 (e): A law enforcement officer, without a warrant, may arrest a person if the officer has probale cause to believe that the person has committed any public offense that makes the person removable from the United States (Arizona 2010a, Article 8 (e)).

[10] "The United States of America is the plaintiff in this action, suing on its own behalf, as well as on behalf of the United States Department of Homeland Security ("DHS"), the Department of Justice ("DOJ"), and the Department of State" [U.S. Complaint].

considered insufficient by U.S. Government, as it is possible to infer from the preliminary injunction petitioned to prevent Arizona to enforce SB 1070 before the final determination about its constitutionality.

The legal debate that arose from SB 1070 issue is developed in two aspects: procedural and substantive. The first aspect questions the states' competence to address an issue about immigration, specifically to establish an immigration policy specific to its territory. In regard to the substantive issues, it inquires into the constitutionality of certain provisions of SB 1070 in the face of individual civil rights, guaranteed in U.S. Constitution.

In the United States, the division of powers between the Federal Government and states has raised intense debates, such as the present about immigration policy (Plascencia 2001, p. 518). The U.S. Constitution is not as objective and expressed as observed in other subjects.[11] Thus, the problem has been solved by U.S. Supreme Court through several cases judged, and today is perceived axiomatic (Vázques-Azpiri 2001, p. 510).

The Supreme Court understands that the power to establish immigration policies—as an issue related to foreign affairs—belongs to the Federal Government, although the Constitution does not expressly determine. Immigration law—as the other foreign affairs subjects—stems from the sovereign power that was transferred to colonies as collective body. Hence, Federal Government must exclusively execute it.[12]

Some of the Constitution's provisions—the Commerce Clause, the Naturalization Clause, and the Migration and Importation Clause—substantiate the Supreme Court's understanding. There are several other theories that deal with this question. In general, what prevails is Federal jurisdiction since the regulation of immigration is an inherent attribute of state sovereignty (Weissbrodt and Danielson 2005, p. 55).

Currently, U.S. immigration law is a complex statutory framework based on Immigration and Nationality Act (INA),[13] which is a compilation of various provisions that enacted the U.S. immigration law. Created in 1952, INA has been constantly refined.[14] It empowers the Department of Justice (DOJ), Department of Homeland Security (DHS), and Department of State (DOS) to administer and enforce the immigration laws (U.S. Citizenship and Immigration Services 2012).[15]

---

[11] On the subject the Constitution lays down that [The Congress shall have Power] "To establish an uniform Rule of Naturalization, and uniform Laws on the subject of Bankruptcies throughout the United States" (United States 1787, Article I).

[12] "Rather, the states individually have "never possessed international powers. Id. Because the federal government's sovereign powers over the entire realm of foreign affairs passed from Great Britain to the colonies "in their collective and corporate capacity as the United States of America" (United States Supreme Court 2012).

[13] U.S.C. article 8 par 1101.

[14] Among the reforms of the INA, the Immigration Reform and Control Act (IRCA) edited in 1986 is one of the most important. Focused on irregular immigration, IRCA reshaped the structure of the Immigration and Naturalization Service (INS)—the federal agency responsible for the issue. It also presents an amnesty plan for irregular immigrants who observe certain criteria.

[15] U.S.C., Article 8, par 1103–1104.

The power to enacted Immigration Law and Immigration Policies within U.S. federated system was one of the main arguments raised by the U.S. Government in petitions against SB 1070:

> In our constitutional system, the federal government has preeminent authority to regulate immigration matters. This authority derives from the United States Constitution and numerous acts of Congress. The nation's immigration laws reflect a careful and considered balance of national law enforcement, foreign relations, and humanitarian interests. [...] Although states may exercise their police power in a manner that has an incidental or indirect effect on aliens, a state may not establish its own immigration policy or enforce state laws in a manner that interferes with the federal immigration laws. The Constitution and the federal immigration laws do not permit the development of a patchwork of state and local immigration policies throughout the country. (U.S. Department of Justice 2012)

Thus, INA represents the result of this power: the establishment of an immigration policy in line with American society's values, in consonance with the Constitution's provision[16] and considering the multiple national interests.

In this context, it is noted that SB 1070 brings to a focus only one of the various interests that must be observed. The fight against irregular immigration—and crime that rises from it—is the central concern of SB 1070. Therefore, Arizona Immigration Policy enforcement may destabilize U.S. immigration system, since it results into a cost to the Immigration Federal Agencies involved and removes those federal agents from the priorities established by the Federal Government, such as terrorism, espionage.

Furthermore, the judicial challenge also emphasized that the Federal Executive has the power to adapt a flexible immigration policy to ensure national interests or for humanitarian reasons. This means that Federal Agencies responsible for immigration law enforcement have a discretion, which allows it to not apply sanctions—whether civil or criminal. Thereby, Arizona's immigration law does not seem to consider this possibility, making the discretion impossible.

Finally, the U.S. argues that Arizona's immigration law puts aside some federal interests, as exposed, and it is contrary to the Supremacy Clause.[17] Also, it prejudices United States foreign affairs, immigration law enforcement, and the discretion granted to agencies responsible for the issue (U.S. Department of Justice 2010).

---

[16] Among Constitutional provisions applicable to the subject:

First Amendment: "Congress shall make no law respecting an establishment of religion, or prohibiting the free assemble, and to petition the Government for a redress of grievances."

Fourteen Amendment: "Section 1. All person born or naturalized in the United States, and subject to the jurisdiction thereof, are citizens of the United States and the State wherein the reside. No State shall make or enforce any law which shall abridge the privileges or immunities of citizens of the United States; nor shall ant State deprive any person of life, liberty, or property, without due process of law; nor deny to any person within its jurisdiction the equal protection of the laws."

[17] Article VI Clause 2: This Constitution, and the Laws of the United States which shall be made in Pursuance thereof; and all Treaties made, or which shall be made, under the Authority of the United States, shall be the supreme Law of the Land; and the Judges in every State shall be bound thereby, any Thing in the Constitution or Laws of any State to the Contrary notwithstanding.

In contrast to these arguments Arizona points out that immigration law should be enforcement by cooperation between federal, state, and local agencies. This argument is based on INA's reforms that established cooperation between these spheres regarding the flows of information concerning immigrants' status. Moreover, Arizona claims that federal structure is inefficient to control irregular immigration, which cause damages to Arizona:

> SB 1070 is Arizona's legitimate and constitutionally permissible response to the crushing personal, environmental, criminal, and financial burdens thrust upon the State as a consequence of illegal immigration and the lack of comprehensive enforcement activity by the federal government and certain Arizona "sanctuary" cities. (Arizona et al. 2010)

According to statistical data presented by Arizona, approximately 50 % of irregular immigrants enter the country through the Arizona's border. It is estimated that irregular immigrants represent 17 % of the prison population in the state. Arizona clearly relates the number of irregular immigrants with the increase in crime rates (Arizona et al. 2010).

Hence, Arizona understands that the "lack of comprehensive enforcement activity by the federal government" sufficiently justifies a harsher immigrations policy and immigration law and is supported by the part of Arizona's population that believes in the relationship between irregular immigration and crime.

In summary, material Arizona's defense claims that SB 1070 was misinterpreted by the Federal Government. Thereby, Arizona's interpretation of the law—also considering the state constitution—is free from defects appointed out by U.S. Petition.

At first, the lower court enjoined Arizona from enforcing some part of SB 1070 (U.S. District Court for the District of Arizona 2010).[18] About the subject, the U.S. Supreme Court has manifested to reaffirm the Federal Government's exclusive power to regulate immigration issues and emphasized that the power extends far beyond the admission of immigrants, inasmuch as it reaches the criteria for residence and expulsion, inter alia. And since this power arises from sovereignty, Arizona's argument—based on inherent authority of the state—should not prevail:

> Because these immigration powers arise from the sovereign authority of the United States, they are not part of the states' police powers. Arizona's claim— that a general and "inherent authority" of states to enforce federal law applies with equal force in the immigration context—must therefore be rejected. (Arizona et al. 2010)

The idea of cooperation in immigration issue stems from the amplitude that can be attributed to the term immigration policy. The meaning attributed by Federal Government on its speech is linked to the sovereignty acts related to immigration subject: admission, discharge, control of immigrants by nationality, etc. However,

[18] It is further ordered preliminarily enjoining the State of Arizona and Governor Brewer from enforcing the following Sections of Senate Bill 1070 (as amended by House Bill 2162): Section 2(B) creating A.R.S. § 11-1051(B), Section 3 creating A.R.S. § 13-1509, the portion of Section 5 creating A.R.S. § 13-2928(C), and Section 6 creating A.R.S. § 13-3883 (A)(5) (U.S. District Court for the District of Arizona 2010).

it is also possible to assign a broad sense—immigration policy as a set of rules that impact immigrants' lives.

The broader meaning gives the grounds for the idea of joint responsibility and cooperation (Plascencia 2001, p. 518), since it is known that the states can edit various rules with high potential to interfere in the lives of immigrants who live in their territory. Labor law issues—reservation of jobs and professions to nationals—are an example of rules that can compose immigration policy in the broad sense.

Moreover, it appears that SB 1070's terms contradict federal immigration policy and Congress' intentions on the subject. Therefore, whenever a conflict takes place—where Federal Government has the power to enact an act and the law enacted has no gaps or omissions that justify the state jurisdiction—federal law must prevail. Finally, the court emphasized that the need to combat social problems arising from irregular immigration does not allow Arizona to exercise federal powers:

> Thus, the rationale advanced by Arizona—that it needs to protect itself from purported social costs related to immigration (Pet. Br. at 2–8)—cannot justify the intrusion on the exclusive federal immigration power worked by Sections 2(B) and 6. (United States Supreme Court 2012)

Therefore, the Supreme Court consolidated the Court of Appeal's decision against SB 1070. It is noteworthy that the legal adequacy was analyzed from the perspective of competence and the hierarchy of norms. An approach to the relationship between immigration and crime rates had no significant place in the legal framework. This is because the legal system language (regular/irregular) does not allow it, and it neither aspires to this discussion, which is gaining ground in criminology and social sciences.

4 Immigration and Crime

The relationship between immigration and crime is approached differently within each paradigm of criminology, according to the methodology of each particular theory. Thus, etiological paradigm analyzes the relationship between immigration and crime under science parameters used in the search for explanations for the causes of crime (Andrade 1995, p. 29). Meanwhile, social reaction paradigm understands this relationship from the perspective of social interaction, taking crime as a society assignment and not as a natural phenomenon (Andrade 1995, p. 32). Finally, it is also possible to explore the relationship on screen from an actuarial perspective wherein it seeks a risk management in order to increase the social control effectiveness and maximum reduction of operating costs (Anitua 2008, p. 815).

Similar to what was observed in the first phase of positive criminology—in which the criminal was studied as a biologically distinct object in relation to the ordinary individual—there are some theories that tries to establish (explain) the relationship between immigration and crime from biological questions. According to those ideas, some immigrant groups were biologically deficient, differentiated; consequently, the increase in crime would be expected whenever these groups enter (Martinez Jr and Lee 2000, p. 488).

This anthropological method is characteristic of Lombroso's research, known as anthropological criminology, which represents the beginning of criminology as a science and the thought of Positive School, whose object was the criminal. Still on this approach—the second phase of the Positive School—the range of causes of deviation has expanded. In addition to individual aspects, physical and social issues were also considered.

Thus, the relationship between immigration and crime could be observed under structural condition (physical) and cultural tradition (social) concepts. Some immigration circumstances lead immigration to settle itself in structurally weak neighborhoods where it is observed a high crime rate and a deficient distribution of opportunities when compared with the most ordinary neighborhoods.

Therefore, it was questioned whether crime arises as a means of overcoming the difficulties of access to ordinary goods, which would come up from unequal distribution (Martinez Jr and Lee 2000, p. 489), and also if structural and social differences between immigrants and the host society could lead the immigrant to deviant behavior. In this framework, the Chicago School's work gains space and prominence.

During the nineteenth and twentieth centuries, Chicago city experienced a huge population growth. This process was spurred by the wave of immigrants who were motivated by the "American dream" and, in order to escape the conflicts taking place in Europe, settled themselves in the United States. Chicago's location facilitated the commercial development of the region and the reception of immigrants. At this time, it is observed the increase in crime rates and the appearance of conflicts between social groups due to culture and social behavior.

It was in this context that Chicago School develops. The initial hypothesis was that there would be a parallel between cities' growth and rising crime. Accordingly, the crime would be related to the social disorganization, which results from the cities' rapid expansion. Cities grow in concentric circles, in which there are areas of crime. The big-city structures favor anonymity and weaken social control over the individual, allowing easier contagion due to contact with the criminal production areas.

In summary, structural differences induce social subgroup (gang) formation—which in this context plays a role of protection and support of legitimate social purpose pursuit. Consequently, the belonging to a subgroup—which promotes subgroup's code that, depending on what subgroup is, can be composed of deviant behaviors—could be seen as the cause of deviant behaviors and crimes.

Regarding the analysis of cultural conflict as a cause of crime, it was observed that cultural relations can only clarify—albeit superficial—the recurrence of certain types of crimes in accordance with the immigration group. In other words, cultural conflicts between the immigrant and the local society do not induce crimes. However, the cultural conflict may—in some cases—justify the repetition of certain crimes in certain immigrant group and also clarify superficially the reason for crimes according to generation immigrants.

Chicago School is the first step in overcoming the etiological paradigm, since it represents a shift in focus, which has considered the structural and social circumstances. Also, there was a strong influence of symbolic interaction thoughts, which encourage the shift of "cognitive interests": the abandonment of the causes of crime and greater interest in the mechanisms of criminalization (Baratta 1999, p. 160).

The relationship between crime and immigration within the paradigm of critical criminology is observed from the standpoint of allocation mechanisms of offender status, which happens in two steps: primary criminalization and secondary criminalization. The first step, primary criminalization, elects the goods worthy of legal protection by criminalizing of detrimental conduct. In turn, the secondary criminalization is the selection of individuals who received the deviant status among the universes of those who committed the deviation (Baratta 1999, p. 161).

The analysis of the relationship between immigration and crime is focused on secondary criminalization. Immigrants, especially irregular immigrants, become one of the factors onto which the society projects a criminal stigma—a scapegoat. Therefore, the probability of immigrant conduct being regarded as deviant increases—this is a consequence of this stigma—since the official control bodies direct their actions to the persecution of these behaviors (Baratta 1999, p. 112).

This situation may be further aggravated when the actuarial method is used for social control purposes. The actuarial speech begins to gain space from the exhaustion of the nation-state, of welfare-state policy, and of Fordism as an industrial production model. In this context, the correctional model was guided towards the formation of disciplined individuals, and the rehabilitation of deviant individuals was sought incessantly by the various power mechanisms (Batista 1955, p. 42).

The correctional model suffers the impacts of theories developed from 1970s, which delegitimize its goals and its instruments (Giorgi 2005, p. 23). In this scenario of correctional model crisis, the actuarial thought emerges as a new trend of social control. The actuarial model promotes a change in "punitive practices' language" (Anitua 2008, p. 815): which go from the formation of disciplined individuals and rehabilitation to a risk management of dangerous social groups in order to redistribute crime as efficiently as possible (Giorgi 2005, p. 9). Traditional techniques of social control are replaced by new ones, which are based on identification, classification, sorting, and management of dangerous groups

The paradigm of risk society[19] encourages the abandonment of permissive structures along the lines of the Enlightenment (Anitua 2008, p. 817). Thus, the

[19] Ulrich Beck describes the paradigm of risk society: "How can the risks and hazards systematically produced as part of modernization be prevented, minimized, dramatized, or channeled? Where they do finally see the light of day in the shape of 'latente side effects', how can they be limited and distributed away so that the neither hamper the modernization process nor exceed the limits of that which is 'tolerable' – ecologically, medically, psychologically and socially" (Beck 2010, p. 22).

actuarial model emerges as a possible answer to the longing for a social control with greater efficiency and lower operating costs.

The use of actuarial methods in the field of social control cannot be considered entirely bad or illegitimate. Indeed, there are some operations—particularly in the field of criminal policy—that can be improved with the use of these methodologies (i.e., policing strategy or allocation of scarce resources).

The problem is when actuarial methodologies take into consideration improper factors that modify the results and remove their legitimacy as social control tool (Young 2002, p. 118). Among the improper factors, fear—fear of crime—is highlighted. Under the fear influence, society is driven to seek greater security, fostering the emergence of populist penal speech (policies) and the false notion that community (us) is against them (criminals/immigrants) (Anitua 2008, p. 816).

These considerations invite us to a reassessment of the relationship between immigration and crime within Arizona's context. From the perspective of the actuarial method, the criminalization of immigrant established by SB 1070 would be justified in actual risk factors, or would it be based on calculations disguised by fear of crime?

In the U.S. context, it is observed that the immigrant profile is close to the stereotype associated with crime by society: male, young, with low educational level. This factor favors the consolidation of the relationship between immigration and increased crime rates, into social consciousness. However, the results of empirical studies show the opposite (Rumbaut and Ewing 2007).

In this regard, it has been developed a series of studies based on official 2000 Census and other data. And the result showed that the incarceration rate[20] of American nationals is five times greater than the rate of immigrants (aliens).[21]

The data collected by 2010 Census were not processed by studies similar to those developed in 2000. Indeed, in late 2010 the prison population was 1,612,395 prisoners, which represents a decrease of 5575 prisoners towards the end of 2009. This reduction of 0.3 % was the first observed since 1972 (U.S. Department of Justice 2010). However, the 2010 Census data, as a whole, seems to endorse the conclusions of previous studies.

Among the prison population recorded in 2010, 95,977 prisoners were not American citizens—which represents a percentage of 5.9 % of prisoners. The number of U.S. prisoners without U.S. citizenship has a decrease of 1.19 % between 2009 Census and 2010 Census data (97,133 alien prisoners in 2009 and 95,977 alien prisoners in 2010) (U.S. Department of Justice 2010).

In the specific case of Arizona, the prison population in 2010 was estimated at 40,130 prisoners, of whom 4762 are not U.S. citizens. Regarding the reduction of

---

[20] The incarceration rate is calculated considering the numbers of those imprisoned from a particular group based on the total population of this group: the number of native Americans arrested based on the total population of native Americans.

[21] American born incarceration rate in 2000 was 3.5 %, meanwhile immigrant (alien) rate was 0.7 %. (Rumbaut and Ewing 2007).

U.S. prison population in 2010, Arizona reproduces the same low trends. Arizona's prison population dropped 1.2 % between 2009 and 2010. However, incarceration rates of prisoners without U.S. citizenship go against this trend, since it had an increase of 31.5 %: from 3259 alien prisoners in 2009 to 4762 in 2010 (U.S. Department of Justice 2010).

Furthermore, it is noted that in 2010 noncitizens represent 9 % of Arizona's population, meanwhile considering only the Arizona prison population, prisoners without U.S. citizenship correspond to 11 % of Arizona's prison population (Statehealthfacts 2012).

The relationship between immigration and crime has not been confirmed from this data, although this data suggest an unwillingness of Arizona and its population to deal with immigration issues, since it appears that the reality presented by Arizona in defense of SB 1070 is not reproduced in other contexts.

As noted by Rúben G. Rumbaut and Walter A. Ewing, Immigration cannot be considered as a cause of crime rate increase—neither as an aggravating circumstance. According to data presented in 2000, young male incarceration rates were lower among immigrants, even among those with lower education levels. Indeed, it was observed that the risk of incarceration among immigrants is as higher the longer they are established in U.S. territory, as well as for their descendants. This trend is a result of social influences and assimilation process observed in the immigration activity (Rumbaut and Ewing 2007).

Therefore, it seems that the efforts to enact SB 1070 are not empirically justified. Thereby, the speech of Arizona's population supporting the law suggests, and the lack of empirical evidence suggests, the influence of fear, which was aggravated after September 11 attacks (Rumbaut and Ewing 2007). In this sense, SB 1070 seems to represent more an unwillingness of Arizona population to manage the risk arising from immigration—which is accentuated by the distorted perception of this risk.

5 Conclusion

The criminalization conducted by Arizona with the enactment of SB 1070 proposes an unwillingness of local society to deal with the immigration issue. Apparently, the local community is not prepared to manage the risks arising from Federal Government decisions about immigration policy.

This local discomfort leads to social conflict that fosters the criminalization of immigrants at the local level. The criminalization process is accentuated by common sense, by which there is a relationship between immigration and crime. Meanwhile, the criminalization process further strengthens this notion in the common sense.

Criminalization has wider limits within the unofficial structures. It can be observed in the common speech and in organizations such as Stand with Arizona (and Against Illegal Immigration). In the context of official bodies of social control, power struggle between local and federal is then a barrier to the local criminalization of immigrants since the states are prevented from establishing a local immigration policy.

The relationship between immigration and crime should be reevaluated. Under the new criminology paradigm, the attention should be on the process and systems of criminalization and no longer on the figure of the offender (criminal), from the viewpoint of Social Reaction theories, as has warned by the Critical Criminology School.

Therefore, it is necessary to reconsider the use of actuarial methods on the criminalization processes. They should not be taken as absolute and isolated methods as they can be distorted by the presence of unrealistic risk factors—such as fear of crime. Thus, the improper use of actuarial methods can generate false (unreal) discourses on the distribution of crime and motivate, in the context of the risk society, misconduct resistance and criminalization based on this false speech.

Empirical data and the above-mentioned social research suggest that, in the case of Arizona, the criminalization of immigrants—whether primary criminalization by issue of SB 1070, whether secondary criminalization by its enforcement by local Arizona's agents—is motivated by an actuarial calculation distorted by fear of crime. Hence, within a risk society context, immigration would be considered as an element of threat (risk) due to the process of modernization, which may justify criminalization—even if it is necessary to ignore the jurisdictional rules, human rights, and international commitments.

References

Andrade VRP (1995) Do paradigma etiológico ao paradigma da reação social: mudança e permanência de paradigmas criminológicos na ciência e no senso comum. BuscaLegis 30: 24–36

Anitua GI (2008) Histórias dos pensamentos criminológicos. Revan, Rio de Janeiro

Arizona (2010a) House Bill 2162. http://www.azleg.gov/DocumentsForBill.asp?Bill_Number=2162. Accessed 6 Aug 2014

Arizona (2010b) Senate Bill 1070. http://www.azleg.gov/DocumentsForBill.asp?Bill_Number=1070. Accessed 6 Aug 2014

Arizona et al (2010) Proposed response to motion for preliminary injunction attached. http://www.ncsl.org/documents/immig/2010ArizonaDismiss.pdf. Accessed 6 Aug 2014

Baratta A (1999) Criminologia crítica e crítica do direito penal: introdução à sociologia do direito penal. Revan, Rio de Janeiro

Batista VM (1955) Introdução crítica à criminologia brasileira. Revan, Rio de Janeiro

Beck U (2010) Sociedade de Risco: rumo a uma outra modoernidade. 34, São Paulo

Edwards JR (2001) Legislation I: immigrantion. In: Ciment J (ed) Encyclopedia of American Immigration: Imigração – Estados Unidos. Sharpe Referenc, United States

Giorgi A (2005) Tolerancia cero: estrategias y prácticas de la sociedade del control. Editorial, Barcelona

Kelsen H (2000) Teoria geral do Direito e do Estado. Martins Fontes, São Paulo

Martinez Jr R, Lee MT (2000) On immigration and crime. In U.S. Departament of Justice. The nature of crime: continuity and change. https://www.ncjrs.gov/criminal_justice2000/vol1_2000.html. Accessed 6 Aug 2014

National Conference of State Legislatures (2012) Arizona's immigration enforcement laws. http://www.ncsl.org/issues-research/immig/analysis-of-arizonas-immigration-law.aspx. Accessed 6 Aug 2014

Plascencia LFB (2001) State, country, and municipal legislation. In: Ciment J (ed) Encyclopedia of American Immigration: Imigração – Estados Unidos. Sharpe Reference, United States

Recueil des Traités des Nations Unies (1966) Pacte international relatif aux droits civils et politiques. http://treaties.un.org/pages/ShowMTDSGDetails.aspx?src=UNTSONLINE&tabid=2&mtdsg_no=IV-4&chapter=4&lang=fr#Participants. Accessed 6 Aug 2014

Rumbaut RG, Ewing WA (2007) The myth of immigrant criminality and the paradox of assimilation: incarceration rates among native and foreign-born men. Spring, Washington

Stand with Arizona (2012) About. https://www.facebook.com/StandWithArizona/info. Accessed 6 Aug 2014

Statehealthfacts (2012) Arizona: population distribution by citizenship status, states. http://www.statehealthfacts.org/profileind.jsp?ind=3&cat=1&rgn=4. Accessed 6 Aug 2014

U.S. Census (2010) 2010 Census Results. http://www.census.gov/2010census/data/

U.S. Citizenship and Immigration Services (2012) Immigration and nationality act. http://www.uscis.gov/portal/site/uscis. Accessed 6 Aug 2014

U.S. Department of Justice (2010) Prisoners in 2010. http://bjs.ojp.usdoj.gov/content/pub/pdf/p10.pdf. Accessed 6 Aug 2014

U.S. Department of Justice (2012) Complaint. http://www.justice.gov/opa/documents/az-complaint.pdf. Accessed 6 Aug 2014

U.S. District Court for the District of Arizona (2010) Order – CV 10-1413-PHX-SRB. http://www.ncsl.org/documents/immig/2010Arizonaboltonruling.pdf. Accessed 6 Aug 2014

United States (1787) Constitution. http://www.senate.gov/civics/constitution_item/constitution.htm. Accessed 6 Aug 2014

United States Supreme Court (2012) Petição n° 11–182 – 2012. www.nilc.org/document.html?id=632. Accessed 6 Aug 2014

Vázques-Azpiri AJ (2001) Legislation II: immigrants in America. In: Ciment J (ed) Encyclopedia of American immigration. Sharpe Reference, United States

Weissbrodt D, Danielson L (2005) Immigration law and procedure. Thomson, St. Paul

Young J (2002) A sociedade excludente: exclusão social, criminalidade e diferença na modernidade recente. Revan, Rio de Janeiro

Zeman S (2001) Civil rights. In: Ciment J (ed) Encyclopedia of American immigration: Imigração – Estados Unidos. Sharpe Reference, United States

Printed by Printforce, the Netherlands